BEYOND THE BARRIO

LATINO PERSPECTIVES

Gilberto Cárdenas, series editor

The Institute for Latino Studies, in keeping with the distinctive mission, values, and traditions of the University of Notre Dame, promotes understanding and appreciation of the social, cultural, and religious life of U.S. Latinos through advancing research, expanding knowledge, and strengthening community.

BEYOND THE BARRIO

Latinos in the 2004 Election

edited by

RODOLFO O. DE LA GARZA,

LOUIS DESIPIO, AND

DAVID L. LEAL

University of Notre Dame Press

Notre Dame, Indiana

Notre Dame, Indiana 46556
www.undpress.nd.edu

Published in the United States of America

Library of Congress Cataloging-in-Publication Data

Beyond the barrio : Latinos in the 2004 elections / edited by
Rodolfo O. de la Garza, Louis DeSipio, and David L. Leal.
p. cm. — (Latino perspectives)
Includes index.
ISBN-13: 978-0-268-02599-1 (pbk. : alk. paper)
ISBN-10: 0-268-02599-1 (pbk. : alk. paper)
1. Hispanic Americans—Politics and government—21st century.
2. Elections—United States. 3. Presidents—United States—Election—2004.
4. United States—Congress—Elections, 2004. 5. United States—Politics
and government—2001–2009. I. De la Garza, Rodolfo O.
II. DeSipio, Louis. III. Leal, David L.
E194.S75B49 2010
323.1168073—dc22
2010008787

To Charles Cotrell, mentor to the first Chicano generation
— *Rodolfo O. de la Garza*

To Jack A. DeSipio, who never quite understood but always supported my interests
— *Louis DeSipio*

To Sidney Verba, who introduced me to Latino politics
— *David L. Leal*

Contents

Acknowledgments

This volume and its predecessors would not have been possible without the willingness of many scholars to participate and offer the unique vantage points of their states. Thanks especially to those who also participated in the original 1988 volume: Luis Fraga, Dario Moreno, and Christine Sierra.

This volume began as a conference held at the University of Texas at Austin in March 2005. The editors would like to acknowledge the support of the university's Irma Rangel Public Policy Institute, Department of Government, and College of Liberal Arts. We wish to thank the staff and graduate students of the Irma Rangel Public Policy Institute, who organized and staffed the conference and helped to produce the manuscript, in particular, Jill Strube, program coordinator, Michael Unger, and Jennifer Lamm. We would also like to thank Jason Casellas, not only for his insightful analysis of New Jersey Latino politics in 2004, but also for this volume's title.

Chapter One

Introduction

A View from the Battleground's Periphery: Latinos and the 2004 Elections

LOUIS DESIPIO AND DAVID L. LEAL

Since 1988 the first two editors of this volume have coordinated collaborative analyses of the influence of the Hispanic population on national and state politics in the United States.[1] More than fifty scholars have contributed to these quadrennial analyses of Latino efforts to shape federal- and state-level politics and political institutions' efforts to bring Latinos into their winning coalitions (de la Garza and DeSipio 1992, 1996, 1999, 2005). Each of the four volumes published thus far has struggled with an ongoing dilemma: how to characterize Latino contributions accurately so that we neither perpetuate the rhetoric claiming a strong and inevitable Hispanic influence in politics today nor undervalue the increasing contribution of Latinos to the national political fabric.

This volume highlights the somewhat confusing and contradictory nature of the Latino constituency in the U.S. political arena. Early in the 2004 presidential campaigns, genuine two-party competition seemed to occur as both parties intensely courted the Hispanic electorate and established strategies for victory that included a central role for Latinos and as each nominee reasonably claimed substantial loyalty among specific Hispanic subgroups. As time progressed, however, we find that the candidates, campaigns, and parties (especially the Democrats) largely neglected and marginalized Latino leaders, voters, and campaign staff in the primaries and in the general election—in particular, John Kerry and his campaign did not make personal connections to Latino leaders or voters—and neither campaign hired many Latinos, relegating them to outreach in Hispanic communities when they did.

In addition, Latino leaders were generally unable to overcome the neglect of the major parties and did not invest extensively in mobilizing Latinos new to the voting process. The Latino vote grew at rates comparable to recent periods between presidential elections, but this growth did not reduce the size of the pool of adults eligible to vote who do not turn out on election day.

Nevertheless, the Latino presence and, more important, its potential as a newly coalescing, sizable, and growing electorate increasingly guides the national political discussion. Nationally, Latinos had a previously unavailable opportunity to shape the selection of the 2004 Democratic presidential nominee in one early primary (Arizona) and one early caucus (New Mexico). In addition, the expectations and potential for Latino influence remained high throughout that race, influencing candidate and campaign strategies; were we to measure only their Election Day influence, we would miss their growing role in shaping the terms of national policy debates and of candidate (and potential candidate) strategies.

This potential has already begun to affect the outcomes of local and state races. Hispanics are increasingly able to use their numbers and organizations to form coalitions with other electorates to elect Latinos to office; in 2004 their participation in key coalitions resulted in the election of two Latinos to the U.S. Senate. This volume highlights the foundation of new forms of Latino politics and successful campaigns by Latino candidates for offices not previously held by Latinos (see, e.g., chapters 3, 4, and 12, this volume).

We acknowledge that not all the states analyzed here saw extensive Latino-focused mobilization or efforts to influence state or national political outcomes. Latino votes were, again, not significant to the outcome of the 2004 presidential race, and Latino voters were ultimately marginalized by the campaigns. Incremental growth in Latino voting and Latino influence has not reached a tipping point; Latinos still do not routinely determine national outcomes, except in the most unusual circumstances, or influence elections as many pundits and campaigns expect early in each election cycle. Nevertheless, we think it is important to continue to chronicle the conduct of the campaigns in these selected states so that we can document the rise of Latino politics in the modern era over time and across the nation. Comparisons across the years for any of the states will allow for an otherwise unavailable portrait of the substantive meaning of contemporary Latino politics.

In this chapter and those that follow, we examine the political consequences of a subtle Latino voice. We begin here with a brief overview of features of the 2004 campaign that were different from those in previous elections. We then provide a narrative of the 2004 campaign to show how Latinos organized and how campaigns and candidates incorporated Latinos and Latino issues into the campaign. This narrative offers critical points of comparison with similar campaign narratives presented in the four previous volumes in this series. The third section of this chapter looks at nonpresidential federal- and state-level races of particular importance in Hispanic communities. We asked that the contributors to this volume also address statewide races, as appropriate, in order to provide a sense of Latino organization and influence at multiple electoral levels. The fourth section measures the influence of Latino votes in the 2004 election at the national level and in states with large Latino populations. This discussion assesses why Latinos constitute a smaller share of the electorate than they do of the national population and examines several measures of the impact of Latino votes on the outcomes of the 2004 national and state elections. It also assesses the role partisanship played in the 2004 election. We conclude the chapter with some observations of long-term opportunities and barriers facing Hispanic electorates and an assessment of how the 2004 campaign altered and reinforced these long-term patterns.

WHAT WAS NEW IN 2004?

The 2004 elections did not change the role Latino voters have played in national elections over the past twenty years. Instead, the patterns of incremental growth in the Latino electorate and instrumental neglect by political parties, candidates, and institutions continued in 2004. That said, several important changes in the structure of the election, in the patterns of Latino participation, and in the electoral outcomes merit comment at the outset so that they do not get lost in the broader narrative of the 2004 campaign. These changes appeared anew in 2004 or became more apparent throughout that campaign compared to previous years, signaling a future for Latino politics that is beyond the barrio—or at least beyond the narrow confines that have characterized it in national campaigns since 1988. Latino politics in 2004 was more national than in the past. First, candidates and campaigns sought Latino votes nationally. Second, the potential of Latino votes shaped the national discourse about electoral outcomes. Third, Latinos had the opportunity to shape the presidential election not just in November but also in the primaries and in key competitive Senate races in states where Latinos are far from the majority.

In terms of the structure of the election, three important changes occurred that, though they do not appear to have affected the 2004 elections, could make a difference in the future. A potentially positive change was the calendar shift of the primaries. Prior to 2004, each party selected its nominee before large numbers of Latinos voted. Democrats changed this in 2004 with a conscious effort to reach out to Latinos (and more broadly to westerners) by scheduling an early primary in Arizona and an early caucus in New Mexico. On the negative side, many states enacted ballot security requirements that increased the likelihood that potential voters would be asked to provide evidence of citizenship, despite little evidence that non-U.S. citizens vote and considerable evidence that many U.S. citizens lack the documentation needed to meet these standards. Latino leaders reported increased levels of intimidation at the polls in states that implemented these requirements. Finally, Latino politics expanded to new destinations: campaigns in battleground states such as Ohio and Pennsylvania saw Latino outreach as major components of state-level campaigns.

As we will demonstrate, Latino voting increased incrementally but at approximately the same rate as that seen between other presidential elections (de la Garza and DeSipio 2006). Guided by exit polls, many analysts find the most interesting change in Latino 2004 voting patterns was a shift to higher levels of Republican presidential voting. While we do see a shift to support President George W. Bush relative to the 2000 election, we are less confident that Bush saw increases at the rates suggested in media accounts.[2] We do, however, see some interesting changes in Latino voting patterns. To the extent that President Bush improved his performance among Latinos, the gains appeared among two segments of the Latino electorate—Tejanos and Protestants, particularly Evangelical and Pentecostal Protestants (DeSipio and Uhlaner 2007; Lee and Pachon 2007). In part, these Protestant Bush voters reflect a more general policy congruence between religious conservative voters and the Republican Party. In addition, the 2004 elections demonstrated that targeted Bush/Republican outreach could translate these policy and ideological connections into higher numbers of Republican Latino votes. This ability to narrowly target Latino outreach efforts (and, evidently, to win votes in close elections based on such efforts) is a new phenomenon.

The 2004 election also saw a dramatic change in Latino representation: two Latinos were elected to the U.S. Senate. Never before had more than one Latino served in the U.S. Senate at any given time, and none had served since 1977. Furthermore, the gubernatorial election of a sitting U.S. senator in New Jersey laid the foundation for a third Latino to join the Senate via the appointment process. One of the newly elected senators was Cuban American, also a first.

LATINOS AND THE 2004 PRESIDENTIAL ELECTIONS: AN OVERVIEW

Between the resolution of the 2000 election and the beginning of the 2004 primary season, national political elites focused on the potential influence of the Latino vote. Matthew Dowd, a pollster and senior consultant to the Republican National Committee (RNC), noted in 2001 that if Bush won the same share of the minority vote in 2004 that he did in 2000, he would lose the election by three million votes, placing Latinos at the center of Republican strategies for 2004 (Kiefer 2001). Dowd's calculations focused on minority populations that Republicans could win: Latinos and Asian Americans. Taking the next step, Bush adviser Karl Rove said that Bush would lose the election unless he raised his share of the Latino vote to 40 percent, from the roughly 35 percent he earned in 2000.

From the first days of his administration, the president engaged in targeted outreach to Latinos, primarily symbolic in nature, including presidential radio addresses in Spanish, a White House Cinco de Mayo celebration, talk of a guest worker program that might evolve into more comprehensive immigration reform, and frequent visits with Mexican President Vicente Fox. Just as the Democrats were beginning the primary season, Bush made a final preelection outreach effort with a renewed immigration proposal, this one more explicitly acknowledging that comprehensive reform would require a path to legalization for unauthorized immigrants (Bumiller 2004).

Contributing to these outreach efforts, the Republican Party recruited Latino Republicans to compete for statewide office. Some candidates were ultimately successful; others were not able to beat white Republicans in party primaries (Marinucci 2003). Examples of these campaigns, respectively, Florida's Mel Martinez and California's Rosario Marin, are discussed below. State and local Republican parties were not as supportive of Latino outreach goals as the national party, a continuing dilemma for Republicans as they try to win more Latino votes.

The Democrats did not cede the Latino vote. In addition to rhetorical appeals, they altered their primary calendar to move Arizona and New Mexico earlier. The Democrats also tapped New Mexico Governor Bill Richardson to deliver a Spanish-language Democratic response to President Bush's State of the Union message (Salinas 2004).

All the Democratic presidential candidates made efforts to win Latino primary votes. In 2003 eight of the nine Democratic candidates spoke to the annual meeting of the National Association of Latino Elected Officials (NALEO); absent was former Senator Carol Moseley Braun. Two—former Vermont Governor Howard Dean and U.S. Representative Dennis Kucinich (D-OH)—addressed the meeting primarily in Spanish (Barabak 2003; Karamargin 2003). The first of the candidate debates sanctioned by the Democratic Party took place in New Mexico and was hosted by Ray Suarez of PBS and Maria Elena Salinas of Univision. Although this debate did not focus on Latino issues per se, several of the candidates used the occasion to highlight their abilities to speak Spanish or to call for a legalization program for unauthorized immigrants. Observers noted, however, that none of the candidates at the debate "offered any new proposals tailored for the Hispanic community" (Balz and VandeHei 2004).

As his campaign developed a sense of inevitability, Governor Dean used this period before the primaries to capture endorsements from prominent Latino leaders, including six of the twenty members of the Congressional Hispanic Caucus. Latino members of Congress differed from their peers in their choice of candidate; Richard Gephardt, who had served as majority and minority leader in the House, received the most congressional endorsements among non-Latinos. No other Democratic candidate had the support of more than two Latino members (Anderson 2003; Eby 2003).

Despite these party and candidate efforts to reach Latino voters and to accentuate the importance of Latino votes in the period before the primaries, the campaigns did not energize Latino voters, nor did Latino voters' preferences coalesce behind a single candidate. Preelection polling did not show a dramatic move to the Republican Party, as some Republican leaders had hoped, but the polls did show some ambivalence toward the Democrats (Hulse 2003; Marrero 2004). What was not discussed at the time was that this ambivalence was felt especially among adults who were less likely to vote in 2004. The core of the Latino electorate remained aligned with the Democratic Party, and by restructuring the primary calendar, the party created an opportunity for Latinos to have a new voice in presidential politics.

The Primaries

Ultimately, as has been the case in each election since 1988 (de la Garza 1992), Latinos proved largely irrelevant to the selection of their parties' presidential nominees. Suspense was completely absent on the Republican side. President Bush faced no opposition in his bid for the Republican renomination. On the Democratic side, Latinos in Arizona and New Mexico could have shaped the selection of the Democratic nominee if they had taken positions distinct from other electorates or if they had voted at unusually high levels. Although California had also moved its primary forward (to early March) in the hope that an earlier primary would increase its voice in the presidential selection process, it had little effect on Hispanic voters.

Iowa and New Hampshire continued to lead the caucus and primary calendar in 2004. New Mexico and Arizona changed the traditional calendar by following in the next wave. New Mexico and North

Dakota held the second wave of caucuses on February 3 (following the January 19 Iowa caucus). Arizona (along with Delaware, South Carolina, Missouri, and Oklahoma) held its primary on February 3, only one week after the January 27 New Hampshire primary. Some pundits characterized February 3 as "Hispanic Tuesday," following the locution of a southern "Super Tuesday" in earlier elections.

New Hampshire and especially Iowa saw the traditional extensive outreach to all potential voters. This outreach included Latino voters, but they make up a very small share of these states' electorates: approximately 12,000 in Iowa and 5,000 in New Hampshire (U.S. Bureau of the Census 2005). The large number of young volunteers from all corners of the country energized the Dean campaign, which was particularly aggressive in seeking Latino voters. Latino Democrats in Iowa reported that they had been contacted multiple times by English- and Spanish-speaking Dean staff.

With the collapse of the Dean campaign after his defeat in New Hampshire (and, conclusively, after his defeat in the Wisconsin primary on February 17), John Kerry became the Democratic frontrunner. Although he participated in collective candidate efforts to win Latino votes, he made small attempts to win them in the early primary states (Avila 2003). Kerry formed a Latino Steering Committee in January; its co-chairs were Henry Cisneros, former Small Business Association director Aida Alvarez, New Mexico House Speaker Ben Lujan, and Los Angeles City Council member Antonio Villaraigosa. In his New Mexico campaign, Kerry tapped Cisneros, as well as Senator Edward Kennedy, as surrogates to reach Latino voters. He also ran some Spanish-language ads in both states (Kasindorf 2004). Overall, however, the Kerry campaign's spending on Spanish-language advertising in Arizona and New Mexico was relatively low (approximately $78,000) compared to the other candidates who courted Hispanics: Dean spent $150,000, and Wesley Clark spent $91,000, all in Arizona (Segal 2004b). There is little evidence that the other Democratic candidates conducted targeted Latino outreach in either state.

The Arizona primary and the New Mexico caucuses offered an opportunity for Latino influence in the selection of the Democratic candidate (Roth 2004). Latinos did not express a voice distinct from other state electorates, however. In Arizona, exit polls indicated that 42 percent of Latinos supported John Kerry, roughly the same level of support of non-Hispanic white (Anglo) voters. In New Mexico, approximately one-third of Latino and Anglo caucus participants supported Senator Kerry. Thus, at least among Latino Democrats in these two states, Latinos reinforced the choices of other electorates. This move toward Senator Kerry also occurred in states with few Latino voters that held primaries and caucuses on these days. Although turnout data on Latino voters or caucus-goers in either of these states is not available, there is no evidence that Latinos participated at unexpectedly high levels.

Primaries in states with large Latino populations were held well after John Kerry had come to dominate the Democratic field (a possible exception is Nevada, which held a February 14 caucus). California's change in its primary date proved futile; by March 2 the nomination race was largely over.

Arizona and New Mexico Latinos voted for Senator Kerry at rates comparable to other electorates; in general, this pattern continued in the two other states that held primaries before Senator Kerry formally wrapped up the nomination in early March. In New York, 67 percent of Latinos and 66 percent of Anglos voted for Kerry. Latinos were more likely than Anglos to support Al Sharpton in New York, but Sharpton's Latino support remained in the single digits. In California, Latinos were somewhat more likely than Anglos to support Kerry (74 percent among Latinos and 64 percent among Anglos).

Despite the revised primary calendar, the Latino voice in the primaries can at best be viewed as subdued. Latino Democrats joined the Kerry bandwagon as it gained steam. Kerry's major opponent, Howard Dean, was effectively out of the race before large numbers of Latino voters were consulted. As a result, it is not possible to say if Latinos would have been a pro-Kerry force in a competitive race or if they were just following other Democrats to the new frontrunner (Sanchez 2004). None of the other candidates who were still active by the time the primary calendar moved to states with Latino voters—most notably, John Edwards and Al Sharpton—caught on among Latino voters. Since Kerry did little to win these Latino votes through active campaigning, extensive elite endorsements, Latino-focused advertising, or substantive outreach on issues of importance to Latinos, it is not possible to say whether he would have been able to energize Latino voters and mobilize Latinos who do not traditionally vote (the majority of the Latino U.S.-citizen adults) in close races, as this one was expected to be (Marelius 2004). As a result, ongoing confusion among pundits about whether Latinos would continue to vote as they traditionally had or would be a swing electorate continued (Lester 2004; Mason 2004; Moreno 2004).

The Postprimary Season

With both nominations sewn up by early March, the candidates had a long period to gear up for the fall campaign. Primarily, each campaign used this time to raise money for its party, focus on key constituencies and states that were expected to be competitive, and undertake certain "bureaucratic" functions (including hiring staff and selecting a running mate in the case of the Kerry campaign).

Most campaign resources were focused on the states perceived to be competitive in the race for Electoral College votes (Shaw 2006). Although this list would narrow later, the spring saw Bush and Kerry speaking to Latinos and other potential voters in Arizona, New Mexico, Colorado, Florida, and Nevada (Garay 2004; Morgan 2004; Radelat 2004; Runningen and Jensen 2004). In other words, they neglected the voters in the states with the most Latino residents: California, Texas, New York, and Illinois. Campaign advertising at this time, including ads primarily in Spanish that targeted Latino voters, targeted these competitive states (Clark 2004; Lang 2004). Both campaigns also began to assemble the leadership networks that would provide the face for the targeted Latino outreach efforts—Viva Bush! and Unidos con Kerry—and the accompanying Web sites and campaign paraphernalia.

Both campaigns ventured beyond the few competitive states to woo Latino elites, however. John Kerry spoke at the annual conferences of the National Council of La Raza and the NALEO, as well as to the League of United Latin American Citizens (LULAC) via satellite. Once selected, vice presidential nominee John Edwards spoke at the annual meeting of the Southwest Voter Registration and Education Project (SVREP). President Bush used satellite technology to attend these events, and his campaign sent surrogates, including White House Counsel Alberto Gonzalez and Secretary of Health and Human Services Tommy Thompson (Associated Press 2004; Balz 2004; Romano 2004).

These meetings offered the venue for the most specific discussion of Latino issues in the campaign. Kerry, in particular, spoke to issues that topped the 2004 Latino issue agenda: education, employment and the labor market, immigration reform, and Iraq and national security.

The Kerry campaign also used this period to select a vice presidential nominee. Among the finalists was New Mexico Governor Bill Richardson (Senior 2004). In addition to his Hispanic heritage, Richardson's potential strengths included his executive branch and diplomatic experience in the Clinton administration and his state and region of residence—New Mexico, a battleground state in the competitive Southwest. Richardson's bluntness often appeared impolitic, leading many to wonder how serious he was in his pursuit of the vice presidency. In fact, despite his status among the handful of names discussed throughout the spring, Richardson insisted that he was not interested in the vice presidency and did not register with the American public. In a June survey, CNN found that voters were most enthusiastic about a Kerry-Edwards or Kerry-Gephardt ticket (CNN 2004). In early July, before Kerry announced his selection of Senator Edwards as the Democratic vice presidential nominee, Governor Richardson withdrew his name from consideration (Coleman 2004). There is no way to evaluate the degree to which discussions of a Richardson candidacy shaped Latino thinking about the campaign. At the time, Richardson was little known outside New Mexico, so it is unlikely that discussions of a Richardson nomination earned Senator Kerry any new Latino support.

Following the pattern of his 2000 campaign, President Bush hired few Latinos for his campaign. Interestingly, he faced little criticism for this neglect. Despite their recently initiated competition for Latino votes, Republican candidates are not held to the same expectations as Democratic candidates for hiring Latinos and assigning them to various roles. John Kerry was routinely lambasted for his low share of Latino staffers. In April, Raul Yzaguirre, president of the National Council of La Raza, denounced the "remarkable and unacceptable absence of Latinos in [the] campaign" (Wilgoren 2004). Yzaguirre noted that Latinos who did work in the campaign were given jobs relating to outreach and not to policy or finance. None of the staff who traveled with Kerry were Latino. Criticisms that the Kerry staff lacked diversity in this pre–general election period spurred the appointment of new African American staff but did not extend to Latinos (Shepard 2004).

This failure to incorporate Latino staff throughout the campaign reflected a broader concern about Kerry that began to be articulated and that would recur throughout the campaign—that the Kerry campaign took Latino votes for granted and did not invest resources in designing a campaign to speak to their policy needs. In April, Alvaro Cifuentes, chair of the Democratic National Committee's (DNC's) Hispanic Caucus, circulated an email in which he charged that "the Kerry campaign has no message out there to the Hispanic community, nor has there been any reach-out effort in any state to the Hispanic electorate, at least with any perceivable sustainable strategy in mind" (Wilgoren 2004). Tangibly, state campaigns neglected to reach Latino voters in Arizona, New Mexico, Nevada, or Florida in late spring (Finnegan 2004). By contrast, Bush had a campaign presence and a Latino outreach effort in each of these states by May, running ads targeted at Latinos in both Spanish and English. When asked about this gap, the Kerry campaign spoke of the need to focus on fund-raising and its future plans to invest in a Spanish-language advertising blitz. In July the Kerry campaign committed $1 million to Spanish-language advertising in Florida, New Mexico, Nevada, Arizona, Colorado, Ohio, Oregon, Washington, Pennsylvania, and North Carolina.

In past elections, the pre–general election period offered Latino leaders the opportunity to organize to enhance the importance of Latino votes or to mobilize nonvoters. Although efforts to increase the number of registered Latino voters were discussed in this period, nonpartisan elite coordination designed to speak to Latino issues or policy needs was not widely achieved. Perhaps this reflects a legacy of the 2000 election and the increased partisan divisions in U.S. society or, perhaps, the absence of nonpartisan leadership in Latino communities; regardless, few Latino voices were heard in this period of the campaign that were not tied to one of the candidates or parties.

Parallel campaign organizations (funded by private donations outside the limits on the candidates and the parties) were able to gear up and set goals during this period. In the lingo of the 2004 campaign, "527 organizations" (named for the section of the tax code that allowed for them to operate as tax-exempt organizations) attempted to mobilize voters. Some of their efforts focused primarily on Latinos; these promised to register one to two million new Latino voters, a number of new registrants comparable to those in the 2000 election (Díaz 2004). Some focused not just on voter registration but also on turnout in the "battleground" states and were funded and organized with an almost military precision. Latinos in the battleground states—especially Florida, New Mexico, and Nevada—benefited from the mobilization efforts of these 527 organizations, but the majority of Latino nonvoters did not.

The Bush campaign committed to high levels of spending on Spanish-language media, both through the campaign itself and through a 527 organization (Progress for America). Overall, the Bush campaign spent a total of $3.3 million and Progress for America spent an additional $476,000. The most prominent of the 527s organized under the auspices of the New Democrat Network (NDN), however, focused on potential Democratic voters. The NDN funded a media campaign to reach Latino voters using Spanish-language media in the battleground states. These efforts began in March with a commitment of $5 million primarily for Spanish-language ad buys (Copp 2004). Ultimately, it spent about $2.3 million; the Kerry campaign spent an additional $1.3 million, the DNC $1.4 million (Segal 2006).

The NDN came to be one of the major loci of Latino outreach, although this may not have been its goal at inception. The Kerry campaign did not articulate a clear strategy to reach out to Latino voters, and Latino leaders did not organize effectively to coordinate Latino outreach efforts. Through advertising, the NDN ultimately did more than either the Kerry campaign or the DNC. With NDN resources in place, the DNC and the Kerry campaign failed to design targeted outreach strategies for Latinos, following the model of the 2000 race. Although it financed and managed "coordinated campaigns" to elect Democrats at various levels of office in competitive areas (e.g., Kerry, Ken Salazar, John Salazar, and Democrats for the state senate and house in Colorado), it did not focus these efforts extensively on states with high concentrations of Latinos.

State-level efforts to mobilize the Latino vote in the battleground states also began to appear in the spring. Viva Bush! served as an organizational structure for state-level Latino mobilization efforts in New Mexico, Arizona, Nevada, California, and Minnesota. The Kerry campaign relied more on groups independent of the campaign, as did Bush in Florida. These included a voter registration organization led by New

Mexico's Bill Richardson (Moving America Forward), which focused on Latinos in New Mexico and Florida, and a national nonethnic organization (America Coming Together), which focused on seventeen states, including a targeted Latino mobilization in Arizona, Colorado, New Mexico, Nevada, and Florida (Finnegan 2004). Overall, Florida saw more of these mobilization efforts than did other states. Because it remained competitive, these efforts continued throughout the campaign season and included not just voter registration but also get-out-the-vote (GOTV) efforts to increase turnout (Kinsler 2004).

The Conventions

While each party sought to use its convention as a tool to promote an image of inclusiveness, their efforts took somewhat different forms. The Democrats named New Mexico Governor Bill Richardson convention chair and created a complete Spanish-language version of the convention Web site. Republicans also ensured a Hispanic voice at their convention, but its role was somewhat more formal and muted than at the Democratic convention. Representative Henry Bonilla served as one of the six deputy permanent chairs of the convention. Although the Republicans were more cautious in their approach, each party trumpeted its diversity; for example, GOP press releases discussed the racial/ethnic diversity of its campaign and constituent base, as well as geographic diversity and the presence of large numbers of veterans (Republican National Committee 2004). Media presentations of the delegates at the Republican convention often focused on the black and Latino delegates, perhaps overstating their actual representation.

Each party saw an increase in the number of Hispanic delegates. Of the 4,300 delegates to the 2004 Democratic National Convention, more than 12 percent were Latino (Torrens 2004). The comparable figure in 2000 was slightly more than 10 percent (DeSipio and de la Garza 2005: 37). Latinos made up the largest minority delegation at the Republican National Convention, increasing from approximately 8.3 percent in 2000 to 9.5 percent in 2004 (Republican National Committee 2004). Based on their share of each party, Latinos were arguably underrepresented at the Democratic convention and overrepresented at the Republican convention.

While each convention offered opportunities for Latinos (especially Latino elected officials) to speak, they were not offered the major speeches that the media covered in its limited capacity. Just two Latinos spoke in prime time at the Democratic National Convention: Richardson and Representative Robert Menéndez (D-NJ) (Root 2004). This low representation in the prime-time slots led to last-minute negotiations that added to the number of Latino speakers overall (Adair and Bousquet 2004). Other Latino Democrats who spoke to the convention included AFL-CIO vice president Linda Chavez-Thompson, National Council of La Raza president Raul Yzaguirre, Los Angeles supervisor Gloria Molina, Los Angeles City Council member Antonio Villaraigosa, U.S. Representatives Hilda Solis, Linda Sanchez, Ciro Rodriguez, and Raul Grijalva, and some state and local elected officials.

To the extent that a widely recognized minority voice was prominent at the 2004 Democratic convention, it was that of Illinois Senate candidate Barack Obama, who electrified the convention on its second night in a prime-time speech. Not only was his speech well crafted; it broke from the structure of each night's theme (frequently focusing on Kerry's military service and national security issues). To the extent that Latinos watched the Democratic convention (about which there are no data), it was this night that spoke most clearly to Latino issues.

Fewer Latino voices were present at the Republican National Convention in New York, although two speakers were given prominent placement in the prime-time lineup. The president's nephew, George P. Bush, addressed the convention in Spanish and English on its opening night. Seeking to unite traditional Republican themes with a Latino outreach strategy, he observed, "Our party has always represented the interests of all people seeking opportunity. We are the home of entrepreneurs, men and women who want to know the pride of accomplishment, the honor of self-sufficiency" (Purdum 2004). Former U.S. Treasurer Rosario Marin joined George P. Bush in prime time.

Columnist and former Republican presidential candidate Pat Buchanan released a new book, *Where the Right Went Wrong* (2004), just before the Republican convention began, undercutting Republicans' efforts to present themselves as a more diverse and inclusive party than in previous years. Among Buchanan's indictments of President Bush was his support for immigration reform that, in some iterations, included a path to permanent residence for unauthorized immigrants in the United States, which caused disquiet among some Republican delegates. At its heart, the book called for a renewed effort in the culture war that Buchanan brought to the floor of the 1992 Republican convention; the power of this sentiment reveals that Latino outreach efforts were questionable for many mainstream Republicans and that the party needed to tread lightly around the issue of inclusion, especially of Latinos, during the convention.

Finally, both conventions offered the opportunity for Latino delegates and party activists to meet possible candidates for the 2008 presidential election, as well as candidates for state office. With the likelihood that there would be no incumbent in either party in 2008, many potential candidates sought inroads among Latino activists. Each convention also saw efforts to connect Latino delegates from throughout the country with ethnic caucuses and to connect delegates to Latino campaign professionals and civic organizations.

The General Election

Ultimately, Latino voters were a footnote to the 2004 general election. The campaigns, the parties, and the 527 organizations focused most of their general election energies on a handful of the battleground states with few Latino residents. Latino communities did not organize to influence the outcome of the presidential race, and the issues of unique importance to Latino communities were not central to either presidential campaign. Perhaps most important, neither candidate made Latino outreach central to his campaign's mission; in particular, the Kerry campaign did less than any recent Democratic nominee to win Latino votes. The Bush campaign, following the model of the 2000 race, did much more than recent Republican candidates and made Latino votes more competitive in two of the battleground states, New Mexico and Florida.

Labor Day 2004—the traditional start of the general election campaign season—saw a tight race in the national polls and a widespread concern that the 2004 race might again result in a contested outcome. Both campaigns anticipated that victory would result from mobilizing voters in one of a handful of battleground states. These competitive states numbered no more than twenty-one in September, with just nine being true toss-ups (Seelye 2004). Of these, Latinos constituted a significant share of the population in six: two states leaning to President Bush—Arizona and Nevada—and four truly unknowns—Colorado, New Mexico, Florida, and New Jersey. By mid- to late October, efforts to win Latino votes narrowed to three of these states: New Mexico, Florida, and Colorado. The competition in Colorado increasingly focused on the Senate race between Ken Salazar and Pete Coors. Thus the opportunities for campaigning in Latino communities and discussing issues of importance to them were few and far between. Most of the campaigns' time and energy focused on the battleground states of the industrial Midwest.

Latinos in New Mexico and Florida did see extensive efforts, including candidate and candidate-surrogate visits, advertising, and voter mobilization efforts by several 527 organizations, to win their votes and ensure that they would vote (DeBose 2004; de Córdoba 2004; Nieves 2004). In New Mexico, for example, field organizers for both campaigns focused on Latino turnout in all of the state's counties. These mobilization efforts, which included door-to-door canvassers and phone banks, were reinforced by advertising campaigns in place since March in the case of the Bush campaign. Latino leaders were happy to see that new registrants in the state had the same proportion of Latinos as did the state voter registration rolls at the beginning of the election year. Considering the socioeconomic disadvantage of Hispanos in New Mexico relative to Anglos, this was thought to bode well for turnout in November. Republican outreach appears to have been somewhat more targeted than was Democratic outreach. In particular, in addition to general outreach, GOP outreach to Hispanos blended with its outreach to places of worship. This Republican effort to mobilize religiously observant Latinos included both Catholics and Protestants.

President Bush and Senator Kerry also competed for Latino votes in Florida. The Florida Latino vote included both Republican-leaning areas (Miami and environs) and Democratic-leaning areas (Orlando and the I-4 corridor). What was interesting in 2004 is that each candidate had to both defend his base and compete in the other candidate's areas of strength (DeBose 2004; de Córdoba 2004). Bush faced certain challenges among Cuban Americans because of new travel restrictions added to the U.S. embargo of Cuba. We discuss this issue later, but it is important to recognize that it forced President Bush to use time and resources to campaign among those who should have been safe Republican voters. The Kerry campaign believed it could win a higher share of Cuban American votes in Miami than had Al Gore in 2000 (de Córdoba 2004). In the central part of the state, the Bush campaign courted Latino voters who had been somewhat reliably Democratic in previous elections, as the 2000 election results suggested that their partisan loyalties might be in flux (Balz and Morin 2004).[3] In particular, the Bush campaign focused on religiously observant Latinos in Orlando and along the I-4 corridor, thus paralleling its efforts in New Mexico.

Although the Kerry Latino campaign in both of these competitive states was well organized on the ground, it was never able to articulate a message to Latino communities—a problem for the campaign throughout the 2004 election. The only consistent Kerry messages to Latinos were (1) that Kerry, like many Latinos, is Catholic and (2) that Kerry's Democratic policy agenda traditionally receives more Latino support than does the Republican agenda (Navarrette 2004a). Kerry never proved a successful messenger when campaigning in Latino communities, and he failed to tailor his message to the specific needs of Latinos.

The candidate's wife, Teresa Heinz Kerry, often spoke to Latino audiences (Agence France Presse 2004), but her intermittent claim of being an immigrant and in some sense a Latina did not always meet a receptive audience (Navarrette 2004b). Kerry's surrogates in the fall campaign, including Henry Cisneros, Antonio Villaraigosa, and Bill Richardson, could speak more directly to Latino concerns, but they did not add excitement to the Kerry campaign. The campaign paid a price for the absence of a Latino message and the dearth of excitement surrounding Kerry in Latino communities.

The Bush campaign was also negligent in terms of developing a Latino message. The president often spoke of his personal connection to Latinos and would occasionally hint at his support for a legalization program as part of comprehensive immigration reform. Beyond this issue, however, he relied on the traditional Republican tropes of moral conservatism, opportunity, and patriotism when speaking to Latino communities. The Bush campaign was able to target these messages to Latino churchgoers, particularly the moral conservative message and particularly in the battleground states. But Bush's failure to craft a distinctive Latino message faced less criticism than did Kerry's neglect.

Both campaigns (and their related 527 organizations) focused their outreach to Latinos through Spanish- rather than English-language media (Segal 2004a). This represents a change from the early period analyzed in our series (de la Garza and DeSipio 1992, 1996); the campaigns now perceive that Spanish-dominant voters are a sizable enough audience to merit considerable investment. These Spanish-dominant Latino voters are largely naturalized U.S. citizens. For their English-dominant children, the ads demonstrate a cultural sensitivity on the part of the candidate. The content of these Spanish-language ads is not very different from the English-language ads (though the visuals vary considerably), so the campaigns must be confident that they are reaching English-dominant Latinos through their nonethnic media purchases.

Nationally, the Kerry campaign spent nearly $1.3 million on Spanish-language advertising and the Bush campaign spent $3.3 million (Segal 2006). The gap is reversed, however, when party and 527 funds are included in the calculations. Overall in 2004, Kerry and the Democrats spent approximately $8.7 million on Latino-focused advertising in the battleground states; 57 percent of this expenditure was used in Spanish-language media. The campaigns and parties each spent around $2.3 million in Florida and $500,000 to $800,000 in New Mexico. Kerry and the Democrats spent about twice as much in Arizona, Nevada, and Colorado as Bush and the Republicans ($775,000 vs. $365,000 in Arizona; $593,000 vs. $315,000 in Nevada, and $395,000 vs. $203,000 in Colorado). The Kerry campaign also spent small amounts on Spanish-language advertising in Ohio, Pennsylvania, Washington, and North Carolina. These funds included both television and radio advertisements, some with content similar to English-language ads and some produced uniquely for Latino communities.

The Spanish-language ads used Latino community settings that were not simply those used in English-language advertising, as had been the case in some previous campaigns. As with the non-Latino advertising, the Spanish-language ads disproportionately focused on national security, the war in Iraq, military service (Kerry's), and economic issues. Several spoke generically about Hispanic contributions to U.S. society.

Although the Kerry campaign and the New Democrat Network (NDN) each ran one commercial that focused on the Cuban community, specifically concerning the new restrictions on travel to Cuba imposed by the Bush administration, these ads were designed for a "generic" Hispanic audience. In addition, Kerry used Bill Richardson as a spokesperson in one ad.[4]

As was the case in 2000, neither campaign hired many Latinos in staff positions and mainly pigeonholed the Latinos they hired to organize and run outreach in the Hispanic communities (Bush-Cheney '04 2004a; John Kerry Campaign Organization 2004). The Kerry campaign hired a director of Hispanic Outreach (Luis Elizondo-Thomson). The Bush campaign took the unusual approach for a modern presidential campaign of not naming a Latino outreach director. It did form a National Hispanic Steering Committee in April. More practically, its media office coordinated Latino media outreach, and staff members Lionel Sosa and Alex Castellanos were often mentioned in the press as the coordinators of Bush's Latino outreach. Latino staff on the Bush campaign included a Southwest field coordinator, a deputy director of voter contact-phones, and a specialty media outreach coordinator. The Kerry campaign, in addition to Elizondo-Thomson, employed Latino staff in field director positions in New Mexico, Arizona, Nevada, Oregon, and Washington, as senior political adviser (primarily focused on community outreach), as deputy press secretary, and as director of Hispanic media (two staff members). In each campaign, Latinos made up less than 5 percent of the national campaign staff.

Similar patterns appear in the Bush and Kerry campaign organizations in Latino battleground states. For example, of the thirty-eight members of the Florida Kerry campaign, the Florida Democratic Party, and pro-Kerry 527 organizations in the state, only two were Latino (Kerry and Allies–Organization, Florida 2005), although it was somewhat more inclusive in New Mexico, with sixteen Latinos appointed to leading staff positions out of the fifty-five similar organizations (Kerry and Allies–Organization, New Mexico 2005). Similarly, the Bush-Cheney state campaigns hired fewer Hispanic staff. In Florida two of forty senior Bush-Cheney staff members were Latinos (Bush-Cheney '04 2004b). In New Mexico four of twenty-two senior staff members were Latinos (Bush-Cheney '04 2004c).

We find this dearth of Latino campaign staff odd. In the 1996 race, the Clinton campaign set what we thought would become the new standard, at a minimum, for Democratic candidates—the employment of Latino staff not just in Latino outreach roles but throughout the campaign as well (DeSipio, de la Garza, and Setzler 1999). This pattern, however, was not the case in 2000 or 2004. In 2004 it is especially telling that the Kerry campaign was unable to identify a strategy to energize Latino voters who might be predisposed to supporting the Massachusetts senator.

In the end, any promises of or expectations for Latino outreach were lost in the exigencies of a campaign highly focused on a handful of states that were primarily non-Latino in population. Certainly the small number of Latinos in battleground states such as Pennsylvania, Wisconsin, and Ohio did receive attention, but it would be difficult to characterize this meager effort as a coordinated Latino campaign. Perhaps if the race had focused more resources on states with large Latino electorates, the candidates or their campaigns would have found more effective strategies to reach Latino voters and speak to the issues of most concern to them. Voter mobilization, probably the greatest electoral need in Latino communities, was neglected in 2004 except in the three states with anticipated close outcomes.

The Electoral College

As the 2000 election taught the nation, the geographic distribution of votes for the candidates can be more important than the number of votes. Voters do not select candidates; they select Electoral College delegates who promise to support the candidate to whom they are pledged. These largely unknown, politically loyal individuals meet without fanfare to elect the president. Table 1.1 lists the number and percentage of Latino delegates for each party from 1992 through 2004.

We offer the caveat that we rely on Latino surnames to identify Latino Electoral College delegates, as we did with Latino campaign staff. If Bill Richardson were a delegate, he might not be counted but for his prominence. This table nevertheless provides a rough estimate and allows us to check for trends over time. In 2004 fewer Latinos were delegates from either party than in 2000. As before, there were more

Table 1.1. Latino Electoral College Delegates, by Party, 1992–2004

	1992		*1996*		*2000*		*2004*	
	Dem.	*Rep.*	*Dem.*	*Rep.*	*Dem.*	*Rep.*	*Dem.*	*Rep.*
Latino	21 (5.7%)	8 (4.8%)	24 (6.3%)	6 (3.8%)	24 (9.0%)	13 (5.0%)	15 (6.0%)	10 (3.5%)
Non-Latino	349	160	355	153	243	258	234	276
Total	370	168	379	159	267	271	252	286

Source: Authors' calculations using standard sources of Latino surnames.
Note: Latino surname lists underestimate the true Latino population by approximately 20 percent.

Democratic (fifteen) than Republican (ten) delegates, but this represents a decline from twenty-four Democrats and thirteen Republicans in 2000. In addition, while the percentage of total Latino delegates had previously increased over time (from 5.39 percent in 1992 to 5.57 percent in 1996 to 6.87 percent in 2000), the 2004 Electoral College was only 4.65 percent Latino.

One explanation for the overall and partisan fluctuations is the specific states the candidates won. The two parties in the same state may have different proportions of Hispanic electors on the ballot, so the basket of states won by each candidate may affect party Hispanic representation in the Electoral College. The switch of New Mexico from the Democrats in 2000 to the Republicans in 2004, for example, reduced the number of Latinos in the Electoral College.

The position of delegate is honorific, and individuals are chosen because of demonstrated party loyalty. Although only a few practical rules constrain the delegate vote, even the closely contested and controversial 2000 election saw only one delegate shift her vote from what was expected of her. That said, a small number of electors could affect the outcome in a close contest; this did not happen in 2000 or 2004, but it cannot be ruled out for the future.

Latino Issues in the National Campaign

Table 1.2 illustrates the mid-October responses of registered voters to a preelection survey administered by the *Washington Post,* Univision, and the Tomás Rivera Policy Institute. The survey asked respondents to identify the single most important issue in their vote for president. The table is different from those in previous volumes, as the events of September 11, 2001, and the war in Iraq significantly changed the public policy priorities of Americans. As DeSipio and de la Garza (2005: 48) noted in the previous volume, *Muted Voices,* "Foreign policy continues to not be a relevant concern among Latinos." But it was an unavoidable part of the 2004 campaign.

Nevertheless, the most important issue for Latinos in 2005 was the economy, with 26.7 percent identifying it as central to their vote choice. The second and third most important issues related to post-9/11 concerns: terrorism (20.2 percent) and the war in Iraq (15.2 percent). It is not entirely clear how to interpret these responses, but one might guess that "terrorism" indicates a voter concerned primarily with security issues, while "Iraq" may indicate a voter concerned that the war was not going well. The fourth most important issue was education (15.2 percent), traditionally the top issue for Latinos: in 2000 Latinos rated education as the most important issue facing the nation and facing Latinos. The next most important issue was health care, followed by immigration and then crime. It is worth noting that while many believe immigration is a high-priority issue for Latinos, this survey confirms the findings of previous research. Latinos do not emphasize the immigration issue, and more generally, Latino issue priorities are quite similar to those of Anglos (DeSipio 2007).

As was the case in recent elections, the candidates discussed few issues in the 2004 presidential race that were unique to the Latino community overall. Cuban Americans in Florida, however, were able to get one uniquely Latino-specific issue on the national table because of Florida's potentially central role in selecting the president. Non–Cuban Americans had long been barred from sending money or prescriptions to Cuba or visiting Cuba. When the Bush administration extended these limits to people in the United States who had close relatives in

Table 1.2. The Single Most Important Issue in Your Vote for President, 2004

Issue	*October 2004 Result (%)*
Economy	26.7
Terror	20.2
Iraq	15.2
Education	15.2
Health	11.1
Immigration	3.5
Crime	1.3
Other	3.0
Don't know	3.9

Source: Question 15 of the *Washington Post*/Univision/TRPI October Election "Survey of Registered Latino Voters in the 2004 Elections."

Cuba or were born in Cuba (although small remittances could continue to be sent), recent Cuban émigrés (the group in U.S. society most likely to be affected by the changes) were outraged and vocal (Glionna 2004).

Interestingly, these new restrictions came in response to calls from Cuban American leaders to tighten the Cuban economic embargo (Wallsten 2004). These limits, and the outrage they engendered, led many to believe that divisions might emerge in the Cuban American vote, with more recent émigrés (who had naturalized) being more likely to support Kerry or not to vote. The Bush campaign was clearly concerned about this possibility and invested heavily in advertising in Miami media markets. The Bush campaign alone spent nearly $1.5 million in Miami (Segal 2006). In contrast, the Kerry campaign spent just $197,000, although this was supplemented with $1.2 million in party and NDN advertising. In the end, there is little evidence that this issue shaped many Cuban American votes (Balz and Morin 2004; chap. 9, this volume). Nevertheless, the possibility of political cleavages among Cuban Americans based on year of migration and communication with relatives in Cuba is one to watch for in the future (García Bedolla and Lavariega Monforti 2006; New Democrat Network 2006).

A second important issue in the 2004 race was the potential for voter intimidation. Although it was not uniquely focused on Latinos, it certainly had the potential to shape the power of their votes. Specifically, critics of the identification requirements included in the Help America Vote Act for first-time voters and state-passed voting identification requirements worried that these limitations could be applied more broadly (Kurlantzick 2004). These requirements disproportionately affect Latinos for three reasons. First, the poor, of whom Latinos are a substantial subpopulation, are less likely to have identification than others in U.S. society. Second, precinct workers may tend to apply the rules unevenly; fears about noncitizen voting (of which there is virtually no evidence on the ground) could cause them to ask Latinos for identification more often than others. Finally, signage at polling places listing identification requirements and, especially, penalties could prove confusing or off-putting for new voters and voters whose first language is not English, again disproportionately reducing Latino votes. In addition, Latino civic organizations identified a significant number of localized efforts to reduce the Latino vote (Hendricks 2004).

Latino organizations responded as they had in previous elections—condemning these policies and setting up phone banks to collect reports of voter intimidation (National Council of La Raza 2004a, 2004b). On Election Day several organizations documented incidences of voter intimidation and rules that disadvantaged minorities. For example, urban and minority voters in Ohio faced long delays in voting and needed court intervention to keep the polls open (Highton 2006; Kennedy 2006). Again, new voting requirements and new forms of intimidation need to be monitored in upcoming elections.

Although Latino leaders would periodically seek to interject specific issues into the campaign, their organizational efforts were weak in 2004. In part, this probably reflected the electoral map of the campaign and its exclusion of the states with the largest Latino populations. As has been the case in recent presidential election cycles, coalitions of Latino organizations raised funds for and implemented national voter registration drives (Gonzales 2004). These voter registration efforts claimed to have registered two million new Latino voters since 2000.

Puerto Rico's taxpayers funded one such effort. The Puerto Rican Federal Affairs Administration claimed to register 322,000 new Latino voters. Its focus on Latinos, rather than just Puerto Ricans, caused some controversy in Puerto Rico.

These Latino-led voter mobilization efforts generally focused on voter registration rather than GOTV efforts. While they certainly added new registered voters to the rolls, they did not add a commensurate number of new voters (discussed later). However, that connection was more likely to be made in the battleground states, especially Florida, where the parties invested heavily in GOTV efforts among the newly registered.

The leaders of the major Latino organizations also sought, as they had in presidential elections since 1984, to craft a consensus document on issues facing Latino communities—the so-called National Hispanic Leadership Agenda.[5] Despite some tentative efforts, no document was produced in 2004, and neither campaign had the opportunity to speak to the leading Latino civic organizations sitting as a collective about a broad Latino-focused agenda in a formal setting. Nor did the campaigns undertake any other effort to shape a cohesive Latino policy agenda using help from leading Latino organizations.

LATINOS AND 2004 NONPRESIDENTIAL RACES

Where Latino influence was limited in the 2004 presidential race, it was felt more dramatically in the year's Senate races. Two Latinos, Mel Martinez (R) in Florida and Ken Salazar (D) in Colorado, were elected to the U.S. Senate. The election of Senator Jon Corzine (D-NJ) to the New Jersey governorship led to the appointment of U.S. Representative Robert Menéndez (D) to the Senate in 2005. Never before had two Latinos served simultaneously in the U.S. Senate, let alone three, and never before had a Latino represented a state other than New Mexico in the U.S. Senate.

The Martinez and Salazar elections reflected the abilities of both candidates to build multiethnic coalitions among voters and to build strong donor bases. Neither Colorado nor Florida Latinos have the numbers or political influence to elect statewide candidates on their own no matter how cohesive their votes. Equally important, and especially so for the Republican Party in the case of the Martinez candidacy, these efforts reflected national party calculations about the need to promote Latino candidacies at the state level in order to build Latino support for non-Latino party candidates. These two candidacies offer models for state-level campaigns to elect Latinos in other states.

Senator Martinez, a naturalized U.S. citizen who migrated from Cuba to the United States while in his teens in 1962, brought a rich set of professional credentials to the Florida Senate race (Barone and Cohen 2006). After an unsuccessful race for Florida lieutenant governor in 1994, Martinez was elected chair of the Orange County, Florida, government, a position whose name was later changed to mayor of the county to reflect its executive responsibilities. In 2001 President Bush nominated Martinez to serve as secretary of the U.S. Department of Housing and Urban Development (HUD). During his service, the Bush administration tapped Martinez to speak to the Spanish-language media on behalf of HUD, as well as about Bush policies more generally. He served as secretary until he resigned in December 2003 to run for the U.S. Senate. The Senate seat was opened when Senator Bob Graham (D) began a presidential campaign and indicated that he would not simultaneously run for reelection. Martinez did not initially seem interested in pursuing the U.S. Senate seat, instead focusing on the governorship in 2006. He eventually entered the race with backing from the White House and leading Senate Republicans, including George Allen and Rick Santorum, then rising stars in their party.

The open Senate seat attracted a large number of candidates from both parties. Martinez was not initially the leading candidate for the Republican nomination. Representative Mark Foley raised over $3 million by June 2003, but he dropped out of the race when the media hinted at his homosexuality. The White House appeared to intercede to discourage some high-profile candidates from pursuing the race, most notably Representative Katherine Harris (who would run and lose in 2006) (Ceaser and Busch 2005: 152).

In the primary, Martinez faced former Representative Bill McCollum, who had lost a Senate bid in 2000. The primary race was ugly.

McCollum attacked Martinez as a trial lawyer and "failed HUD secretary." Martinez defended his work as a lawyer, spoke of his rags-to-riches successes, and attacked McCollum as anti-family because of his support for a hate crimes bill. The Martinez campaign ran one commercial that tied McCollum to the "radical homosexual agenda" because of his support for a hate crimes bill, which the campaign later withdrew at the request of Florida Governor Jeb Bush. Throughout the race, Martinez maintained the support of the White House and national Republican leaders. Because of this support, state Republican politicians and activists may have worried that a failure to support Martinez could result in negative consequences (see chap. 9, this volume).

Despite the vitriol of the race, Martinez won the primary handily (45 percent to 31 percent). He won all sections of the state but did especially well among the largely Cuban Republican electorate in Miami-Dade County. In Miami-Dade, Martinez took nearly four in five votes.

The negativity of the Republican primary continued through the general election, though backed by considerably more money. Martinez spent nearly $13 million, and his Democratic opponent, Betty Castor, a former legislator and president of the University of South Florida, spent $11.5 million. The race was interrupted by four hurricanes and was overshadowed by the hard-fought presidential race, which consumed opportunities to advertise and potential campaign volunteers. Martinez accused Castor of being soft on terrorism because of a controversy surrounding a University of South Florida professor. Castor sought to present herself as an "independent Democrat" and Martinez as a rubber stamp for the White House. Martinez continued to tap his own success story as a key message in his campaign. Like McCollum, Castor tried to attack Martinez based on failures at HUD during his term.

Unlike the Republican primary, the vote in the general election was very close. Martinez won by fewer than 83,000 votes. Cuban American votes were especially important to the Martinez victory, though his appeal did not necessarily extend to non-Cuban Latinos. In the end, however, Martinez did better among Latino voters than did President Bush; CNN analysis of the National Exit Poll showed that President Bush carried 56 percent of Florida Latino votes and Martinez won 60 percent.

Colorado also elected a Latino senator in 2004. Attorney General Ken Salazar defeated Peter Coors, heir to the brewery of the same name, somewhat more decisively than Mel Martinez defeated Betty Castor—51 percent to 47 percent. Salazar, whose brother also won an open House seat from Colorado, tapped the iconography of rural Colorado as well as his Hispanic roots to win the Senate seat for the Democrats (Florio 2004). Salazar's victory is even more remarkable considering that John Kerry lost the state by a 52 to 47 percent margin.

The Colorado Senate seat opened with the retirement of Senator Ben Nighthorse Campbell (R), a decision that came as something of a surprise. Initially, each party saw a large pool of candidates for the open seat. On the Democratic side, several of the initially leading candidates withdrew and endorsed Attorney General Salazar. The Republican Party saw a more competitive race between Coors Brewing chair Pete Coors and U.S. Representative Bob Schaffer. Although Coors was the odds-on favorite, he proved a less than adept campaigner with a policy agenda and corporate history—mostly notably, a proposal to lower the Colorado drinking age and the Coors company's support of Colorado's gay pride festival—that made him suspect to many Republican primary voters (Greene 2004). Ultimately, Coors won the primary by a healthy margin, but he entered the general election without the advantage that a Republican candidate would have expected in recent Colorado elections (Florio and Bartels 2004; Barone and Cohen 2006).

The fall campaign was fractious and ultimately proved one of the few Democratic victories. Throughout the campaign, polls suggested that it was a toss-up. Salazar won the fund-raising battle, raising nearly $10 million for his race compared to Coors's $7.8 million. Salazar ran independently of the Kerry campaign and stressed his deep family ties to Colorado. He focused his campaign on environmental issues, health care, and tax equity. Salazar did not place issues framed in terms of the Latino community at the center of his agenda (see chap. 4, this volume), running a decidedly nonethnic campaign from start to finish.

The tone of Salazar's campaign adopted that of the Republican primary; he continued to attack Coors and emphasize his inexperience. He noted in particular Coors's inconsistent positions on education vouchers. When Coors attacked Salazar for being a lawyer, claiming there were already too many lawyers in the Senate, Salazar responded that there were too many multimillionaires in the Senate. Although Coors tried to galvanize moral conservatives by discussing his support for the Family Marriage Amendment, the legacy of the primary undermined this approach. Coors also focused on his support for President Bush and for the war in Iraq, though he undercut this position somewhat in October by saying that he might not have voted for it in 2003 had he known what he knew in 2004.

Salazar won the race with a comfortable margin—51 to 47 percent. CNN analysis of National Election Poll data indicates that the Salazar victory was the result of minority voters. He carried 80 percent of the black vote and 72 percent of the Latino vote, while losing the white vote by the same margin he won statewide—51 to 47 percent. Salazar did slightly better among Colorado Latinos than did John Kerry but not quite as well in the small Colorado African American community. Kerry lost the white vote in Colorado by a 54 to 44 percent margin. Ultimately, Salazar owed his victory to urban and suburban voters, but he was able to keep the gap sufficiently narrow in rural areas to ensure his victory. John Kerry, for example, took just 35 percent of the rural vote; Ken Salazar was able to win 45 percent.

Two new Latino members joined the U.S. House of Representatives after the 2004 election.[6] Henry Cuellar won a seat by defeating a fellow Latino Democrat and incumbent U.S. representative, Ciro Rodriguez, in the Texas 2004 primary. John Salazar (Ken Salazar's older brother) defeated Republican Greg Walcher in an open-seat race in Colorado, a seat previously held by a Republican. The 2004 elections therefore resulted in a net increase of one Latino member in the U.S. House of Representatives.

Despite Cuellar's claim that a primary challenge was not an unusual occurrence in South Texas, it was highly unusual in the House and brought a great deal of attention to the race. Rodriguez was at a relative disadvantage because the district had been significantly redrawn in 2003 as part of a GOP mid-Census effort to weaken Texas Democratic House incumbents. The redistricting entailed moving several heavily Hispanic counties out of the district and moving more of Laredo (Cuellar's hometown) into the district. Though both were Democrats, the two candidates offered distinct views on policy. The more conservative Cuellar had endorsed President Bush in 2000 (but supported John

Kerry in 2004) and had served as Republican Governor Rick Perry's appointed secretary of state in 2001, while Rodriguez had the most liberal voting record of Texas's six Latino members of Congress (Barone and Cohen 2006).

The race proved very close, with Rodriguez initially winning by 145 votes of the approximately 50,000 cast. Rodriguez carried the parts of the district around his San Antonio base and Cuellar the parts around his hometown of Laredo. After a recount, a judicial challenge, and an appeal, Cuellar won the primary by 58 votes (Off the Kuff 2004). He then won an easy victory in the general election, garnering 59 percent of the vote. In the same election, President Bush won 53 percent of the votes in that district.

Democrat John Salazar's Colorado congressional victory came in a Republican-leaning district; President Bush carried the district by 10 percentage points or more in 2000 and 2004, and Republicans had a six percentage point registration advantage. The post-2000 redistricting had added some Democratic areas and Latino population concentrations, however, improving Salazar's chances. The incumbent did not run in 2004; Scott McInnis (R) announced in 2003 that he would not seek reelection after having served six terms.

Salazar was a sitting member of the Colorado assembly, but he was probably better known in the district for organizing against a developer's efforts to sell San Luis Valley water rights for use in Denver (Barone and Cohen 2006: 330; Reid 2004). A great advantage, Salazar's candidacy lacked competition in the primary. His general election opponent, Greg Walcher, faced stiff primary competition, including a strong race by the brother-in-law of the retiring representative.

In the general election, Salazar positioned himself as a centrist and emphasized his ties to the district and his occupation as a farmer. In addition, several high-profile policy issues worked to his advantage. Walcher had supported a 2003 state initiative to issue $2 billion in bonds for water projects that was highly unpopular in the rural parts of the state; Salazar noted at most of his campaign appearances, "Walcher stood on the side of urban interests while I was fighting for the rural areas here in the 3rd District" (Reid 2004), not a claim that a Democrat could routinely make. Walcher tried to attack Salazar on social conservative issues such as abortion and gay marriage,[7] but ultimately these issues did not drive the election in the district. Salazar focused on agricultural issues, repeal of the estate tax, and the rights of gun owners (Draper 2004).

Ultimately, Salazar won with 51 percent of the vote, which was significantly better than John Kerry's 44 percent in the district. The excitement generated by his brother's Senate campaign and the similar message about the Salazar brothers that the two campaigns promoted undoubtedly assisted his victory. John Salazar's campaign, however, deserves significant credit for being able to raise more than $1.6 million. Walcher raised $1.5 million.

Table 1.3 provides financial data for House campaigns that involve a Latino candidate. The first row shows the money raised by Latino incumbents in three election cycles: 1995–96, 1999–2000, and 2003–4. Over time, Latino incumbent fund-raising increased, although the rate of growth slowed in the last four years (11.8 percent) in comparison to the 1996–2000 cycle (107 percent). The average amount, $853,000, is about $160,000 less than that raised by the average House incumbent. Because many incumbents run unopposed, we also calculate the funds raised by Latino incumbents facing major party candidates. This was slightly more ($941,000), which represented a small and possibly meaningless decline ($60,000) from the previous presidential election cycle.

Most challengers raise significantly less money than incumbents, and this is also true for Latino challengers and those who challenge Latino incumbents. Major party challengers to Latino members of Congress raised $85,043, a $23,000 decline from the previous presidential election cycle. Furthermore, Latino challengers to non-Latino incumbents raised less money in 2003–4 than in 1999–2000. Nevertheless, Latino challengers to Latino incumbents showed an average increase of $90,000 (to an average of $227,788) in comparison to 1999–2000. This suggests that perhaps political competition in Latino districts is increasing as serious Latino challenges to non-Latino incumbents are on the decline.

In open seat elections, we see considerable spending increases over time. In the 1995–96 campaign Latino open-seat candidates raised almost half a million dollars on average. This declined considerably in 1999–2000 (to less than $100,000 on average) but then increased in 2003–4 to $752,573. Even this amount is less than the average $1.2 million that all open-seat candidates raised.

Table 1.3. Campaign Fund-Raising, 1995–1996, 1999–2000, 2003–2004

	1995–1996	*1999–2000*	*2003–2004*	*% Change 1996–2000*	*% Change 2000–2004*	*% Change 1996–2004*
Incumbents, average for:						
Latino incumbents	$368,758	$762,881	$853,103	+106.8	+11.8	+131.3
Latino incumbents facing major party opponents	$339,215	$1,057,283	$941,508	+211.7	-11.0	+177.6
All incumbents	$725,677	$900,026	$1,130,426	+24	+25.6	+55.8
General election challengers to incumbents, average for:						
Major party challengers to Latino incumbents (all ethnicities)	$57,143	$108,688	$85,043	+90.2	-21.8	+48.8
Latino challengers to Latino incumbents	$28,026	$135,848	$227,788	+384.7	+67.7	+712.8
Latino challengers to non-Latino incumbents	NA	$364,944	$226,910	—	-37.8	—
All challengers to incumbents	$262,813	$364,944	$267,253	+38.9	-26.8	+1.7
General election to open seats, average for:						
Latino candidates	$480,545	$78,017	$752,573	-83.8	+864.6	+56.6
All candidates	$640,000	$1,080,944	$1,204,340	+68.9	+11.4	+88.2

Sources: 1995–96 data from de la Garza and DeSipio 1999: table 1.5; 1999–2000 data from de la Garza and DeSipio 2004: table 1.11; 2003–4: authors' calculations of Federal Election Commission data available at www.fec.gov/finance/disclosure/srssea.shtml (accessed May 13, 2007); and Barone and Cohen 2005.
Note: In 2000 one Latino incumbent (California's Matthew Martinez) lost in a party primary and, consequently, did not run in the general election. If he is excluded from the average, the amount raised by Latino incumbents rises to $794,521. In 2003–4 nominees for both parties were incumbents due to redistricting in one Texas race. For the calculations in table 1.13, both candidates in these races were coded as incumbents rather than challengers or open seats.

Latinos also saw gains at other levels of elective office. The number of Latinos in state-level elective office increased, particularly in the lower houses of state legislatures. Prior to the election, 161 Latinos served in state assemblies and 61 in state senates (NALEO Educational Fund 2004a). After the election, the number of Latinos in lower legislative houses increased to 171, and the number in state senates decreased by one to 60 (NALEO Educational Fund 2004b).

The 2004 election saw a final dimension of Latino influence: a dramatic growth in spending by Latino political action committees (PACs). The role of PACs and 527s is growing in U.S. national elections, and Latino leaders are using these new tools to raise and spend campaign money. Latino PAC spending grew from $605,000 in 2000 to slightly more than $1.8 million in 2004 (Russell 2005). Republican Latinos seeking to support Latino Republican candidates formed the largest Latino PAC in 2004—the Latino Alliance. Its president is columnist and unsuccessful Bush nominee for secretary of labor, Linda Chavez. It spent nearly $700,000 in 2004. The second largest Hispanic PAC in 2004—the Hispanic Democratic Organization—supported Democrats running for office. The third largest Latino PAC—the U.S.-Cuba Democracy PAC—focused its money on "candidates running for the United States Congress, who oppose any economic measures that directly or indirectly finance and prolong the repressive machinery of the Castro regime" (U.S.-Cuba Democracy PAC 2004).

A review of the expenditures of these PACs at opensecrets.org suggests the first two spent relatively little money directly on candidates. Instead, they spent money to raise money and support staff and offices. The U.S.-Cuba Democracy PAC, on the other hand, spent most of its resources on candidate contributions and made those contributions in a very bipartisan manner. While Latinos therefore tapped a new resource for political influence in 2004, the impact of party-focused PACs was limited because they did not expand the financial resources available to candidates running for office.

The state ballot initiative most relevant to Latinos in 2004 was Arizona's Proposition 200, the Protect Arizona Now initiative. It received a great deal of national media attention and would have prohibited "public benefits" for unauthorized immigrants. Following the logic of California's 1994 Proposition 187, Proposition 200 added new prohibitions on services to unauthorized immigrants, including a requirement that voters prove their U.S. citizenship and, according to its critics, requirements that local public officials deny authorized immigrants access to parks, libraries, or emergency services, such as fire departments (Kammer 2004; National Council of La Raza 2004c). The Arizona campaign in support of Proposition 200 grew from concerns about increasing unauthorized migration that resulted from enforcement efforts on the California-Mexico border. While national and state Latino leaders strongly opposed the proposition, it is not so clear that this outrage spread to Latino voters. Supporters of Proposition 200 were careful to limit their ire to unauthorized migrants and not, as had been the case in California in 1994, expand the rhetoric to a more general incitement of Latinos (see chap. 5, this volume). Ultimately, the proposition passed with 56 percent of the statewide vote. Latinos only narrowly opposed the initiative, by a 47 to 53 percent margin.

Colorado voters considered a ballot issue that, had it passed and spread to other states, would have served Latino interests. Amendment 36 would have changed Colorado's allocation of Electoral College votes to a proportional system (Johnson 2004). Although this proposal was ultimately rejected by voters, it opens the possibility that states will consider alternatives to what is now the dominant winner-take-all pattern of allocating Electoral College votes. Changes like this would increase competition in states that are now solidly in the hands of one of the parties—the states in which the vast majority of the Latino population resides—and increase the incentive for candidates and parties to invest in voter mobilization in solidly partisan areas.

LATINO VOTES AND NATIONAL ELECTIONS

Expectations of Latino influence build from a recognition that the size of the Latino population is growing rapidly and will continue to do so for the foreseeable future. This perception is generally correct, but it masks population characteristics that dampen the Latino political voice. Table 1.4 shows that Latinos make up 14.2 percent of the U.S. population and 12.6 percent of the voting-age population (VAP). In the parallel volume discussing the 1996 election, *Awash in the Mainstream,* de la Garza and DeSipio (1999) noted an overall Latino population of 28.4 million individuals; the comparable figure in 2004 was just over 40 million. Of these, 27 million are of voting age, and 16 million are voting age U.S. citizens. Compared to other racial and ethnic groups in the United States, however, Latinos have a higher share of the population who either cannot or do not participate in electoral politics. Latinos make up just 8.2 percent of the *U.S. citizen* voting age population. This noncitizenship challenge helps to explain why Latino political power does not match the size of the Latino population: 11 million Latino adult noncitizens currently cannot vote.

Although political districts in the United States are based on overall population and elected officials are tasked with representing these districts, it is also true that politicians are more likely to respond to those who elected them to office or who might be expected to exercise the vote in the next election. Latinos may constitute a significant and growing share of the population, but this is no guarantee that political repre-

Table 1.4. National Overview, United States, 2004

Total U.S. population[a]	285,691,501
Total Latino population[a]	40,459,196
% Latino of total U.S. population[a]	14.2
% Mexican American of Latino population[a]	64.0
% Puerto Rican of Latino population[a]	9.6
% Cuban American of Latino population[a]	3.6
% Other Hispanic of Latino population[a]	22.9
Voting age population (VAP)[b]	215,694,000
Latino VAP[b]	27,129,000
% Latino of VAP[b]	12.6
Citizen VAP	197,006,000
Latino citizen VAP	16,088,000
% Latino citizen VAP	8.2
Latino adult noncitizens[b]	11,041,000

Source: U.S. Census Bureau.

[a] Based on the 2004 American Community Survey.

[b] Based on Current Population Study 2004: table 2 (White alone and Hispanic).

sentation is inevitable or even likely. Relying on population size alone to generate political power—what de la Garza (1996) called "el cuento de los números"—is risky and built on an unclear understanding of political representation.

The Latino Vote in 2004

In 1976 there were about 2 million Latino voters, or 2.4 percent of the electorate. By 2004 this had grown to 7.6 million voters and 6 percent of the electorate (see table 1.5). Although these estimates are based on self-reported Census data and may therefore overestimate the vote, it is clear that the number and share of Latino voters is increasing across the decades. In no year has the number of Latino reported voters or their share of the national vote decreased or remained static. Translating this growth into real power to move politicians away from the traditional "piñata politics" toward policy substance is a continuing challenge for the Latino political community and one that was not resolved in the 2004 election. On the contrary, the nature of the 2004 election and its focus on a handful of battleground states—largely states with few Latinos—ceded influence to electorates in those states providing little influence for the growing Latino population.

The self-reported voting levels in table 1.5 indicate that Latino leaders did not achieve their goal of increasing the Latino electorate by two million voters between 2000 and 2004. The increase in the number of Latinos voting nationally was nevertheless larger (1.6 million) than in any previous quadrennial period and could have led to a more dramatic increase in the Latino share of the vote. The non-Latino vote also increased more than in previous quadrennial periods, so the Latino share of the national vote increased only from 5.4 to 6.0 percent.

Latino Nonvoting

Despite the increase in the number of voting Latinos, the overall pattern of relatively low rates of registration and turnout among Latinos relative to whites and African Americans continued in 2004 (table 1.6). In 1980 Latinos were about seventeen percentage points less likely to be registered than Anglos and eight points less likely to be registered than

Table 1.5. Latino Vote as a Percentage of the Total Vote, 1976–2004[a]

	1976	*1980*	*1984*	*1988*	*1992*	*1996*	*2000*	*2004*
Total vote	86,698,000	93,066,000	101,878,000	102,224,000	113,866,000	105,017,000	110,836,000	125,736,000
Latino vote[b]	2,098,000	2,453,000	3,092,000	3,710,000	4,238,000	4,928,000	5,934,000	7,587,000
Latino percentage of the total vote[c]	2.4	2.6	3.0	3.6	3.7	4.7	5.4	6.0%

Source: U.S. Bureau of the Census 1978, 1982, 1985, 1989, 1993, 1998, 2002, 2006.

[a] Voting estimates rounded to the nearest thousand.

[b] Latinos can be of any race.

[c] Based on Current Population Survey (CPS) estimates. CPS data may overestimate actual voting levels by as much as 20 percent. However, there is no evidence that different national origin groups misreport voting at different rates (U.S. Census 1990c).

African Americans. By 2004 these figures were about 16 percent and 10 percent, respectively. This suggests that registration gaps, relative to the size of the U.S. citizen population, are essentially unchanged over the past twenty-four years.

Even larger voting gaps are visible, and Latinos are again the least likely of these three racial/ethnic groups to participate.[8] In 1980 Latinos were nineteen percentage points less likely than Anglos and eight points less likely than African Americans to vote. By 2004 the respective gaps were eighteen points and thirteen points.

Because these data consist of U.S. citizen respondents over the age of eighteen—the voting age population—lower levels of U.S. citizenship in Latino communities cannot explain the differences. Youth may

Table 1.6. Voting and Registration Rates for White, Black, and Latino U.S. Citizens, 1980–2004

	White	*Black*	*Latino*
% registered (citizens)			
1980	70.8	61.7	53.3
1984	72.1	68.6	58.9
1988	71.1	67.0	56.6
1992	74.0	67.2	58.5
1996	72.0	66.4	58.6
2000	71.6	67.6	57.3
2004	73.6	68.7	57.9
% voting (citizens)			
1980	63.1	52.0	44.1
1984	64.0	57.8	48.0
1988	61.9	53.5	45.9
1992	67.1	56.9	48.2
1996	59.5	53.0	44.0
2000	61.7	56.9	45.1
2004	65.4	60.0	47.2

Source: U.S. Bureau of the Census 1982, 1985, 1989, 1993, 1998, 2002, 2006. Unless otherwise noted, all calculations of the citizen population are the authors'.

explain some of the gap. VAP Latinos are more likely to be in their twenties or thirties, whereas Anglos and African Americans are more likely to be older. In addition to relative youth among adults, scholars have noted a variety of socioeconomic factors that depress Latino turnout, in particular, low levels of formal education and low household and individual incomes (Rosenstone and Hansen 1993). While these dynamics are relevant to the participation of every group, Latinos are the most youthful group and have especially low levels of education and income (DeSipio 1996). Table 1.7 illustrates how these factors play a role in the participation of Latino, Anglo, and African American citizens.

For all groups, age is positively associated with voting. The one exception is the highest age category, as mobility and health problems can interfere with participation at this stage in life. This means that a relatively youthful group (such as Latinos) will be disadvantaged on Election Day. The data show that about 19 percent of Latino citizens are in the 18–24 age group, compared to 12 percent of Anglos and 16 percent of African Americans. Even within the same age groups, we see that Latinos are less likely to participate. For the youngest group, ages 18 to 24, only 33 percent of Latinos voted, compared to 47 percent of both Anglos and African Americans. These patterns are consistent with those of previous elections.

A similar pattern applies to education and income. Latinos are more likely to occupy the lower categories, and individuals in such categories have the lowest turnout rates. For example, about 13 percent of Latinos have less than a ninth-grade education, compared to 2.8 percent of Anglos and 4.4 percent of African Americans. Turnout is very low for this group as a whole: 37.2 percent for Latinos, 39.4 percent for Anglos, and 45.6 percent for African Americans. In terms of income, 18.2 percent of Latino U.S. citizen adults are in the lowest three categories, compared to 7.8 percent of Anglos and 23 percent of African Americans. The average turnout rate across these three categories is lowest for Hispanics, however: 33.6 percent, compared with 49 percent for Anglos and 55.7 percent for African Americans.

Non-U.S. citizenship is a barrier that disproportionately disenfranchises Latinos (and Asian Americans). In 2004, 11.0 million of 27.1 million Latino adults were ineligible to participate electorally because

Table 1.7. Turnout Rates and Share of Adult Citizen Population for Age, Education, and Income Cohorts of Latinos, Non-Latino Whites, and Non-Latino Blacks, 2004

	Latino Adult		*Non-Hispanic White Adult*		*Non-Hispanic Black Adult*	
	Turnout Rate (%)	*Population Share (%)*	*Turnout Rate (%)*	*Population Share (%)*	*Turnout Rate (%)*	*Population Share (%)*
Age						
18–24	33.0	(18.9)	47.5	(12.0)	47.1	(15.8)
25–44	45.2	(43.3)	61.5	(35.2)	59.3	(40.5)
45–64	56.2	(27.0)	72.0	(34.6)	65.3	(31.6)
65–74	57.9	(6.6)	74.4	(9.4)	68.6	(7.1)
75+	55.7	(4.2)	69.9	(8.7)	61.9	(5.0)
Education						
Less than 9 years	37.2	(12.5)	39.4	(2.8)	45.6	(4.4)
9–12 years, no diploma	30.5	(15.7)	40.6	(7.6)	45.3	(15.2)
H.S. graduate	42.7	(32.0)	58.3	(32.4)	56.3	(35.3)
Some college	56.1	(27.1)	71.7	(28.8)	66.7	(29.7)
B.A. or equivalent	66.5	(9.2)	80.7	(18.9)	72.6	(10.8)
Advanced degree	78.1	(3.6)	86.6	(9.5)	78.7	(4.5)

Table 1.7. Turnout Rates and Share of Adult Citizen Population for Age, Education, and Income Cohorts of Latinos, Non-Latino Whites, and Non-Latino Blacks, 2004 *continued*

	Latino Adult		*Non-Hispanic White Adult*		*Non-Hispanic Black Adult*	
	Turnout Rate (%)	*Population Share (%)*	*Turnout Rate (%)*	*Population Share (%)*	*Turnout Rate (%)*	*Population Share (%)*
Family Income (per year)						
Less than $10,000	34.6	(6.0)	39.4	(2.4)	50.6	(10.6)
$10,000–$14,999	35.2	(6.1)	50.2	(2.8)	55.0	(7.0)
$15,000–$19,999	42.2	(6.1)	57.3	(2.6)	61.5	(5.4)
$20,000–$29,999	45.8	(13.0)	60.5	(8.1)	61.2	(12.3)
$30,000–$39,999	45.2	(13.7)	64.9	(9.7)	67.5	(11.0)
$40,000–$49,999	47.4	(9.1)	72.4	(8.3)	66.8	(7.3)
$50,000–$74,999	59.8	(17.7)	74.6	(20.2)	73.6	(15.1)
$75,000–$99,999	66.2	(7.8)	80.1	(12.9)	77.2	(6.9)
$100,000–149,999	67.7	(5.0)	83.5	(10.8)	76.3	(4.9)
$150,000 and over	70.7	(2.0)	83.7	(6.8)	79.3	(1.9)
Not reported	34.7	(13.7)	55.6	(15.4)	42.7	(17.5)

Source: Authors' compilations based on U.S. Bureau of the Census 2006: tables 2, 6, 9.

Note: Figures in parentheses are the share of the adult citizen population made up of that age, education, or income cohort.

they were not U.S. citizens (U.S. Bureau of the Census 2005).[9] However, the effect of noncitizenship on the potential impact of Latino votes varies considerably by state (table 1.8). The state with the highest share of noncitizen adults is New Jersey. Almost 48 percent of the 906,000 Latino adults in this state were not citizens, which serves to counteract the relatively high (58.3 percent) level of voting by New Jersey Latino adult citizens. In the state of New Mexico, by contrast, only 10.7 percent of adults are not citizens, and the state has the highest voting percentage for both Latino adults and Latino adult citizens. This relatively high percentage of Latino citizens is long-standing and illustrates the importance of political context and history. Migration to New Mexico is relatively low, and Anglos are a relatively small share of the population; these unique factors help to explain the significant political power possessed by the Hispanos of this state.

In certain states with large concentrations of Latinos, the total number of ineligible Latino adults is higher even than the total Latino population of many other states. For instance, there are 3.7 million noncitizen adults in California and 1.5 million in Texas. New Mexico is in its own category; its substantial Latino population consists mainly of citizens, and only about 58,000 noncitizen adults reside in the state (although statewide and congressional elections in New Mexico can be very close, and even a few hundred or a few thousand votes in either direction have made a difference). In Florida, perhaps the most important battleground state in the union, almost a million Latino adults are not citizens, many of whom are not Cuban (a notoriously Republican subgroup) and may favor Democratic candidates if given the franchise.

Table 1.8 shows the latent voting power of Latinos, a power that is unrealized because of low voter turnout among the eligible population. Across all the states, about half of Latino citizen adults turned out to vote. This ranged from 41.6 percent in Texas to 58.3 percent in New Jersey. In aggregate terms, almost 2.2 million eligible Latinos did not vote in Texas and about 2.4 million did not vote in California, two states with extraordinarily large citizens of Latino descent.

Of course, demographics and citizenship cannot tell the entire turnout story. As Verba, Schlozman, and Brady (1995) and Rosenstone and Hansen (1993) found, civic skills and mobilization can bring individuals to the polls despite low socioeconomic status (SES). On the

Table 1.8. Latino Turnout and Noncitizenship by State, 2004

State	*All Latino Adults*	*All Latino Adult Citizens*	*Adult Latinos Who Voted*	*% of Adult Latinos Voting*	*% of Adult Latino Citizens Voting*	*Number of Noncitizen Adults*	*% of Noncitizen Adults*
Arizona	1,160,000	629,000	296,000	25.5	47.1	531,000	45.8
California	8,127,000	4,433,000	2,081,000	25.6	46.9	3,694,000	45.5
Colorado	574,000	361,000	165,000	28.7	45.7	213,000	37.1
Florida	2,422,000	1,444,000	824,000	34.0	57.1	978,000	40.4
Illinois	1,031,000	608,000	294,000	28.5	48.4	423,000	41.0
New Jersey	906,000	475,000	277,000	30.6	58.3	431,000	47.6
New Mexico	544,000	486,000	276,000	50.7	56.8	58,000	10.7
New York	1,976,000	1,346,000	613,000	31.0	45.5	630,000	31.9
Texas	5,232,000	3,688,000	1,533,000	29.3	41.6	1,544,000	29.5

Source: Authors' compilations based on U.S. Bureau of the Census 2006: table 4a.

other hand, Latinos are not particularly likely to have occupations and affiliations that promote such skills, and they are not often targeted by mobilization campaigns because of their reputation for relatively low turnout (de la Garza and DeSipio 1993, 2006; for a different conclusion based on recent Los Angeles County voting data, see Barreto, Segura, and Woods 2004); these assumptions help to create a self-fulfilling prophecy of low participation. Elections that focus on Latino mobilization and issues or candidates who speak to Latino policy needs can overcome these patterns (Shaw, de la Garza, and Lee 2000; Pantoja, Ramírez, and Segura 2001; Barreto 2005; Nuño 2007). Scholars and community organizations have identified successful models for Latino and immigrant mobilization that can dramatically increase Latino turnout (Green and Gerber 2004; Ramírez 2005; Michelson 2006). The 2004 presidential race for the most part, however, did not generate widespread efforts to mobilize Latinos.

Table 1.9 illustrates some of the reasons nonvoters offer for not turning out on Election Day. Although these responses are not expressed in social-scientific language, they provide important evidence for why so many Latinos do not make it to the polls. The first point to note is the large number of nonvoters of all ethnicities and races. Almost 20 million Latinos, 52 million Anglos, and 11 million African Americans did not vote in 2004. The reasons that individuals do not engage vary by race and ethnicity, however. For Latinos, the most significant explanation was lack of U.S. citizenship (56.5 percent), an obstacle for a much smaller percentage of the Anglo (6.3 percent) and African American (14.4 percent) populations. While the latter two figures are larger than some might have anticipated (contrary to most media and political discourse, immigration is not an entirely Latino phenomenon), the table points out the significant electoral obstacles posed by current immigration and naturalization laws.

After citizenship, the next most serious obstacle is the voter registration requirement; more than one-third of Latinos said this was the reason they did not vote in 2004. In contrast, more than two-thirds of Anglos and African Americans found them onerous. This points out how voter registration requirements are obstacles to potential voters of all races and ethnicities, and a change in these laws might benefit millions (Alvarez and Ansolabehere 2002; Keyssar 2000).

Table 1.9. Reasons for Not Voting, by Race and Ethnicity, 2004

	Latino	*Non-Hispanic White*	*Non-Hispanic Black*
Total aggregate	*19,542,000*	*51,844,000*	*10,894,000*
	%	%	%
Total nonvoters			
Not U.S. citizen	56.5	6.3	14.4
U.S. citizen, not registered	34.7	71.1	67.1
Registered, did not vote	8.8	22.7	18.5
Registered voters			
Too busy, conflicting schedule	23.5	18.9	20.7
Not interested	10.5	10.8	10.0
Illness or disability	10.7	16.2	16.5
Did not like candidates or campaign issues	7.3	11.1	6.4
Out of town	6.3	9.9	5.5
Forgot	6.1	3.0	3.9
Transportation problems	1.6	1.9	4.2
Inconvenient polling place	1.5	3.2	2.6
Registration problems	10.9	6.2	7.2
Bad weather conditions	0.2	0.5	0.3
Other	11.6	10.8	9.8
Don't know or refused	9.8	7.6	13.0

Source: Authors' compilation based on U.S. Bureau of the Census 2005: tables 2, 12.

In addition, another significant percentage of respondents indicated that they were in fact registered but simply did not vote. What are the reasons? Political scientists might note the effects of SES, but individual respondents are unlikely to provide such explanations. Nevertheless, we find that the data reveal few significant differences by race and ethnicity. The most popular explanation is busyness and unspecified schedule conflicts, and the responses are in approximately the same range for all racial/ethnic groups. Other commonly cited reasons include a lack of interest, illness or disability, being out of town, disinterest in the candidates or campaign issues, and unspecified problems with registration (despite knowing they were registered). An important issue, registration problems are slightly more likely to affect Latinos, which could reflect a lack of knowledge of the political system.

The 2004 Latino Vote in the States with Large Latino Populations

For decades Latino political activists have hoped that growing population numbers will translate into higher levels of political influence in Washington, D.C., and state capitals. Usually they are disappointed because parties and elected officials respond to voter preferences and sometimes only to those voters who are part of their winning coalitions. A large population alone is not enough to ensure substantive political representation.

To understand better the potential for Latino influence at the state level, we examined the change in the number of Latino voters in selected states from 2000 to 2004 (table 1.10). A growing Latino electorate at least has the potential to increase its political influence, whereas a declining or static minority population is unlikely to attract the attention of elected officials.

The first point to note is that the number of Latino voters increased by 27.9 percent over four years, from 5.9 million in 2000 to 7.6 million in 2004. Due to the Electoral College system, however, overall votes matter much less than do state-level returns. When we examine state data, we see significant variation. No state saw a decline in the Latino voter population; however, one state (Colorado—a battleground state, at that) experienced single-digit growth while four states in the study saw growth rates above 30 percent (California, Illinois, New Jersey, and

New Mexico, as well as the remaining "other" states). With the exception of some of the "other" states, none of these was one where we would have predicted a sizable increase in Latino voting based on candidate and campaign outreach. Clearly, these growth rates do not map well with the states we identified as having competitive and noncompetitive elections.

We can compare these growth rates to the data collected in the volume on the 1996 election (de la Garza and DeSipio 1999). From 1992 to 1996 the number of Latino voters increased by 16.3 percent, from 4.2 million to 4.9 million. In those years, one state saw its Latino electorate decline by 5.4 percent (Colorado), and only two states saw an increase of over 30 percent (New York and New Jersey). VAP growth was therefore much larger in terms of absolute numbers and relative percentages in the early 2000s than in the early 1990s.

In both time periods, the state with the fastest-growing Latino electorate was New Jersey (43.6 percent in 1992–96 and 54.7 percent in 2000–2004). In addition, the state at the bottom end of the scale in both time periods was Colorado, although 2004 saw a positive change, which contrasts with the decline in the early 1990s. One of the differences is the significant increase in the rate of growth in California (13.7 percent vs. 30.3 percent) and Arizona (4.8 percent vs. 19.8 percent). While Arizona has long been considered a Republican state in presidential voting, the Democrats have gained ground in large part as a result of the increasing Latino population, and California has become a safely Democratic state because of Latinos (Fraga, Ramírez, and Segura 2005). In addition, a Democratic "Southwest strategy" based on consolidating New Mexico and Colorado and winning Arizona and Nevada may be on the horizon.

Another notable, but perhaps less electorally significant, change is the growth in the "other" category. This electorate grew by 18.3 percent from 1992 to 1996, but it increased by 27.9 percent in 2000–2004. This likely reflects the increasingly dispersed Latino population across the "new destination" states (see chap. 12, this volume). With Latino populations and electorates increasing in states such as North Carolina and Tennessee, for the first time many parts of America are experiencing a population hitherto largely concentrated in the Southwest, Florida, and a few northern and midwestern urban areas. Some of this growth reflects new migrants, but quite a lot is due to "internal migrants" who

Table 1.10. Latino Vote, 2000 and 2004, National and Selected States

	2000 Vote	*2004 Vote*	*Change (%)*
Arizona	247,000	296,000	19.8
California	1,597,000	2,081,000	30.3
Colorado	158,000	165,000	4.4
Florida	678,000	824,000	21.5
Illinois	218,000	294,000	34.9
New Jersey	179,000	277,000	54.7
New Mexico	191,000	276,000	44.5
New York	502,000	613,000	22.1
Texas	1,300,000	1,533,000	17.9
Other	864,000	1,228,000	42.1
Total	5,934,000	7,587,000	27.9

Sources: Authors' calculations based on U.S. Bureau of the Census 2002: table 4a; 2006: table 4a.
Note: Current Population Survey data collected monthly through a household survey of approximately 50,000 households and rely on self-reporting of voting and voter eligibility in the weeks after the election. These data likely overestimate actual voting levels, perhaps by a significant amount.

are moving from established Latino metropolitan areas. Although this population growth is large in terms of percentages, it is still small in terms of absolute numbers, so the electoral impact is likely to be minimal in the years to come. Nevertheless, the very presence of Latinos in these states may well change the political debate and certainly adds a new element to the traditional black-white racial paradigm.

Latino Partisanship and Candidate Choice

National Results

Despite relatively clear evidence of non-Cuban Latino loyalty to the Democratic Party, Republicans have long claimed Latinos as the lost tribe. Ronald Reagan famously stated that "Hispanics are Republicans, they just don't know it yet" (Republican National Committee 2007). The Bush candidacies were premised, in part, on the assertion that Latinos were beginning to reconsider their allegiances (DeSipio and de la

Garza 2005). Bush garnered about 35 percent of the Latino vote in 2000, which equaled the previous high for Republicans (the 1984 contest between Ronald Reagan and Walter Mondale), which raised party hopes high for 2004. As we have suggested, the rhetoric of the 2004 campaign focused, in part, on a Latino electorate in flux that might result in further gains for the Republicans.

As demonstrated in table 1.11, however, no pattern of Latino partisan change is evident since the early 1960s. At first glance, a significant decline in Latino voting for Democratic candidates appears to occur over the past four decades; from a high of 85 percent in 1960, the Democratic proportion dropped to approximately 56 to 62 percent in 2004. This, however, compares apples and oranges because of changes in the Latino population itself and in the ways pollsters sample Latinos. The surveys of the 1960s and 1970s only included Mexican Americans, whereas today's surveys include a broader range of Latinos, including Republican-leaning Cuban Americans. As pollsters became more accurate in their sampling of Latinos (de la Garza 1987), samples moved beyond residents of urban neighborhoods and included suburban Latinos who were less liberal, therefore discovering that the political landscape looks different outside of urban Los Angeles or San Antonio. Polling in the 1960s and 1970s showed Mexican American support for Democratic presidential candidates in the 80 to 90 percent range. Once pollsters began to survey Latinos more accurately, this support appeared to "drop" to the 60 to 70 percent range.

With these caveats in mind, no other clear patterns are apparent over time. While many are searching for a larger story, such as Latino movement toward the GOP, the data are resistant to such simplifications. Instead, Latino support is more like a narrowly bounded roller coaster, much like overall American public opinion. Candidates who are more popular with Anglos are more popular with Latinos, and vice versa. For example, Reagan may have received Latino support in the mid-30s in 1984, but this was not the start of a trend. Latino support for George H. W. Bush in 1988 fell to the low 30s, and support for Bob Dole in 1996 fell into the 20 percent range. Although Latino support for the GOP increased with George W. Bush at the top of the ticket in 2000 and 2004, this may well prove to be driven by personality and circumstance rather than "un nuevo dia" (Marbut 2005).

Table 1.11. National Latino Voting Patterns, 1960–2004

Latino Electorate by Year	*Democratic Vote (%)*	*Republican Vote (%)*	*Other Vote (%)*
1960			
Mexican Americans[a]	85	15	—
1964			
Mexican Americans[a]	90	10	—
1968			
Mexican Americans[a]	87	10	—
1972			
Mexican Americans[a]	64	36	—
Mexican Americans[b]	85	15	—
1976			
Mexican Americans[b]	92	8	—
Latinos[c]	82	18	—
1980			
Latinos[c]	56	37	7
1984			
Latinos (CBS)[d]	66	34	—
Latinos (NBC)[e]	68	32	—
Latinos (ABC)[e]	56	44	—
1988			
Latinos (CBS)[d]	70	30	—
Latinos (ABC)[f]	70	30	—
Latinos (NBC)[f]	69	31	—
Latinos (L.A. Times)[f]	62	38	—
1992			
Latinos (VRS)[g]	62	24	14
Latinos (L.A. Times)[h]	53	31	16
1996			
Latinos[g]	72	21	6
2000 Latinos			
ABC[i]	62	35	—
CBS[i]	66	29	—
CNN[j]	62	34	3
Los Angeles Times[i]	61	38	1
New York Times[i]	67	31	2
USA Today[i]	64	32	2

Table 1.11. National Latino Voting Patterns, 1960–2004 *continued*

Latino Electorate by Year	*Democratic Vote (%)*	*Republican Vote (%)*	*Other Vote (%)*
2004 Latinos			
NEP (CNN-initial)[j]	53	44	2
NBC NEP (revised)[k]	58	40	
WCVI (revised)	64	35	

Sources: [a] Garcia and de la Garza 1977: 101–3.

[b] Gann and Duignan 1986: 210.

[c] CBS News/New York Times exit poll in "Opinion Roundup" (1989: 24).

[d] CBS News/New York Times exit poll in "Opinion Roundup" (1989, 25).

[e] Balz 1987: 32.

[f] "Opinion Roundup" 1986: 26.

[g] Voter Research and Surveys exit poll (most of the networks and wire services used this exit poll in 1992 and 1996).

[h] *Los Angeles Times,* November 5, 1992.

[i] Relies on data collected by the Voter News Service Consortium. Each news agency, however, develops its own analysis methodology and weighting. "Other vote" includes percentage of votes for Ralph Nader and Pat Buchanan.

[j] www.cnn.com/ELECTION/2000/results/index.epolls.html. ABC, AP, CBS, CNN, Foxnews, and NBC were part of the National Election Pool (NEP) and used exit polls from Edison Media Research and Mitofsky International. The NEP data reported in table 1.10 were obtained from CNN (www.cnn.com/ELECTION/2004/pages/results/states/US/P/00/epolls.0.html).

[k] Revised NBC (www.bizjournals.com/sanantonio/stories/2004/11/29/daily42.html).

Initial results from the 2004 election seemed to indicate that President Bush had indeed made significant inroads among Latinos. National Election Pool (NEP) analysis of the returns stated that Bush won 44 percent of their vote, suggesting that the growing numbers of Latino voters might not benefit the Democratic Party as previously expected. Subsequent analysis by Leal and colleagues (2005) and others suggests that this figure was too high. Evidence offered to challenge these results questioned the NEP methodology. First, multiple surveys with rigorous methodologies in the months leading up to the election generally found that Kerry won twice the number of votes compared to Bush, and there was no reason to expect any significant change in the final days of the campaign. No specific events transpired that would have moved Latino voters to Bush, and Latino respondents across all demographic categories reported strong Kerry support. A possible exception, non-Catholic Latinos, had been the target of Republican outreach, particularly in New Mexico, but the mid-October *Washington Post*/TRPI/Univision National Survey of Latino Voters showed this group reporting only slightly higher than average voter mobilization contacts. In addition, this group constituted only about 18 percent of the Latino electorate. Second, actual voting data from Texas counties with a high percentage of Latinos showed Kerry with a comfortable lead over Bush. Due to the very high share of the Latino vote in these counties, the NEP finding of an evenly divided Tejano vote does not appear to be accurate.

While NEP defended this number after the election, NBC would later revise the figure to 40 percent, and most analysts who follow the issue agree that 38 to 40 percent is more realistic. This was also reminiscent of the situation in 2000, when exit pollsters initially claimed that Bush won 40 percent of the Latino vote but eventually adjusted this number to 35 percent. The quality of journalistic reporting on Latinos is so mixed that some newspaper articles today still repeat the 44 percent figure.

State Results

Although we have concerns about the accuracy of exit poll measures of Latino candidate choice, they offer the only available tool to assess state-by-state Latino voting patterns and thereby assess Latino influence in electoral outcomes. We believe that these data should be interpreted with some caution, and we note particular areas of concern below (table 1.12).

The NEP state-level results show that John Kerry won the majority of Latinos in all states but Florida. Kerry comfortably won the Latino vote in Illinois, New York, Colorado, and California. His share of the Latino vote did not exceed 60 percent in New Jersey, New Mexico, or Texas, however, which is low for a Democrat (see also chap. 2, this volume).

Bush did best among Latinos in Florida, receiving 56 percent of the vote. This was most likely due to the predominantly Republican Cuban American population, but it may also reflect the more general popularity of then-Governor Jeb Bush among many Latinos. This margin is narrow for a Republican and demonstrates that Florida's Latino community is rapidly diversifying.

Table 1.12. Exit Polls of Latino Presidential Candidate Choice

	Kerry (%)	*Bush (%)*	*Nader (%)*	*Latino Share (%)*
Latinos nationally				
NEP	53	44	2	8
NEP (NBC revised)	58	40		
Los Angeles Times	54	45		5
WCVI[a] exit poll	65	33	2	Not reported
WCVI exit poll (revised)	64	35		
Latinos by state				
Arizona NEP	56	43		12
California NEP	63	32		21
Colorado NEP	68	30	—	8
Florida NEP	44	56	—	15
Illinois NEP	76	23		8
New Jersey NEP	56	43	1	10
New Mexico NEP	56	44	1	32
New York NEP	75	24	1	9
Texas NEP	50	49		20

Notes: ABC, AP, CBS, CNN, Foxnews, and NBC were part of the National Election Pool (NEP) and used exit polls from Edison Media Research and Mitofsky International. The NEP data reported in table 1.11 were found at the CNN Web site. The *Los Angeles Times* California exit poll data were found at www.latimes.com/media/acrobat/2004-12/15267247.pdf.
[a] William C. Valasquez Institute.

Bush also did quite well in Texas, where he had served as governor before his 2000 presidential election. As state chief executive, Bush cultivated positive relationships with Tejanos and refused to campaign against immigrants or countenance those who did, such as Pete Wilson of California. This contrast won Bush Hispanic support in Texas during his gubernatorial campaigns; Kerry made little effort to campaign in the state. We are dubious, however, of the 49 percent NEP figure, in large part because Kerry earned a significantly higher share of the vote in high-concentration Latino areas of the state (Leal et al. 2005). While the Latinos in such areas may well be more Democratic than Latinos who live among non-Latinos, a high share of Texas's Latino population resides in these high-concentration areas. Therefore, it would be difficult to see the source of the high number of Bush votes in the state.

Latino Influence on the 2004 Presidential Race

The ability of Latino communities to shape a state's Electoral College delegation is not simply a function of the share of votes for each candidate. Even a 90 to 10 margin for one candidate may mean little if Latino voters constitute only a small percentage of the electorate or if the non-Latino electorate supports one of the candidates by a margin larger than the size of the Latino electorate. The last column of table 1.12 indicates the Latino share of the state vote for selected states. Again, we see a great deal of variation between the states. Of the nine states with significant Latino populations, the lowest percent included Illinois and Colorado (8 percent each) and the highest was New Mexico (32 percent). In the upper-middle range were California (21 percent) and Texas (20 percent); in the lower-middle range, Florida (15 percent), Arizona (12 percent), New Jersey (10 percent), and New York (9 percent).

We assess two measures of possible Latino influence on the outcome of the 2004 presidential race (see also chap. 2, this volume). The first is a baseline measure for Latino influence: what would have happened in the state races if no Latino had voted. Clearly, this is only a thought experiment. Latinos are integral to the body politic and are growing as an electorate, not shrinking or disappearing. The "no Latino voted" model, however, provides a measure of the minimum level of Latino influence. If the non-Latino electorate is sufficiently large and sufficiently cohesive, Latino votes simply do not matter in presidential politics and Latino influence is largely absent. The second measure is Latinos' importance to the winning candidate's margin of victory. We therefore assess whether the outcome would have changed if Latinos did not vote for the candidate who won each state's popular vote but continued to vote for the losing candidate at the levels estimated by the exit polls. In previous analysis, we have used a third measure of influence: a change in the result of a presidential race in a state either because Latinos voted in higher numbers than would be expected based on normal quadrennial population growth or because Latinos voted more cohesively than would be expected based on the results of recent elections. We have found only one example of this form of influence, the most rigorous, between 1988 and 2000: Arizona in 1996. We did not find any examples in 2004.

As is evident in tables 1.13 and 1.14, Latino votes made little difference in the allocation of these nine states' Electoral College delegates. In the thirty-six state-level races for presidential electors in the nine states with large Latino populations in the 1988 through 2000 elections, the results in twenty-five would have been no different if no Latino voted (DeSipio and de la Garza 2005: 27–31). In three states (Illinois, New York, and Texas) the popular vote margin was larger than the entire Latino vote, meaning that it was impossible for Latino voters to make a difference (see table 1.13). In all states, the net Latino vote for the winner did not provide the winning margin. While Bush won by only 6,988 votes in New Mexico, it was non-Latinos who provided the margin. Fewer Latino votes would serve to increase the electoral competitiveness of some states but probably not enough to turn any Republican or Democratic states into battleground states. For instance, without Latino voters in California, Kerry's margin would have declined from about 1.2 million to about 700,000 votes.

The situation was different in 2000 because of the very close results in Florida and New Mexico and because each state narrowly selected the candidate of choice of the majority of its Latinos. In both states, the outcome would have changed without any Latino voters. Gore would have won Florida, Bush would have won New Mexico, and Gore would have won the presidency in the Electoral College. That this did not occur in 2004 does not mean that Latinos are becoming less influential but that Latino influence is contingent—as it almost always is—on the voting behavior of non-Latinos.

A significant share of the electorate may provide little political power for Latinos if non-Latinos are united behind another candidate. In table 1.14 we assess what would have happened if Latinos had not supported the winning candidate. The first part shows the overall Bush and Kerry vote in each state and the Bush margin of victory (or loss) in

Table 1.13. Latino Influence on Award of Electoral College Votes

	Electoral Winner	*Popular Vote Margin*	*Latino Vote*	*Estimated Latino Vote for Winner*	*Estimated Latino Vote for Loser*	*Net Latino Vote for Winner*	*Result Had No Latino Voted*
2000							
Arizona	Bush	96,311	247,000	81,510	165,490	-83,980	No change
California	Gore	1,293,774	1,597,000	1,117,900	479,100	+638,800	No change
Colorado	Bush	145,521	158,000	38,710	119,290	-80,580	No change
Florida	Bush	537	678,000	335,610	342,390	-6,780	Gore wins state
Illinois	Gore	569,605	218,000	NA	NA	NA	No change
New Jersey	Gore	504,677	179,000	102,030	76,970	+25,060	No change
New Mexico	Gore	366	191,000	126,060	64,940	+61,120	Bush wins state
New York	Gore	1,704,323	502,000	404,110	97,890	+306,220	No change
Texas	Bush	1,365,893	1,300,000	539,500	760,500	-221,000	No change
2004							
Arizona	Bush	210,770	296,000	127,280	168,720	-41,440	No change
California	Kerry	1,235,659	2,081,000	1,311,030	769,970	+541,060	No change
Colorado	Bush	99,523	165,000	49,500	115,500	-66,000	No change
Florida	Bush	380,878	824,000	461,440	362,560	+98,880	No change
Illinois	Kerry	545,604	294,000	223,440	70,560	+152,880	No change
New Jersey	Kerry	241,427	277,000	154,560	122,440	+32,120	No change
New Mexico	Bush	5,988	276,000	121,440	154,560	-33,120	No change
New York	Kerry	1,351,713	613,000	459,750	153,250	+306,500	No change
Texas	Bush	1,694,213	1,533,000	751,170	781,830	-30,660	No change

Sources: Exit polls: authors' compilations based on published sources; turnout data: authors' calculations based on U.S. Bureau of the Census 2002: table 4a; 2006: table 4a.
Note: "Estimated Latino Vote for Winner" is calculated by multiplying major state exit poll data for the state's winning candidate.

terms of absolute votes and percentages. The second part calculates the Latino vote for the winning candidates and then shows the winner's margin had no Latino voted for the winning candidate. The results show that three states might have switched had no Latino voted for the winning presidential candidate in 2004. Bush would have won California, and Kerry would have won Florida and New Mexico. In the other states, no change would have occurred. This suggests that in three states the Latino votes received by the winning candidate were enough to make the difference, although it is somewhat arbitrary to subtract Latino votes from the winner's total but not the loser's total.

CONCLUSION

As was the case in several of the recent presidential election cycles analyzed in this series, the structure of the 2004 campaign did not work to the advantage of Latino outreach or Latino influence. Latinos were the target of outreach to the extent that they resided in competitive states. Thus Latinos in Arizona, New Mexico, and Nevada saw some attention in the primaries (less than we would have predicted), and Latinos in Colorado, New Mexico, Florida, Pennsylvania, and Ohio were the targets of candidate and party attention in the general election.

The winner-take-all nature of awarding Electoral College votes largely eliminated any argument about Latino influence in these states, with the candidate of choice of the majority of Latino voters losing in all these states but Florida and Pennsylvania (and there winning by well more than the number of Latino votes). As was the case in the 1988, 1996, and 2000 races, the vast majority of Latinos did not see or hear much (or any) outreach, whether Latino-targeted or not, and had little incentive to vote in the presidential race (or, in most cases, in state or local races). Latino-led outreach was largely absent, and no comprehensive national strategy was undertaken to move Latino permanent residents toward U.S. citizenship or to transport nonvoting Latino registered voters to the polls.

Despite these issues, the standard story of the lack of Latino influence is no longer adequate. The importance of Latinos goes beyond their simple contribution to the winning coalitions in the states. Their presence in the electorate now shapes certain strategic decisions in both parties. To simply claim that Latinos were politically inconsequential in 2004 because their vote played no role in the election's outcome is to neglect the broad change in the importance of Latino voters and the more amorphous "Latino community" to national politics.

As we document here, the 2004 election presents a new role for Latinos in national elections, whether or not the competitiveness of state

Table 1.14. Latino Influence and the 2004 Elections

Margin between Bush and Kerry, Selected States

	BushVote	*Kerry Vote*	*Bush Margin of Victory*[a]	*Absolute Difference as % of State Vote*
Arizona	1,104,294	893,524	210,770	10.6[b]
California	5,509,826	6,745,485	-1,235,659	10.1
Colorado	1,101,255	1,001,732	99,523	4.7
Florida	3,964,522	3,583,544	380,978	5.0
Illinois	2,345,946	2,891,550	-545,604	10.4
New Jersey	1,670,003	1,911,430	-241,427	6.7
New Mexico	376,930	370,942	5,988	0.8
New York	2,962,567	4,314,280	-1,351,713	18.6
Texas	4,526,917	2,832,704	1,694,213	23.0

Latino Votes as a Share of the Winning Margin

	Winning Candidate	*Latino Vote for Winning Candidate*	*Winner's Margin Had No Latino Voted for Winner*	*Impact*
Arizona	Bush	127,280	83,490	No change
California	Kerry	1,311,030	-75,371	Bush wins state
Colorado	Bush	49,500	50,023	No change
Florida	Bush	461,440	-80,462	Kerry wins state
Illinois	Kerry	223,440	322,164	No change
New Jersey	Kerry	155,120	86,307	No change
New Mexico	Bush	121,440	-115,452	Kerry wins state
New York	Kerry	459,750	891,963	No change
Texas	Bush	751,170	943,043	No change

Sources: U.S. Bureau of the Census 2006: table 4; exit polls from the National Election Pool (NEP), Edison Media Research and Mitofsky International.

[a] For ease of presentation, we represent the margin as the Bush vote minus the Kerry vote. Thus a plus represents a Bush victory and a minus a Kerry victory.

[b] These Latino vote totals for the winning candidates are derived from U.S. Bureau of the Census Current Population Survey Data, which overestimate turnout, and from exit polls.

elections makes their votes count. First, as was the case in 2000, Latinos factored into calculations to achieve victory in 2004 for both parties. Second, the Latino electorate is more national than it has been at any time in the past. The Kerry campaign, for example, reached out to Pennsylvania and Ohio Latinos just as it did to their coethnics in New Mexico and Florida. With the dispersion of Latino migration over the past decade to parts of the country where Latinos did not previously reside, a new Latino electoral presence will only grow in future elections. Third, outreach—in particular, Republican outreach—grew more sophisticated in 2004. The adeptness of the Bush campaign in reaching specific subsets of Latinos was not new; Republican "Latino" campaigns have long had Cuban as well as generally Latino components. What was new in 2004 was the very explicit and evidently successful effort to build Latinos into their outreach to religious conservatives. Future races will likely see similar parsing of Latino voters, at least in competitive states. With the steady growth of the Latino electorate, it is likely that all future races will see candidate and campaign efforts to win pieces of the national Latino vote. Here, the Democrats can learn from the Republicans.

Fourth and finally, national and state party calculations about the importance of nominating Latino candidates for statewide offices are based on the great potential of the Latino electorate. Election to state office requires the formation of multiracial coalitions because no state has a Latino electoral majority. The nomination of Secretary Martinez in the U.S. Senate race in Florida made this connection explicit, but the desire to win Latino partisan loyalties adds an incentive for state party leaders to nominate Latino candidates who can build these coalitions. Thus 2004 is a harbinger of a new arena for Latino politics—the potential to add candidates considered national in stature to the pool.

As we look to the future, several questions arise both from the 2004 elections and from the subsequent national political dialogue. First, we question the degree to which the new levels of Republican outreach to Latinos will continue in the absence of President Bush. As DeSipio and de la Garza (2005) noted, Bush altered the rhetoric of the Republican Party directed to Latinos, at least in national elections, and the data we present here demonstrate that he won some new Latino votes as a result. Thus we cannot be sure whether the changes we have identified are party-driven (and more permanent) or candidate specific (and more fragile).

Second, and relatedly, both the 2000 and 2004 races saw less incendiary rhetoric surrounding issues of concern to Latinos, especially immigration, immigrant incorporation, and bilingual education. In light of the immigration reform debate that followed the 2004 race and the passage of Proposition 200 in Arizona, however, this detente may disappear.

Third, 2004 created a new form of Latino leadership: three Latino U.S. senators. They are joined by a Latino elected leadership with a national presence, such as New Mexico Governor Bill Richardson (an early presidential candidate in the 2008 contest) and Los Angeles Mayor Antonio Villaraigosa (elected in 2005). Never before have so many Latino leaders been elected by multiracial electorates. These officeholders, as well as leaders from other sectors of U.S. society, could change the pattern documented in this series; Latinos may finally take the lead in overcoming the barriers to their electoral influence.

Fourth, 2006 saw an unprecedented outpouring of Latinos making demands, demonstrating against H.R. 4437 and for immigration reform. At this writing, the hopes of these several million peaceful protesters have been dashed. Their hopes and anger could serve as the foundation for equally unprecedented levels of naturalization and voting, especially if national leaders are unable to reach a compromise that ensures a path to legalization for unauthorized immigrants in the United States.

ORGANIZATION OF THIS BOOK

We organized this volume to mirror previous books in the series (de la Garza and DeSipio 1992, 1996, 1999, 2005; also see de la Garza, Menchaca, and DeSipio 1994). The chapters that follow this national overview and Robert Erikson's analysis of the variability in the state-level Latino vote and measurement of Latino influence in the national election (chap. 2) analyze outreach to Latinos and Latino efforts to shape electoral outcomes in the key states of Latino residence. Our goal here is to provide nuance and texture to what is often presented in popular discussions and the media as an undifferentiated "Latino politics." Instead, as we will show, Latino leaders and Latino voters have widely different opportunities to shape electoral outcomes based on where they reside. For instance, the odds that nonvoters will receive encouragement to register and vote, or that permanent residents will find motivation to naturalize, vary in part according to national political calculations and the organization of local elites. Without detailed attention to the local realities of Latino politics, it is not possible to understand the process of building an electorate and creating the foundation for empowerment and influence.

Chapters 3, 4, and 5, respectively, analyze New Mexico, Colorado, and Arizona, the three states with the oldest Latino populations in the country. Until recently, these states were less affected by immigration than were those with the largest Latino electorates. The Latino populations of these three southwestern states consist almost entirely of people of Mexican or Spanish origin and ancestry. Moving into the last months of the campaign, each of these states appeared to be up for grabs and received disproportionate attention from the campaigns. In New Mexico and Arizona, Latinos had the opportunity to influence not only the general election but also the selection of the Democratic nominee. Colorado Latinos did not have the potential to influence the primary, but they proved key to the 2004 election of a Latino senator and to the net gain of a Latino in the U.S. House of Representatives.

In chapters 6 and 7 we move to two states with large populations, including large numbers of Latinos: Texas and California. Like New Mexico, Arizona, and Colorado, many in the Latino communities of these states can trace their ancestry to family members who happened to reside in territories that made the transition from Mexican to U.S. rule in the mid-1800s. International and domestic migration have much more substantially influenced these two states, however. Thus the Latino populations are not just more numerous but also more heterogeneous. Neither of these states proved central to the candidates or party political calculations in 2004. In California, however, the Democrats could not be so confident about their chances without the steady growth of Latino voting over the past two decades and its strong Democratic partisanship (Fraga, Ramírez, and Segura 2005).

The final section of state-level analyses, chapters 8 through 12, looks at states where Latino population growth and the potential for Latino influence is a twentieth- and twenty-first-century phenomenon: New York, Florida, Illinois, New Jersey, and states with newly emerging Latino populations and Latino electorates. The Latino populations in general and the Latino voting populations in particular are more heterogeneous in these states than in the others. Florida's electorate, for example, is made up not just of the Miami-area Cuban Americans for which the state's electorate is known but also of migrants from other parts of the Americas in the Miami, Orlando, and Tampa areas. Puerto Ricans and Dominicans dominate New York's Latino electorate but are joined by Latinos of other origins. Illinois's Latino electorate has traditionally consisted of Puerto Ricans and Mexicans, but the Mexican American share has been growing in recent years. Like New York, New Jersey's Latino population includes a high share of Puerto Rican and Dominican Latinos but also a large Cuban American population. Of these states, only Florida saw significant and sustained competition for Latino votes in the presidential race.

Latino politics in states with emerging Latino populations is a new addition to the series. As will be evident, the Latino population is small in these states, with an even smaller share of the electorate, but it has an advantage that Latinos in the states with more established communities do not: their political reach is coalescing as sophisticated models have emerged and candidate and campaign institutions have developed outreach strategies to garner Latino votes. Thus the Latino politics of these emerging states can be jump-started just as Latino votes make a difference. We see various patterns in the states under examination, but we hope to establish a baseline for future analysis of this new locus of Latino politics.

We conclude the volume with Rodolfo de la Garza's assessment of how the 2004 race fits into the broad spectrum of Latino and national politics. Finding evidence of both continuity (long-standing patterns of neglect and the dearth of Latino leadership) and change (the new national focus of Latino campaigns and the dispersion of the loci of Latino politics on the ground) reinforces the notion that Latino politics have moved beyond the barrio.

NOTES

1. In this chapter and throughout the volume, we use the terms *Latino* and *Hispanic* interchangeably to refer to individuals who trace their origin or ancestry to the Spanish-speaking nations of Latin America and the Caribbean.

2. We accept the assessment of Leal, Barreto, Lee, and de la Garza (2005) that Bush likely received 38 to 40 percent of the Latino vote.

3. In the interests of intellectual disclosure, it should be noted that the editors of this volume participated in the design of the survey discussed in this article.

4. A complete inventory of 2004 Spanish-language campaign advertising through September 2004 can be found in Segal 2004a.

5. See, e.g., National Hispanic Agenda '88.

6. A third new member (California's Jim Costa) was elected in 2004 and is counted by some as a Latino member of Congress. Costa represents a Latino-majority district in the Central Valley. Costa is of Portuguese-Azorean ancestry and is not Latino by the definition used here. It should be noted that Costa, along with Californian Dennis Cardoza, are members of the Congressional Hispanic Caucus. Devin Nunes, also from California, is a member of the Congressional Hispanic Conference. Like Costa, Cardoza and Nunes are of Portuguese-Azorean ancestry.

7. John Salazar is pro-choice and opposed a constitutional amendment banning gay marriage. He also opposes gun control.

8. Asian Americans are somewhat less likely than Latinos to register or vote. This gap widens in multivariate models that account for socioeconomic status, which generally predict that Asian Americans would vote at higher rates than Latinos.

9. Many in this population can be moved relatively quickly into voting eligibility. Of the 11 million non-naturalized immigrants, approximately 5.1 million are legal permanent residents currently eligible to naturalize (Passell 2007). It is this group of naturalization-eligible Latino adults that a rigorous Latino outreach effort might target in the years before a competitive election. Future immigration reforms may qualify some of the remaining 6 million Latino adults to legalize and later naturalize.

REFERENCES

Adair, Bill, and Steve Bousquet. 2004. "Hispanic Democrats Enjoy Clout, but They Wish for More Limelight." *St. Petersburg Times,* July 31.

Agence France Presse. 2004. "Kerry's Wife Slams Bush Treatment of Latinos." Agence France Presse, September 13.

Alvarez, R. Michael, and Stephen Ansolabehere. 2002. *California Votes: The Promise of Election Day Registration.* New York: Demos.

Anderson, Nick. 2003. "Dean Gaining Support among Latino Leaders." *Los Angeles Times,* December 17.

Associated Press. 2004. "Presidential Contenders Plan Teleconferences to Delegates." Associated Press News Wire, July 7.

Avila, Oscar. 2003. "Hispanic Leaders in the Spotlight: Cisneros Seen as Standard-Bearer." *Chicago Tribune,* July 16.

Balz, Dan. 2004. "Kerry Makes an Appeal to Blacks and Hispanics." *Washington Post,* June 30.

Balz, Dan, and Richard Morin. 2004. "Crucial Florida Vote May Hinge on Burgeoning Latino Population." *Washington Post,* October 16.

Balz, Dan, and Jim VandeHei. 2004. "Democratic Rivals Focus Attacks on Bush." *Washington Post,* September 5.

Barabak, Mark Z. 2003. "Latino Political Clout Has Candidates Brushing up on Their Spanish." *Los Angeles Times,* June 30.

Barone, Michael, with Richard E. Cohen. 2006. *The Almanac of American Politics 2006.* Washington, DC: National Journal Group.

Barreto, Matt. 2005. "Ethnic Cues: The Role of Shared Ethnicity in Latino Political Participation." Ph.D. diss., University of California, Irvine, 2005.

Barreto, Matt, Gary Segura, and Nathan Woods. 2004. "The Effects of Overlapping Majority-Minority Districts on Latino Turnout." *American Political Science Review* 98 (February): 65–75.

Buchanan, Pat. 2004. *Where the Right Went Wrong: How Neoconservatives Subverted the Reagan Revolution and Hijacked the Bush Presidency.* New York: Thomas Dunne Books.

Bumiller, Elisabeth. 2004. "News Analysis: Border Politics as Bush Woos 2 Key Groups with Proposal." *New York Times,* January 8.

Bush-Cheney '04, Inc. 2004a. "President George W. Bush–Campaign Organization." http://www.gwu.edu/~action/2004/bush/bushorg.html. Accessed January 9, 2007.

———. 2004b. "President George W. Bush–Campaign Organization, Florida." www.gwu.edu/%7Eaction/2004/bush/bushorgfl.html. Accessed January 9, 2007.

———. 2004c. "President George W. Bush–Campaign Organization, New Mexico." www.gwu.edu/%7Eaction/2004/bush/bushorgnm.html. Accessed January 9, 2007.

Ceaser, James, and Andrew E. Busch. 2005. *Red over Blue: The 2004 Elections and American Politics.* Lanham, MD: Rowman and Littlefield.

Clark, Lesley. 2004. "Kerry Pours $1 Million into Hispanic TV Ad Blitz: Democrat John Kerry Back on the Air with Spanish-Language Ads, but Bush Campaign Says He's Late to the Game." *Miami Herald,* July 13.

CNN. 2004. "Edwards Tops Kerry Veep Poll: Gephardt Would Be Respondents Second Choice." CNN, June 29.

Coleman, Michael. 2004. "Richardson Makes It Official: N.M. Won't Supply the VP." *Albuquerque Journal,* July 2.

Copp, Tara. 2004. "Ads Mark Opening of Battle for Hispanic Voters." Scripps Howard News Service, March 5.

DeBose, Brian. 2004. "Martinez Looks to Hispanic Support." *Washington Times,* October 27.

de Córdoba, Jose. 2004. "The Kerry Campaign Seeks a Cuban American Beachhead: Bush's Travel Restrictions Could Create an Opening for the Democrat in Florida." *Wall Street Journal,* September 20.

de la Garza, Rodolfo, ed. 1987. *Ignored Voices: Public Opinion Polls and the Latino Community.* Austin: Center for Mexican-American Studies Press.

———. 1992. "From Rhetoric to Reality: Latinos and the 1988 Election in Review." In *From Rhetoric to Reality: Latino Politics in the 1988 Elections,* ed. Rodolfo O. de la Garza and Louis DeSipio, 171–80. Boulder, CO: Westview Press.

———. 1996. "El Cuento de los Números and Other Latino Political Myths." In *Su Voto es Su Voz: Latino Politics in California,* ed. Aníbal Yáñez-Chávez, 11–32. San Diego: Center for U.S.-Mexico Studies.

de la Garza, Rodolfo O., and Louis DeSipio, eds. 1992. *From Rhetoric to Reality: Latino Politics in the 1988 Elections.* Boulder, CO: Westview Press.

———. 1993. "Save the Baby, Change the Bathwater, and Scrub the Tub: Latino Electoral Participation after Seventeen Years of Voting Rights Act Coverage." *Texas Law Review* 71 (June): 1479–539.

———, eds. 1996. *Ethnic Ironies: Latino Politics in the 1992 Elections.* Boulder, CO: Westview Press.

———, eds. 1999. *Awash in the Mainstream: Latino Politics in the 1996 Elections.* Boulder, CO: Westview Press.

———, eds. 2005. *Muted Voices: Latinos and the 2000 Elections.* Lanham, MD: Rowman and Littlefield.

———. 2006. "Reshaping the Tub: The Limits of the VRA for Latino Electoral Politics." In *The Future of the Voting Rights Act,* ed. David L. Epstein, Richard H. Pildes, Rodolfo O. de la Garza, and Sharyn O'Halloran, 139–62. New York: Russell Sage Foundation.

de la Garza, Rodolfo, Martha Menchaca, and Louis DeSipio. 2004. *Barrio Ballots: Latino Politics in the 1990 Elections.* Boulder, CO: Westview Press.

DeSipio, Louis. 1996. *Counting on the Latino Vote: Latinos as a New Electorate.* Charlottesville: University of Virginia Press.

———. 2007. "Drawing New Lines in the Sand: An Early Assessment of the Medium- and Long-Term Consequences of the 2006 Immigrant Rights Protests." Paper presented at Understanding the Immigration Protests of Spring 2006: Lessons Learned, Future Trajectories Conference, Berkeley, CA, April.

DeSipio, Louis, and Rodolfo O. de la Garza. 2005. "Between Symbolism and Influence: Latinos and the 2000 Elections." In *Muted Voices: Latinos and the 2000 Elections,* ed. Rodolfo O. de la Garza and Louis DeSipio, 13–60. Lanham, MD: Rowman and Littlefield.

DeSipio, Louis, Rodolfo O. de la Garza, and Mark Setzler. 1999. "Awash in the Mainstream: Latinos and the 1996 Elections." In *Awash in the Mainstream: Latino Politics in the 1996 Elections,* ed. Rodolfo O. de la Garza and Louis DeSipio, 3–46. Boulder, CO: Westview.

DeSipio, Louis, and Carole Jean Uhlaner. 2007. "Immigrant and Native: Mexican American Presidential Vote Choice Across Immigrant Generations." *American Politics Research* 35, no. 2 (March): 176–201.

Díaz, Elvia. 2004. "Latino Registration Drive Planned: Groups Seek 500,000 New Voters in the U.S." *Arizona Republic,* April 2.

Draper, Electra. 2004. "Profile: John Salazar." *Denver Post,* October 14.

Eby, Charlotte. 2003. "Congress' Top-Ranking Latino Endorses Dean." *Sioux City Courier,* December 28.

Finnegan, Michael. 2004. "Kerry's Low Profile May Cost Crucial Latino Votes." *Los Angeles Times,* May 3.

Florio, Gwen. 2004. "Salazars Are Valley Forged: Roots Run Deep for Political Brothers." *Rocky Mountain News,* April 9.

Florio, Gwen, and Lynn Bartels. 2004. "Two Originals, One Colossal Race: Native Sons Set for High Stakes Senate Battle." *Rocky Mountain News,* August 11.

Fraga, Luis Ricardo, Ricardo Ramírez, and Gary Segura. 2005. "Unquestioned Influence: Latinos and the 2000 Election in California." In *Muted Voices: Latinos and the 2000 Elections,* ed. Rodolfo O. de la Garza and Louis DeSipio, 173–93. Lanham, MD: Rowman and Littlefield.

Garay, Annabelle. 2004. "Presidential Candidates Court Hispanic Voters." Associated Press, May 5.

García Bedolla, Lisa, and Jessica Lavariega Monforti. 2006. "Social Context and Exile Politics: A Look at Cubans and Cuban Americans." Paper presented at the annual meeting of the American Political Science Association, Philadelphia, August–September.

Glionna, John M. 2004. "Bush's Cuban American Support May Be Slipping: New Limits on Travel and Remittances to Cuba Have Turned Some Former Backers against the President, Surveys Show." *Los Angeles Times,* September 21.

Gonzalez, John Moreno. 2004. "Millions Added to the Rolls." *Newsday,* October 7.

Green, Donald, and Alan S. Gerber. 2004. *Get Out the Vote! How to Increase Voter Turnout.* Washington, DC: Brookings Institution.

Greene, Susan. 2004. "Bitter Infighting May Leave Scars on State GOP." *Denver Post,* August 11.

Hendricks, Tyche. 2004. "Coalition of Latino Groups Sound Alarm over Intimidation of Voters." *San Francisco Chronicle,* October 27.

Highton, Benjamin. 2006. "Long Lines, Voting Machine Availability, and Turnout: The Case of Franklin County Ohio in the 2004 Presidential Election." *PS: Political Science and Politics* 65, no. 8 (January): 65–68.

Hulse, Carl. 2003. "Democrats Design Agenda in Bid to Hold Hispanic Support." *New York Times,* June 11.

John Kerry Campaign Organization. 2004. "John Kerry Campaign Organization–General Election Edition." www.gwu.edu/~action/2004/kerry/kerrorggen.html. Accessed January 9, 2007.

Johnson, Kirk. 2004. "Coloradans Consider Splitting Electoral College Votes." *New York Times,* September 19.

Kammer, Jerry. 2004. "Arizona's Prop. 200 Is Dividing State." *San Diego Union-Tribune,* October 16.

Karamargin, C. J. 2003. "Latinos Meet, Dems Rush In." *Arizona Daily Star,* June 29.

Kasindorf, Martin. 2004. "Parties Target Hispanics in 4 Battleground States." *USA Today,* July 19.

Kennedy, Robert F., Jr. 2006. "Was the 2004 Election Stolen? Republicans Prevented More than 350,000 Voters in Ohio from Casting Ballots or Having Their Votes Counted—Enough to Put John Kerry in the White House." *Rolling Stone,* June 1.

Kerry and Allies–Organization, Florida. 2005. "Kerry General Election Florida Campaign Organization." Typescript. Eric M. Appleman/Democracy in Action. www.gwu.edu/~action/2004/kerry/kerrgenfl.html. Accessed January 7, 2007.

Kerry and Allies–Organization, New Mexico. 2005. "Kerry General Election New Mexico Campaign." Typescript. Eric M. Appleman/Democracy in Action. www.gwu.edu/~action/2004/kerry/kerrgennm.html. Accessed January 7, 2007.

Keyssar, Alexander. 2000. *The Right to Vote: The Contested History of Democracy in the United States.* New York: Basic Books.

Kiefer, Francine. 2001. "Bush Plans 2004 Wedding with Hispanics." *Christian Science Monitor,* May 18.

Kinsler, Laura. 2004. "Number of Hispanic Voters Rises as Groups Seek Them." *Tampa Tribune,* July 18.

Kurlantzick, Joshua. 2004. "2000, the Sequel: In Theory, the Help America Vote Act was Congress' Attempt to Prevent the Catastrophes of the Last Election from Happening Again. In Fact, It May Have Made Things Even Worse." *New Republic,* October 2.

Lang, Thomas. 2004. "The Longer View." *Columbia Journalism Review,* June 17.

Leal, David, Matt Barreto, Jongho Lee, and Rodolfo de la Garza. 2005. "The Latino Vote in the 2004 Election." *PS: Political Science and Politics* 38: 41–50.

Lee, Jongho, and Harry Pachon. 2007. "Leading the Way: An Analysis of the Effect of Religion on the Latino Vote." *American Politics Research* 35, no. 2 (March): 252–72.

Lester, Will. 2004. "Pollster: Hispanic Vote Holding Steady." Associated Press, March 26.

Marbut, Robert G., Jr. 2005. "*Un Nuevo Dia?* Republican Outreach to the Latino Community in the 2000 Campaign." In *Muted Voices: Latinos and the 2000 Elections,* ed. Rodolfo O. de la Garza and Louis DeSipio, 61–83. Lanham, MD: Rowman and Littlefield.

Marelius, John. 2004. "'Hispanic Tuesday' Could Be a Misnomer: Democratic Candidates Face Voter Indifference." *San Diego Union-Tribune,* February 1.

Marinucci, Carla. 2003. "Latina, Former Bush Appointee, Joins GOP Field to Unseat Boxer." *San Francisco Chronicle,* December 3.

Marrero, Pilar. 2004. "America's New Soccer Moms: Latinos a Swing Vote in 2004." Pacific News Service [January 28].

Mason, Julie. 2004. "Democratic Pollster Says Bush's Hispanic Support Stagnant." *Houston Chronicle,* March 12.

Michelson, Melissa R. 2006. "Mobilizing the Latino Youth Vote: Some Experimental Results." *Social Science Quarterly* 87 (December): 1188–206.

Moreno, Dario. 2004. "A Growing Hispanic Electorate Still Favors GOP." Globe Newspaper Co., March 7.

Morgan, David. 2007. "Bush Courts Latinos in Southwest Visits." Reuters, March 27.

NALEO Educational Fund. 2004a. *2004 Election Profile: General Election November 2, 2004.* Los Angeles, CA: NALEO Educational Fund.

———. 2004b. *2004 Election Profile: Latinos and Congress and States Houses after 2004: A State-by-State Summary.* Los Angeles, CA: NALEO Educational Fund.

National Council of La Raza. 2004a. *Latino Community Organizations to Air Concerns over Upcoming Election: Groups Contend That Ensuring the Right to Vote Should Not Be a Partisan Issue* [October 21]. Washington, DC: National Council of La Raza.

———. 2004b. *Protecting the Latino Vote in 2004 Election: Community-Based Efforts Key to Increasing Size of Latino Electorate* [October 26]. Washington, DC: National Council of La Raza.

———. 2004c. *NCLR Strongly Opposes Anti-Immigrant Ballot Initiative: Proposition 200 Will Have Grave Consequences for Arizona.* Washington, DC: National Council of La Raza.

National Hispanic Agenda. 1987. *National Hispanic Agenda '88 Preliminary Draft: September 10, 1987.* Washington, DC: National Hispanic Agenda.

Navarrette, Ruben. 2004a. "Kerry and the Latino Vote: Hurdles and Opportunity." *Seattle Times,* June 23.

———. 2004b. "Teresa, Drop the Shtick." *Dallas Morning News,* August 13.

Nelson, Michael, ed. 2005. *The Elections of 2004.* Washington, DC: CQ Press.

New Democratic Network. 2006. *Survey of Cuban and Cuban American Resident Adults in Miami-Dade and Broward.* Miami: New Democrat Network.

Nieves, Evelyn. 2004. The Fight Is on Over N. Mexico's Hispanics." *Washington Post,* October 20.

Nuño, Stephen. 2007. "Latino Mobilization and Vote Choice in the United States." *American Politics Research* 35, no. 2 (March): 273–93.

Off the Kuff. 2004. "Cuellar Finally Wins CD28." July 12. www.offthekuff.com/mt/archives/cat_election_2004.html. Accessed January 8, 2007.

Pantoja, Adrian, Ricardo Ramírez, and Gary M. Segura. 2001. "Citizens by Choice, Voters by Necessity: Patterns in Political Mobilization by Naturalized Latinos." *Political Research Quarterly* 54, no. 4 (December): 729–50.

Passell, Jeffrey S. 2007. *Growing Share of Immigrants Choosing Naturalization.* Washington, DC: Pew Hispanic Center.

Pickler, Nedra. 2004. "Kerry Puts $1 M into Spanish-Language Ads." Associated Press, July 12.

Purdum, Todd S. 2004. "Upbeat Republicans Revive Bush Theme of Compassion." *New York Times,* September 1.

Radelat, Ana. 2004. "Dems, GOP Both Vie for Hispanic Swing Votes." Gannett News Service, April 13.

Ramírez, Ricardo. 2005. "Giving Voice to Latino Voters: A Field Experiment on the Effectiveness of a National Non-Partisan Mobilization Effort." *Annals of the American Academy of Political and Social Science* 601: 66–84.

Reid, T. R. 2004. "Democrats Eye Colorado and See a Chance to Tweak Republican Noses." *Washington Post,* October 9.

Republican National Committee. 2004. "Nearly One in Five Delegates to the 2004 Republican National Convention Is a Veteran or Active Military Personnel." GOP.COM News Releases, August 16.

———. 2007. "Hispanic Team." www.gop.com/Teams/Hispanic/. Accessed June 10, 2007.

Romano, Lois. 2004. "Kerry: Bush Has Neglected Latin America: Presidential Candidate Courts Hispanics by Promising Jobs, Better Education." *Washington Post,* June 27.

Root, Jay. 2004. "Hispanics Missing from Convention Podium, Some Complain." *Fort Worth Star Telegram,* July 29.

Rosenstone, Steven J., and John Mark Hansen. 1993. *Mobilization, Participation, and Democracy in America.* New York: Macmillan.

Roth, Bennett. 2004. "Democratic Candidates Adjust Efforts to Draw Hispanic Vote." *Houston Chronicle,* February 2.

Runningen, Roger, and Kristen Jensen. 2004. "Kerry Courts Hispanic Vote, Pushes Education Plan in California." Bloomberg, May 5.

Russell, Joel. 2005. "Power PACs: Hispanic Political Action Committees Nearly Tripled Their Campaign Contributions during the 2003–04 Election Cycle." *Hispanic Business* (March): 16–18.

Salinas, Maria Elena. 2004. "Richardson Response Hones in on Hispanics." *Fresno Bee,* January 25.

Sanchez, Jennifer W. 2004. "Hispanic Voters Wanted More than 'Lousy Spanish.'" *Albuquerque Tribune,* February 4.

Seelye, Katherine. 2004. "Some Swing States Appear to Be Swinging to the President." *New York Times,* September 29.

Segal, Adam J. 2004a. "Bikini Politics: The 2004 Presidential Campaigns' Hispanic Media Efforts Cover Only Essential Parts of the Body Politic: A Select Group of Voters in a Few Battleground States." Typescript. Washington, DC: Johns Hopkins University Hispanic Voter Project.

———. 2004b. "Presidential Spanish-Language Political Television Advertising Set Records in Early Primaries: Democrats and Republicans Poised to Reach All-Time High for Presidential General Election Spending on Media Aimed at Hispanic Voters." Typescript. Johns Hopkins University Hispanic Voter Project, Washington, DC.

———. 2006. "Total Spanish-Language TV Spending by Market in the 2004 Presidential Election." Johns Hopkins University Hispanic Voter Project, Washington, DC.

Senior, Jennifer. 2004. "The Life of the Party?" *New York Times Sunday Magazine,* May 9.

Shaw, Daron R. 2006. *The Race to 270: The Electoral College and Campaign Strategies of 2000 and 2004.* Chicago: University of Chicago Press.

Shaw, Daron, Rodolfo O. de la Garza, and Jongho Lee. 2000. "Examining Latino Turnout in 1996: A Three-State, Validated Survey Approach." *American Journal of Political Science* 44 (April): 338–46.

Shepard, Scott. 2004. "Election 2004: Kerry Campaign Adds Staff, Diversity." *Atlanta Journal Constitution,* April 17.

Torrens, Claudia. 2004. "Latinos: More than 600 Will Attend Convention to Show Strength." *New York Daily News,* July 18.

U.S. Bureau of the Census. 2005. *Voting and Registration in the Election of November 2004.* www.census.gov/population/www/socdemo/voting/cps2004.html. Accessed January 12, 2007.

U.S.-Cuba Democracy PAC. 2004. "Statement of Purpose." www.uscubapac.com/. Accessed June 16, 2008.

Verba, Sidney, Kay Lehman Schlozman, and Henry E. Brady. 1995. *Voice and Equality: Civic Voluntarism in American Politics.* Cambridge, MA: Harvard University Press.

Wallsten, Peter. 2004. "Poll of Hispanic Voters: Bush Paying Price for Cuban Policies." *Miami Herald,* March 2.

Wilgoren, Jodi. 2004. "Some Blacks and Hispanics Criticize Kerry on Outreach." *New York Times,* April 30.

Chapter Two

Hispanic Voting in the American States

The Case of 2004

ROBERT S. ERIKSON

Hispanic political influence across the United States is diverse (de la Garza and DeSipio 2005). Some states contain large concentrations of Hispanics; others do not. Moreover, Hispanic Americans themselves are ethnically and politically diverse: recent arrivals come from Mexico, the Caribbean, and, increasingly, Central and South America. Whereas the aggregate number of Hispanics is increasing, their influence lags, in part because (except for Puerto Ricans) many of those who are recent arrivals lack citizenship. Even among Hispanic U.S. citizens, the voting rate is below average in a nation with a deplorably low rate of turnout compared to other democracies. In presidential politics, Hispanic influence is limited due to Hispanic concentration in states where no group is pivotal because the presidential vote tends to be one-sided and the Electoral College vote is certain.

The positive side of this equation is the tremendous potential influence of the Hispanic population on U.S. politics. Their rate of participation can only grow with further assimilation into American culture.

We can await the impact of the disproportionate number of Hispanics who are young—currently under or barely over the age of voter eligibility—when they mature politically. Their future voting patterns and the likely fluidity of Hispanics' partisan choices only increase the relevance of the Hispanic vote in future elections.

This chapter examines the Hispanic vote in the United States from the perspective of the 2004 presidential election. The aim is to analyze state voting patterns in that election, now fading into the past, but also to explore how changes in state-level Hispanic voting can affect the future of U.S. politics. It also asks what the state-level patterns of turnout and vote choices among Hispanics in 2004 tell us about the long-term influence of Hispanic voting power on U.S. elections.

These questions are addressed by merging the two common data sets regarding state-level voting in 2004. For Hispanic turnout in the states, the data set is the U.S. Census's November 2004 Current Population Survey (CPS) and its report of state-level voter turnout in 2004. For Hispanic vote choices in the states, the dataset is the collection of state-level National Election Pool (NEP) exit polls conducted for the television networks and the Associated Press by Edison Media Research/Mitofsky International. From these data, I compare the turnout rates and the partisan vote by state among Hispanics and whites, with an eye toward answering questions about Hispanic voting power. I use data simulations of counterfactual scenarios involving changes in Hispanic turnout and voting patterns and their hypothetical effect on the 2004 outcome.

Although these data sources contain certain flaws, they are nonetheless useful. The "raw" 2004 exit polls were notorious for inflating the Democratic vote in 2004, and their leakage on Election Day created the widespread but mistaken belief that Kerry had defeated President Bush. Importantly, the reported exit polls used here are not the notorious raw or early returns. Rather, they are the clean postelection data, reweighted to reflect the states' voting electorate and to correct for actual election results. These data make it possible to estimate the behavior of different voting groups made up of actual election day voters rather than the claimed intentions or reports of voting behavior in surveys on the days immediately before or after the election.

In this analysis, the exit poll data have been linked to the CPS of voter participation. The analysis of CPS respondents is restricted to self-reported citizens only. The CPS has its flaws, too, in that it greatly inflates voting participation rates. If one were to take the self-reports of voting participation in the November 2004 CPS, a full 64 percent of U.S. adult citizens cast ballots. The basic ethnic breakdown shows 47 percent of Hispanic adult citizens and 67 percent of white (non-Hispanic) adult citizens turned out to vote. The 64 percent voting rate among all citizen survey respondents is higher than the official tally of 55 percent voting among the U.S. voting age population. One prominent study suggests that the actual voting rate among adult eligible voters was 60 percent, where "eligible" was defined to exclude noncitizens and felons but to include citizens abroad (McDonald 2004). By this standard, the CPS figure of 64 percent voting among citizens is only modestly inflated. Of course, whatever the degree of inflation in the CPS numbers, they indicate clearly that Hispanic turnout lagged considerably behind that of whites.

The first question is, what were the actual turnout rates of whites and Hispanics in 2004? We observe that in the CPS, the ratio of Hispanic to non-Hispanic white citizens is .109, indicating that among citizens, whites outnumber Hispanics about ten to one. Among self-reported voters in the CPS, the ratio of Hispanics to non-Hispanic whites is a lower .076. When talking about reported voters rather than both voting and nonvoting citizens, the ratio of Hispanics to whites declines by 70 percent. It follows that with citizens in the denominator, Hispanic turnout is about 70 percent that of whites. If we accept the CPS's reported proportions for all respondents, whites, and Hispanics among both citizens and voters and adjust the inflated turnout percents by taking 60 percent as the net turnout rate for all citizens, the turnout rates for white and Hispanic citizens are 64 percent and 45 percent respectively, for a 19-point gap.[1]

The second question is, what were the presidential vote percentages for whites and Hispanics? According to the national exit poll, whites voted 41 percent for Kerry to 58 percent for Bush. As is well known, the national exit poll undercounted the Kerry vote among Hispanics as 53 percent Kerry and 44 percent Bush. If this account were true, it would have been a remarkable Republican gain over past elections. The problem with the National Exit Poll is that by chance, a disproportionate number of its highly Hispanic sample precincts were in Florida, which includes a pro-Republican Cuban population. The more accurate estimate is the net vote from aggregating the state exit polls (and properly weighing by the number of voters). This new estimate, based on a larger sample than the national poll, is a Hispanic vote that was 40 percent for Bush and 58 percent for Kerry.[2] In terms of the major-party vote in the (adjusted) exit polls, Kerry won 41.8 percent among non-Hispanic whites and 59.2 percent among Hispanics.

The first section of this chapter discusses the variation by state in comparison with the white non-Hispanic vote, in terms of both turnout rate and candidate choice. The second section presents various counterfactual scenarios regarding shifts in Hispanic turnout or candidate choice. It extends the counterfactuals to examine Electoral College implications whereby gains for one party among Hispanics are offset by an equal number of votes gained among non-Hispanic whites. The third and final section develops the conclusions from this exercise.

STATE VARIATION IN THE HISPANIC VOTE

Hispanic voting behavior is not uniform across the states. Turnout rates vary, as do the divisions of candidate choice. Why is this so? Are there fifty-one separate stories about the Hispanic vote? Is the variation idiosyncratic, or can we account for it in some way? As de la Garza (2004) has emphasized, Hispanic voting behavior varies across the states for reasons beyond the fact that Hispanic settlements in the states vary by national origin.

There is a pattern across states that can be described as follows. As a general tendency, while Hispanic voting behavior differs from white voting behavior across the states, the differences are systematic. In general, while Hispanic turnout rates are lower, the Hispanic rate is highest where the white turnout rate is the highest. In general, the Democratic (Kerry) vote among Hispanics was higher in states where whites voted most heavily Democratic. In other words, whatever causes white turnout to rise or fall, or whites to vote Republican rather than Democratic, works for Hispanics in the state as well. The difference is that Hispanic turnout rates are almost always lower. In addition, Hispanics almost always vote more Democratic than their white non-Hispanic counterparts. At the same time, these are only tendencies, as there is variation in Hispanic voting patterns that cannot be statistically accounted for by the pattern among whites. Importantly, even after accounting for common trends among whites and Hispanics and adjusting for measurement error in the occasionally small state samples of Hispanics, the voting tendencies of Hispanics show more variation across states than do those of whites.

Hispanic Voter Turnout

We turn first to state variation in turnout, comparing Hispanics and non-Hispanic whites in the November 2004 CPS. This massive survey following the 2004 election has sufficient samples of Hispanics in thirty of the fifty states to record relevant participation data. For these thirty states, we can obtain percentages of Hispanic (and non-Hispanic white) respondents who report U.S. citizenship, voting registration, and decision to vote in 2004.

Figure 2.1 displays the proportion of adult Hispanic citizens who reported being registered to vote on the vertical (Y) axis as a function of the proportion of adult non-Hispanic whites who reported being registered on the horizontal (X) axis. This figure contains several important features. First is the elongation of the graph. As the X- and Y-axes were drawn to a common scale, the graph is elongated vertically. This is to accommodate the fact that in terms of registration rates, there is more Hispanic than white variation across the states.

Second, registration rates are (except for the Ohio sample) higher among whites than Hispanics. (Nationally, according to CPS data, the gap is 20 percentage points, as the registration rates are 47 percent for Hispanics and 67 percent for non-Hispanic whites.) Moreover, the two sets of registration rates track each other. The higher the rate of voter registration among white citizens, the higher the rate of voter registration among Hispanic citizens. In terms of a statistical equation predicting the Hispanic registration from the white registration rate, we find:

Hispanic Registration Rate (if a citizen) = −37.82 + 1.25 White Registration Rate (if a citizen)
Adjusted R squared = .255.

Figure 2.1. Hispanic Registration Rate by White Non-Hispanic Registration Rate in Thirty States

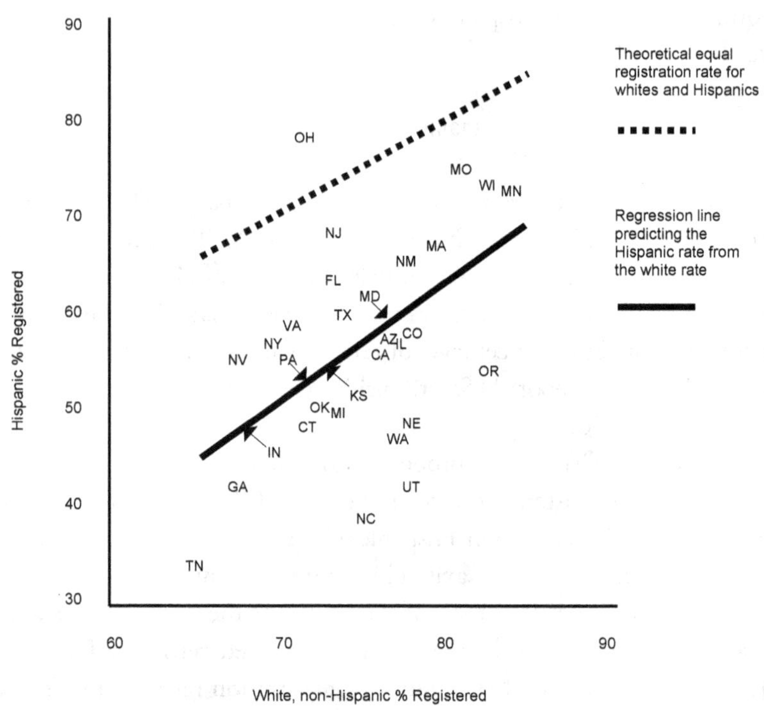

Source: November 2004 Current Population Survey. U.S. Census Bureau.

If we are willing to tease a causal interpretation from this relationship (statistically significant at the .01 level), it would be that whatever the state-level variables (culture, etc.) that cause whites to register also cause Hispanics to register and have a greater impact on Hispanic registration. We might even infer that general appeals to voter registration have a stronger impact among Hispanics than Anglos.

The final remark about figure 2.1 is that even after 25 percent of the variance in Hispanic registration rates can statistically be accounted for by the white registration rate in the state, the residual (unaccounted for) variance in the Hispanic registration rate is still four times that among whites. While some of the wobble in the Hispanic registration rate is due to fluctuation in the small CPS Hispanic samples in states with small Hispanic populations, this fact is an indication that state differences like those reported in this volume do matter.[3]

Next we turn from registration to voting. Figure 2.2 shows Hispanic voting rates among *registered* Hispanics as a function of white voting rates among *registered* whites. First we note that both Hispanics and whites are more likely to vote if registered than to register if a citizen. It is more difficult to get citizens to register than to get registered voters to show up at the polls for a presidential election. (Across the CPS national sample, 82 percent of registered Hispanics turned out to vote in 2004, compared to 89 percent of whites.)

Looking specifically at the state-to-state differences in figure 2.2, we see the same patterns for voting as we saw for registration, but even stronger. In terms of voting rates among registered voters, the state-to-state variance for Hispanics is thirteen times that for whites. In some states, the Hispanic voting rate (once registered) is on par with whites', and in fact in several states Hispanic registrants vote at a higher rate. Yet in other states (especially Tennessee and North Carolina) hardly more than half the Hispanic registrants actually voted. Let us consider the regression equation describing the Hispanic voting rate as a function of the white rate:

Hispanic Voting Rate (if registered) = –146.99 + 2.56 White Voting Rate (if registered)
Adjusted R squared = .486

Half of the variance in the Hispanic voting rate among registered voters can statistically be accounted for by the white voting rate. The state-level forces that encourage or discourage whites to vote (if registered) have the same effect on Hispanics. Given the coefficient of 2.56, their effects must in fact be much larger. We might infer that efforts to encourage (or repress) the vote generally in a state have a much bigger impact among Hispanics than among whites.

As the final observation regarding figure 2.2, we note that even when we account for half the variance in the Hispanic voting rate as

Figure 2.2. Hispanic Voting Rate among Registered Voters by White Non-Hispanic Voting Rate among Registered Voters in Thirty States

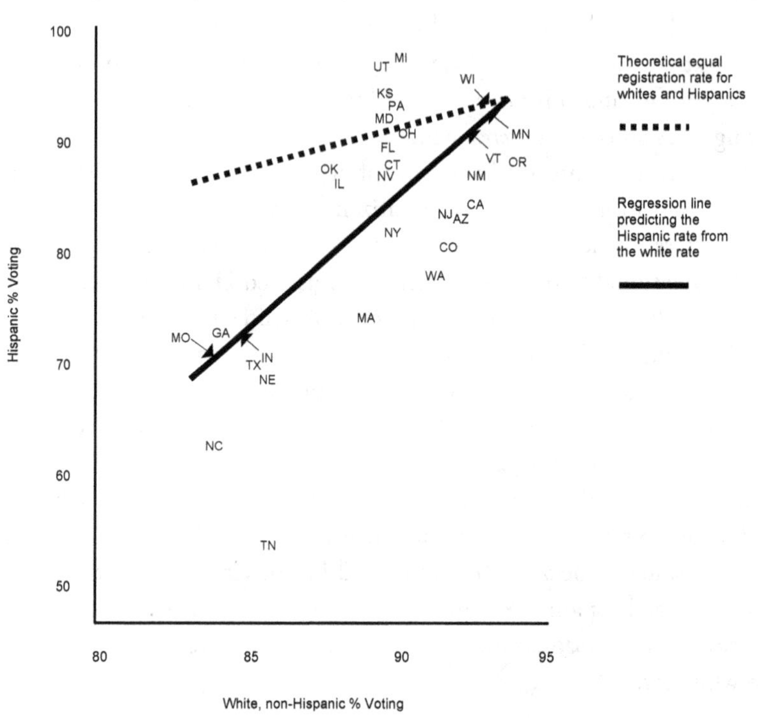

Source: November 2004 Current Population Survey. U.S. Census Bureau.

statistically explained by the white voting rate, the residual unexplained variance is still seven times the variance in the voting rate among whites. Even if we accept that some of the Hispanic variance is due to sampling variance with a small sample, Hispanic voting rates are far more variable.[4] In most states the white voting rate among those registered is in the high 80s or low 90s. Register an Anglo, and he or she will almost always vote for president. Register a Hispanic, and the likelihood of voting still depends to a surprising degree on the state in which he or she resides.

Figure 2.3. Hispanic Voting Rate among Adult Citizens by White Non-Hispanic Voting Rate among Adult Citizens in Thirty States

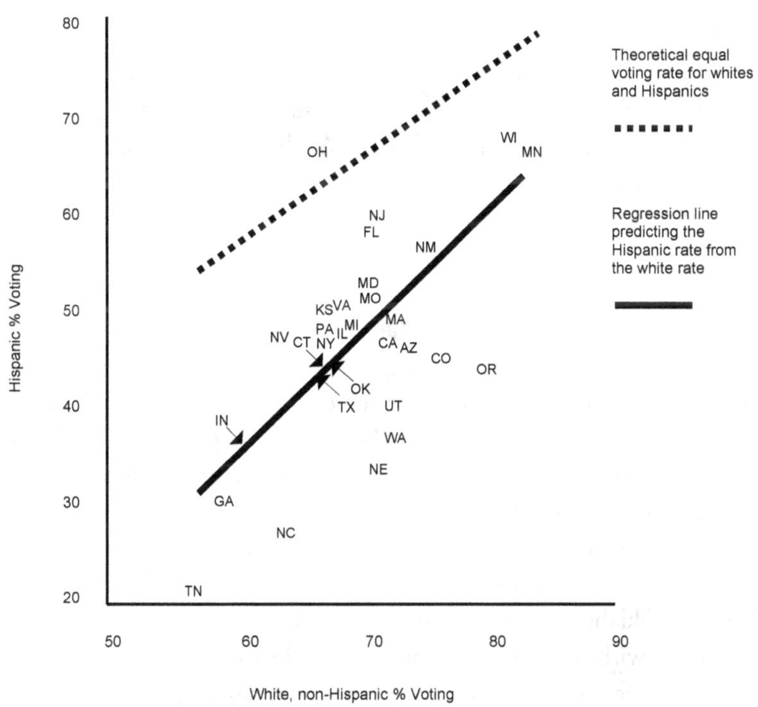

Source: November 2004 Current Population Survey. U.S. Census Bureau.

Figure 2.3 combines the registration decision and the vote decision to present the Hispanic and white voting rates among citizens in the thirty states of the 2004 CPS sample. We see the patterns we have learned to expect. In almost all states, the net voting rate is higher among whites. The variance is higher for the Hispanic rate. The regression equation predicting the Hispanic net voting rate from the white net voting rate shows a slope greater than 1.0, and the residual variance in the Hispanic net voting rate is almost three times that of the non-Hispanic white voting rate:

Hispanic Voting Rate (if a citizen) = –47.81 + 1.40 White Voting Rate (if a citizen)
Adjusted R squared = .400

From this analysis of state-level participation data, we can form several conclusions. Statewide rates of Hispanic voting participation are more variable than the comparable rates for whites, especially when it comes to whether registrants will vote. At the same time, participation (registration and voting) rates for Hispanics track those for whites. Even when taking the rates for whites into account, the state-level variation for Hispanics is greater.

Hispanic Partisan Voting

As we shift from turnout to the voting decision, we also shift from the thirty states with reported turnout figures for Hispanics in the CPS to the twenty-one states with reported Hispanic voting in the 2004 exit polls. Figure 2.4 presents the relationship between the Hispanic Democratic vote and the white vote according to the state exit polls. As expected, the Hispanic vote is more Democratic than the white vote, although Oklahoma is a mysterious exception.

Just as with participation, the state-level variance is greater for Hispanics than for whites. The variance of the state-level Hispanic vote is 2.5 times that of the variance in the white vote. This tells us something important and surprising. When we think of which states are Democratic and which are Republican in their presidential voting, variation in the vote of white voters mainly drives the distinction. Since Hispanics are fewer in numbers, their impact on the total vote goes largely undetected. As figure 2.4 shows, however, there is greater diversity in the Hispanic vote. This can be only partly explained by the differences between the more Republican Cuban Americans and their more Democratic counterparts in Mexican American and other Latino communities.

As with participation, the Hispanic voting pattern tracks the white voting pattern—as if whatever makes whites vote for a party has the identical effect on Hispanics, only magnified. The equation is:

Hispanic % Democratic = 16.67 + 1.00 White % Democratic
Adjusted R squared = .378

The coefficient of precisely 1.00 means that on average, the Hispanic vote tends to be the same as the white vote, except about 17 points more Democratic. This tracking of the Hispanic vote to the white vote helps to account for much of the state variation. For instance, Hispanics in Texas vote less Democratic than Hispanics elsewhere, but this can be explained by the fact that whites also vote less Democratic in Texas than elsewhere.

Figure 2.4. Hispanic Democratic Vote for President by White Non-Hispanic Democratic Vote for President in Twenty-one States

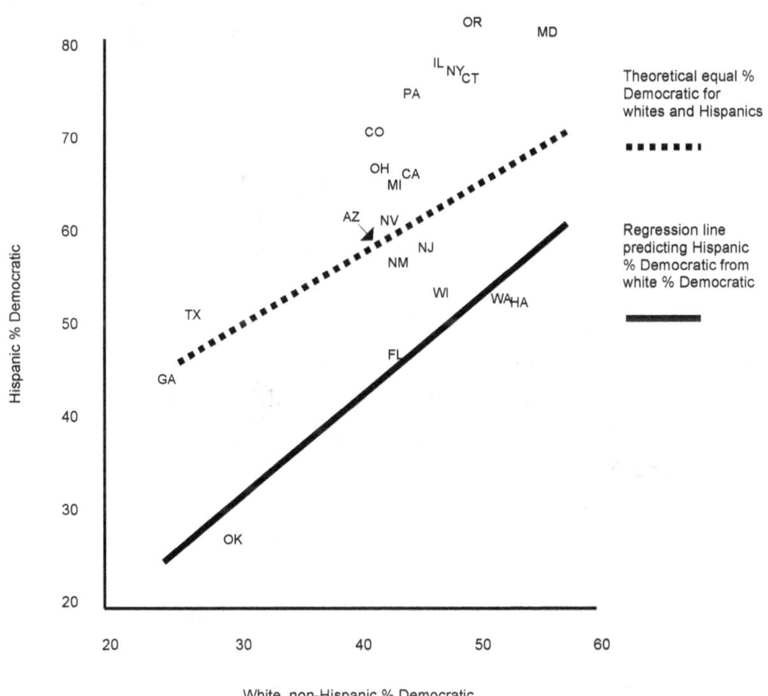

Source: NEP 2004 Exit Polls.

Overall, the white vote statistically "explains" one-third of the variance in Hispanic voting in the states—but a considerable amount is not explained and is idiosyncratic to the states. The unexplained variance in the Hispanic vote remains 1.5 times the total variance in the white vote. Even with an adjustment for sampling error due to the small Hispanic samples in some state exit polls, the residual variance in the Hispanic vote (unexplained by the white vote) exceeds the observed variance in the white vote.[5] There can be no doubt that the Hispanic vote varies more by state than does the white vote.

Hispanics, Blacks, and Whites

So far, I have compared Hispanic turnout with white turnout and Hispanic voting with white voting. It is useful to add state participation rates and state-level voting behavior among African Americans to the mix. Figure 2.5 shows the details comparing black and Hispanic participation rates with those for non-Hispanic whites. Figure 2.6 does the same for presidential vote choice comparing black and Hispanic voters on the vertical axis with white voting behavior on the horizontal axis.

Figure 2.5 reveals that the African American voting rate (as percent of citizens) exceeded that for Hispanics in twenty-six of the thirty states from the CPS survey. Similarly, the white voting rate exceeded that for blacks in twenty-six of the states. This hierarchy is not surprising. Like the Hispanic voting rate, the black voting rate has more variance than the voting rate for whites. But what is different is that the black voting rate depends little if at all on the white rate. Whatever generates state-to-state differences in participation rates by African Americans, it is distinct from that which predicts white participation.[6]

Figure 2.6 shows 2004 presidential voting for the three groups in the fifteen states with data for both groups. As one would expect, in all fifteen states blacks in the exit polls voted more Democratic than both whites and Hispanics, typically in the 80 or 90 percent range. Unlike the state-level Hispanic vote, the state-level black vote is typified by its low variance. The variance of the black vote is one-third that of the white vote and one-eighth that of the Hispanic vote. Thus we see a crucial distinction between the black and Hispanic minorities when com-

Figure 2.5. Hispanic and Black Democratic Voter Turnout by White Non-Hispanic Democratic Voter Turnout in Thirty States with Reports of Both the Hispanic and Black Turnout

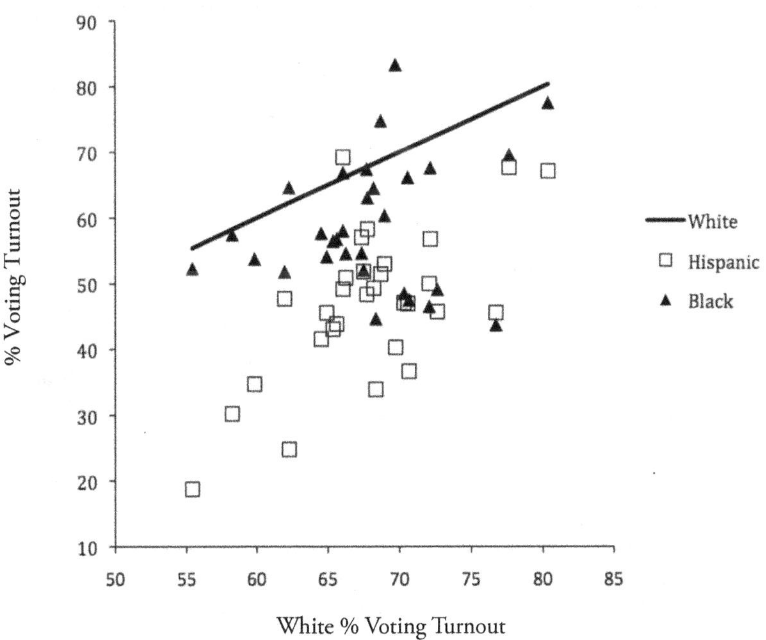

Source: November 2004 Current Population Survey. U.S. Census Bureau.

paring across states. Blacks are not only more one-sided (Democratic) in their voting behavior, they are also more uniform in that behavior. Across all states, African American voters are decidedly Democratic in their presidential voting. Compared to African Americans, Hispanic voters do not comprise one political community.

SIMULATING COUNTERFACTUALS: WHAT IF . . . ?"

The influence of the Hispanic vote in presidential elections depends on its impact on the Electoral College. As DeSipio and de la Garza (2005)

Figure 2.6. Hispanic and Black Democratic Vote for President by White Non-Hispanic Democratic Vote for President in Fifteen States with Exit Poll Reports of Both the Hispanic and Black Vote

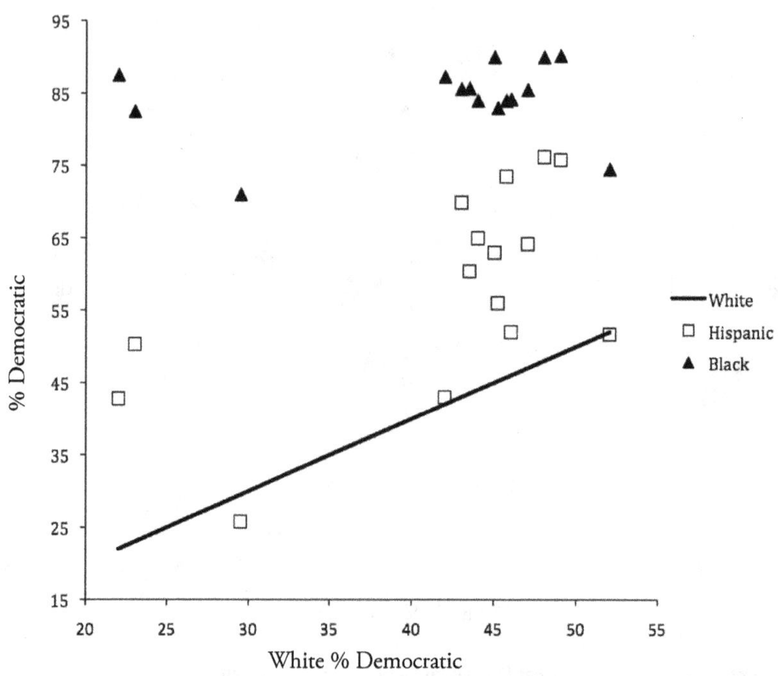

Source: NEP 2004 Exit Polls.

demonstrate for earlier elections (1988–2000), the Latino vote has rarely been pivotal in determining states' Electoral College winners. Was the situation different in 2004?

We can ask a series of what-if questions regarding hypothetical shifts in the Hispanic vote. For instance, what would happen if the Hispanic vote were neutralized either because of 100 percent nonvoting or because Hispanics' vote choices exactly mirrored those of non-Hispanics. We could ask, what if turnout increased, perhaps to white levels, or if the Hispanic voting electorate were to, say, double in size? We can also ask what would happen with large shifts in the vote. It has been argued, for instance, that the actual 2004 voting rate among Hispanics is considerably larger than the exit poll estimates—about two-to-one for Kerry. We can also consider magically large shifts in the Hispanic vote. For instance, suppose Latinos were to become just as one-sidedly Democratic as African Americans. Alternatively, suppose Karl Rove's dream is realized and Hispanics vote even more Republican than the general population.

We start with the actual Democratic vote among Hispanics, estimated from exit polls for twenty states and—more shakily—from the predictions based on the presidential vote in the remaining ten states with CPS participation data for Hispanics.[7] To estimate the Hispanic proportions of the voting electorates in the thirty states, we use the Hispanic proportions of state voters in the CPS. The realism of the simulations depends on the accuracy of these sets of state-level figures, plus (depending on the simulations) the turnout rates in the CPS. Thus, they should be taken with more than the usual grain of salt even as they expand the imagination.[8]

Six Simulations of Counterfactual Scenarios

I conduct six simulations involving hypothetical shifts in the net vote. These are as follows:

1. Hispanic percent Democratic equals the white non-Hispanic percent Democratic in the state.
2. Hispanic turnout rate matches the white turnout rate in the state.
3. Hispanic turnout doubles in each state.
4. Hispanics vote 8 percentage points more Democratic than in 2004 while the non-Hispanic vote stays the same.
5. Hispanics vote 28 percentage points more Democratic than in 2004 (averaging about 87 percent) while the non-Hispanic vote stays the same.
6. Hispanics vote 28 percentage points less Democratic than in 2004 (averaging about 31 percent) while the non-Hispanic vote stays the same.[9]

The results are summarized in table 2.1. The simulated state scenarios are shown in the six panels of figure 2.7. The striking thing about

Table 2.1. Counterfactual Simulations of the 2004 Presidential Elections Examining the Hispanic Vote

	National Vote as Democratic Percent of Two-Party Vote (%)	*Electoral College Switches (Electoral Votes)*
Actual Vote	48.8	—
Hispanic % Democratic = white % democratic in state	48.1	None
Hispanic turnout rate[a] = white turnout rate in state	49.0	R→D NM (5)
States' Hispanic turnout doubles	49.4	R→D NM (5)
Hispanic % Democratic increases by 8 percentage points in all states	49.2	R→D NM (5)
Hispanic % Democratic increases by 28 percentage points in all states	50.5	R→D NM (5) NV (5) FL (25)
Hispanic % Republican increases by 28 percentage points in all states	47.1	D→R WI (10)

[a] Percent voting among citizens.
[b] Number of Hispanic voters doubles.

these results is that our counterfactual assumptions lead to very little change in either the national vote or the Electoral College result. If Hispanics were to vote like whites, the Democratic vote would be depressed further but by less than one percentage point and with no change to the Electoral College. If Hispanics were to vote at the same rate as whites and for the same candidate as they did in 2004, the change in the vote would also be less than one point, but this would flip one state, New Mexico, in the Electoral College. Even if we double the size of the His-

Figure 2.7. Six Simulations of Counterfactual 2004 Outcomes with Alternative Scenarios for the Hispanic Vote

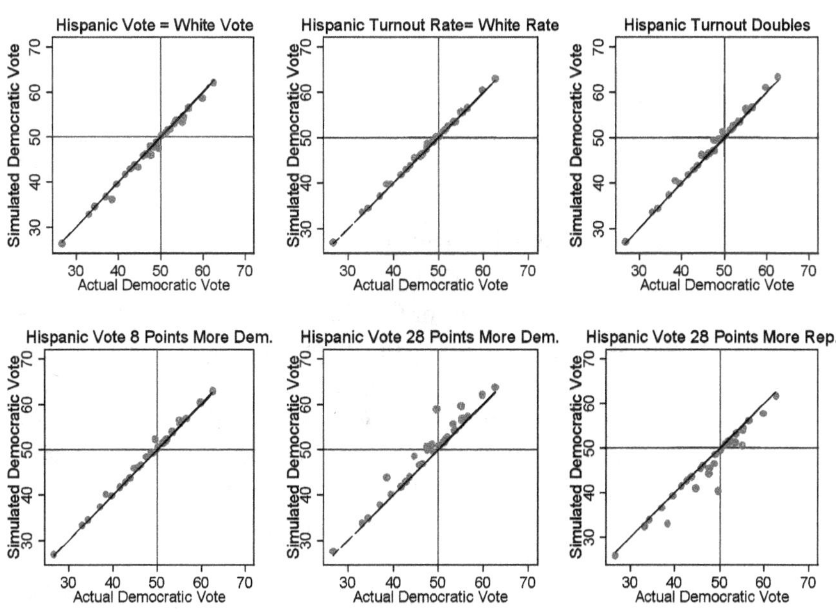

panic electorate or add eight percentage points to the Hispanic Democratic vote in all states (enlarging the Democratic vote among Hispanics slightly beyond the 2000 figures), the net vote changes by less than one point and only New Mexico flips.

It is worth noting that an eight-point shift by Hispanics in all states would add only New Mexico to the Democratic column, not enough to have shifted the 2004 verdict from Bush to Kerry. An eight-point shift would have meant an even greater share of the Hispanic vote going to Kerry than went to Gore in 2004. If Hispanics had maintained their 2000 level of support for the Democratic candidate in 2004, it still would not have been enough to change the Electoral College outcome.

Why do these counterfactual shifts, seemingly at the fringe of realistic changes in Hispanic behavior, create so little movement in the net outcome? For shifts in the vote choice, the net vote change represents the gap between the actual and the counterfactual vote percentage (e.g., eight points more Democratic in all states) multiplied by the percent of Hispanics in the voting electorate (e.g., .06 x .076 nationally). For shifts in turnout, the net vote change represents a similar multiplication of small numbers. The conclusion therefore is that even a rather large change in the number of Hispanic voters, or their vote choice, would have little impact on presidential politics.

But we can also consider a truly large change in the vote choices of Hispanics. Consider the scenario in which the Hispanic vote increases by 28 percentage points in favor of the Democrats (fifth panel of figure 2.7).[10] In this simulation, the Hispanic vote would be as strong as the African American vote for the Democratic Party. As table 2.1 shows, the majority of the resultant national vote would tip to Kerry. If Hispanics had voted by this scenario in 2004, the Democrats would have captured Nevada and Florida in addition to New Mexico (winning the Electoral College majority by a comfortable margin), but still fallen short in states like Arizona and Colorado.

The last panel of figure 2.7 shows the result if Hispanics had become 28 percentage points more Republican. This Republican fantasy leads to only one additional state, Wisconsin, swinging to the Republicans. This result illustrates that in 2004 Hispanics generally did not supply the margin of victory in states where the Democrats carried.

Simulating Offsetting Hispanic and Non-Hispanic Vote Shifts

Close observers of the Hispanic vote are aware that the Electoral College works against Hispanic influence on U.S. presidential elections. Hispanics tend to reside in those states with the most Electoral College delegates (such as California, Texas, and New York), which are usually noncompetitive in close presidential elections. Florida, with its politically unique Cuban American population, is the exception.

This imbalance can affect the thinking of political strategists. Suppose, for instance, an issue such as "immigration reform" could push Hispanics to vote, say, X percentage points more Democratic across all states while pushing non-Hispanics to vote slightly more Republican in all states by a lesser amount that offsets the Democratic surge among Hispanics in a vote-neutral way. (In other words, after the shift, the net national vote remains the same.) Would this vote-neutral shift affect the balance of partisan control of the states?

We can readily simulate such outcomes in the states. Suppose that our new issue drives Hispanics to vote 10 percentage points more Democratic while driving non-Hispanics to vote 0.66 points more Republican. This scenario generates a vote-neutral offset at the national level but provides mixed results at the state vote level. Given the 2004 vote starting point, the net result should not surprise given our earlier simulations: the Democrats retake New Mexico, while the Republicans flip Wisconsin.

Next, suppose the issue drives Hispanics to vote a full 20 points more Democratic, while non-Hispanics move an offsetting 1.32 points in the opposite direction. This shuffling of the vote produces no changes in Electoral College outcome. If we get truly revolutionary and allow a 30-point Democratic gain for Hispanics with a 1.96 non-Hispanic offset, the Democrats do not gain any states beyond New Mexico, while the Republicans add Pennsylvania in addition to Wisconsin.

For the sake of completeness, we can also examine what would happen if Hispanics voted more Republican while non-Hispanics move more Democratic in a vote-neutral way. Hispanic Republican shifts of 10 or 20 percent have no effect on the Electoral Vote map, but a shift of 30 points more Republican by Hispanics and an offsetting 1.96 points more Democratic by non-Hispanics leads to an ironic result: the Democrats win Ohio.

These scenarios inform us about the possible impact of newly relevant issues that further the political divide between Hispanic Americans and non-Hispanic Americans. For instance, would the development of anti-immigrant or anti-Hispanic wedge issues change the political landscape as far as which party wins which states? Based on the analysis here, if non-Hispanic votes moving in one partisan direction are offset by Hispanic votes moving in the other, there would be little net impact on presidential politics. We should be cautious about thinking we know in advance what a new wedge issue would bring, however. The outcome could differ from the limited set of counterfactual scenarios applied to rerun the 2004 election as I have done above.

CONCLUSION

At the state level, Hispanic voting behavior is more variable than one might think; in fact, it is more variable than the vote among blacks and non-Hispanic whites. Registration and turnout rates across the states vary more for Hispanics than for whites, and the Democratic vote percentage across the states varies more for Hispanics than for whites. These observed tendencies are sufficiently large that they cannot be explained by sampling error of small state samples. Registration, turnout, and vote choice varies for Hispanics across the states in a manner correlated with the same variables for whites in the states. Such state-level tendencies for Hispanics are partly—but only partly—"explained" by similar tendencies among whites.

This variability offers a strong reason for analyzing the Latino vote at the state level. Latino voting varies across states even more than for the white majority. At the same time, the small sample sizes for some states examined here produce anomalies that might be sampling error. For instance, as discussed above, the exit poll data show that Oklahoma Hispanics are just as Republican in their presidential voting as Oklahoma whites. This might be more a mirage than a true pattern.

Various "what if" simulations of the 2004 presidential vote suggest that it would have taken major changes in the Hispanic vote to have changed the election result beyond shifting a state or two and would not have shifted the Electoral College majority to Kerry. Hispanics are not that different from others—or numerous enough in the voting booth—to expect them to be pivotal in a moderately close election such as 2004. Like most other politically relevant groups, Hispanics move in tandem with other segments of society from one election to the next.

This conclusion is similar to DeSipio and de la Garza's assessment of Hispanic influence in previous presidential elections. It is difficult to see the Latino vote holding the balance of power since such voters are rarely pivotal in determining a state's electoral vote winners. Some might draw the conclusion that ultimately Latinos have little reason to engage in presidential politics. That would be wrong for several reasons.

To start, it cannot be denied that the Hispanic vote is often crucial in elections for state and local offices. Moreover, it follows that when the Latino vote is pivotal for statewide office, that same balance could plausibly occur in future presidential elections. In other words, contrary to the specific scenarios examined here where the starting point is the set of 2004 vote divisions in the states, we can imagine different scenarios in which the vote for president mimics more closely the vote for statewide office. For instance, suppose voters realign for presidential elections so that heavily Latino states such as Arizona, Colorado, and Nevada become pivotal rather than (as it turned out) safely Republican as in 2004. Then the influence of the Latino vote on the outcome greatly increases over the scenarios here based on a 2004 alignment.

Suppose Hispanics were to withdraw from presidential politics, for some reason choosing irrevocably not to vote for president. The result would be that Hispanics, currently underrepresented in Washington, would see their influence decline toward zero. By this reasoning, Hispanics' current level of influence on national policy is largely due to their showing up at the polls and voting for president. The flip side is to imagine the result if Hispanic Americans grow in numbers and spread more evenly across the states from their current concentration in a few large noncompetitive states. This is not hypothetical, as the population of vote-eligible Hispanics is growing, with a pool of younger than average potential voters who, given historical patterns, will vote more frequently as they mature politically. The potential exists, therefore, for the Hispanic vote to both grow and become more fluid in its vote choice.

NOTES

1. This differential is similar to that in 2000. See de la Garza and DeSipio 2005, especially table 1.2.

2. Anna Maria Arumi of NBC News computed this adjustment and reported it in NBC's "First Read" of December 4, 2004. Arumi stated, "Through the luck of the draw, four Hispanic precincts were in Florida and three of those were in Miami-Dade County. This demonstrates some of the clustering effects you can have in a national sample of 250 precincts when you are looking at breakouts of subgroups like Hispanics—in this case an overrepresentation of

Cuban opinion in the overall Hispanic numbers. . . . To ameliorate this clustering problem I aggregated the 50 state polls which were collected from a total of 1,469 precincts and looked at the Hispanic data in this much larger sample, which yielded smaller, but still significant, Bush gains among Hispanics: 40 percent for Bush to 58 percent for Kerry." For additional discussion, see the "First Read" of Friday, December 3, 2004, from Elizabeth Wilner, Mark Murray, Huma Zaidi, and Aaron Inver at www.msnbc.msn.com/id/6531105/ and the authoritative source mysterypollster.com: "Correcting the 'Correction'" by Mark Blumenthal, December 6, 2004, retrieved from www.mysterypollster.com/main/2004/12/correcting_the_.html.

The William C. Velasquez Institute conducted its own exit poll of Hispanics, which shows Hispanics breaking 65.4 percent for Kerry to 33 percent for Bush. See its report at www.wcvi.org/press_room/press_releases/2004/us/exit_poll_120204.html. The institute's vote breakdown is in line with the Hispanic vote reported in preelection polls. For more on the disputed Hispanic vote in 2004, see Leal et al. 2005.

3. Based on sampling theory and the assumption of simple random sampling, it is possible to estimate the statistical reliabilities of the state estimates of registration rates for samples of white citizens and Hispanic citizens. For white citizens, the estimated reliability approaches 1.0, a result of the large state samples. For Hispanic citizens, the estimated reliability is .82, meaning that about 82 percent of the observed variance in states' registration rates by Hispanics is true and the remaining 18 percent is error. Even with this adjustment, the residual state-level registration rate is about three times greater for Hispanics than for whites.

4. Based on the assumption of simple random sampling, the reliability of the state estimates of voting rate among Hispanic registrants is .78, meaning that the observed variance should be discounted by about one-fifth.

5. Adjusted for sampling error based on the numbers of Hispanics in the state exit polls and assuming random sampling, the reliability of the Hispanic vote is .85.

6. Black voting rates correlate slightly (significant barely at .05) with Hispanic voting rates.

7. For the simulations, we exclude Hawaii, which has Hispanic exit poll data but no report of Hispanic data on turnout in the CPS.

8. One potential source of error is that the proportion of Hispanics in the exit polls as weighted are slightly larger than the proportion of respondents reported voting in the CPS state samples.

9. The changes of 8 and 28 percentage points are arbitrary selections.

10. In instances where this scenario predicts over 100 percent Democratic, the simulated vote is reset to 100 percent Democratic.

REFERENCES

de la Garza, Rodolfo. 2004. "Latino Politics." *Annual Review of Political Science* 7: 91–123.

de la Garza, Rodolfo, and Louis DeSipio, eds. 2005. *Muted Voices: Latinos and the 2000 Elections.* Lanham, MD: Rowman and Littlefield.

Leal, David, Matt Barreto, Jongho Lee, and Rodolfo de la Garza. 2005. "The Latino Vote in the 2004 Election." *PS: Political Science and Politics* 38: 41–50.

McDonald, Michael P. 2004. "Up, Up and Away! Voter Participation in the 2004 Presidential Election." *Forum* 2, no. 4. www.bepress.com/forum/vol2/iss4/art4. Accessed August 20, 2008.

Chapter Three

Hispanic Politics in a Battleground State

New Mexico in 2004

CHRISTINE MARIE SIERRA

AND F. CHRIS GARCIA

Early in the 2004 presidential campaign, New Mexico, a small state of about 1.9 million people with only five Electoral College votes, appeared primed to receive national attention from the candidates, the political parties, and the media. In the 2000 presidential election, Democrat Al Gore won the state over George W. Bush by only 366 votes, the closest margin in the country. Given the much-anticipated competitiveness of the 2004 presidential contest, New Mexico appeared destined to be a battleground state once again. Early signs that President George W. Bush and the Republican Party would aggressively court the Hispanic vote virtually guaranteed that "the land of enchantment" would find itself prominently in play in the presidential contest.

That Hispanics in New Mexico would figure prominently in the 2004 presidential race was to be expected given their prominence in the state and its electoral system. According to the 2000 U.S. Census, Hispanics accounted for 42 percent of the state's population—the highest percentage in any state in the nation. *Nuevomexicano* prominence also reflected their relatively high proportion of the state's eligible electorate. Census figures estimated that Hispanics constituted just over 37 percent of the state's voting age citizen population—again, the largest proportion of any state's electorate (U.S. Census Bureau 2005). Added to these impressive demographic characteristics is a long-standing *nuevomexicano* profile as a politically engaged and participatory population that can claim near-parity in its representation in the state legislature as well as significant numbers of local and statewide officials. To be sure, New Mexico would find itself at the center rather than at the margins of presidential politics in 2004, and *nuevomexicanos* promised to be an integral part of that electoral equation.

A prevalent theme that emerges in scholarship on Hispanic politics in New Mexico is one of exceptionalism. That is, both the history and the contemporary patterns of political behavior that characterize Hispanic politics in New Mexico differ from those found in other states. Though discrimination and inequality have affected the status of Hispanics in New Mexico, the Hispanic population, in general, has not been as excluded or marginalized from political power as have Latinos in other states. Indeed, studies have generally found that the New Mexico Hispanic electorate participates at levels somewhat comparable to the Anglos in the state and significantly higher than those of Latinos in other states (Garcia and Sierra 2005). All in all, a unique set of historical and demographic factors have assisted the *nuevomexicano* quest to remain "integral and central to the politics of the state throughout its history" (Garcia and Sapien 1999: 75).

One key demographic feature that sets apart the Hispanic population of New Mexico is its high rate of citizenship. Approximately 89 percent of Hispanic adults in New Mexico are U.S. citizens; most not only have been born in the United States but also are native to the state (U.S. Census Bureau 2000, 2004). Hence New Mexican Hispanics are not disadvantaged by citizenship as a requirement for voting, as are Hispanics in other states with large noncitizen populations. Moreover, most of them share in the *nuevomexicano* narrative that New Mexico is their homeland—their turf—where long-standing incorporation in the political system has fostered relatively high rates of Hispanic political participation and maintained a strong Hispanic presence in the state's political leadership.

KEY FINDINGS FROM PREVIOUS ELECTIONS

In line with the theme of New Mexico Hispanic exceptionalism, studies of previous presidential elections have found the Hispanic electorate an integral part of electoral outcomes. But playing an integral role in elections has not necessarily translated into a pivotal role for Hispanics in presidential contests—that is, producing the presidential winner in the state. Previous studies in Rodolfo de la Garza and Louis DeSipio's Latino election series have shown that New Mexico Hispanics are involved throughout election cycles as voters, party activists, and candidates for federal, state, and local office. Hispanic voters in New Mexico have been longtime Democratic supporters—60 to 70 percent of them are affiliated with the Democratic Party and upwards of 60 percent vote for Democratic presidential candidates. Whether the Hispanic vote has been decisive in the vote for president has varied, however, depending on electoral circumstances.

Sierra (1992) characterized Hispanic voting in the 1988 presidential contest as important but not pivotal, as Hispanics voted for Democrat Michael Dukakis, who lost the state to Republican George H. W. Bush. Although Garcia and Sapien (1999) summarized Hispanic voting in the 1992 presidential contest as simply contributing to Democrat Bill Clinton's margin of victory, they found that the Hispanic vote proved "crucial" to Clinton's 1996 victory in the state. Similarly, Garcia and Sierra (2005) found the Hispanic vote essential to Democrat Al Gore's razor-thin victory (366 votes) over Republican George W. Bush in 2000. At the same time, they noted that Gore's winning margin had to come from additional sectors of the electorate, such as African American or Native American voters. In other words, the Hispanic vote was necessary but not sufficient to carry the state for Al Gore.

Data on Hispanic registration and voting rates over previous presidential elections generally find Hispanics in New Mexico an engaged electorate but not without qualification. Garcia and Sapien (1999: 98) point out that the low turnout of Anglo Dole supporters made the Hispanic vote critical to Clinton's 1996 victory. Hispanics constituted reliable voters but did not turn out in record numbers. In comparing registration and voting rates from 1980 to 2000, Garcia and Sierra (2005) found a "widening gap" between Hispanic and Anglo rates of registration and voting. Even more dramatic were the lower rates of voter turnout for both Anglos and Hispanics from 1988 to 2000, suggesting that "New Mexico has not been immune to the general pattern of American disengagement from the electoral process" over time (128).

Despite some potentially troubling aspects of Hispanic participation rates over the long term, Hispanic engagement in electoral politics in New Mexico remains apparent. Given the predicted closeness of the presidential contest in 2004, the major political parties and their presidential candidates treated New Mexico, with its significant bloc of Hispanic voters, as though it might prove pivotal in the election.

THE 2002 MIDTERM ELECTION

The 2002 midterm election added an important feature to the political landscape of New Mexico: the election of Bill Richardson as governor. Richardson, a Democrat, was well known to voters in the state, having served several terms in the U.S. Congress as the representative from New Mexico's Third Congressional District. Born to an Anglo Boston banker father and a Mexican mother, Richardson's Hispanic identity and fluency in the Spanish language helped him to connect with his heavily Hispanic constituency in the northern part of the state. He left Congress when President Bill Clinton appointed him U.S. ambassador to the United Nations in 1997. One year later Clinton asked him to take over as secretary of energy. These positions helped to raise Richardson's profile in national politics, so much so that his name circulated in the national media as a potential vice presidential running mate for Al Gore in 2000. However, controversy associated with alleged security breaches at the national laboratories under his watch as energy secretary brought negative publicity that ultimately closed that door (Garcia and Sierra 2005).

An ambitious politician, Richardson turned his sights on the New Mexico governorship shortly thereafter. His Republican opponent in the gubernatorial election was John Sanchez, a successful Hispanic businessman who had defeated New Mexico's powerful Speaker of the House in a stunning upset in 2000. The one-term state representative, however, was no match for Richardson and his aggressive and well-financed campaign. Richardson defeated Sanchez decisively by a margin of 55.5 to 39.0 percent of the total vote (Green Party candidate David Bacon received 5.5 percent). Notably, Richardson drew a 75 percent level of support from Hispanics (23 percent voted for Sanchez) while running competitively with Sanchez among Anglo voters (46 percent to 48 percent, respectively).

Richardson won in twenty-four of New Mexico's thirty-three counties. He won resoundingly in the north-central counties, a Democratic stronghold with Hispanic voting majorities. In addition, he won several counties in the southern part of the state that, despite sizable Hispanic populations, generally lean toward the Republicans. Adding to his impressive victory, the Democrats recaptured Bernalillo County, the seat of the state's largest urban population (Albuquerque), its two adjacent counties, as well as seven mostly Anglo counties in the eastern part of the state that usually vote Republican (Sierra 2003). With an expansive geographic base of support in Hispanic, Anglo, and Native American areas, Bill Richardson would wield substantial power in New Mexico and draw on his popularity and stature as the nation's only Hispanic governor to insert himself into Democratic presidential politics in the 2004 election.

The reelection of New Mexico's senior senator, Republican Pete Domenici, also took place in the 2002 midterm election. His challenger was Gloria Tristani, granddaughter of New Mexico's former longtime Democratic U.S. Senator, Dennis Chavez. She proved no match for the five-term incumbent, as Domenici easily defeated her, 65 percent to 35 percent. Exit polls showed Domenici with broad support across virtually all demographic groups, including 63 percent support from Hispanics (Sierra 2003).

Domenici's reelection illustrates another long-standing trait of New Mexico's Hispanic electorate. Although partisanship and ethnicity are factors in voter choice, New Mexicans will cross party and ethnic lines to vote for a candidate of their liking. As in his previous reelection bids, Domenici's popularity in New Mexico and the formidable advantages of incumbency (such as name recognition and a substantial campaign war chest) drew crossover votes from Hispanics.

BILL RICHARDSON: A KEY PLAYER IN PRESIDENTIAL POLITICS

Within months of taking office as governor, Richardson received headlines for his political ambitions and broad public policy agenda for the state. His ambitious agenda, which included promoting economic development and tourism, was not without personal political implications. As an example, his image appeared on a huge billboard in Times Square in New York City. Albuquerque columnist Larry Calloway remarked that "millions will see the 70-foot panoramic shot of northern New Mexico's Ghost Ranch cliffs with Gov. Bill Richardson in the left foreground wearing a loose shirt and a bolo tie." Republican state party chairman John Dendahl decried the whole thing as "shameless self-promotion." Observed Calloway, "The Republican point . . . is that Broadway Bill is already off and running for president or vice president at our [i.e., public] expense" (Calloway 2003).

Republican and Democratic lawmakers also criticized Richardson's extensive travel and time spent out of the state. They complained that, as governor, he needed to spend more time attending to the state's business. Undaunted by such criticism, Richardson countered that his actions were meant to elevate New Mexico in the national spotlight in order to advance its political standing and economic well-being. He boldly championed several actions designed to bring more attention to New Mexico and its Hispanic voters in his party's presidential politics. He worked to bring the first official, nationally televised debate among the contenders for the Democratic presidential nomination to New Mexico. Kate Nelson of the *Albuquerque Tribune* commented that the Democratic National Committee chose for its first sanctioned debate "not a power town but the little Duke City [Albuquerque]—thanks to behind-the-scenes wrangling by Richardson" (Nelson 2003). The televised debate, scheduled for early September, 2003, brought media exposure to Albuquerque and drew the participation of eight out of nine announced presidential candidates.

Richardson also convinced the state party to move the date of New Mexico's 2004 presidential primary from June to early February in order for New Mexican voters to influence the choice of the party's nominee. The date change was accompanied by a change in name—a presidential preference caucus. Despite the reference to a caucus, voting would take place along the lines of a party-run primary election, as was done previously.

Nelson (2003) credited Richardson's "wrangling" with this move as well. She observed, "New Mexico Democrats will finally get a chance to weigh in on the party's candidate before the rest of the nation winnows the field." In a slick publication produced by the state Democratic Party, Richardson touted New Mexico's bellwether status in choosing presidential winners and, especially, the significance of the Hispanic vote in New Mexico. Richardson pointed out that New Mexicans had voted for the national popular vote winner in twenty-two of twenty-three past presidential elections. Moreover, since 1984 state voting for president had virtually mirrored national vote results. Richardson maintained that New Mexico's role in choosing the next president promised to take on even greater significance due to the "enduring strength" of the state's Hispanic voters (*New Mexico Chooses* 2003: 1).

Indeed, Richardson and Democratic Party activists dubbed February 3, 2004, "Hispanic Tuesday" or "Martes Latino," as Arizona and New Mexico would hold their presidential primaries on the same day. In the state party publication, Richardson declared, "New Mexico and Arizona will test the candidates' ability to attract Hispanic voters. Those who win in the Southwest will demonstrate that they can win across the nation" (*New Mexico Chooses* 2003: 3).

Another Democratic Party decision would place New Mexico's governor squarely in the center of the party nominating process. Drawing support from some presidential candidates (Nelson 2003) as well as black and Hispanic Democrats who lobbied on his behalf (Brazile 2003), Richardson was named permanent chair of the 2004 Democratic National Convention. Hence the New Mexico governor found himself on yet another national stage from which he could tout his ambitious political and partisan agenda and speak to the importance of Hispanics—and New Mexico—in national politics.

To carry his agenda forward, Governor Richardson established his own political action committee, Moving America Forward (MAF). Through the money it raised and the political events and voter registration drives it sponsored, MAF would be among the most important PACs and 527 organizations operating in New Mexico during the 2004 election. Its general objective was to help elect Democrats from the top of the ticket to lower offices, but it also worked to increase the presence of ethnic minorities in electoral politics in New Mexico and beyond.

MAF announced it would focus its activities on four battleground states with large Hispanic populations: New Mexico, Arizona, Florida, and Nevada (Fecteau 2003). The multistate effort would sponsor training and events to recruit more Hispanics, Native Americans, and young people to run for public office and work in political campaigns. MAF also directed attention specifically toward Latinas; partnering with Emily's List, a national pro-choice women's PAC, they trained Latinas interested in working on campaigns or running for public office at no cost to attendees (Torres 2003). Ultimately, Richardson wanted to build the political infrastructure needed to influence national politics. In his words, "We must position ourselves to advance the national Hispanic and Democratic agenda, and garner the financial and political resources necessary to build a national mobilization campaign" (Andersen 2003).

It was not difficult to see that Bill Richardson was on the move to make a name for himself as he touted the virtues of both his state and his party during the presidential campaign season. Talk of his candidacy as a potential vice presidential running mate in 2004 or a presidential candidate in 2008 would again gain traction in political and media circles. One prominent Albuquerque journalist went so far as to claim that while Richardson may not be the party's "MVP—Most Valuable Politician—he's well on his way to becoming its MVH: Most Valuable Hispanic" (Nelson 2003).

THE 2004 PRESIDENTIAL PRIMARY RACE: THE DEMOCRATS

Nothing precipitated the extraordinary attention to New Mexico voters as much as Richardson's "big idea" of having New Mexico join six other states in holding their presidential primaries immediately after the contests in Iowa and New Hampshire. Because New Mexico moved toward the front of the line of state primaries and caucuses, virtually all the Democratic presidential hopefuls sent paid staff to New Mexico to set up field operations and, in some cases, open campaign offices, mostly in Albuquerque, the state's largest city. Drawing largely on the extensive coverage of the primary campaign in Albuquerque's local newspapers, we constructed a time line of public campaign events and candidate visits beginning in June 2003 and extending to February 2, the day before the Democratic presidential preference caucus was held.

Howard Dean, former governor of Vermont, visited the state first, holding a rally and fund-raiser in Santa Fe, the state capital, at the end of June. Dean was also the first candidate to open statewide offices in New Mexico (in Albuquerque, Santa Fe, and Las Cruces). His organization appeared to be the most formidable, hiring more staff than the other campaigns and holding numerous fund-raisers, house parties, and "meet-ups" during New Mexico's primary season. The candidate himself visited the state five times from June to December 2003.

Perhaps a political junkie's dream, the candidates descended on the Duke City in unprecedented fashion in early September; eight of the nine announced Democratic presidential candidates came to New Mexico for the first official, televised debate sanctioned by the Democratic National Committee (DNC). Debate participants included Senator Bob Graham (FL), Representative Richard Gephardt (MO), Senator John Kerry (MA), former Senator John Edwards (NC), former Senator Carol Moseley Braun (IL), Senator Joseph Lieberman (CT), Representative Dennis Kucinich (OH), and Howard Dean. Retired General Wesley Clark had not yet declared his candidacy, and inclement weather in New York prevented the Reverend Al Sharpton from attending the debate (Nagourney and Wilgoren 2003).

The Congressional Hispanic Caucus sponsored the debate, held on the University of New Mexico campus, and Univision and PBS jointly televised it. Speaking in English and briefly in Spanish, Governor Richardson welcomed the candidates and the live and television audiences to the first bilingual debate among presidential candidates in U.S. politics, a historic moment. Two prominent Latino journalists, Ray Suarez (of the *Jim Lehrer News Hour* on PBS) and Maria Elena Salinas (news anchor for Univision), were the moderators. Some questions were put to the candidates in Spanish, but most were in English. Candidate responses were in English, with a few daring souls inserting Spanish here and there in a few of their answers. The debate then was not truly bilingual, but Univision translated it into Spanish for its viewing audience.

A number of issues were addressed, with the war in Iraq dominating. Immigration appeared to be the only Latino-specific issue addressed, however, with a number of candidates expressing support for a legalization program for undocumented immigrants. Notwithstanding few references to Latino-specific concerns or issues, Adam Segal of the Hispanic Voter Project at Johns Hopkins University claimed, "It shows how much importance the party leadership at the very highest levels is placing on [Hispanic] outreach" (Fecteau 2003). Perhaps more symbolic than substantive, the first "bilingual debate" among presidential contenders certainly brought national attention to the Hispanic electorate in New Mexico and the nation.

Shortly thereafter, the Democratic National Committee held a Hispanic leadership summit in Albuquerque. The DNC's intention was to draw about one hundred Hispanic leaders and activists to discuss Hispanics' role in the 2004 election. The DNC's choice of Albuquerque for the national summit drew this remark by Leslie Hoffman of the Associated Press: "Democrats continue to court the coveted Hispanic vote using New Mexico as a favored pulpit." According to Hoffman, Richardson had lobbied for this event to be held in New Mexico (Hoffman 2003). DNC Chairman Terry McAuliffe attended the event to "show the party's commitment to the Hispanic community," to discuss how the party could assist Hispanic communities, and to "get the vote out in 2004" (Garcia 2003). Clearly, New Mexico offered the Democrats an arena in which to both showcase and test their strategies for connecting with and mobilizing Hispanic voters.

The candidates' campaigns varied in organization, resources, and time spent in New Mexico. Based on our compilation of press reports on campaign staff, endorsements, and events, the candidates who actively campaigned in the state (which excludes Moseley Braun and Sharpton) used some form of Hispanic inclusion and outreach. Several candidates placed Hispanics in key staff positions, and prominent Hispanics in New Mexico politics, especially state and local officeholders, publicly endorsed their preferred candidate and showed their support at rallies and events in the state (although Richardson himself did not endorse any candidates during the primary).[1]

Campaign road shows included appearances in Hispanic areas in various parts of New Mexico, replete with the symbolic inclusion of

Hispanic culture, such as the use of Latino music at campaign events and the insertion of Spanish (usually only phrases) in stump speeches. Surrogate campaigners also came to the state, including Hispanic celebrities or politicians popular with Hispanic voters, such as Henry Cisneros and Massachusetts Senator Edward Kennedy, who gave a rousing speech on Kerry's behalf at a packed union hall in Española, an old Hispanic town and gateway to the Hispanic north. Joe Monahan, political observer and blogger on New Mexico politics, commented, "You can't do much better than a visit by a Kennedy," in relation to outreach to Hispanics (Limon 2004: A4). The major candidates also ran Spanish-language ads on television.

As of early January 2004, the *Albuquerque Journal* reported that Democratic candidates had visited the state twenty-six times (President Bush had also visited the state once). In other words, a presidential candidate was "live and in person somewhere in New Mexico" every two weeks on average (Linthicum 2004a: A1, A6.) In addition, the campaigns set up ten offices in Albuquerque, Santa Fe, and Las Cruces; hired thirty-two staffers; and spent $1 million (the governor's estimate) in New Mexico (Linthicum 2004a: A7).

Candidate momentum during the New Mexico primary season generally resembled what occurred nationally, especially for the Dean and Kerry campaigns. A poll in early September 2003 showed Howard Dean leading among the Democratic candidates. In mid-January 2004 a poll showed Dean had maintained the lead but had not extended it. Rather, Wesley Clark was a strong second, only two percentage points behind Dean. John Kerry ran far behind with the rest of the candidates. At the same time, the poll indicated that Dean was drawing more Hispanic support than Clark, whose military credentials were thought to have broad appeal to Hispanics in New Mexico. In fact, Hispanics were reported to be Dean's "single largest group of supporters," whereas Anglo voters favored Clark over Dean (Coleman 2004a). Notably, a sizable number (34 percent) of those polled indicated they were still undecided.

A third poll of likely New Mexico Democratic voters was conducted one week after Kerry's victories at the Iowa caucus and the New Hampshire primary. Although his New Mexico campaign organization was slow to get off the ground, his momentum clearly influenced New

Table 3.1. Democratic Party Candidates for President, New Mexico Pre-Primary Polls, 2004 (percent)

Candidates	*Sept. 8–10, 2003*[a]	*Jan. 12–15, 2004*[b]	*Jan. 28–29, 2004*[c] *Total*	*Hispanic*
Kerry	10	8	31	34
Dean	18	18	15	13
Clark	n/a	16	14	
Edwards	1	4	7	
Lieberman	14	8	3	
Gephardt	7	7	1	
Kucinich	3	6	2	
Undecided	38	34	27	
None	9			
Number of observations	203	401	500	

Source: Albuquerque Journal/Research and Polling, Inc.
[a] Sample: Registered Democrats. Margin of error: +/– 7 percentage points.
[b] Sample: Registered Democrats (likely voters). Margin of error: +/– 5 percentage points.
[c] Sample: Registered Democrats who voted in the last two primary and general elections, according to voting records. Margin of error: +/– 4.5 percentage points.

Mexico preferences. Kerry surged ahead in the New Mexico poll (31 percent) and left Dean and Clark competing for a distant second place (15 percent and 14 percent, respectively); the poll indicated that Hispanics also now favored Kerry over the others. The only potential silver lining on an impending dark cloud of defeat for Dean—the candidate to campaign first in New Mexico and to establish what most regarded as the best organization—and the other candidates was the still substantial percentage of likely New Mexican Democratic voters who remained undecided less than one week before they were to vote (27 percent).

Voting results produced John Kerry as New Mexican Democrats' *numero uno* to do battle with President Bush in November. Kerry won handily, finishing with 42.5 percent of the total vote. Wesley Clark came in second with 20 percent and Howard Dean third with 16 percent. Rounding out the field were John Edwards with 11 percent, Dennis Kucinich with 5.5 percent, and Joe Lieberman with 2.5 percent of the votes cast. Among New Mexico's twenty-six pledged delegates to the national convention, sixteen went to Kerry, five to Clark (who dropped out of the race after New Mexicans voted), and five to Dean (Linthicum 2004b: E3). A University of New Mexico survey of caucus voters after the election showed that while Anglos and Hispanics both preferred Kerry, the strength of their support was different: Hispanics voted 50.3 percent for Kerry, 23.5 percent for Clark, and 14.0 percent for Dean; Anglo voters gave 36.9 percent of their votes to Kerry, 20.2 percent to Clark, and 16.3 percent to Dean (Atkeson 2004: table 9).

Bill Richardson's "big idea" appeared to pay off for New Mexico. State party Democrats were entirely elated with the outcome: the attention drawn to the state, the level of interest and mobilization shown by New Mexico Democratic voters, and the enhanced profile for the governor, who pulled off what his party proclaimed a success (Linthicum and Nash 2004: A1). Over 102,000 total votes were cast—fewer than votes cast in previous state-run June primaries but about twice the targeted (and low) threshold party elites had set (Linthicum 2004b). It remained to be seen how much of John Kerry's primary battle in the state would serve as a "practice run" for his national campaign in terms of Hispanic outreach and mobilization.

THE "OTHER" PRIMARY

Notwithstanding the Democratic caucus on February 3, a June 1 state-run primary was slated for all other candidates—Republicans, third party candidates, and Democrats running for federal, state, and local office. For Republicans, the primary season was mostly spent putting the party's state apparatus in place to run the president's reelection effort in New Mexico and to support Republican candidates running for various offices throughout the state. John Sanchez, the former state representative who ran unsuccessfully for governor in 2002 against Bill Richardson, was named Southwest regional chairman of Bush's reelection campaign across five southwestern states, including New Mexico

("Sanchez to Chair Bush Campaign" 2003). U.S. Senator Pete Domenici was named chair of the Bush-Cheney '04 campaign in New Mexico (Coleman 2004b).

Compared to the Democrats, the Republicans held relatively few campaign events in the state from early January to early June, but they included high-profile visits by President Bush, his father, Laura Bush, and Vice President and Mrs. Cheney. Tellingly, Bush's first visit was to Roswell, a small town of slightly over 45,000 in conservative southeastern New Mexico. His speech addressed energy policy, the economy, and the "war on terror." Uniformed cadets from the New Mexico Military Institute stood behind the president onstage. Though Hispanics constitute 44 percent of the city's population, no Hispanic emphasis was apparent at the event. Rather, the Republicans were targeting the city's predominantly Anglo conservative Republican base (Coleman 2004c). Bush visited Albuquerque three months later for an invitation-only event at which he touted a strong national economy, home ownership, and his fight against terrorists (Nash and Linthicum 2004).

These two visits essentially revealed an important element of the GOP mobilization strategy for 2004: do not neglect the state's larger urban areas, which tend to favor Democrats, but pay special attention to the smaller, rural, mostly Anglo and Republican-voting communities of New Mexico. In a similar vein, Vice President Cheney's first two visits to the state in 2004 were to Albuquerque and Artesia, a southeastern town of only 10,700, 45 percent Hispanic. Both visits were fund-raisers among the party faithful, with no visible Hispanic outreach. Cheney's $1,000-a-plate fund-raiser in Albuquerque netted an estimated $250,000 for the Bush-Cheney reelection campaign (Reed 2004). The Artesia fund-raiser emphasized the oil and gas interests in the region and benefited the successful reelection effort of Republican congressman Steve Pearce (Romo 2004).

Several members of Bush's cabinet and high party officials also visited the state to tout administration policies. The day before the Democratic caucus, Marc Racicot, chairman of Bush's national reelection campaign, led a Republican rally in Santa Fe at the State Capitol. The rally was to flex Republican muscle amid all the hoopla over the Democratic caucus and "to remind New Mexicans that Democrats aren't the only ones seeking the presidency this year." Racicot also took the opportunity to announce that internal dissension within the state Republican Party ranks had been resolved (Miles 2004a).

Headlines the day after the June 1 primary featured State Senator Richard Romero winning the Democratic nomination for U.S. House District 1. He would do battle for the second time with the incumbent, Republican Heather Wilson, who ran unopposed in the primary (Lenderman and Romo 2004). With the primary season over, Democrats and Republicans geared up for what was to be an extraordinary mobilization effort of New Mexico voters by both parties and presidential tickets.

DRAWING THE BATTLE LINES

Soon after John Kerry emerged as the Democratic Party's standard-bearer, a poll of New Mexican registered voters indicated that a close race with George W. Bush was under way. Asked if they had a "favorable or unfavorable impression" of the presidential candidates, poll respondents placed Kerry just ahead of Bush in their favorability ratings (44 percent to 43 percent, respectively). Bush drew the largest percentage of "unfavorable" responses (38 percent to 24 percent for Kerry), most likely because voters were more familiar with him as the incumbent president. At the same time, a higher percentage of voters stated they did not know Kerry or would not say how they rated him (14 percent to only 4 percent for the president).

At first glance, favorability ratings among Hispanics suggested Kerry held a strong lead over Bush, 55 percent to 44 percent. Even more hopeful for the Kerry camp was that the candidate enjoyed a 70 percent favorability rating in north-central New Mexico, the heart of the Hispanic Democratic base (Miles 2004b). This poll offered some optimism for the Republicans as well; if they could peel off upwards of a third of the Hispanic vote, New Mexico could easily end up in the "red" rather than the "blue" column.

Organizationally, the Republicans jumped in front of the Kerry campaign in New Mexico. Top GOP staff arrived in January 2004 to set up a statewide infrastructure to run both the Bush-Cheney reelection campaign and "Victory 2004," the RNC's effort to elect Republican candidates running for federal and state legislative offices. According to J. Scott Jennings, executive director for the Bush-Cheney campaign in New Mexico, the GOP intended not only to reelect the president but also to build a "comprehensive, grassroots, precinct-level organization," a political infrastructure that would strengthen the state party in the long-term (Atkeson, Carrillo, and Walker 2005: 125). The GOP effort became highly centralized, however, with national staff "calling the shots" (Atkeson, Carrillo, and Walker 2005: 125). The GOP strategy also included outreach to Hispanics. Organized as the Viva Bush Coalition, the party provided opportunities for Hispanic Republicans, from prominent politicians and celebrities to local party activists, to solicit the support of Hispanic voters for the president's reelection.

Three local New Mexicans, two of them Hispanic, served as field directors for the Victory 2004 campaign, supervising voter registration and mobilization throughout the state. According to Christopher Atencio, northern field director for Victory 2004, Hispanic outreach was a "big part of everything we did." In Rio Arriba County, the largest county in the north and where Atencio himself has family, "everything [was] geared to Hispanics." The GOP's outreach strategy included getting people to register to vote and, most important, working through friendship and family networks to get people to switch parties, or at least to vote for Bush. Toward these ends, Atencio worked with GOP party officers (many of whom were Hispanic) in the northern counties and towns under his jurisdiction (Atencio 2007). He faced a formidable challenge, as he worked in heavily partisan Democratic areas, but the mere assignment of Atencio to work in "enemy territory" underscored another element of the Republican 2004 strategy: do not concede any area, city, or town to the Democrats; work them all for the Republican cause.

The central New Mexico field director, Scott Darnell, pointed to the party's "extremely successful" voter registration effort at the New Mexico State Fair, under the direction of a longtime New Mexico Hispanic family, the C. de Bacas. Darnell mentioned the State Fair effort as an example of the party's outreach to Hispanics in Albuquerque, as the fair draws Hispanic families from across the state (Darnell 2007). Both field directors assessed the GOP voter registration efforts as quite successful, as voter registration numbers for Republicans increased beyond their stated goal. GOPNM set a goal of registering 30,000 new Republican voters and achieved an estimated 50,000 registrants (Atkeson, Carrillo, and Walker 2005: 125).

Although, as in the primary season, John Kerry was slow to put his campaign organization in place (Finnegan 2004), Governor Bill Richardson's efforts to "Move America Forward" with his PAC bolstered the Democratic effort in the state. According to Vanessa Alarid, executive director of the Democratic Party of New Mexico (DPNM), the state party followed an organizational strategy that complemented rather than duplicated the mobilization efforts of Richardson's PAC. As she explained, because MAF's top priority was voter registration, the state party did not engage in this effort. Rather, it concentrated on voter mobilization—that is, get-out-the-vote (GOTV) activities. Hence, the party "backed off" certain tasks that were covered by MAF and put money and other resources into other outreach activities, such as building its new voter database (Alarid 2005).

MAF hired more than ninety paid staff members to do site and door-to-door registration, with an emphasis on Hispanic and American Indian areas, including the pueblos. In Albuquerque, seeing MAF workers registering voters in front of grocery stores in various middle-income or working-class areas was common. MAF also set up a phone bank to determine if some adults remained unregistered in a household with registered voters. In the end, MAF claimed 27,921 newly registered Hispanics and American Indians, surpassing its goal of 25,000. Of these, an estimated 18,000 were Hispanic and 10,000 were American Indian (Atkeson, Carrillo, and Walker 2005: 128).

Two Latino interest groups also engaged in voter registration activities. The Southwest Voter Registration and Education Project (SVREP), based in San Antonio, Texas, sent Victor Landa to New Mexico in March 2004 to train New Mexicans to register voters and organize registration drives in seventeen communities "chosen for their high number of unregistered Hispanics"[2] and to register voters on site at public places and events rather than walk door-to-door. SVREP claimed to register 20,000 new voters in the state. The Southwest Organizing Project (SWOP), a Chicano community organization based in Albuquerque, also engaged in voter registration, targeting unregistered members and young Hispanics (Atkeson, Carrillo, and Walker 2005: 128).

Although not specifically Hispanic, the Albuquerque affiliate of the national network Association of Community Organizations for Reform Now (ACORN) also engaged in voter registration, especially in poor and minority communities in Albuquerque. ACORN-NM became embroiled in controversy when one of its canvassers was caught forging voter registration applications. The Republican Party aggressively pursued this and other cases through litigation, claiming that voter fraud presented a serious problem in this election. Indeed, the party had lawyers in every county to fight voter fraud (Atencio 2007).

MAF, SVREP, SWOP, and ACORN were just part of the constellation of Democratic interest groups active in the New Mexico presidential contest. A plethora of 501c(3), c(4), and 527 organizations played a major role in voter registration and GOTV efforts on behalf of the Democratic Party. Depending on the activities their tax status allowed, these organizations assumed much of the party-building work that parties previously funded through soft money.[3]

The Kerry campaign for the presidency sent three top staffers to New Mexico, all of whom were Hispanic. Moses Mercado was state director, Ruben Pulido Jr. was campaign spokesman, and Irma Esparza served as director of the Coordinated Campaign, the Democratic Party's overall effort to support the other Democratic candidates running for office in the state. Two native New Mexican Anglos, Lieutenant Governor Diane Denish, the first woman to be elected to that position, and John Pound, a trial lawyer and longtime Democratic Party activist, were named co-chairs of the Kerry campaign.

New Mexicans were keenly interested in whether Kerry would choose their governor as his vice presidential running mate. The Albuquerque media followed Richardson's activities closely, noting his numerous trips out of state on the campaign trail (Nash 2004), at a "Boston VIP" meeting with party officials in his role as chair of the upcoming national party convention (Coleman 2004d), and as host to the party elite and public officials who held meetings in the state. In early July, after much speculation, Richardson announced that he had requested that his name be removed from a list of potential running mates. He had met with Kerry in Phoenix earlier in the week "to discuss the vice presidential search." Richardson aides explained that Kerry never offered Richardson a spot on the ticket but that he had been under consideration (Coleman 2004e). Whether Richardson was, in fact, on Kerry's short list was never officially confirmed—a question that generated much intrigue among political pundits and media in the state (see Coleman 2004f).

Between the Democratic caucus and the national convention, Kerry visited the state twice as his party's designated presidential nominee. His second visit was with John Edwards, just days after he had announced Edwards as his vice presidential running mate. Thousands greeted the Democratic presidential ticket at the National Hispanic Cultural Center in Albuquerque. A beaming Governor Richardson introduced them to the excited throng: "Today we are making history . . . because for the first time in our state's long proud existence, a presidential candidate and a vice presidential candidate are here together" (Lenderman and Nash 2004: A1). Although Richardson misspoke (in the 2000 presidential campaign, George W. Bush and Dick Cheney appeared together in southern New Mexico), his enthusiasm reflected what, in fact, was evident: New Mexicans were drawing unprecedented attention in the presidential battle this time around.

THE NATIONAL CONVENTIONS

New Mexico's delegates to the Democratic National Convention were "fired up" when they arrived in Boston the last week in July. Their governor presided as chair over the convention, they were seated near the center stage, and the governor and interest groups, intent on showing them a good time, provided plenty of amenities (Lenderman and Coleman 2004). As is typical in New Mexican politics, Hispanics were well represented among the delegation. Regular delegates totaled thirty-seven, of whom seventeen were Hispanic, sixteen were Anglo, two were Native American, and two were African American, one of whom was Afro-Latina (Farrauto 2007). New Mexicans enjoyed the national spotlight. Richardson delivered a major foreign policy speech, and other New Mexican leaders addressed the convention. They returned ready to fight "with the gloves off" (Pickler and Riechmann 2004).

The Republicans lost no time countering the Democratic hoopla. Vice President and Mrs. Cheney visited Rio Rancho, a rapidly growing area just outside Albuquerque, the day after the Democratic convention's conclusion. In the month between the national party conventions, President Bush visited Albuquerque twice and made important appearances in southern (Las Cruces) and northwestern (Farmington) New Mexico. For their part, the Democratic candidates, along with spouses, children, and New Mexico politicians, took a train ride through the Hispanic north, with a rest stop in Albuquerque. New Mexico's battleground status even drew visits from Independent presidential candidate Ralph Nader and the Libertarian Party's Michael Badnarik.

New Mexico sent twenty-four delegates to the National Republican Convention, held in New York City at the end of August. Among them were thirteen Anglos, seven Hispanics, two African Americans, and two Native Americans (Coleman 2004g; Atencio 2007). Whereas Hispanics made up 45 percent of the New Mexico Democratic delegation, they were 29 percent among the Republicans. Heather Wilson, the Republican incumbent seeking reelection in Congressional District 1, was a featured speaker at the New York convention.

THE FALL CAMPAIGN: DOWN TO THE WIRE

Preelection polls showed a close presidential race in New Mexico. Early in the race, Kerry ran ahead of Bush (Zogby Interactive 2004; American Research Group 2004), but during and after the Republican National Convention, Bush began to claim a narrow lead in some polls. It was a very close race, as the candidates appeared to change leads several times between August and October. In fact, underscoring the tightness of the race, the results of various polls of registered and likely New Mexican voters were within their margins of error.

Ethnic differences between Anglo and Hispanic preferences were apparent (table 3.2). A majority of likely Anglo voters consistently favored Bush, whereas likely Hispanic voters consistently favored Kerry. Despite Kerry's lead among Hispanics, the numbers were potentially troublesome in that Democratic presidential candidates drew higher levels of Hispanic support at comparable points in time during previous elections (Garcia and Sapien 1999; Garcia and Sierra 2005; also see Atkeson, Carrillo, and Walker 2005: 124).

Table 3.2. New Mexico Presidential Preference Polls by Ethnicity, 2004 (percent)

	Aug. 27–Sept. 1, 2004[a]		*Sept. 15–16, 2004*[b]		*Oct. 26–29, 2004*[c]	
Candidates	*Anglo*	*Hispanic*	*Anglo*	*Hispanic*	*Anglo*	*Hispanic*
Bush (R)	55	32	59	27	56	32
Kerry (D)	34	52	32	62	36	59
Nader (I)	1	1	1	3		
Other party	3	0	1	--		
Undecided	5	12	7	8		
Won't say	1	2				
Number of observations	908		625		1,140	

[a] *Source:* Albuquerque Journal/Research and Polling, Inc. Sample: Registered New Mexico voters, who said they are likely to vote, and asked, "If the Presidential election were held today, for whom would you vote?" Margin of error: +/– 3%.

[b] *Source:* Santa Fe New Mexican/KOB-TV Statewide Poll/Mason-Dixon Polling & Research, Inc. Sample: Registered New Mexico voters, who said they are likely to vote. Margin of error: +/– 4%.

[c] *Source:* Albuquerque Journal/Research and Polling, Inc. Sample: Registered New Mexico voters, who said they were likely to vote or already had cast early in-person or absentee ballots. Margin of error: +/– 3%.

The ground war incorporated a bilingual approach, with both presidential campaigns running radio and television ads in English and Spanish. Direct mail from the parties and interest groups also appeared in both languages. At election's end, the Republican National Committee and the Bush-Cheney campaign were estimated to have spent $3.4 million on radio and television ads; the estimated total expenditure of the Democratic National Committee and the Kerry-Edwards campaign was $4.1 million (Atkeson, Carrillo, and Walker 2005).

Republican Party Outreach Efforts

Republicans worked hard to get out the vote with targeted personal contact through coalitions of local groups. Voter contact through phone banking, walking door-to-door, and other efforts matched individuals with common interests. Hence, person-to-person contact matched Evangelical Christians to other Evangelicals, veterans to veterans, gun owners to gun owners, and so forth. The matching, targeted strategy applied to Hispanics as well. The Viva Bush Coalition sought to get Hispanic community leaders involved in approaching fellow Hispanics to vote for the president. Organization for the Bush-Cheney campaign revolved around the idea of "trust"—in other words, "reach out to someone you know and get them to support the ticket. People will listen to someone they know and trust" (Atencio 2007).

The Republican message to Hispanics emphasized "faith and family." Volunteers went into Hispanic neighborhoods and spoke to folks about social values and "family values." According to Scott Darnell, Republican field organizer for Albuquerque, family values meant, first and foremost, the issues of abortion and gay marriage, then tax cuts, economic opportunity, education, and the No Child Left Behind Act. The war on terror also figured into the Republican message to Hispanics (Atkeson, Carrillo, and Walker 2005: 126). All in all, Darnell maintained that "family values" was a message that worked well with the Hispanics they approached. He claimed that Hispanics were especially drawn to Bush's opposition to abortion and gay marriage. At the same time, Darnell admitted that as party workers canvassed in primarily Democratic Hispanic neighborhoods, some welcomed them, but others slammed their doors shut (Darnell 2007).

Events for Hispanics were held in various areas throughout the state. Republican organizers were especially pleased with campaign visits by Small Business Administration head Hector Barreto, former U.S. Treasurer Rosario Marin, White House counsel and fellow Texan Alberto Gonzales, and the president's nephew, George P. Bush. Republican support in the Hispanic north energized the party. As a campaign organizer said, "When Hector Barreto entered Española on a campaign trip for Bush/Cheney, the streets were lined with people holding and waving Bush/Cheney signs." It was quite a sight for Española, in the heart of the Democrats' Hispanic base in the north (Atencio 2007). Republican enthusiasm was also evident in other northern places, namely, Santa Fe and Taos, whipped up by the fact that "Republicans in the north get very little visibility [or] a chance to celebrate, so they were very enthusiastic that such Republican events were taking place" (Darnell 2007).

Republican outreach came largely through volunteer efforts. The Bush-Cheney campaign and the GOP hired a couple of dozen paid staff in New Mexico, but the party relied heavily on about fifty thousand volunteers statewide (Atencio 2007). Republican efforts were assisted by 527 organizations, especially the Swift Boat Veterans for Truth, which ran television ads disputing and disparaging Kerry's decorated war record in Vietnam. But far more 527s aligned with the Democrats worked the state for Kerry than did Republican interest groups for Bush. The Republican National Hispanic Assembly organized in New Mexico and the Latino Coalition spent over $11,000 on television and radio ads. But no other national Hispanic organizations worked the state on behalf of Bush-Cheney (Atencio 2007; Atkeson, Carrillo, and Walker 2005).

Democratic Party Outreach Efforts

While Republicans sought votes in all corners of the state, the Democratic mobilization strategy focused on GOTV efforts in Democratic strongholds and the state's more populous and urban areas, especially Bernalillo County (Albuquerque). The Democrats' Coordinated Campaign targeted "any precinct that was at least 65 percent Democratic, conceding in particular Southeastern portions of the state, a mistake they lamented in hindsight" (Atkeson, Carrillo, and Walker 2005: 127).

Because New Mexican Hispanics are part of the Democratic base, the party's GOTV efforts "automatically" included them (Alarid 2005). However, the party did engage in some specific Hispanic outreach—over and above what was done in general for Democratic voters. Vanessa Alarid, executive director of DPNM, implemented a Hispanic caucus within the party, wherein Hispanic party activists across the state but primarily from Albuquerque and Rio Arriba, Taos, and Santa Fe Counties were asked to enlist five new participants in election activities. The caucus was informal, with a network of about fifty persons.

Following a "three-by-three" strategy, DPNM contacted Hispanic households prior to October with three knocks (visits) on their doors, three phone calls, and three pieces of mail. Mailings to Hispanics specifically were "persuasion . . . pieces that stressed family values." In contrast to a Republican-defined "family values" agenda, the Democratic message spoke of the importance of family and addressed issues such as education, health care, child care, and jobs. References were not made to abortion or gay rights issues. DPNM also organized bus tours in the northern and southern parts of the state with members of the Congressional Hispanic Caucus. State and local Hispanic public officials met with the congressional members along the way (Alarid 2005).

A variety of interest groups assisted the Kerry campaign and the Democratic Party in their outreach efforts. According to one study, thirty-six interest groups engaged in at least one type of voter communication activity (e-mail, mail, personal contact, phone call, or newspaper, magazine, radio or television ads) on behalf of the Kerry campaign and the Democrats; in contrast, the study identified ten interest groups as "Republican allies" (Atkeson, Carrillo, and Walker 2005). Among these "Democratic allies," three were either Hispanic organizations or Hispanic oriented. MAF focused on "getting new and low propensity voters, especially Hispanics, American Indians, and newly registered voters to the polls" (Atkeson, Carrillo, and Walker 2005: 128). ACORN "hired citizens to visit homes in highly Hispanic neighborhoods with a nonpartisan GOTV message" (131). Adding to the mobilization mix were national Hispanic nonpartisan groups, such as the National Association of Latino Elected and Appointed Officials (NALEO) and the Southwest Voter Registration and Education Project (SVREP). In the end, one organizer for Albuquerque's Southwest Organizing Project (SWOP) noted that the "national mobilization efforts made it difficult for local groups to compete and that many people were simply turned off by 'overkill'" (128).

THE ROLE OF CHURCHES IN THE CAMPAIGN

Two starkly contrasting portraits can be painted for the role of churches in the Republican and Democratic presidential campaigns. Evangelical Christian and conservative Catholic churches were critically important and integral to Republican efforts to mobilize their base. Conservative churches served as targets of GOTV activities, and individual members of the congregations formed the backbone of the volunteer army that mobilized voters across the state. Volunteers from the Mormon Church and the "home-school movement" in Farmington helped with voter registration in their respective churches (Atencio 2007). Reports of Catholic priests endorsing President Bush from the pulpit surfaced in Española and San Juan Pueblo (Alarid 2005; Atencio 2007).

According to its executive director, the New Mexico Right-to-Life Organization (RTL) targeted Catholic churches, including predominantly Hispanic Catholic churches, across the state. The organization tried to convince people to "vote for life," meaning for pro-life candidates, regardless of party affiliation. On Sundays, RTL placed leaflets on cars in church parking lots with information on where Bush, Kerry, and other candidates stood on abortion and related issues (Dulce 2005), a tactic that was met with protest by a number of parish priests in Albuquerque.

Several Albuquerque pastors reported that they had the RTL literature removed from cars and destroyed. Some acknowledged that they were offended by the content in the fliers. One Hispanic priest referred to the RTL as "a front of the national Republican party." All indicated that having campaign literature distributed on church property could jeopardize the Church's tax-exempt status (Catholic Clergy 2005). At the same time, a number of Catholic churches provided their congregations with a document prepared by the United States Conference of Catholic Bishops. "The Challenge of Faithful Citizenship" addressed the pro-life stance of the Church along with a social gospel message on various other issues (USCCB 2004).

As local institutions, churches in general were largely marginal to the electoral activities of the Democrats. DPNM executive director Alarid indicated that they did not approach Hispanic Catholic or most other churches per se, except for black churches. Two religiously oriented groups did work for Kerry: Catholics for Kerry and People of Faith for Kerry. Alarid did not consider them very effective. Moreover, the Democratic Party had no strategy to integrate faith communities (even progressive ones) into the campaign. For example, according to Alarid, "The Michigan folks requested a 'faith video' from the Kerry campaign. They were told that none were available. In stark contrast, the Bush/Cheney campaign distributed faith videos at K-Mart stores." In the end, Republicans highlighted religious issues, but the Democrats had no answer (Alarid 2005).

SUMMARY OF CANDIDATE AND SURROGATE VISITS

A content analysis of campaign coverage in New Mexico's leading newspapers identified a total of 76 candidate and surrogate visits to the state beginning shortly after the Democratic presidential caucus in early February until the November election. Democrats accounted for 42 of these visits, or 56 percent of the total; Republicans accounted for 34, or 45 percent of the total. John Kerry visited seven times, and President Bush made six visits.

The authors also examined the visits for Hispanic content: was the event held in a heavily Hispanic area? was Hispanic culture evident in the staging of the event? and was there a Hispanic emphasis to the visit (i.e., did the speech(es) emphasize the Hispanic population and its concerns)? Twenty-one visits had some Hispanic content (28 percent of the total), but only ten had a Hispanic emphasis (13 percent of the total number of visits). Democratic visits had more Hispanic content than Republican visits, but in Hispanic emphasis, they came out the same at five visits each. To be sure, New Mexico's Hispanic population figured into the mobilization strategies for both parties, but most events that featured the presidential and vice presidential candidates and/or their surrogates carried no special emphasis to connect directly with Hispanic voters in substance or message. Generic stump speeches were more common than messages specifically tailored to Hispanic audiences.

ELECTION OUTCOME AND ANALYSIS

When the state canvassing board met three weeks after the election to officially certify the vote counts, New Mexico changed its presidential colors from blue to red. Both the turnout and the candidate choice numbers showed that New Mexico had deserved its designation as a closely contested battleground. George W. Bush eked out a close popular vote victory over John Kerry by a margin of 5,988 votes, or 0.8 percent of all the votes cast. The official numbers were as follows: Bush, 376,930 (49.8 percent); Kerry, 370,942 (49 percent); Nader (Independent), 4,053 (0.5 percent); Badnarik (Libertarian), 2,382 (0.3 percent); Cobb (Green), 1,226 (0.2 percent); and Peroutka (Constitution), 771

(0.1 percent). As it has in every election but one since becoming a state, New Mexico's popular vote for president went in the same direction as that of the nation.

The significant attention focused on the state during the campaign probably resulted in higher turnout in New Mexico than across the nation; 56.5 percent of those of voting age in New Mexico cast a ballot, compared to 50.8 percent nationwide. Seventy percent of registered voters participated in 2004; in 2000, only 63 percent of registered voters actually voted. A total of 775,301 New Mexicans voted in the election, casting a vote for at least one item on the ballot.

In 2000 Democratic candidate Al Gore had won the state's five electoral votes by the slimmest of margins among voters who are registered as Democrats—a 1.7 to 1 proportion. Now, four years later, the Republican candidate had increased his margin just enough to win the state's electoral votes. Did the extraordinary attention and record high dollars spent on the state make the difference, especially among the Hispanics of New Mexico?

Overall, turnout increased from 2000 to 2004 by 9.5 percentage points—from 47.0 percent of the voting age population to 56.5 percent. An examination of patterns of voting at the county level reveals that turnout was higher across the regional and ethnic boards. For example, turnout increased by 9.5 percent in predominantly Anglo counties and by 10.9 percent in predominantly Hispanic counties. In majority Anglo counties, the increase was 9.7 percent, compared to an increase of 8.3 percent in the majority Hispanic counties. This indicates that there were no significant differentials in turnout rates from 2000 to 2004 between Hispanic and Anglo areas.

We also detect little difference when we examine the direction of the 2000 and 2004 votes across mostly Hispanic and mostly Anglo counties. The percentage of the Republican vote increased strikingly over the Democratic vote in twenty-four of the state's thirty-three counties, however. Most notably, among the predominantly and the majority Hispanic counties, the Democratic increase was greater than the Republican increase in only one county—Taos.

Looking at the increase in votes cast for president in the 2000 election compared to the 2004 election again shows the dramatic increase in the Hispanic vote for the Republican candidate. Kerry's Hispanic vote was 9,103 votes more than Al Gore had received four years earlier.

In contrast, Bush's support among Hispanics in his second campaign increased by 45,191 votes. Therefore, the 2004 increase in total Hispanic voter turnout resulted in an approximate 36,000-vote advantage for the Republican candidate. True, Kerry had beaten Bush among Hispanics by about 29,000 votes, but that "comfort margin" disappeared rapidly (exit poll data reported that Hispanics accounted for 32 percent of the total votes cast for president).

In New Mexico the CNN exit poll concluded that Bush received 44 percent of the Hispanic vote, 56 percent of the white vote, and 33 percent of the "other" (mostly Native American) vote. The 44 percent Hispanic vote for Bush in New Mexico was identical to the number reported nationally for Latinos. Just as the latter was hotly disputed, there were also doubts that the New Mexico Hispanic vote was accurately caught by the exit polls. Although a statewide exit poll was not conducted, an important indicator of the accuracy of the national exit poll's report for the state is its congruence with an independent exit poll taken in Bernalillo County. Historically, the voting results in Bernalillo County are very close to those of the statewide totals, especially given that almost one-third of the state's population and 32 percent of its registered voters reside in this county.

According to the Research and Polling exit poll for Bernalillo County, Hispanics voted 43 percent for Bush and 57 percent for Kerry. The director of the poll, Brian Sanderoff, stated that while Kerry won among "progressive" Latinos, he did not run nearly as well among New Mexico's more conservative, rural Hispanics. He suggested that this might well have been a result of the so-called family values issue positions (Barabak 2005). Another credible explanation for Bush's popularity with Hispanics lay in additional exit poll data that showed 21 percent of New Mexico Hispanics claimed "strong leadership" mattered most to them as they cast their votes; fully 83 percent of these voters supported the president (Atkeson, Carrillo, and Walker 2005: 132). Finally, Sanderoff's poll showed that among all voters surveyed, the war in Iraq, the economy, and terrorism ranked as the top three most important issues facing the nation. Given New Mexico's heavy dependence on defense-related industry and the strong military presence in the state, "staying the course" with the incumbent president may have held sway with New Mexican voters, including the state's Hispanics.

All the House incumbents running for reelection in New Mexico's three congressional districts also won. In the First Congressional District race, the Hispanic Democrat, Richard Romero, lost to incumbent Republican Heather Wilson by a larger margin than in 2002 (54 percent to 46 percent). In this race, 90 percent of the votes cast in the First District came from Bernalillo County; the Hispanics in this county supported the Hispanic challenger Romero (52 percent) over Wilson (48 percent). This was one of the most expensive House races in the nation: Wilson spent about $3.3 million, Romero around $2 million (Massey 2004).

Republican and Democratic partisans pointed to additional factors to explain Bush's victory in the state. Republican operatives noted that Bush's personality and personal style were more *simpatico* to Hispanics. In addition, while Kerry waxed philosophical on various issues, Bush delivered a simple message, for example, "protect American families" (Atencio 2007). Putting resources behind a campaign that emphasized candidates over issues was the better strategy: "Issues do not galvanize voters as well as candidates do" (Darnell 2007). Finally, and perhaps most important, Republicans were "smarter" in their mobilization strategy (Darnell 2007). The Republicans worked to remain competitive in Democratic areas while investing significant resources in mobilizing their base in smaller, rural areas of the state (Lenderman 2004d). Furthermore, while Democratic-oriented 527s were "more vocal," the Republican outreach effort "matched scripts to values" (Darnell 2007), working through coalitions of local groups and social networks to get out the vote.

The Bush win had an extra sting for Democrats, especially Hispanic Democrats, in New Mexico. Governor Richardson had worked on many fronts to secure victory for the Democratic presidential ticket. That the Hispanic governor was not able to deliver the Hispanic vote for Kerry in his own state was a source of some embarrassment. Richardson demurred, stating he had attended about thirty rallies for Kerry. He also observed, "A vote for president is a very personal vote. . . . It's not easy to transfer your political popularity to another candidate. I tried very hard to transfer my political capital to [Kerry]" (Terrell 2004b).

The executive director of DPNM pointed fingers at a faulty mobilization strategy that, she maintained, ultimately took Hispanics for granted. Not enough effort was directed to mobilizing Democratic strongholds, including the Hispanic north. And conceding small, rural areas to the Republicans (with a minority but still substantial numbers of Hispanics) may have been a mistake (Alarid 2005). Finally, the Democrats' heavy reliance on 527 activity, which was dominated by out-of-state organizations with "professional" (i.e., paid) organizers who "parachuted" in for the election ultimately did not match the Republicans' effective use of local volunteers, organizations, leaders, and networks to enlist voter support.

To conclude, Hispanics in New Mexico most certainly figured into the process and outcome of presidential politics in 2004. In terms of outcome, a majority voted for Kerry, but not enough to give him a victory in the state. Indeed, while mobilizing their conservative and largely Anglo base, the Bush-Cheney campaign drew enough Hispanics into their camp to assure victory. Perhaps the lesson of 2004 in New Mexico is that the intense competition generated in a battleground state requires not only huge investments of resources but also substantive and more effective strategies to mobilize Hispanic voters. The next presidential election will test whether Bush's popularity with Hispanic voters was indicative of short-term electoral circumstances or shifting partisan politics with long-term consequences.

NOTES

1. Governor Bill Richardson remained "neutral" during the primary season, choosing not to endorse any candidate. He served, rather, as a host to all when they visited the state. Support for Howard Dean, Wesley Clark, John Edwards, and John Kerry came from some heavy hitters, including Albuquerque Mayor Martin Chavez for Dean; former U.S. Ambassador to Spain and New Mexico influential Ed Romero for Clark; State Attorney General Patricia Madrid for Edwards; New Mexico Speaker of the House, Ben Lujan, for Kerry; and the sitting and former Presidents Pro-Tem of the state senate, Richard Romero and Manny Aragon, respectively, for Gephardt, who later dropped out of contention. As late as the end of January 2004, however, the press reported only one Hispanic, District Court Judge Ernesto Romero, among the endorsers for Lieberman. Dennis Kucinich had no Hispanic endorsers listed for his campaign, though he did have some well-known liberals in his corner: Green Party activist and former candidate for governor David Bacon and actress Shirley MacLaine,

who owns a home in the Santa Fe foothills. Interestingly, Kucinich's organization in the Hispanic north was reportedly made up of former Raza Unida Party activists (Green 2004).

2. These included Hobbs, Las Cruces, Silver City, Zuni, Gallup, McKinley, and Santa Fe Counties.

3. Illustrative of the numerous Democratic allies at work in the state, the following organizations formed the America Votes Coalition: America Coming Together (ACT), the League of Conservation Voters, Moving America Forward (MAF), NARAL Pro-Choice America, MoveOn.org, and the Southwest Young Voter Alliance. The purpose of the coalition was to provide a communications network for these groups in order to maximize their efficiency and reduce unnecessary duplication in their GOTV efforts (Atkeson, Carrillo, and Walker 2005: 127).

REFERENCES

Alarid, Vanessa. 2005. Executive Director, Democratic Party of New Mexico. Interview by Christine Marie Sierra. Democratic Party Headquarters, Albuquerque, NM, May 31.

American Research Group, Inc. 2004. "Kerry Maintains Lead over Bush among Likely Voters in New Mexico." August 20. www.americanresearchgroup.com. Accessed January 30, 2009.

Andersen, Shea. 2003. "Wanted: Aspiring PAC Campers." *Albuquerque Tribune,* September 10.

Atencio, Christopher. 2007. Northern Field Director, Victory 2004. Interview by Christine Marie Sierra. Albuquerque, NM, April 4.

Atkeson, Lonna Rae. 2004. New Mexico Caucus Voter Survey Executive Summary. July 20. www.unm.edu. Accessed January 30, 2009.

Atkeson, Lonna Rae, Nancy Carrillo, and Mekoce Walker. 2005. "New Mexico Presidential Race 2004: The Battle for Five Electoral Votes." In *Dancing without Partners: How Candidates, Parties and Interest Groups Interact in the New Campaign Finance Environment,* ed. David B. Magleby, J. Quin Monson, and Kelly D. Patterson. Provo, UT: Center for the Study of Elections and Democracy, Brigham Young University.

Barabak, Mark Z. 2005. "Democrats Push for a New Frontier." *Los Angeles Times,* April 18.

Brazile, Donna. 2003. Informal conversation with Christine Marie Sierra. Center for American Women and Politics, Rutgers University.

Calloway, Larry. 2003. "Media-Friendly Governor Setting N.M. Apart." *Albuquerque Journal,* March 2, B3.

Catholic Clergy. 2005. Confidential telephone interviews by Christine Marie Sierra. Albuquerque, NM.

Coleman, Michael. 2004a. "Dean, Clark Lead in New Mexico." *Albuquerque Journal,* January 18, A1, A3.

———. 2004b. "Domenici to Lead N.M. Bush Campaign." *Albuquerque Journal,* January 27, p. A6.

———. 2004c. "Bush Presses His Agenda in N.M." *Albuquerque Journal,* January 23, A1–A2.

———. 2004d. "Richardson a Boston VIP: City Rolls out Red Carpet for Convention Chairman." *Albuquerque Journal,* June 25, A1–A2.

———. 2004e. "Gov. Tells Kerry 'No': Richardson Wants Off Any VP List." *Albuquerque Journal,* July 2, A1, A5.

———. 2004f. "Kerry Screener Gives Richardson Good V.P. Ratings." *Albuquerque Journal,* July 15, A10.

———. 2004g. "Delegates Headed to GOP Party." *Albuquerque Journal,* August 29, A1, A3.

Darnell, Scott. 2007. Central New Mexico Field Director, Victory 2004. Interview by Christine Marie Sierra. Albuquerque, NM, April 16.

Dulce, Dauneen. 2005. Executive Director, New Mexico Right to Life Organization. Telephone interview by Christine Marie Sierra. May 20.

Farrauto, Matt. 2007. Executive Director, Democratic Party of New Mexico. Democratic National Committee, 2004 Delegate Information. E-mail to Christine Marie Sierra, June 25.

Fecteau, Loie. 2003. "Governor: Hispanics Hold Key to 2004." *Albuquerque Journal,* July 27, B4.

Finnegan, Michael. 2004. "Kerry's Low Profile May Cost Crucial Latino Votes." *Nation,* May 3. www.latimes.com/. Accessed February 2, 2009.

Garcia, F. Chris, and Bianca Sapien. 1999. "Recognizing Reliability: Hispanos and the 1996 Elections in New Mexico." In *Awash in the Mainstream: Latino Politics in the 1996 Election,* ed. Rodolfo O. de la Garza and Louis DeSipio, 75–100. Boulder, CO: Westview Press.

Garcia, F. Chris, and Christine Marie Sierra. 2005. "New Mexico Hispanos in the 2000 General Elections." In *Muted Voices: Latinos and the 2000 Elections,* ed. Rodolfo O. de la Garza and Louis DeSipio, 101–29. Lanham, MD: Rowman and Littlefield.

Garcia, Patricia L. 2003. "Democrats Open Their Hispanic Summit." *Albuquerque Journal,* September 26. www.abqjournal.com/news/state/aphisp09-26-03.htm. Accessed February 2, 2009.

Green, Jordan. 2004. "Kennedy in Española: Democratic Patronage in Northern New Mexico." *Rio Grande Sun,* February 3.

Hoffman, Leslie. 2003. "City to Host Hispanic Summit." *Albuquerque Journal,* September 25. www.abqjournal.com/. Accessed February 2, 2009.

Lenderman, Andy. 2004a. "Oh, So Close! Bush Has Slight Lead in N.M." *Albuquerque Journal,* September 5, A1, A8.

———. 2004b. "Poll: Kerry Gains Edge over Bush." *Albuquerque Journal,* October 6, A1, A3.

———. 2004c. "Down to the Wire: President Holds Slight Lead over Kerry in N.M. Race." *Albuquerque Journal,* October 31, A1, A10.

———. 2004d. "Rural Emphasis Won for Bush." *Albuquerque Journal,* November 21, B2.

Lenderman, Andy, and Michael Coleman. 2004. "DNC Delegates Fired Up." *Albuquerque Journal,* July 25, A1–A2.

Lenderman, Andy, and Kate Nash. 2004. "Kerry, Edwards Hear Wild N.M. Greeting: President-VP Candidate Visit a First for N.M." *Albuquerque Journal,* July 10, A1–A2.

Lenderman, Andy, and Rene Romo. 2004. "Romero, Wilson Again." *Albuquerque Journal,* June 2, A1, A3.

Limon, Iliana. 2004. "Hispanic Voters to Fore: N.M. Showered with Lots of Attention." *Albuquerque Tribune,* January 28, A1, A4.

Linthicum, Leslie. 2004a. "N.M. Vote Attracts Candidate Attention." *Albuquerque Journal,* January 4, A1, A6–A7.

———. 2004b. "Kerry Official Winner in N.M." *Albuquerque Journal,* February 14, E3.

———. 2004c. "Cheney: 'I Really Like This Crowd.'" *Albuquerque Journal,* August 1, A1–A2.

Linthicum, Leslie, and Jeff Jones. 2004. "Lawyer Loses Bid for Open Cheney Rally." *Albuquerque Journal,* July 31, A1, A6.

Linthicum, Leslie, and Kate Nash. 2004. "Gov.'s Push for Early Caucus Puts N.M. on 'Political Map.'" *Albuquerque Journal,* February 4, A1, A9.

Massey, Barry. 2004. "N.M. Race among Most Expensive." *Albuquerque Journal,* December 7, D3.

Miles, David. 2004a. "GOP Leaders Campaign for Bush." *Albuquerque Journal,* February 3, A4.

———. 2004b. "Bush, Kerry Almost Tied in N.M. Popularity." *Albuquerque Journal,* March 23, A1–A2.

Nagourney, Adam, and Jodi Wilgoren. 2003. "In First Encounter, Democrats Hit Bush over Jobs and Iraq." *New York Times,* September 5, A1, A16.

Nash, Kate. 2004. "Guv Away from N.M. for 54th Time since July." *Albuquerque Journal,* June 25. www.abqjournal.com/. Accessed June 25, 2004.

Nash, Kate, and Leslie Linthicum. 2004. "Bush Woos N.M. Again." *Albuquerque Journal,* March 27, A1, A8.

Nelson, Kate. 2003. "Guv's Tactics Turn N.M.—and Him—into Clout Machine." *Albuquerque Tribune,* July 1, A3.

New Mexico Chooses: Guidebook. 2003. Albuquerque: Democratic Party of New Mexico.

Pickler, Nedra, and Deb Reichmann. 2004. "Gloves Are Off: Bush, Kerry Trade Barbs as Election Officially Starts." *Albuquerque Journal,* July 31, A1, A6.

Reed, Ollie, Jr. 2004. "Chow and Cheney." *Albuquerque Tribune,* February 17, A3.

Romo, Rene. 2004. "Cheney Raises Money, Presses Agenda in Artesia." *Albuquerque Journal,* March 16, D3.

"Sanchez to Chair Bush Campaign." 2003. *Albuquerque Journal,* July 11, B3.

Sierra, Christine Marie. 1992. "Hispanos and the 1988 General Election in New Mexico." In *From Rhetoric to Reality: Latino Politics in the 1988 Elections,* ed. Rodolfo O. de la Garza and Louis DeSipio, 43–68. Boulder, CO: Westview Press.

———. 2003. "Hispanic Politics in New Mexico: A Look at Recent Elections." *New Mexico Report,* Spring: 1–6. Albuquerque: Southwest Hispanic Research Institute, University of New Mexico.

Terrell, Steve. 2004a. "Bush Holds Slim N.M. Lead." *Santa Fe New Mexican,* September 21, A1, A4.

———. 2004b. "Our Final Answer?" *Santa Fe New Mexican,* November 4, B1, B3.

Torres, Winter. 2003. Correspondence to Joe Montano and the Hispanic Roundtable. E-mail to Christine Marie Sierra, Albuquerque, NM, August 8.

United States Conference of Catholic Bishops (USCCB). 2004. "The Challenge of Faithful Citizenship: A Catholic Call to Political Responsibility." USCCB, Washington, DC.

U.S. Census Bureau. 2000. American FactFinder, Fact Sheet: New Mexico. Summary File 2 (SF2) and Summary File 4 (SF4).

———. 2005. Current Population Survey. Table 4a, "Reported Voting and Registration of the Total Voting-Age Population, by Sex, Race and Hispanic Origin, for States: November 2004." Internet Release Date May 25, 2005.

Zogby Interactive. 2004. "Battleground States Poll." August 2. http://online.wsj.com/public/resources/documents/info-battleground04.html. Accessed February 2, 2009.

Chapter Four

Emerging Pattern or Unique Event?

The Power of the Nonracial Campaign in Colorado

ERIC GONZALEZ JUENKE
AND ANNA CHRISTINA SAMPAIO

In the end, it came down to two brothers from Colorado's San Luis Valley. After all the talk of a tight presidential race, the power of the first time voters, 527 groups, Amendment 36, voter intimidation, and voter fraud, *the* story of the 2004 election in Colorado concerned two Latino farmers earning historic victories on Election Day. Ken Salazar and his older brother, John, became the first Latino senator and U.S. Representative, respectively, to be elected in the state of Colorado.[1] That these victories took place in Colorado and not in states such as New Mexico or California that have larger bases of Latino voters and long records of electing Latinos to Congress creates new questions for those who study Latino politics. The answers to these questions may uncover the beginning of a new pattern in Latino politics, or they may simply reveal a blip on the screen, a unique event of no long-term consequence to Latinos in the United States.

This chapter targets a number of puzzles regarding the condition of Latino politics in Colorado in 2004. The most intriguing question surrounds the ability of Ken and John Salazar, both Democrats, to win tightly contested elections in a moderately conservative state that supported George Bush by 9 percentage points (145,000 votes) in 2000. To be sure, John Kerry and the Democrats made some gains in the state, losing to Bush by only 5 percentage points (100,000 votes),[2] but further analysis of the results reveals that Ken Salazar outgained Kerry (his statewide ticket partner) in sixty-two of Colorado's sixty-four counties. This feat required the Salazars to run campaigns that differed from the typical Latino Democrat, campaigns that we label "nonracial." Turning the tables on (or borrowing from) the Republican playbook to skim Latino voters from the Democrats, these candidates were able to appeal to Latino voters while converting a large number of non-Latinos.

The successes of these campaigns, we argue, speak to some of the fundamental issues in Latino politics in the twenty-first century, making the Salazars a metaphor for the strategic fluidity of race and ethnicity in a changing national environment. Is the nonracial campaign the best way for Latinos to achieve descriptive representation in the new century? More specifically, is this the best strategy for electing Latinos to national and statewide seats in Republican-dominated areas? If so, what impact will these Latino elites have on policy? Are Latino voter preferences changing, and what does this mean for the two major parties at the national level?

COLORADO LATINOS AND COLORADO POLITICS: ETHNICITY AND INFLUENCE

It has been difficult to measure a consistent Latino impact in Colorado during the most recent national elections (Hero 1996; Hero and Jaramillo 2005; Hero, Jaramillo, and Halprin 1999). On the one hand, Latinos are a substantial part of Colorado's fast-growing population. They represent about 17 percent of the total population (735,601 of 4,301,261 in 2000; U.S. Census Bureau 2000) and were responsible for about 31 percent of the population growth in the state from 1990 to 2000.[3] Prior to 2004, however, their status as the state's largest nonwhite population had not been translated into significant political influence in statewide elections. True enough, Hero and Jaramillo (2005) predict a greater future role for Latino voters in their analysis of the 2000 elections. The authors demonstrated that greater Democratic outreach to Latinos may have played a role in flipping the state senate to the Democratic Party (Hero and Jaramillo 2005). Beyond this, however, the authors found that the majority of Colorado Latinos in 2000 had a great deal of potential but very little influence.

Data from the Current Population Survey (CPS 2005) present a fairly clear picture of why Latinos in 2004 failed to turn their growing numbers into elite influence. U.S. citizenship continues to play a substantial role in dampening Latino influence. Whereas 98 percent of adult whites and 92 percent of adult blacks in Colorado are U.S. citizens, only 63 percent of Latinos who are eighteen or older are citizens (CPS 2005). Further, after excluding noncitizens, we see a registration gap between blacks and Latinos and their white counterparts. Seventy-nine percent of white citizens eighteen or over are registered to vote, compared to 59 percent of blacks and 57 percent or Latinos (CPS 2005).

Once we examine turnout among registered voters, the gap between whites, blacks, and Latinos shrinks (but it is still present): turnout rates are 92 percent, 84 percent, and 81 percent, respectively (CPS 2005). At each stage of the voting process (including gaining citizenship and the right to vote, registering, and turning out), Latinos lag behind other major groups, producing a staggering final statistic; of those in each group who are eighteen years or older, 71 percent of whites, 46 percent of blacks, and only 29 percent of Latinos actually vote (CPS 2005). Should it be a surprise, then, that despite their apparent numerical clout, Latinos lack significant and consistent political influence at the state level? The 2004 election was more of the same for the vast majority of Latino voters in the state but not for the two brothers from the San Luis Valley.

The party affiliations of Colorado voters in general have been fairly stable over time. That is, since 1984 there have been more registered Republicans than Democrats, and their relative share has changed only slightly (Hero and Jaramillo 2005: 133). Independents have always been a large part of the voting population in the state, making up about a third of the electorate in each election (Hero and Jaramillo 2005: 133). In the 2004 election these numbers remained stable: 30 percent of registered voters were Democrats, 36 percent were Republican, and 33 percent were Independent. In short, registered Republicans outnumbered Democrats by approximately 188,000 voters. This creates challenging races, especially for Democrats, in most parts of the state and makes small groups like Latinos prime targets for candidate messages (Guerra and Fraga 1996).

Although Colorado has only nine electoral votes, the apparently tight 2004 presidential race made it a battleground state. Contributing to this national attention was the prospect of electoral reform in the shape of Amendment 36. This amendment to the state constitution would have exchanged Colorado's winner-take-all system of allocating electoral votes for a proportional allotment system. Because the national presidential race appeared to be so close, this amendment garnered increased attention as November approached. In the end, the amendment was voted down by a substantial margin, but its relationship to the tight presidential race before the election was important for Latinos because it increased the perception that their votes made a difference in the state.

Aside from the proposed Amendment 36, the 2004 election in Colorado was devoid of specifically "Latino" issues. No immigration initiatives, education proposals, or language policy decisions clouded the tight races for the president, the Senate, or the House. As we note above, the within-state races were interesting for the major parties, if lacking a particular Latino dynamic.

THE BROTHERS SALAZAR AND THE NATURE OF THEIR CAMPAIGNS

One of the most important themes emerging from the victories of both John Salazar (in the Third Congressional District) and his brother Ken Salazar (for the Senate) is the nonracial nature of their campaigns and their appeal to the rural Republican counties in Colorado. Specifically, both Salazars successfully orchestrated campaigns that captured enough Independents, moderate Republicans, and even Bush supporters to win the Third Congressional District seat, where registered Republicans outnumbered registered Democrats by approximately 17,000, and the statewide vote for Senate, in which registered Republicans outnumbered registered Democrats by approximately 188,000.

For Ken Salazar, this meant targeting rural Republican and Independent voters early in the primaries and promoting a policy agenda that highlighted the interests of rural and urban Colorado.[4] This practice of deemphasizing the racial character of the campaign while appealing to broad segments of the state was the same strategy he employed successfully in his 1998 bid for attorney general, when he became the first Latino in Colorado to win a statewide race. After winning this campaign, Ken Salazar underscored the nonracial character of that effort: "I am the attorney general for *all* of Colorado," and "the fact that I'm the first Hispanic elected statewide sends a good signal to all people in Colorado that it's really a land of opportunity" (Bartels 2004).

A key component to constructing a nonracial campaign was the Salazars' ability to package themselves and their policy platforms in a manner that would appeal to Independent and moderate Republicans: they highlighted the interests of rural Colorado without invoking tensions or unwarranted racial attention on issues such as immigration. In both the Third Congressional District and across the state, Independents accounted for almost a third of the registered voters; hence any candidate able to draw even half of them would likely win the election. Ken Salazar's campaign outlined support for a set of policy issues consistent with the Democratic National Committee's platform, including enhanced homeland security, strengthening international coalitions, revitalizing the nation's manufacturing sector to create more jobs, and expanding health care coverage. Although Salazar's positions were centrally focused on the three themes of security, jobs and the economy, and health care, he also promoted policy on key rural issues such as water, the environment, agriculture, and rural development. More notable is the way in which the issues of interest to rural Colorado were featured prominently in his top three themes and the way he wove together conservative discourse with support for Democratic issues.

For example, in his policy paper, "Jobs and the Economy," Salazar maintained, "As a small businessman and farmer, I know that private enterprise, not government, creates jobs. But government policies and priorities can make a difference to families and businesses, and

Washington has an obligation to act responsibly, and fairly, when it comes to federal spending, the deficit, and tax and fiscal policy." At the same time, in his appeal to Independent rural voters, he asserted, "I will also be an independent voice for agriculture and our rural economy and small towns" (K. Salazar 2004a). As such, he advocated a plan of "fiscally conservative policies" such as pay-as-you-go spending and "responsible, common sense tax cuts" combined with support for tax credits for companies that retained manufacturing jobs in the United States. In addition, the largest portion of his policy agenda on jobs was dedicated to "Revitalizing Rural Colorado." This included redirecting farm supports to family farmers, protecting Colorado's water for "downstream users," maintaining and expanding roads to connect rural towns, rebuilding rural health care, supporting renewable energy development, providing rural investment tax credits, and investing $1 billion in a new initiative to bring capital to rural communities.[5]

John Salazar's campaign mirrored that of his brother. Although he coined the phrase "Send a Farmer to Washington" as their slogan, the disproportionate focus on rural Colorado was less unique in John's campaign because the Third Congressional District encompassed twenty-eight Western Slope counties that were primarily agricultural and because John Salazar was an active potato farmer. Like Ken Salazar, John Salazar also outlined support for key Democratic Party issues, including public education, the war in Iraq, fighting for veterans, creating jobs, improving Colorado's economy, and providing affordable access to health care. However, he wove these together with an appeal to rural voters highlighting management of natural resources, serving as a strong voice for rural Colorado, and protecting Colorado's water as key policy items.

Equally significant to both Salazar campaigns was the relative inattention to issues traditionally relevant among Latino voters and other ethnic minorities—namely, education and immigration (Pew Hispanic Center 2004; Tomás Rivera Policy Institute 2004). While both identified support for public education as one of their top policy issues, neither their ads nor their position papers mentioned bilingual education, migrant education, or in-state tuition for undocumented children, despite the high profile of these issues in Colorado over the previous two years. In addition, neither Salazar prioritized immigration as a key concern. While Ken Salazar included a brief paragraph supporting stronger border enforcement and a crackdown on "illegal human trafficking" in a statement titled "Immigration" that was subsumed under "Other Issues" (K. Salazar 2004c), John Salazar offered no policy statement or position paper on this issue. This was significant because both the state of Colorado and the Third Congressional District were experiencing a substantial growth in the Mexican immigrant population and because their scant attention suggests an effort to refocus attention from their Latino background toward their farming history. Finally, the Web sites for both campaigns were available in *English only,* without Spanish translations. This is of particular interest given that both the Democratic and Republican National Parties provided Spanish translations on their Web sites, as did Ken Salazar's opponent, Pete Coors.

In cultivating this focus, both candidates had to resist their opponents' attempts to effectively racialize their campaigns and mark them as Latino candidates by questioning their positions on immigration. In particular, as the election drew closer, the television ads run in support of the Republican candidate, Greg Walcher, in the Third Congressional contest became more racially charged. In one of two such ads, Walcher charged John Salazar with supporting government subsidies for illegal immigrants because Salazar voted in favor of a bill to allow undocumented children to apply for in-state tuition in higher education.

Despite these challenges, both Salazars maintained a considerable silence on specific racial issues and did not invoke their Hispanic heritage to mobilize voters. In fact, both Ken and John Salazar regularly invoked their rural ranching roots, donning cowboy hats, boots, and denim at public functions, while rarely mentioning their family's important position in the history of Latinos in the area (the Salazars were among the original settlers of Santa Fe, New Mexico). This position was facilitated further by the lightness of their complexions and the absence of a Spanish accent, making it easier for voters to perceive them as white and more difficult for opponents to cast them as nonwhite. In effect, both brothers reflected the unique racial and ethnic dynamic of Colorado's "Hispano" population drawn primarily from the Spanish colonial settlements in New Mexico, with clear roots in farming and many generations of settlement in Colorado. As such, this population is culturally, politically, and economically distinct from the more recent working-class Mexican immigrant population that exhibits more temporary settlement and limited English proficiency.

While the Salazar brothers' campaigns can be described as nonracial, notable efforts were made throughout the state to target, register, and mobilize Latinos. Among both the Democratic and Republican Parties and nonpartisan groups, Colorado was largely regarded as a battleground state where effective mobilization of new and Latino voters could make the difference in November, especially in tight races. In the end, the national and state parties, political action committees, and newly formed 527s conducted most of the targeted outreach to Latinos. In fact, as we discuss below, the Latino outreach that did take place in relation to the Salazar campaigns was largely outsourced to these organizations.

LATINO OUTREACH

The Democratic Party

The Democratic Party's Latino outreach efforts in Colorado were concentrated largely in the hands of the Coordinated Campaign, through which the Democratic National Committee (DNC) and the Democratic Senatorial Campaign Committee (DSCC) channeled money to the Colorado Democratic Party. The Kerry-Edwards '04 campaign also had an extensive grassroots, media, and advertising team focused on Latinos, as did the DNC;[6] however, their work in Colorado was primarily concentrated in managing television and radio ads, while the Coordinated Campaign largely orchestrated the more traditional elements of outreach and fieldwork (e.g., targeted mobilization, direct mail, door knocking, phone banks, get-out-the-vote [GOTV] efforts) (Dominguez 2005).[7]

Overall, the Coordinated Campaign was responsible for developing a comprehensive outreach and field plan for all the candidates that had invested in it, including outreach to key demographic groups of which Latinos were central. To participate in the Coordinated Campaign, candidates had to buy in with an initial investment, on which the DNC and DSCC (through the Coordinated Campaign) would spend large sums on their campaigns via media buys, fieldwork, and GOTV.[8] Rarely were individual candidates promoted through these outreach efforts; rather, the Coordinated Campaign typically promoted the party's presidential candidate together with others who had invested in the campaign.

Altogether, the Latino outreach efforts of the Coordinated Campaign built on many of the hallmarks of traditional fieldwork. This included targeting voter contact among Latinos (identifying key voters and their locations, developing a message), implementing the message through a combination of direct mail, phone banks, media buys (primarily Spanish print, radio, and television ads), door knocking, and GOTV. In addition, they initiated other important outreach efforts to local Latino elected officials (who would then mobilize their constituents), as well as earned media events such as the Nueva Esperanza bus tour detailed below.

However, there were several notable nuances in their use of more traditional outreach strategies. For example, the bilingual direct mailings organized by the Coordinated Campaign were sent to Latinos who were "likely voters" as well as Latinos who were registered but had never voted. This proved a more expensive strategy because it increased the scope of the mailings, but the idea was to reach out to those who were disaffected and bring them to the party. Moreover, the Democratic Party organizers we spoke with acknowledged that this effort may have yielded a small return on the 2004 election (both because it was aimed at less likely voters and because it was bilingual), but it was part of a larger effort to strengthen the party's long-term relationship with Latinos, especially those who were not currently active (Rodriguez 2005).

The state Coordinated Campaign also recruited several Latinos from out of state to help orchestrate and implement their outreach efforts. Campaign consultants estimated that fifteen to twenty professional Latinos were brought in to work in various capacities, such as communication, GOTV, and advance work. In addition, the DNC paid for approximately one hundred more Latinos from out of state to boost outreach and GOTV efforts in Latino communities in the last several weeks of the campaigns. Their goal was both to bring in political operatives from out of state who had strong experience working campaign cycles across the country and to "at least get people who look like us" to represent their outreach efforts in these Latino communities (Rodriguez 2005).[9]

To understand the impact of the Coordinated Campaign's outreach efforts for Colorado candidates it is important to note that those candidates who decided to invest in the campaign typically had very limited outreach efforts of their own. That is, candidates who bought into the Coordinated Campaign were free to spend their individual campaign funds on other efforts such as television ads highlighting just their candidacy. Rather than invest heavily in a separate outreach campaign of their own, both Salazars bought into the Coordinated Campaign—a strategy that would allow them to reach out to other segments of their constituency while the Coordinated Campaign targeted Latino outreach.

Funding

The Democratic Party's support for both Ken and John Salazar was best documented in the unprecedented fund-raising, independent expenditures, and in-kind contributions to their campaigns. Overall, Ken Salazar's campaign raised more than $9.5 million; his opponent, Pete Coors, raised just over $7.6 million, including a personal loan for $1.45 million (Center for Responsive Politics 2004a; Federal Election Commission 2004a). On the other hand, John Salazar and his opponent, Greg Walcher, each raised virtually the same amount—just over $1.6 million (Center for Responsive Politics 2004a). Despite this, John Salazar won his seat with 50.55 percent of the votes to Walcher's 46.56 percent, and Ken Salazar defeated Pete Coors 51.30 percent to 46.53 percent (Colorado Secretary of State 2004b).

A more detailed breakdown of Ken Salazar's funding reveals that nearly 80 percent of the campaign money came from individual contributions, 10.4 percent came from PAC contributions, and 9.7 percent came from other sources (Center for Responsive Politics 2004b; Federal Election Commission 2004a). Of the PAC contributions, the largest portion (approximately 40 percent) came from labor unions, with a significant amount coming from unions and associations representing rural farming interests such as the American Sugar Beet Growers Association, the Great Lakes Sugar Beet Growers, the National Association of Wheat Growers, and the National Farm Union (Center for Responsive Politics 2004b; Federal Election Commission 2004a).The most significant spending came from the Democratic Senatorial Campaign

Committee, which contributed close to $500,000 in party coordinated expenditures (via the Coordinated Campaign) and approximately $2.3 million in independent expenditures on behalf of the candidate (Center for Responsive Politics 2004b; Federal Election Commission 2004a).

John Salazar's fund-raising revealed a similar pattern, albeit on a smaller scale. Of the money raised in his campaign, approximately 63 percent came from individual contributions, 36 percent from PAC contributions, and less than 1 percent from other sources (Center for Responsive Politics 2004c; Federal Election Commission 2004b, Federal Election Commission 2004c). Of the PAC contributions, approximately 50 percent came from groups representing labor, and, much like Ken Salazar's campaign, agriculture and farm PACs figured prominently in this list (Center for Responsive Politics 2004c; Federal Election Commission 2004b, Federal Election Commission 2004c).

Thus the funding patterns of both John and Ken Salazar suggest something of a symbiotic relationship between the construction of a nonracial campaign and their appeal to rural agricultural communities. That is, as both distanced themselves from an explicitly Hispanic candidacy and emphasized their relationship to rural farmers, they drew the support of agricultural and farm associations while still benefiting from significant contributions from Latino political officials, Latino professionals, and Latino PACs that the Democratic Party's Coordinated Campaign mobilized.

The Republican Party

The Republican Party's outreach to Latinos in Colorado mirrored that of the Democratic Party with their 96-Hour Victory Campaign (more commonly referred to as Victory 2004), which operated much like the Democrats' Coordinated Campaign (Campbell 2005).[10] In addition to serving as the political bridge between the Republican National Committee (RNC) and the Colorado Republican Party (CRP), the Victory Campaign engaged in much of the same targeted mobilization of likely Latino voters, coupled with message development, mailings, and traditional fieldwork such as precinct walking and phone banking. Indeed, both the Democratic Party's Coordinated Campaign and the Republican Party's Victory Campaign orchestrated highly publicized bus tours through the state as part of their Latino outreach strategies and mobilized locally based grassroots efforts. Among Democrats, these groups were commonly called Unidos con Kerry, and among Republics they were Hispanics for Bush (Campbell 2005; Cerveny 2005).

Despite these similarities, the two parties differed in several important aspects of their efforts to reach out to Latinos in the state. First, the Republican Party did not have a high-profile Latino on the statewide ballot, thereby affecting their ability to energize and mobilize Latino voters. The most prominent Latino GOP candidate was Roland Chicas, a Guatemalan from New York with strong business ties in Colorado, who challenged incumbent Representative Dianne DeGette in the First House District (the most heavily Democratic House District in the state). The relative indifference of the Republican Party to this race and to Chicas's candidacy was demonstrated in the lackluster fundraising and relative obscurity of this race. While Chicas raised slightly more than $17,000 throughout the primary and general election, the Republican Party spent no direct money on his candidacy and only $2,500 indirectly through an independent Republican organization (Federal Election Commission 2004d). In the end, DeGette easily defeated Chicas, 74 percent to 23 percent (Colorado Secretary of State 2004b).

A second and substantive difference between the two parties relates to their targeted mobilization and outreach to likely Latino voters via local churches. That is, the Republican Party Victory Campaign (along with state-level Republican campaigns across the country) worked to identify likely Republican Latino voters by comparing church lists in largely Latino areas with voter files compiled by the secretary of state in order to target unregistered churchgoers (Campbell 2005). In addition, churches (especially the Catholic churches in Colorado) contributed to these outreach efforts by delivering targeted political messages to their congregants.

Specifically, Colorado Springs Bishop Michael J. Sheridan and Colorado Archbishop Charles Chaput delivered messages to Catholic churchgoers warning them that support for abortion or same-sex marriage is incompatible with the teachings of the church. Beginning in early May 2004, Bishop Sheridan said that Catholics who vote for politicians who support abortion, same-sex marriage, stem cell research, or euthanasia should not receive communion (Florio 2004). Moreover, in a pastoral letter to the 125,000 Catholics in Colorado Springs, Sheridan maintained that "any Catholic politicians who advocate abortion, stem cell research, any form of euthanasia, or same-sex marriage ipso facto place themselves outside full communion with the Church and so jeopardize their salvation," as do any Catholics who vote for them (*Telegraph* 2004).

A final point of comparison between the Republican and Democratic Party outreach to Latino voters in Colorado pertains to their fieldwork and media strategies. While the Democratic Party Coordinated Campaign and the DNC focused a good deal of their Latino outreach on fieldwork—hiring 15 to 20 professional Latino political operatives and 100 to 200 paid Latino interns to design and execute these strategies—Republican efforts led by the RNC seemed to be more heavily concentrated on targeted media buys. Specifically, the Bush-Cheney '04 campaign's Hispanic media team and the RNC produced and distributed several Spanish- and English-language television and radio ads aimed at Latino voters in the state. In fact, the director of the Democratic Party Coordinated Campaign estimated that the Republican Party outspent Democrats in the state two to one in Spanish-language television and radio advertising (Dominguez 2005).[11]

Thus, while both parties engaged in fairly traditional methods of outreach to Latinos, some important innovations punctuated their strategies, such as the increased reliance on churches and people from outside the state. Of particular importance here is the reliance of individual candidates, Ken Salazar and John Salazar, on the Democratic Party (and specifically the Coordinated Campaign) and independent organizations to mobilize Latino voters in their races. This outsourcing of Latino outreach effectively freed the candidates to both distance themselves from highly racialized issues and to position themselves in such a way as to capture both Independents and conservative voters in their races.

ANALYSIS OF THE ELECTION RESULTS

We examine the election results at two levels. First, we look at the county returns for the presidential and Senate races, testing for the effect of potential Latino votes on the results for both campaigns. Because it is difficult to make inferences about individual voting behavior using county-level returns, we also look at National Election Pool (NEP) exit poll data (Edison/Mitofsky 2005). This second analysis has the potential to support or rebut the county-level findings and allows us to ask different questions about individual attributes and vote choices.

We return to the two questions of import in 2004: Did Ken Salazar's nonracial candidacy contribute to his ability to outperform John Kerry? and Did John Salazar's House candidacy have any bearing on the presidential or Senate outcomes? There are a variety of reasons why these questions could be answered in the affirmative. The Salazars' strategy was to hold on to Latino voters while appealing to rural non-Latino conservatives, requiring them to pick up voters that Kerry could not persuade, either because of the Bush campaign's ability to woo more Latinos than other Republicans have in the past or because Kerry held no appeal for rural voters from the Salazar brothers' area of the state. It is important then to test for differences in the effects of factors that explain the Kerry vote and those that explain Ken Salazar's. As to the second question, based on the story so far, we expect that non-Latino support was the critical factor in Ken Salazar's victory and that this support came from his brother John's electoral district.

KERRY AND SALAZAR AT THE COUNTY LEVEL

Data and Hypotheses

We develop a general model to predict the percent of the vote for each candidate at the county level. The model (see table 4.1) includes measures of party affiliation, the percentage of the voting age population (VAP) that is Latino—*% Latino VAP*—the total Latino population in the county, the percent of the votes in 2000 that went to Ralph Nader, and the percent of total turnout.[12] We expect Kerry and Salazar to do better in counties with a higher percentage of Latino voters and more registered Democrats and in counties with more Latinos.[13] The other variables require a bit of explanation.

The year 2000 was the "Nader election," and although Nader supporters do not appear to be completely responsible for Al Gore's losses in Colorado, he did take a substantial number of votes away from the Democratic candidate (Hero and Jaramillo 2005). Ten Colorado counties gave Nader more than 10 percent of their votes in 2000 (with San Miguel at a high of 17 percent), making the inclusion of a "Nader" variable crucial for analyses of the 2004 election. Because Nader support had all but vanished in 2004, with former supporters throwing much of their weight behind John Kerry, we expect that the variable *% Nader in 2000* has a positive relationship with the Kerry vote in 2004, after controlling for the percentage of Democratic voters.

Next, because of projected record turnout figures in the state of Colorado and because these projections appear to have been accurate, it is important to measure the turnout of Latino voters.[14] At this time there is no good measure (or even an estimation) of Latino turnout across counties, so we control for this using a measure of overall turnout. This is regrettable, as one of the questions surrounding this close election is whether Latino turnout could have had an effect on the outcome (and if voter registration and mobilization drives were successful), but the overall turnout figures are still useful. While we expect that this variable will be significant, we do not have a directional expectation, given that Bush and Kerry (as well as Salazar and Coors) would all benefit from increased turnout.

Finally, we test for separate effects in John Salazar's electoral district. A dummy variable for the counties in John's district (N = 29) is included to control for regional and/or ballot effects (the two cannot be disentangled at this level). This is one of the key variables of interest because it tests for the effects of the Salazar campaign strategy. Salazar's nonracial campaign was tailored to the farmers and families of Colorado's rural west. In addition to this, the benefit of having his brother's name on the ballot strengthens the expectation of significant gains in this part of the state. For Kerry, however, these rural western counties are expected to decrease his vote percentage, all else equal, as the Bush campaign's message hit home (as it did in 2000).[15]

Also included in the models is an interaction of the *% Latino VAP* with the House District 3 dummy. The variable is important for two reasons. First, it tests for separate Latino effects in John Salazar's House district, specifically for John Kerry. If Kerry is at an overall disadvantage in this part of the state, we expect that he will get some boost from counties in the region with a higher percentage of Latinos, all else equal (because of the "Salazar effect"). Alternatively, the variable provides the opportunity to test the success of the nonracial campaign for Ken Salazar because voter ethnicity should become less of a factor in these counties (if his strategy is successful). We expect this interaction variable to be negative for Salazar (to essentially cancel out the overall positive effect of *% Latino VAP*).

Results

Table 4.1 displays the results of the models used to explain John Kerry's percentage of the vote at the county level. Using ordinary least squares regression (OLS), we estimate the parameters of one model without the House District 3 dummy and interaction variable and another model containing these terms. Because we are interested in teasing out the effects of the Ken Salazar and John Kerry results, a variable for the percentage of the county that voted for Ken Salazar is included as a control here (and vice versa in the Salazar model). The key here is to demonstrate what factors affected each candidate's share of the vote, *beyond what his ballot partner received.*[16]

The results generally reflect the expectations. All else equal, the variables *% Salazar, total Latino population,* and *% Nader in 2000* are positive and significant. Moreover, in House District 3 counties (John Salazar's district), Kerry starts at a 5 percentage point disadvantage compared to other counties in the state, reflecting the strength of support for George Bush in this region. However, as the percentage of the Latino VAP in these counties increases, Kerry's share of the vote increases. We cannot determine if this is a Salazar effect, but the evidence is at least consistent with such a phenomenon. That is, after controlling for party share, Ken Salazar, and other important factors, *in John Salazar's electoral district,* Kerry received a boost in counties with higher a percentage of Latino VAP. Last, the finding that the variable *% Democrat* is insignificant is noteworthy, especially in the context of the results presented in table 4.2.

The models in table 4.2 are used to explain Ken Salazar's share of the vote at the county level. After controlling for the *% Kerry* vote in each county, only two variables help explain variation in the Salazar shares. The results for these two variables, however, reveal an interesting

Table 4.1. Explaining the Kerry Vote at the County Level

	Model 1		*Model 2*	
	Coefficient	*t-score*	*Coefficient*	*t-score*
% Democrat[a]	–.01	0.15	.001	0.02
% Salazar	.84**	7.50	.77**	7.46
% VAP Latino	.002	.0	-.09	1.11
House District 3[b]	...	...	–5.29**	3.64
HD 3 * % VAP Latino	...	...	.20*	2.35
Latino population (1000s)	.06**	2.91	.06**	3.15
% Nader in 2000	1.02**	3.70	1.35**	5.03
% total turnout	–.19+	1.75	–.21*	2.05
Constant	8.00	.94	12.52	1.52
N	63		63	
Adj. R^2	.93		.94	
F statistic	147.05**		134.47**	

OLS Estimation: Dependent Variable = % Kerry Vote.
Statistical significance: + < .10 * < .05 ** < .01; all models estimated using STATA 8.
[a] Colorado has a substantial number of "Independent" voters (approximately 30%). To control for partisan voters, we recalculate *% registered Democrats* as a percentage of "major party" voters (Republican/Democrat). This makes *% Democrat* the inverse of *% Republican.*
[b] House District 3 was John Salazar's electoral district. It contains twenty-nine of Colorado's sixty-four counties.

relationship. First, the coefficient for *% Democrat* is positive and significant. This suggests that, all else equal, Salazar is picking up extra Democratic support beyond what he shares with Kerry. Recall that in table 4.1, Kerry was unable to generate Democratic support beyond what he shared with Salazar. Second, after controlling for party share and Kerry support, *% Latino VAP* is positively and significantly associated with *% Salazar.* This is important, because it partially separates what occurred at the state level (with control of both chambers switching to the Democrats) from what Salazar was able to achieve with Latino support. Third, Ken Salazar's overall vote share does not seem to be related to his brother's House race, nor does it appear to be connected to any non-Latino support in this region of the state, at least based on county results.

Table 4.2. Explaining the Salazar Vote at the County Level

	Model 1		*Model 2*	
	Coefficient	*t-score*	*Coefficient*	*t-score*
% Democrat[a]	.20**	3.98	.19**	3.71
% Kerry	.60**	7.50	.66**	7.46
% VAP Latino	.12*	2.53	.14+	1.87
House District 3[b]	...	...	2.25	1.54
HD 3 * % VAP Latino	...	...	–.07	.86
Latino population (1000s)	.01	.29	–.01	.50
% Nader in 2000	.32	1.26	.07	.23
% total turnout	.13	1.35	.14	1.43
Constant	2.77	.38	.64	.08
N	63		63	
Adj. R^2	.94		.94	
F statistic	161.66**		122.78**	

OLS Estimation: Dependent Variable = % Salazar Vote.

Statistical significance: + < .10 * < .05 ** < .01; all models estimated using STATA 8.

[a] Colorado has a substantial percentage of "Independent" voters (approximately 30 percent). To control for partisan voters, we recalculate *% registered Democrats* as a percentage of "major party" voters (Republican/Democrat). This makes *% Democrat* the inverse of *% Republican.*

[b] House District 3 was John Salazar's electoral district. It contains twenty-nine of Colorado's sixty-four counties.

The findings thus far suggest that Ken Salazar was able to get support from counties with higher percentages of Democrats and Latinos, in addition to whatever amount of support he shared with John Kerry. The next logical step in disentangling the results from these two campaigns (one successful, Salazar; one not, Kerry) is to look at what factors explain their differences at the county level. In table 4.3 we do this using the same models employed in tables 4.1 and 4.2, but the dependent variable is now the *difference* between the vote share for Ken Salazar and the vote share for John Kerry *(% Salazar – % Kerry).*[17] This difference is precisely what we are interested in explaining.

In table 4.3 the effects of the nonracial campaign and a familiar family name become more apparent. Here, positive coefficients represent

Table 4.3. Explaining Salazar Gains

	Coefficient		*t-score*
% Democrat[a]	.09+		1.76
% VAP Latino	.13		1.53
House District 3[b]	4.73**		3.20
HD 3 * % VAP Latino	–.17*		1.98
Latino population (1000s)	–.05*		2.49
% Nader in 2000	–.91**		4.97
% total turnout	.21*		1.98
Constant	–8.44		1.02
N		63	
Adj. R^2		.47	
F statistic		8.80**	

Dependent Variable = Difference between % Salazar and % Kerry
Statistical significance: + < .10 * < .05 ** < .01; all models estimated using STATA 8.
[a] Colorado has a substantial percentage of "Independent" voters (approximately 30 percent). To control for partisan voters, we recalculate *% registered Democrats* as a percentage of "major party" voters (Republican/Democrat). This makes *% Democrat* the inverse of *% Republican.*
[b] House District 3 was John Salazar's electoral district. It contains twenty-nine of Colorado's sixty-four counties.

Ken Salazar further outperforming John Kerry at the county level, and negative coefficients indicate a decrease in the gap between the two candidates' vote shares (Salazar comes closer to Kerry's numbers). For example, in counties with a higher Nader vote in 2000 (a negative coefficient), John Kerry and Ken Salazar were closer to having equal vote shares. In contrast to this, Salazar has an average edge of 4.73 percentage points over Kerry in his brother John's electoral district. Whether it is because of the shared family name on the ballot, voter confusion, or a special connection with the people from these counties, Ken Salazar picks up substantial and significant (extra) support in the House district in which his brother campaigned (and won).

Even further, in his brother's region of the state, Ken Salazar creates distance from John Kerry as the percentage of Latino VAP goes *down.* That is, as the percentage of *non*-Latinos increases in these western rural counties (the inverse of *% Latino VAP* decreasing), the distance between Salazar and Kerry gets bigger.[18] Figure 4.1 clearly illustrates this relationship. As the *% Latino VAP* increases in the rest of the state, Ken Salazar increases his vote share over John Kerry. John Salazar's House district shows a different relationship. Here, Ken increases the distance between himself and John Kerry as the percentage of non-Latinos increases. These relationships are evidence of two things. First, Ken Salazar's gains in his brother's region are attributed to counties with more *non*-Latinos. Second, in other counties in the state, Salazar made huge gains over Kerry in places with larger Latino populations. The next section examines these issues at the individual level.

KERRY AND SALAZAR AT THE INDIVIDUAL LEVEL

Using the exit polling data from the NEP (Edison/Mitofsky 2005), we develop similar tests for support for John Kerry and Ken Salazar at the individual level (N = 2,000+).[19] The models are very similar to the ones employed previously, including measures of a respondent's party iden-

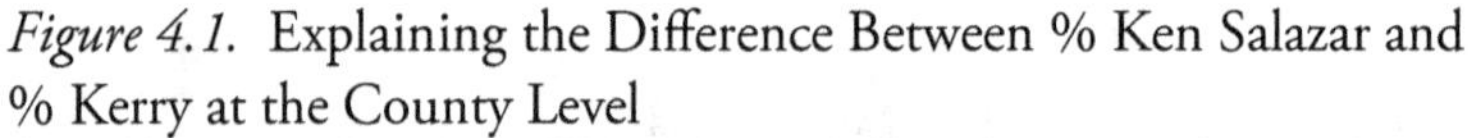

Figure 4.1. Explaining the Difference Between % Ken Salazar and % Kerry at the County Level

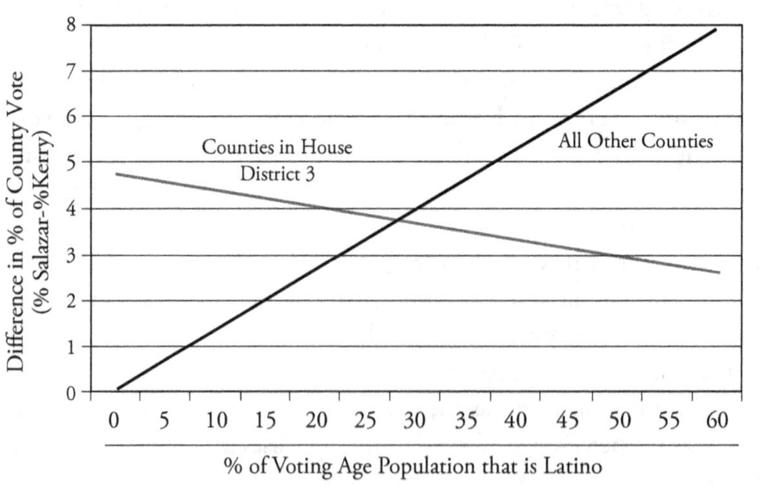

tification, ethnicity or race, and vote choice for the president and senator. The probit estimations, however, also include measures of a respondent's age, income, and education level. The latter three variables are calculated using ordinal scales. The remaining variables are dummies representing each category and vote choice.

Because the results are generally consistent with the county-level analyses, we summarize them briefly. Latino, black, Democratic, Independent, more highly educated, of lower income, or younger respondents are more likely to vote for John Kerry. Once a person's senatorial vote is known, however, the respondent's Latino ethnicity is no longer significant in calculating the probability of a Kerry vote (similar to the interpretation of the results in table 4.1). This reinforces the idea that Kerry was unable to court Latino voter support beyond what was shared with Ken Salazar.

Finally, much like the county-level findings (although more definitive), the results of the individual-level models do not reject the "family connection" and "nonracial" hypotheses. Figure 4.2 clearly illustrates the actual effects of these variables. The figure shows the difference in the predicted probabilities of a Ken Salazar vote due solely to the manipulation of the interaction terms. Much like the county-level findings, the individual-level results show that *outside* of his brother's district, Ken Salazar receives a substantial increase in support from Latino voters. Conversely, in House District 3, a person's Latino ethnicity has very little influence (if any) on his or her vote for Salazar. We suggest that due to the success of his nonracial campaign, being a non-Latino in this region (an "Anglo" in this case) has just as much influence on the probability of a vote for Ken Salazar as being a Latino. The combination of multilevel evidence is, in sum, compelling (see Juenke and Sampaio 2008).

DISCUSSION

In 2004 the general history of Latino voter influence in state and national elections in Colorado was characterized as "more apparent than real" (Hero and Jaramillo 2005). However, the focus of this chapter is not Latino masses but rather the success of two Latino elites who chose

Figure 4.2. The Effects of Family and a Non-Racialized Campaign on the Salazar Vote

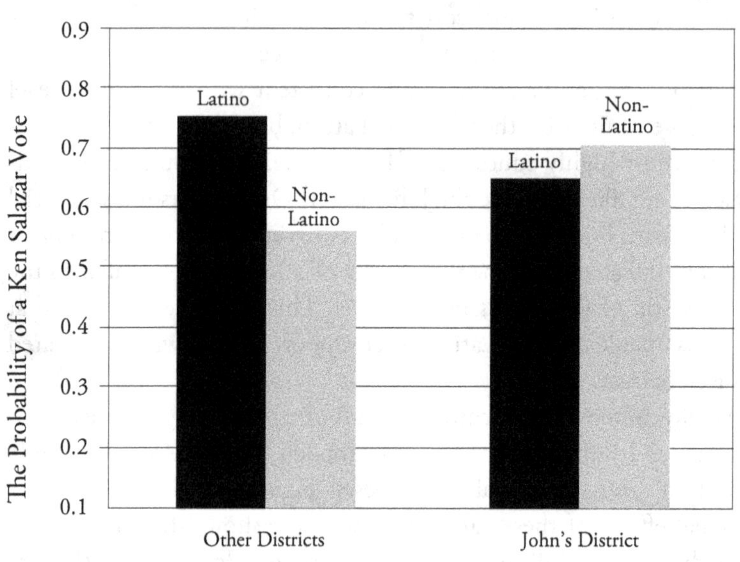

to do something different and relatively new. With a mix of foresight and good timing, Ken Salazar and John Salazar capitalized on the strength of their Latino backgrounds, as well as a strong commitment to the rural conservative values of their neighbors in the western part of the state. To a large degree, they simply stayed true to their roots as farmers and reaped the rewards, but they were also careful not to alienate their core Democratic and Latino constituencies. We argue that they were able to accomplish this feat by not emphasizing their Latino background while simultaneously not disowning it. Both strategies were intentional and crucial to their significant success in 2004.

The evidence at both the county and individual levels supports these contentions. The Latino vote was crucial to Ken Salazar's success outside of his brother John's region. Conversely, the non-Latino vote was just as crucial to his victory inside his brother's region. At this time, it is difficult to gauge whether John helped Ken more or whether it was the other way around. Further, it is hard to discern whether the effect was due to the shared name and shared background or whether it was because the brothers ran almost identical campaigns.

Either way, the Salazars appear to have provided a valuable lesson for those interested in Latino politics in Colorado. First, they showed Democrats how to win in a Republican state without having to expend an inordinate amount of energy and money targeting Latino voters and nonvoters. They also showed Republicans that Latino candidates (and possibly even Latino voters) can have tremendous influence in the state when the campaign is packaged correctly. Perhaps the future of Latino politics in Colorado begins with the success of these relatively mainstream elites and not, as has been predicted, with the growing masses of both Latino voters and nonvoters. The next campaign season will offer a better picture of these trends. Whether the results from this election prove an emerging pattern or a unique event remains to be seen.

NOTES

The authors would like to thank Jenny Wolak for her valuable input.

1. In addition, Ken Salazar became the first Latino Democrat elected to the U.S. Senate in almost thirty years and one of only five Latinos ever elected to that office. In 2004 Republican Mel Martinez also ran a successful campaign for the U.S. Senate in Florida.

2. These gains go beyond the "Nader effect" present in the 2000 election, as demonstrated below.

3. Authors' calculations based on census data (U.S. Census Bureau 1990, 2000).

4. As we pointed out in the previous section, a cursory review of party affiliation and voting history in Colorado reveals why this targeted mobilization of moderate Republicans and rural voters coupled with a nonracial approach was an essential strategy for any Democrat (much less a Latino) to win a statewide election. However, the strategy was not without detractors, especially among members of the state Democratic Party, including many Latinos in the party leadership. This tension was best revealed in the race between Ken Salazar and a younger African American/Japanese American candidate named Mike Miles during the state Democratic Party convention. Miles effectively mobilized the liberal and urban sectors of the state party, and participation in the Democrats' state caucuses and assemblies in the weeks before the primary surpassed turnout in 2000 and 2002. Moreover, at the State Democratic Convention on

Saturday May 22, the tension between Miles and Salazar and their divergent campaign strategies came to a head as 51 percent of delegates voted for Miles over Salazar, relegating Salazar to second place on the primary ballot (Couch 2005). In the end, this tension proved a relatively minor obstacle for Salazar as he proceeded to beat Miles in the August primary with over 70 percent of the vote (Colorado Secretary of State 2004b).

5. Ken Salazar's position on health care mirrored this practice. That is, in addition to supporting some of the hallmarks of the Democratic Party's proposed reforms of health care, such as providing tax credits to small businesses to cover all their employees or expanding the Children's Health Insurance Program, he included an expansive agenda on rural health care in his position papers. He proposed increasing the number of health care professionals in rural areas, increasing the funding for rural health centers by $225 million, increasing funding for the National Health Service Corps to help cover shortages in rural areas, improving rural technology to bring specialty care to rural clinics, and preserving VA medical services for rural veterans (K. Salazar 2004b).

6. Within the Kerry-Edwards '04 campaign, there was a Hispanic Grassroots Team, a Hispanic Media Team, and a Hispanic Advertising Team. The Hispanic Grassroots Team was made up of Luis Elizondo-Thomson (Hispanic outreach director), Paul Rivera (senior political adviser), and Moses Mercado (New Mexico state director). The Hispanic Media Team consisted of Fabiola Rodriguez-Ciampoli (director of Hispanic media) and Luis Miranda (deputy press secretary for Hispanic media). Finally, the Hispanic Advertising Team was composed of one person, Lorena Chambers, a consultant from Chambers, Lopez and Gaitán in Arlington, Virginia (a position held by Armando Gutierrez early in the campaign). In the Democratic National Committee, Nelson Reyneri served as director of Hispanic outreach, Melissa Diaz was director of Hispanic media, Ellen Moran directed the DNC's independent expenditures, and James Aldrete served as the DNC media consultant (Segal 2004).

7. Some notable exceptions to this included the Unidos con Kerry groups established in Colorado through Hispanic Outreach from the Kerry-Edwards '04 campaign. This program reflected a mostly grassroots effort that initiated Latino community house parties and letter-writing campaigns aimed at local newspapers.

8. The Coordinated Campaign operating in Colorado served as the mechanism to channel funding from the DNC and the DSCC but not the Democratic Congressional Campaign Committee (DCCC), whose money was spent on work through independent expenditures in the 2004 election (telephone interview with Maria-Therese Dominguez).

9. The success of out-of-state actors may vary across the states. This raises questions for future study, and we hope this volume provides guidance on some of the factors responsible for success and failure of outside actors in presidential campaigns as they relate to Latino politics.

10. Outside of Colorado specifically, several Latinos had attained high-profile positions with the Republic Party in the Southwest region. Most notable are John Sanchez, Republican Party Southwest regional chairman; Rudy Fernandez, Republican Party Southwest regional political director; and Danny Diaz, Republican Party regional press secretary (Appleman 2004).

11. This was confirmed in an interview with Wanda Padilla, editor in chief of *La Voz,* the largest and oldest bilingual newspaper in Colorado (Padilla 2005).

12. We recalculated the percentage of registered Democrats as a percentage of "major party" voters (Republican/Democrat). This makes *% Democrat* the inverse of *% Republican* and excludes "Unaffiliated" or "Independent" voters.

13. Colorado has many sparsely populated counties, creating misleading group percentages (e.g., Crowly has a similar percentage of Latino VAP as Adams and Denver Counties—20 to 25 percent—but the Latino population is higher in these two counties by about 100,000). After controlling for percent Latino, we expect counties with a higher concentration of Latinos (mostly urban areas) to support the Democratic candidates.

14. Although it should be noted that the Colorado secretary of state uses an odd formula for voter turnout that uses a category of registered voters called "active voters" as its divisor (Colorado Secretary of State 2004a), this smaller group of registered voters creates bloated turnout figures very close to 100 percent. We recalculate the voter turnout figure using all registered voters and all ballots cast in the county. These numbers still provide evidence of a big turnout during the 2004 election (a county average of 71 percent).

15. Bush beat Gore in twenty-two of twenty-nine counties in House District 3 during the 2000 cycle, most of them by very wide margins (authors' calculations based on data from the Federal Elections Project 2005).

16. It should be noted that leaving Ken Salazar's or John Kerry's share of the vote out of the respective models does not significantly change the results except that *% Latino VAP* is positive and significant (when explaining Kerry's share). This difference, however, reinforces the fact that Kerry made no gains among these counties above what he and Salazar shared.

17. This can be done two ways: (1) using each candidate's percentage of the vote across counties or (2) using the raw number of votes each candidate received and then using these to create a percentage of all votes cast in the county. The second method is preferable, but each produces results that are almost identical (the variables correlate at the .99 level and estimate similar parameters). We use the first method in the results presented here.

18. The slope for *% Latino VAP* in John Salazar's House district is calculated by adding the base coefficient (.13) to the interaction coefficient (–.17), which equals –.04.

19. Due to space constraints, we are unable to produce the full individual-level results here. See Juenke and Sampaio 2008 for an in-depth look at consistent but more detailed evidence at the individual level.

REFERENCES

Appleman, Eric. 2004. "Bush-Cheney '04, Inc. Colorado Leadership." www.gwu.edu/~action/2004/bush/bushorgco.html. Accessed February 3, 2009.

Bartels, Lynn. 2004. "Salazar Hispanic Background 'Plays Well.'" *Rocky Mountain News,* August 18.

Campbell, Colin. 2005. Director 96-Hour Victory Team. Personal correspondence with Anna Sampaio, Denver, CO, February 7.

Center for Responsive Politics. 2004a. "Congressional Races in 2004: Colorado." www.opensecrets.org/states/election.asp?State=CO&year=2004. Accessed February 3, 2009.

———. 2004b. "Congressional Races in 2004: Colorado: Ken Salazar." www.opensecrets.org/politicians/. Accessed February 3, 2009.

———. 2004c. "Congressional Races in 2004; Colorado: John Salazar." www.opensecrets.org/politicians/. Accessed February 3, 2009.

Cerveny, Curt. 2005. Republican Political Consultant. Personal correspondence with Anna Sampaio, Politically Direct Campaign Resources. February 1.

CNN.com. 2000. "2000 Election Exit Poll Results." www.cnn.com/. Accessed February 3, 2009.

———. 2005. "2004 Election Exit Poll Results: Colorado." www.cnn.com/ELECTION/2004//pages/results/states/CO/P/00/epolls.0.html. Accessed February 3, 2009.

Colorado Secretary of State. 2004a. "November 2, 2004, General Election Results." www.sos.state.co.us/pubs/elections/main.htm. Accessed February 2005.

———. 2004b. "August 2004, Primary Election Results." www.sos.state.co.us/pubs/elections/primary/COLORADO-CUMULATIVE.htm. Accessed February 2005.

Couch, Mark. 2005. "Miles Wins Top Line on Ballot." *Denver Post,* May 22, sec. 1A.

Dominguez, Marie-Therese. 2005. Telephone interview with Anna Sampaio, Democratic Party Coordinated Campaign, Denver, CO, February 8.

Edison Media Research and Mitofsky International. 2005. "National Election Poll: Colorado." Inter-University Consortium for Political and Social Research, University of Michigan, Ann Arbor. www.icpsr.umich.edu/org/announce.html#nep. Accessed February 3, 2009.

Federal Election Commission. 2004a. "FEC Disclosure Report: Salazar for Senate." http://query.nictusa.com/cgi-bin/com_rcvd/C00397679/. Accessed February 3, 2009.

———. 2004b. "FEC Disclosure Report: John Salazar for Congress." http://query.nictusa.com/cgi-bin/com_rcvd/C00393033/. Accessed February 3, 2009.

———. 2004c. "FEC Disclosure Report: John Salazar for Congress: Committees Who Gave to This Candidate: Independent Expenditures against Candidate." http://query.nictusa.com/cgi-bin/can_give/H4CO03167/. Accessed February 3, 2009.

———. 2004d. "FEC Disclosure Report: Roland Chicas for Congress." http://query.nictusa.com/cgi-bin/com_rcvd/C0039805/. Accessed February 3, 2009.

Federal Elections Project. 2005. "2000 Election Data by State." Center for Congressional and Presidential Studies, American University. http://spa.american.edu/ccps/pages.php?ID=12. Accessed February 2005.

Florio, Gwen. 2004. "Politics Takes Place at Pulpit." *Rocky Mountain News,* June 1.

Greg Walcher for Congress. 2004. Television ad: "Illegal Alien Amnesty." www.n-email.com/he/vo.asp?FileID=7676&MemberID=19407750. Accessed February 3, 2009.

Guerra, Fernando, and Luis Ricardo Fraga. 1996. "Theory, Reality, and Perpetual Potential: Latinos in the 1992 Election." In *Ethnic Ironies: Latino Politics in the 1992 Elections,* ed. Rodolfo O. de la Garza and Louis DeSipio, 131–45. Boulder, CO: Westview Press.

Hero, Rodney. 1996. "An Essential Vote: Latinos and the 1992 Elections in Colorado." In *Ethnic Ironies: Latino Politics in the 1992 Elections,* ed. Rodolfo O. de la Garza and Louis DeSipio, 75–94. Boulder, CO: Westview Press.

Hero, Rodney, and Patricia Jaramillo. 2005. "Latinos and the 2000 Elections in Colorado: More Real than Apparent, More Apparent than Real?" In *Muted Voices: Latinos and the 2000 Elections,* ed. Rodolfo O. de la Garza and Louis DeSipio, 130–48. Lanham, MD: Rowman and Littlefield.

Hero, Rodney, Patricia Jaramillo, and John C. Halprin. 1999. "Similar Behavior, Different Results: Latinos and the 1996 Elections in Colorado." In *Awash in the Mainstream: Latino Politics in the 1996 Election,* ed. Rodolfo O. de la Garza and Louis DeSipio, 101–16. Boulder, CO: Westview Press.

Juenke, Eric Gonzalez, and Anna Christina Sampaio. 2008. "Deracialization and Latino Politics: The Case of the Salazar Brothers in Colorado." *Political Research Quarterly,* online ed. prq.sagepub.com/pap.dtl. December 24.

King, Roxanne. 2004. "APC Members Urge Archbishop Chaput to Continue Speaking out on Catholics and Politics." *Denver Catholic Register,* May 19, Local News sec.

Kirkpatrick, David D., and Laurie Goodstein. 2004. "Groups of Bishops Using Influence to Oppose Kerry." *New York Times,* October 12.

Padilla, Wanda. 2005. Editor in Chief, *La Voz.* Telephone interview with Anna Sampaio, Denver, CO, March 3.

Rodriguez, Geronimo. 2005. Telephone interview with Anna Sampaio, Democratic Party Coordinated Campaign, Denver, CO, February 7.

Salazar, Ken. 2004a. "Creating Jobs and Economic Opportunity." Ken Salazar for U.S. Senate. No current URL, February 2009.

———. 2004b. "Ensuring Quality, Affordable Health Care." Ken Salazar for U.S. Senate Web site. No current URL, February 2009.

———. 2004c. "Other Issues," Ken Salazar for U.S. Senate." Ken Salazar for U.S. Senate Web site. No current URL, February 2009.

Salazar, John. 2004. "Most Important Issues." Salazar for Congress Web site. No current URL, February 2009.

Segal, Adam. 2004. "Bikini Politics: The 2004 Presidential Campaigns' Hispanic Media Efforts Cover Only the Essential Parts of the Body Politic: A Select Group of Voters in a Few Battleground States." Hispanic Voter Project, Johns Hopkins University, Baltimore, MD.

Tankersley, Jim. 2004. "Hispanics Slam Bush." *Rocky Mountain News,* September 21.

Telegraph. 2004. "Voting for Kerry 'Will Jeopardize Your Salvation,' Catholics Told." *Telegraph,* May 15. www.telegraph.co.uk/news. Accessed February 3, 2009.

U.S. Department of Commerce. Bureau of the Census. 1990. American FactFinder. http://factfinder.census.gov/servlet/DatasetMainPageServlet?_program=DEC&_lang=en. Accessed February 3, 2009.

———. 2000. American FactFinder. http://factfinder.census.gov/servlet/DatasetMainPageServlet?_program=DEC&_lang=en. Accessed February 3, 2009.

Chapter Five

Battleground Voters in a Battleground State?

Latinos in Arizona and the 2004 Presidential Election

MANUEL AVALOS, LISA MAGAÑA, AND ADRIAN D. PANTOJA

In 2004 there was considerable optimism going into the campaign that Arizona might become one of the swing states that both political parties would target. To that end, the possibility was very real that the candidates might target Latino voters during the campaign. Coupled with a controversial statewide proposition known as the Arizona Taxpayer Citizen Protection Act, or Proposition 200, which would have required proof of citizenship to vote, the potential for Latino political mobilization seemed imminent.

With this backdrop to the election, we discuss how the campaign was conducted, focusing on potential and real Latino political mobilization, the impact of Proposition 200, and how Arizona played out as a potential swing state in the election. Despite significant increases in Arizona's Latino population—from 18.8 percent in 1990 to 25.3

percent in 2000—the effect of the Latino vote on presidential elections in the state has been slight. Previous analyses of presidential elections since the early 1990s have documented a history of low turnout among potential Latino voters, which has limited their impact on the outcome of presidential campaigns (Avalos 2005, 1999, 1996).

It is a truism of American politics that individuals participate either because they have the resources to "go to politics" or because "politics comes to them" through mobilization efforts (Rosenstone and Hansen 1993). A number of recent works have noted the importance of voter mobilization drives for bringing Latinos to the polls (Pantoja and Woods 1999; Ramírez 2005, 2007; Shaw, de la Garza, and Lee 2000). Despite being a key factor in fostering political engagement, voter mobilization campaigns by political parties, candidates, and interest groups have not historically targeted Latinos (Michelson 2003; Ramírez 2005, 2007). A study by Verba, Schlozman, and Brady (1995) found that 56 percent of non-Hispanic whites reported being asked to become involved in politics, compared to 40 percent of African Americans and 25 percent of Latinos. Other studies similarly find low levels of political contact by partisan and nonpartisan groups (Shaw, de la Garza, and Lee 2000).

Nonetheless, in recent years Latinos have been making significant political strides across the nation as a result of increases in naturalization and voter participation. A number of factors have contributed to this change, but it is most often attributed to a rise in anti-immigration sentiment and negative Latino reactions to ballot initiatives such as Proposition 187 in California (Pantoja, Ramírez, and Segura 2001). The growth of the Latino electorate in states with significant numbers of electoral votes, a belief among many that the "Latino vote is up for grabs," and a polarized electorate has led presidential candidates from both parties to try to win the Latino vote. Much has been made about these efforts, in particular, those of George W. Bush, who used his Spanish-speaking skills and Spanish-language ads to attract Latino voters (Nicholson, Pantoja, and Segura 2006). Not to be outdone, Democratic candidates Al Gore and John Kerry also employed Spanish-language media ads and other symbolic gestures in their campaigns.

Although Latinos in Arizona have overwhelmingly registered as Democrats (70 to 75 percent throughout the 1990s), the state has become increasingly conservative and Republican. Among the overall electorate in 2004, registered Republicans outnumbered registered Democrats in Arizona 43 percent to 38 percent, with 19 percent registered as Independents. Despite the fact that the Latino share of the Arizona electorate increased over the decade, from 9 percent in 1990 to 13 percent in 2004, in only one presidential election might the Latino vote have determined the outcome. This took place in 1996, when 76 percent of Arizona Latino voters supported Bill Clinton; without this support, Bob Dole would likely have won the state (de la Garza and DeSipio 1999: 33).

Latino voters were poised to be important players in deciding what was projected to be a close election. The media focused on the battleground states many considered key to winning the election. Four battleground states had sizable Latino populations: New Mexico, Nevada, Florida, and Arizona. Republican Party chairman Ed Gillespie noted, "A slight shift among Hispanic voters in these states can tip the Electoral College" (Kasindorf 2004). Prior to the election, Bush's and Kerry's efforts to win the Latino vote generated much excitement in these states. Four months before the election, a *USA Today* article noted, "This handful of strategic states is getting most of the specialized ads in Spanish, on which the campaigns and allied groups are expected to spend up to $17 million. And these states are targeted for most of the doorbell ringing to get out the vote in Hispanic communities" (Kasindorf 2004). Turnout in these states was anticipated to be high in general and among Latinos in particular, as the Republican and Democratic Parties, along with interest groups, would be carrying out intensive media campaigns and get-out-the-vote (GOTV) drives in Latino communities.

As the election neared and Bush maintained a double-digit lead over Kerry in Arizona, the fanfare surrounding the importance of the Latino vote diminished. Bush did not need them to carry the state, and Kerry could not count on them to win it. By October it became clear that projections of a tight race in Arizona were too optimistic. Both parties began to redeploy staffers to more competitive states, such as Ohio, leading some state Republicans to declare, "It's over in Arizona. John Kerry will not carry Arizona" (Kamman and House 2004). Kerry supporters countered by insisting they had a strong "ground game" and that grassroots efforts to court the Latino vote were going to continue (Sauerzopf 2004). In addition, some Democrats hoped that Proposition 200 would galvanize Latino voters.

PROPOSITION 200

A decade after the passage of Proposition 187 in California, Arizona's Proposition 200, a move to block undocumented immigrants from receiving public services, developed as a backdrop to the 2004 election. The heightened concern about undocumented immigration has in part been due to a downturn in the state economy, the increasing influx of immigrants in what is now the busiest undocumented immigration corridor into the United States, and the incredible growth of the Arizona Latino population (of which close to 40 percent are noncitizens) between 1990 and 2000.[1]

With increasing numbers of Latino immigrants in Arizona and mounting frustration among many Arizonans with the country's failed immigration enforcement policies in a post-9/11 environment, a citizen group, Protect Arizona Now, successfully placed a citizen's initiative (Proposition 200, the "Arizona Taxpayer Citizen Protection Act") on the ballot for the 2004 general election. Proposition 200 would require (1) proof of citizenship when registering to vote, (2) ID at polling places, (3) proof of immigration status when applying for state public welfare benefits, and (4) government workers to alert immigration officials of suspected undocumented immigrants seeking benefits.

Protect Arizona Now received substantial financial support from three national anti-immigrant groups: Federation for American Immigration Reform (FAIR), Americans for Better Immigration, and POP.STOP. Inc. The goal of this coalition was to use Arizona's vote to spread their restrictionist agenda, which included a militarized border, a significant decrease or end to legal immigration, deportation of undocumented immigrants, and opposition to amnesty or guest worker proposals (Crawford 2004).

Resistance to Proposition 200 came from a broad-based coalition of bipartisan political leaders and organizations representing business, labor, health care, the Latino community, political groups, various religious denominations that formed the No on 200 Arizonans for Real

Immigration Reform (ARIR) committee. Former Arizona Attorney General Grants Woods chaired the committee, and it received substantial monetary support from the Service Employees International Union. Also joining the opposition to Proposition 200 were Democratic Governor Janet Napolitano and Republican U.S. Senator John McCain, as well as Latino advocacy groups (Alianza Indígena sin Fronteras, Arizona Hispanic Community Forum) and organizations such as the Arizona Chamber of Commerce, the ACLU of Arizona, AFL-CIO Arizona, the Arizona Democratic Party, and the Arizona Education Association (Diaz 2004). The ARIR committee focused its campaign on what it perceived as "unintended" consequences—specifically, the significant cost to government to implement the act (Marson 2004).

OUTCOME

The final vote count showed that President Bush defeated John Kerry by about 211,000 votes, or a 54.2 to 43.8 percent margin. Proposition 200 passed by a 44.6 to 44.4 margin. More than two million Arizona voters cast ballots in the 2004 presidential election, shattering previous turnout records. Statewide, about 478,000 more voters cast ballots in the 2004 election than in 2000, a gain of nearly 31 percent (Kamman 2004). Voter turnout of 77.1 percent easily exceeded the 71.8 percent of registered voters who cast ballots in 2000 and virtually tied the turnout in the 1992 contest between Bill Clinton and George H. W. Bush, when 78 percent of the electorate voted. Voter registration, promoted heavily by partisan and nonpartisan groups, also saw a significant increase (21.6 percent) in comparison to the 2000 presidential election. Across the state, turnout was especially high in Republican-dominated areas, which gave Bush wide margins of victory. The margin of victory in Maricopa County, about two points higher than the GOP registration advantage, was especially meaningful because the county accounts for about 60 percent of all votes cast in the state.

As in previous years, turnout among the Latino electorate was significantly lower than overall statewide and county turnout percentages (see table 5.1). According to the U.S. Census, only 47 percent of the Latino citizen population eighteen years and older turned out to vote in the 2004 contest.

Table 5.1. Voter Characteristics of Latinos in Arizona, 1992–2004

Characteristic	*1992*	*1994*	*1996*	*1998*	*2000*	*2004*
Percent total population	19	20	21	21	25	28
Percent citizen of population 18 or older	53	56	56	61	67	55
Percent of the electorate	9.0	9.8	10.9	10.6	15.0	13.2
Percent registered[a]	41.4	42.1	57.9	41.5	49.3	57.8
Percent turnout[b]	40.2	31.9	41.1	41.5	40.1	47.1

Source: U.S. Census, *Voting and Registration in the Election of November 1992–2004.*
[a] U.S. citizen population 18 years and older.
[b] Of those registered who are 18 and older.

Table 5.2 presents the results from the 2004 canvas of the vote for selected precincts in the most heavily populated state legislative districts (13–16) in Maricopa County. The table compares precincts with a 70 percent or higher Latino voting age population ($N = 39$) with precincts in the same legislative district with a 70 percent or higher non-Hispanic white voting age population ($N = 28$). While the majority of Latinos voted for John Kerry by a 68 to 31 percent margin, voter turnout in Latino precincts was more than 28 percent lower than county and statewide averages and 24 percent lower than heavily populated Anglo precincts in the same legislative districts.

An analysis of the vote on Proposition 200 in heavily populated precincts in metropolitan Phoenix reveals that, while the majority of Latinos (56 percent) voted against Proposition 200, 44 percent voted in favor of it. Moreover, Proposition 200 did not mobilize large numbers of the Latino electorate to the polls on Election Day. Turnout in the Latino precincts in Phoenix (50.7 percent) was markedly lower than the heavily populated Anglo precincts (73.5 percent) in the same legislative districts and more than 37 percent lower than the affluent homogeneous Anglo precincts (87.7 percent) in Scottsdale and Fountain Hills. How might we explain this low turnout and the relatively low opposition to Proposition 200 by the Latino electorate?

Table 5.2. Canvas of the 2004 Vote for Selected Precincts in Maricopa County (percent)

Precincts	*Latino VAP*	*Registered Dem*	*Registered GOP*	*Voter Turnout*	*Vote Kerry*	*Vote Bush*	*Vote Prop 200*
70+% Latino precincts, Districts 13–16	74.4	58.3	14.9	50.7	67.9	30.8	44.3
70+% Anglo precincts in Districts 13–16	18.2	42.1	32.4	73.5	73.5	43.3	53.4
Maricopa County	22.1	31.2	43.5	78.2	41.7	56.0	57.5
Statewide	21.3	37.9	43.2	78.0	43.8	54.2	55.6

Source: Authors' calculations based on Arizona election data.

Economic self-interest might explain why many Latinos voted for Proposition 200. Since the vast majority of Latinos who live in legislative districts 13–16 are working class, one could argue that Latinos are as inclined as any other voters to protect their economic livelihoods. Although the opposition focused on government services for undocumented immigrants, the proposal offered blue-collar, working-class voters the chance to express their frustration over competing with undocumented workers willing to accept lower pay.

Exit poll results of 1,881 voters conducted for the Associated Press by Edison Media Research and Mitofsky International lends some support for the economic self-interest argument. These results revealed that support for Proposition 200 was highest among the lowest wage earners. Nearly three-fourths (72 percent) of voters making less than $15,000 voted for it, as did almost two-thirds (60 percent) of respondents earning $50,000 or less. In contrast, voters earning between $100,000 and $200,000 were the only demographic group to vote no on Proposition 200 (with 55 percent opposed). The exit poll also revealed that three out of five voters with less than a college degree favored the proposition, as opposed to 50 percent among those with a college or postgraduate degree (Associated Press 2004). Latinos are disproportionately represented among those with lower incomes and education.

A second argument focuses on the role of ideology in immigration policy. Previous research has suggested that partisanship was a strong determinant of voter choice on California's Proposition 187 (Cain and MacDonald 1996; Salvanto 1997). Precinct-level results in table 5.2 reveal that while predominantly Latino precincts in legislative districts 13–16 (precincts with 58 percent registered Democrats) opposed Proposition 200 by a 56 to 44 percent margin, predominantly Anglo precincts within these same legislative districts (precincts with 42.1 percent registered Democrats) voted in favor of Proposition 200 by a 53 to 47 percent margin. This provides evidence supporting both the partisan and the social conflict–racial/ethnic diversity theories.

Tolbert and Hero (1996) examined the county-level racial composition of the 1994 California electorate to determine how demographics affected electoral opinion on Proposition 187 in the fifty-eight counties voting on the initiative. Their findings confirm the contextual effects of race on the vote for Proposition 187. They argued that "bifurcated counties with above average Latino populations and an electorally dominant white population" can account for support for Proposition 187 in the same way that homogeneous counties with small numbers of minorities ensured support for the initiative (Tolbert and Hero 1996: 816). Our examination of precincts within bifurcated legislative districts 13–16, as well as precinct results in homogeneous Anglo legislative district 8, confirms the ethnic/racial diversity argument. Despite this finding, however, ethnic/racial diversity theory cannot explain why 44 percent of Latino voters supported Proposition 200.

Finally, the media campaign in support of Proposition 200 was markedly different from the one carried out on behalf of Proposition 187 in California. The media campaign for the latter was filled with racially charged images of hoards of illegal immigrants invading the state. The media campaigns behind Proposition 200 were relatively tame and frequently included persons of diverse racial and ethnic backgrounds speaking on behalf of the initiative. Absent were images of gritty INS footage showing undocumented immigrants crossing into Arizona. The absence of a racially charged campaign in Arizona may have quelled the anticipated Latino backlash.

What is clear from the analysis of the Latino vote on Proposition 200 is that the Latino community was divided. It therefore appears that although the majority of Latinos voted against Proposition 200, greater voter mobilization of the Latino electorate would not have changed the overall outcome of the vote.

Exit poll results by Edison Media Research and Mitofsky International (2004) reveal that the overwhelming support for Proposition 200 came from the following groups:

- Republicans (70 percent);
- ideologically conservative voters (70 percent);
- voters who made their decision to vote more than a month before Election Day (64 percent);
- voters who identified terrorism and moral values as the most important issues in the election (64 percent); and
- white males (60 percent).

CONCLUSION

Did Latinos vote in record numbers in Arizona? To the extent that turnout may have increased, was it attributable to voter mobilization efforts and/or Proposition 200? These are difficult questions to answer considering the paucity of attitudinal and behavioral data on Latinos in Arizona. In order to determine the extent and consequences of voter registration and mobilization efforts, one must rely on the accounts of interest groups, political activists, and party leaders to make an assessment of their activities. This is problematic, of course, since the political parties and some interest groups are not forthcoming about their political activities. From the information provided, there is little evidence of any meaningful, sustained efforts by the Republican or Democratic Party to target Latino voters in the state. Perhaps as a result of the comfortable lead Bush maintained in the state, neither party considered Latino voters essential to carrying it. One of the largest anti-Bush voter mobilization entities, America Coming Together (ACT), did create Spanish-language voter mobilization fliers targeting Arizona's Latino voters, but it also transferred its resources out of the state in the final two weeks of the campaign.

The existing studies on Latino political participation reveal that Latino voters respond more positively to the mobilization efforts of Latino activists (Shaw, de la Garza, and Lee 2000) and to live telephone calls than to direct mail or robotic telephone calls (Ramirez 2005). Yet, in Arizona, there is an absence of indigenous Latino organizations capable of targeting and mobilizing large numbers of Latino voters. Consequently, if Latino voters in the state were going to be targeted in a meaningful way, it would have to be undertaken by national Latino advocacy groups such as the National Association of Latino Elected Officials (NALEO), Southwest Voter Registration and Education Project (SVREP), and the National Council of La Raza (NCLR). Although Arizona was included in NALEO's "1-888-Ve-Y-Vota" campaign, a toll-free number for voters seeking information about their polling place or to report voter intimidation, the organization did not carry out any voter mobilization drives in Arizona in 2004. SVREP, the largest Latino voter mobilization organization, claims to have registered 7,342 Latinos in the state in 2004. They offer no evidence or records that analyze the effectiveness of their GOTV drives, however. NCLR provided limited funding ($10,000) to an advocacy group in Arizona called Chicanos por la Causa. The money was given to the Tucson/Pima County office for a voter registration and mobilization project. A total of 836 Latinos were registered on the south side of Tucson, a high-density Latino area. The registration efforts included a civic education component that stressed the importance of voting. The director of the project estimates that of the 836 Latinos registered, over 70 percent voted on Election Day.

In the end, Arizona did not prove to be a battleground state, nor did Latinos become the anticipated "battleground voters" as evidenced by the lack of voter registration and mobilization campaigns in Hispanic communities. Whether Proposition 200 leads to an increase in Latino naturalization and political participation in the future remains to be seen. Empirical studies of the effects of California's Proposition 187 on the Latino electorate were carried out a few years after the initiative's passage, and it may similarly take time for research to pinpoint whether there is a Latino reaction against anti-immigrant initiatives. While the Latino political tsunami has yet to hit Arizona, it may be slowly brewing below our vision.

NOTE

1. The 2000 census count revealed that the population in Arizona grew more than three times as fast as the rest of the nation. During the 1990s, Arizona's population increased by 1.5 million, and the Latino population in Arizona increased by an amazing 88 percent (from 688,000 in 1990 to over 1.2 million in 2000). In addition, the Latino population increased its proportion of the statewide population from 18.7 percent in 1990 to over 25 percent in 2000 (U.S. Census 2000).

REFERENCES

Associated Press. 2004. "Prop. 200 Won Support from Blue-Collar Workers." *Arizona Republic,* November 3.

Avalos, Manuel. 1996. "Promise and Missed Opportunity: The 1992 Latino Vote in Arizona." In *Ethnic Ironies: Latino Politics in the 1992 Elections,* ed. Rodolfo de la Garza and Louis DeSipio, 95–110. Boulder, CO: Westview Press.

———. 1999. "Less Is More: Latinos in the 1996 Election in Arizona." In *Awash in the Mainstream: Latino Politics in the 1996 Elections,* ed. Rodolfo O. de la Garza and. Louis DeSipio, 117–36. Boulder, CO: Westview Press.

———. 2005. "Will More (Votes) Continue to Equal Less (Influence)? Arizona Latinos in the 2000 Elections." In *Muted Voices: Latinos and the 2000 Elections,* ed. Rodolfo O. de la Garza and Louis DeSipio, 149–62. Lanham, MD: Rowman and Littlefield.

Cain, Bruce, and Karin MacDonald. 1996. "Nativism, Partisanship and Immigration: An Analysis of Prop. 187." Paper presented at the Annual Meeting of the American Political Science Association, San Francisco, CA.

Crawford, Amanda J. 2004. "Prop. 200 Gains Fans, Foes Nationwide." *Arizona Republic,* October 22, B1.

de la Garza, Rodolfo, and Louis DeSipio, eds. 1999. *Awash in the Mainstream: Latino Politics in the 1996 Elections.* Boulder, CO: Westview Press.

Diaz, Elvia. 2004. "66% in State Favor Anti-Immigrant Issue." *Arizona Republic,* September 10, B1.

Kamman, Jon. 2004. "Arizona's Election Turnout Set Record." *Arizona Republic,* November 16. www.azcentral.com.

Kamman, Jon, and Billy House. 2004. "Kerry Pulls Ads in Arizona, Focus Shifts to More Competitive States." *Arizona Republic,* September 23. www.azcentral.com.

Kasindorf, Martin. 2004. "Parties Target Hispanics in 4 Battleground States." *USA Today,* July 20, A1.

Marson, Barrett. 2004. "No on 200 Group Targets 'Unintended' Outcomes." *Arizona Daily Star,* September 10. www.azcentral.com.

Michelson, Melissa. 2003. "Getting out the Latino Vote: How Door to Door Canvassing Influences Voter Turnout in Rural California." *Political Behavior* 25: 247–63.

Nicholson, Stephen, Adrian D. Pantoja and Gary M. Segura. 2006. "Political Knowledge and Issue Voting among the Latino Electorate." *Political Research Quarterly* 59: 259–71.

Pantoja, Adrian, and Nathan Woods. 1999. "Turning out the Latino Vote in Los Angeles County: Did Interest Group Efforts Matter?" *American Review of Politics* 20: 141–62.

Pantoja, Adrian, Ricardo Ramírez, and Gary Segura. 2001. "Citizens by Choice, Voters by Necessity: Patterns in Political Mobilization by Naturalized Latinos." *Political Research Quarterly* 54: 729–50.

Ramírez, Ricardo. 2005. "Giving Voice to Latino Voters: A Field Experiment on the Effectiveness of a National Nonpartisan Mobilization Effort." *Annals of the American Academy of Political and Social Science* 601: 66–84.

———. 2007. "Segmented Mobilization: Latino Nonpartisan Get-Out-the-Vote Efforts in the 2000 General Election." *American Politics Research* 35: 155–75.

Rosenstone, Steven J., and John Mark Hansen. 1993. *Mobilization, Participation, and Democracy in America.* New York: Macmillan.

Salvanto, Anthony M. 1997. "Initiatives as Running Mates: The Impact of Candidate-Centered Initiative Campaign." Paper presented at the Annual Meeting of the Western Political Science Association, Tucson, AZ.

Sauerzopf, Marty. 2004. "Groups Are Pushing Hard to Mobilize Latino Voters." *Arizona Republic,* October 26. www.azcentral.com.

Shaw, Daron, Rodolfo de la Garza, and Jongho Lee. 2000. "Examining Latino Turnout in 1996: A Three-State Validated Survey Approach." *American Journal of Political Science* 44: 332–40.

Tolbert, Caroline, and Rodney Hero. 1996. "Race/Ethnicity and Direct Democracy: An Analysis of California's Illegal Immigration Initiative." *Journal of Politics* 58: 806–18.

U.S. Census. 2000. Factfinder 2000 Data. http://factfinder.census.gov/servlet/DatasetMainPageServlet?_program=DEC&_lang=en. Accessed August 22, 2008.

Verba, Sidney, Kay L. Schlozman, and Henry E. Brady. 1995. *Voice and Equality: Civic Volunteerism in American Politics.* Cambridge, MA: Harvard University Press.

Chapter Six

A Candle in the Wind?

Latinos and the 2004 Elections in Texas

JESSICA LAVARIEGA MONFORTI

The 2004 elections seem to have been a mix of contradictions for Texas Hispanics.[1] Despite the enormous presence of Hispanics in the state, and therefore the potential for ethnic bloc voting and strong Latino leadership, Tejanos (Texas Latinos) did not play a major role. This is because party leaders concluded very early on in the presidential campaigns that Texas would continue to be a "red state," as it had been in the past (Martinez 1996; Montoya 2005). Consequently, the Bush-Cheney and Kerry-Edwards campaigns, as well as the media, gave very little attention to Texas and Tejanos. Action at the congressional and state House levels, due, in part, to redistricting, offered interesting opportunities for Hispanics at the local level, however.[2] Elections for positions such as county sheriff and county clerk, which are often ignored in the broader political landscape, provided opportunities for political gains among Texas Hispanics, and women in particular.

What is the significance of the opportunities for political gains among Texas Hispanics? Did political parties, electoral campaigns, or organizations pursue and mobilize Latino voters and/or candidates in Texas? If so, how was this done? Did Hispanic voters in Texas play an influential role in the 2004 elections?

A review of the various stages of the 2004 elections reveals the answers we seek. The context and dynamics of the campaigns, along with the political actions of the Hispanic community, are extremely important considerations (Guerra 1992). According to Shapiro (2005: 5), "What matters most for real-world politics are observable indications of Latino political power, including high rates and levels of political participation." Therefore, this chapter reviews the political involvement of Hispanics in Texas in the various components of the 2004 elections: the presidential contest, statewide races, and other salient congressional, state, and local races. I pay specific attention to the role of the Republican and Democratic Parties throughout the analyses, as the parties often set the context of the elections and the participation they generate. The final section of the chapter synthesizes these findings in an effort to examine why the potential strength of the Hispanic vote in Texas was largely disregarded.

THE CONTEXT OF HISPANICS IN TEXAS AND THE 2004 ELECTIONS

In the 2004 presidential election, 63.8 percent of the nation's eligible voters (U.S. citizens eighteen years of age and older) cast ballots. In Texas, turnout among eligible voters was lower than this (about 57 percent). Turnout among voting-eligible Tejanos was an even lower 41.6 percent.

In 2003 the U.S. Census Bureau reported that approximately 35 percent of Texas's population is of Hispanic or Latino ethnicity.[3] Approximately 2,170,000 Hispanics were registered to vote in Texas in 2004, constituting 22.4 percent of the state's registered voters. In the 2004 election 70.6 percent of registered Hispanics voted—in comparison to 82.1 percent of registered voters statewide (U.S. Bureau of the Census 2005). According to the Texas Legislative Council, 61.5 percent of all Texans voted for Bush in the 2004 presidential election while 38.5 percent voted for Kerry. Further, in statewide contests, voters across Texas showed more support for Republican than Democratic candidates, 59.1 percent to 40.9 percent.

The National Exit Poll (NEP) found that Latinos split their votes nearly evenly between President Bush and Senator Kerry. According to this poll, the results of which have been called into question (Leal et al.

2005), Kerry carried 50 percent of Texas Hispanic votes and Bush carried 49 percent. Even if this poll overstates Latino votes for Bush by several percentage points, as I suspect, Bush improved his performance among Latino voters compared to his 2000 race.

Given the scholarly doubts about the accuracy of the NEP in measuring Texas's Hispanic votes, I offer another tool for analysis. Hispanics in Texas are concentrated in high numbers in several counties with large populations: Bexar (which includes the San Antonio metropolitan area), Dallas, El Paso, Harris (which includes the Houston metropolitan area), and Hidalgo (which runs along part of the U.S.-Mexico border in southeastern Texas). Hispanics constitute the highest percentage of several additional counties that have low numbers of total residents. These counties are located on the state's southern border: Jim Hogg, Maverick, Starr, Webb, and Zavala. Alternatively, Hispanics in Texas have the lowest numbers and percentages in Armstrong, Cass, Delta, King, Lamar, Loving, Newton, Roberts, Sabine, and Tyler Counties, which are largely located in the northern and eastern parts of the state. I assess changes in support for Democratic and Republican presidential candidates in these four types of counties as a way to assess the actual vote in counties where Hispanics are present in large numbers and where Hispanics are largely absent. I compare the Republican share of the county vote in 2004 to that of 1992. The year 1992 is selected as a comparison election because it was the last statewide election before George Bush ran for governor and became either a statewide candidate or an influence on the statewide vote.

Republicans gained votes in all four types of counties in comparison to 1992, although these gains were more pronounced in counties with low numbers and low percentages of Hispanics (see table 6.1). On average, the Republican share of the county vote increased relative to the 1992 election by nearly 60 percent in counties with high numbers and high percentages of Hispanics. In counties with the lowest numbers and lowest percentage of Hispanics, the Republican share of the vote increased by much higher levels: 190 percent and 162 percent, respectively.

It is important to note that the high-concentration Hispanic counties show relatively low levels of support for Bush compared to the statewide vote. In none of these counties does the Bush share of the vote exceed 43 percent, and in two cases it is in the mid-20s. Admittedly,

Table 6.1. Voter Distribution from 1992 and 2004 Presidential and Vice Presidential Candidates and County (percent)

County	*Vote for Clinton-Gore '92*	*Vote for Kerry-Edwards '04*	*Change in Vote for Democrats*	*Vote for Bush-Quayle '92*	*Vote for Bush-Cheney '04*	*Change in Vote for Republicans*
Counties with the Highest Number of Hispanics						
Harris	38	44.6	6.6	43	54.8	11.8
Bexar	42	44.4	2.4	41	54.8	13.8
El Paso	50	56.1	6.1	35	43.2	8.2
Hidalgo	58	54.9	-3.1	30	44.8	14.8
Dallas	35	49	14	39	50.3	11.3
Total			26			59.9
Counties with the Lowest Number of Hispanics						
Loving	20.8	15	-5.8	32.3	81.3	49
Roberts	20.4	9.1	-11.3	63.4	91	27.6
King	28.6	11.5	-17.1	41.8	87.8	46
Armstrong	27	16.9	-10.1	54.8	82.7	27.9
Delta	43	30.1	-12.9	30	69.5	39.5
Total			-57.2			190

Table 6.1. Voter Distribution from 1992 and 2004 Presidential and Vice Presidential Candidates and County (percent) *continued*

Counties with the Highest Percentage of Hispanics						
Starr	83	74.0	–9.0	13	26.0	13.0
Webb	58	56.9	–1.1	31	42.7	11.7
Maverick	61	59.3	–1.7	27	40.1	13.1
Jim Hogg	72	65.1	–6.9	23	34.5	11.5
Zavala	79	74.8	–4.2	15	24.9	9.9
Total			–22.9			59.2
Counties with the Lowest Percentage of Hispanics						
Tyler	47	34.3	–12.7	32	65.1	33.1
Lamar	39	30.6	–8.4	36	69	33
Sabine	49	31.8	–17.2	32	67.6	35.6
Newton	59	44.1	–14.9	22	55.4	33.4
Cass	47	38.4	–8.6	34	61.3	27.3
Total			–61.8			162.4
Total Vote Change, 1992–2004			–115.9			471.5

Source: Website of the Texas Secretary of State.

these counties have small overall populations, so they added relatively few votes to either Bush's or Kerry's statewide totals. In two of the counties with the largest numbers of Hispanics (El Paso and Hidalgo), the Bush share of the 2004 vote was in the low-to-mid 40 percent range. These counties have 78 and 88 percent Hispanic populations, respectively. These findings confirm doubts about the accuracy of the statewide exit poll estimates for candidate preference among Hispanics. The Bush vote was much higher in the counties with the lowest numbers of Hispanics and in the counties with the lowest percentage of Hispanics.

THE PRESIDENTIAL ELECTIONS AND TEJANOS

The presidential primaries, which are open primaries in Texas, were held on March 9, 2004.[4] Five Democratic candidates were on the ballot: Howard Dean, John Edwards, John Kerry, Dennis Kucinich, and Al Sharpton. Kerry won 67 percent of the vote and 183 delegates, followed by Edwards with 14 percent of the votes and 10 delegates; all the other candidates received less than 6 percent of the votes. According to exit polls conducted by Edison Media Research and Mitofsky International,[5] 73 percent of Hispanic voters in Texas supported Kerry in the primary, while 13 percent supported Edwards and 7 percent voted for Dean.[6] Therefore, Hispanic voters were only slightly more supportive of Kerry than the overall Democratic primary voters in Texas. George Bush received 92.5 percent of the vote in the Republican primary, with the remaining 7.5 percent listed as "uncommitted."

Turning to the general presidential election in November, Texas has thirty-four Electoral College votes and 12,041,793 registered voters. Three candidates were on the ballot in Texas: George Bush, John Kerry, and Michael Badnarik, a Libertarian from Austin. Exit poll data collected on Election Day in Texas was contested because of issues involving the sampling methodology, so it is difficult to be sure about the Latino electorate in this state and nationally (Leal et al. 2005). Despite such problems, according to the Edison Media Research and Mitofsky International exit polls, approximately 20 percent of the voters in Texas were Hispanic. However, we can examine data from Texas counties with the highest number and percentage versus the lowest number and percentage of Hispanics in the state (table 6.2).

Table 6.2. Texas Voting in 2004, in Percent (number of votes in parenthesis)

County	2004 Voter Registration	2004 Turnout Total	Statewide Democrats	Kerry Support	Statewide Republicans	Bush Support
Counties with the Highest Number of Hispanics						
Harris	16.6	67.8	45.7	44.9	54.3	55.0
	(1,605,783)	(1,088,793)		(475,865)		(584,723)
Bexar	45.3	62.5	47.3	44.7	52.7	55
	(767,501)	(479,646)		(210,946)		(260,687)
El Paso	67.9	51.5	59.7	56.5	40.3	44
	(326,964)	(168,404)		(95,142)		(73,261)
Hidalgo	78.8	48	59.4	55	40.6	45
	(236,313)	(113,439)		(62,369)		(50,931)
Dallas	12.4	69.2	49.8	49.3	50.2	51
	(998,035)	(691,083)		(336,475)		(346,091)
Counties with the Highest Percentage of Hispanics						
Starr	94.4	39.2	78.3	73.8	21.7	26.0
	(25,291)	(9,904)		(7,199)		(2,552)
Webb	87.4	47.7	65.4	57.1	34.6	43
	(88,093)	(42,030)		(23,654)		(17,753)
Maverick	88.3	43.6	64.3	59.6	35.7	40
	(22,899)	(9,974)		(5,948)		(4,025)
Jim Hogg	89.7	58.6	73.7	65.4	26.3	35
	(3,588)	(2,104)		(1,344)		(712)
Zavala	88.5	20.2	78.2	75	21.8	25
	(6,926)	(3,474)		(2,332)		(777)

Table 6.2. Texas Voting in 2004, in Percent (number of votes in parenthesis) *continued*

County	*2004 Voter Registration*	*2004 Turnout Total*	*Statewide Democrats*	*Kerry Support*	*Statewide Republicans*	*Bush Support*
Counties with the Lowest Number of Hispanics						
Loving	8.9	4.2	27.6	16.7	72.4	83
	(192)	(81)		(13)		(65)
Roberts	2.8	77.9	11.9	9.1	88.1	91
	(652)	(508)		(46)		(461)
King	3.5	7.2	18.2	11.6	81.8	88
	(2,153)	(156)		(18)		(137)
Armstrong	2.3	70.2	18.3	17.1	81.7	83
	(1,419)	(996)		(170)		(826)
Delta	1.5	63.3	35.6	30.3	64.4	70
	(3,282)	(2,077)		(629)		(1,447)
Counties with the Lowest Percentage of Hispanics						
Tyler	1.4	64.8	42.9	34.5	57.1	66
	(12,198)	(7,903)		(2,659)		(5,043)
Lamar	1.2	67.2	37.2	30.7	62.8	59
	(26,137)	(17,562)		(5,338)		(12,054)
Sabine	1.1	70.7	39.0	32	61.0	68
	(6,659)	(4,708)		(1,476)		(3,138)
Newton	1	66.8	54.3	44.3	45.7	56
	(8,631)	(5,764)		(2,514)		(3,159)
Cass	.8	73.6	44.9	38.5	55.1	62
	(16,326)	(12,015)		(4,630)		(7,383)

Source: Author's calculations based on Texas elections data.

The vote choice among voters in high percentage and high number Hispanic counties is very interesting. Counties with the highest percentages of Hispanics voted solidly for Kerry, whereas counties with the highest numbers of Hispanics were split; that is, they supported both Bush and Kerry. Counties with the lowest number and percentages of Hispanics strongly supported Bush. George Bush, however, had a positive history with the voters of his home state, including Hispanics. Bush was elected governor of Texas on November 8, 1994, and he was reelected by a landslide in 1998. In those campaigns, Bush demonstrated an ability to win votes from historically Democratic groups in Texas, including, to some extent, Hispanics. Some have argued that he continued to appeal to Latino voters in his initial presidential bid and subsequent reelection; others question this theory (Gimpel 2003, 2004). However, we need to ask if Hispanic voters were mobilized in Texas in 2004, and if so, what strategies were used and by whom.

LATINO OUTREACH DURING THE CAMPAIGNS

The conventional wisdom is that several factors mobilize voters: issues and events, community groups, civic organizations, political parties, and the issues surrounding the presidential campaigns (Michelson 2003, 2006). In the 2004 elections in Texas, the Southwest Voter Registration Education Project (SVREP) and the Democratic and Republican Parties tried to mobilize Latinos.[7] SVREP had a national strategy that included targeting Texas Latinos as well as Hispanics in thirteen others states: Arizona, California, Colorado, Florida, Georgia, Idaho, Nevada, New Mexico, North Carolina, Oregon, Oklahoma, Utah, and Washington.

According to Texas Democratic Party staffers, outreach to the Hispanic community was limited. Local party entities received little or no funding from the national or state level; local party fund-raising events elicited a total of $17,000. At the state level, the Democratic Party was dealing with internal conflict between its various factions: Mexican American Democrats (MAD),[8] Tejano Democrats,[9] and the rest of the majority-Anglo executive party leadership. The focus of this conflict was the lack of Hispanics in staff and executive positions within the party infrastructure, as well as differing opinions regarding election procedures at the state convention and the outcome of those elections.

Despite these internal struggles and limited funds, local Democratic Party offices in South Texas engaged in a mobilization effort in the few Democratic strongholds left in the state by touring the major cities in the region by bus. Efforts were coordinated across local party entities to urge registered Hispanic voters to go to the polls, but because of their lack of available funds, staffers relied on free media coverage in both English and Spanish to publicize its tour before, during, and after each city's rally.[10] In interviews I conducted, staffers appeared to be frustrated with the lack of state-level support for these efforts.

After repeated attempts to bring John Kerry or John Edwards to the Rio Grande Valley for a speaking engagement to "rally the troops" and gain media attention,[11] it was Teresa Heinz Kerry who made an appearance and engaged in fundraising activities in mid-October. Heinz Kerry, speaking in Spanish, stated, "No se olviden que su voto es su voz" (Don't forget that your vote is your voice), and the crowd responded with chants of "Si, se puede!" (Yes, we can!) (Ovaska 2004). Elected officials from Cameron and Hidalgo Counties, including U.S. Congressmen Lloyd Doggett (D-Austin) and Rubén Hinojosa (D-Mercedes), who faced Republican challengers as a result of the controversial Texas redistricting, were onstage with Heinz Kerry (Bernstein 2004). While turnout at the civic center for Heinz Kerry was less than expected and many were disappointed that neither Kerry nor Edwards chose to campaign in the valley, local party leaders said they were "satisfied" with the rally. In response to the efforts of local Democrats, local newspapers reported that Hidalgo County Republican chair Hollis Rutledge said that Kerry does not understand the economy or culture of the Valley (Ovaska 2004). Nevertheless, Kerry-Edwards won the valley by a margin of 17 percentage points.

The Republican Party of Texas employed a very different strategy.[12] According to reports, a three-pronged approach was used: (1) talking about Bush's history with Hispanics in Texas in a positive light, (2) relying on Republican strength in the state, and (3) spreading a message about family values and moral issues through churches, especially Catholic churches, in high-density Hispanic areas. The last two strategies are most important as they explain why the Bush-Cheney campaign spent little effort, time, and energy in Texas and how they worked their Hispanic strategy in the state with the limited resources they chose to utilize.

The use of the "Catholic" strategy by the GOP and conservative groups is well documented. For example, Texas Republican Party chair Tina J. Benkiser and treasurer Susan Howard Chrane promoted Republican candidates, including President George W. Bush, by distributing literature and seeking votes at an Austin church event in March 2004 (Conn 2004). Further, according to the *National Catholic Reporter,* Republican National Convention delegates and other Bush supporters gathered on September 2 for what was called "the Catholic Outreach Rally" on the closing day of the convention. A retired bishop of Corpus Christi, Texas, offered the benediction at the rally: "Help them," Bishop Rene Gracida asked God, "to achieve the election of George W. Bush as president of this great nation" (Feuerherd 2004). Furthermore, Focus on the Family, a conservative group, reached out extensively to the Hispanic community using opposition to abortion rights and gay marriage as a cornerstone. This group aired ads on about two hundred Spanish-language radio stations and provided information to about thirteen thousand churches in an effort to lure Hispanic voters to support Bush (Puzzanghera 2004). Some link this strategy of reaching out to Hispanic communities through the churches to Bush's history in Texas (Curiel 2004). For example, it was reported that

> Cisneros, president and chief executive of American City Vista, a San Antonio company that builds urban housing, said the outreach at churches, particularly among Latino Catholics, appeared to help Bush, who enjoyed strong support from Latinos when he was governor of Texas. "The conversion of Latinos, if you will, has to be a top priority in their playbook," Cisneros said of Bush and his aides. "And because they're from Texas, they get it." (Puzzanghera 2004)

Finally, a select group of conservative bishops within the Church, for example, Archbishop Charles Chaput, from a diocese in Denver, Colorado, asserted that a vote for a pro-choice candidate is a moral failing that Catholics must confess before receiving communion (Dowd 2004; Kirkpatrick and Goodstein 2004; Toner 2004).[13] According to Kirkpatrick and Goodstein:

> The efforts of Archbishop Chaput and his allies are converging with a concerted drive for conservative Catholic voters by the Bush campaign. It has spent four years cultivating Catholic leaders, organizing more than 50,000 volunteers and hiring a corps of paid staff members to increase Catholic turnout. The campaign is pushing to break the traditional allegiance of Catholic voters to the Democratic Party, an affiliation that began to crumble with Ronald Reagan 24 years ago. (2004: 1)

Many priests followed Archbishop Chaput's lead, and parishioners at some Catholic churches in South Texas (part of the Diocese of Brownsville) were told specifically that they would "go to hell" if they voted for a pro-choice candidate like Kerry.

Despite both parties' efforts, it was clear that Hispanics across the state felt that both the Republican and Democratic presidential candidates largely ignored them. Some thought this indifference might be related to the fact that Texas was not a battleground state; rather it was largely considered a Republican state (Gimpel 2003, 2004; Navarrette 2004). In the end, voter turnout was low across the state, especially in the counties with the highest Latino populations—with the exception of Zavala County, where voter turnout increased significantly. Although Democratic staffers stated that they lost about five percentage points among Hispanics in 2004 as compared to 2000, they argued that the majority of Hispanic voters still supported the Kerry-Edwards ticket over Bush-Cheney. The major question is whether this loss of support among Hispanics for Democrat candidates in this election marks a permanent departure from politics as usual for Tejanos. Will Republican gains continue to be sustained or grow in the 2006 and 2008 elections? Unfortunately, these are questions that cannot be addressed at the time of this writing.[14]

REDISTRICTING AND CONFLICT IN URBAN AREAS

As King, Engstrom, and Riddlesperger (2004: 1) have stated, "Redistricting is the most purely political of all legislative activities as it reallocates political influence." The authors go on to say that "redistricting in the wake of the reappointment following the 2000 census was highlighted in several states by overt efforts to manipulate the partisan composition of the congressional delegation. This effort reached its peak in 2003 when the legislatures of Texas and Colorado attempted to redistrict congressional seats for a second time in the decade" (2).

During the first redistricting process in 2001, the Texas legislature was deeply divided along partisan lines. The result was that the legislative session closed without passing redistricting legislation; Governor Rick Perry (R) declined to call a special session to deal with the issue, and court cases were filed. In *Balderas et al. v. State of Texas* (Civil No. 6:01-CV-158), the U.S. District Court for the Eastern District of Texas issued an order adopting districts for the 2002 elections. The U.S. Supreme Court affirmed this decision on June 17, 2002. The outcome was a map that provided Republicans with the best chance since the 1870s to take control of both chambers of the Texas legislature, as well as pick up several seats in the Texas congressional delegation (Stutz 2002). King, Engstrom, and Riddlesperger (2004: 5) have argued that it was the Republican strategy to "revisit the issue of congressional district lines after the election of 2002, as the new state legislative districts would likely result in Republican majorities in both chambers in 2003." Former U.S. Representative Tom DeLay (R-Sugarland) was a moving force behind many of these efforts. As Republican Whip in 2001–2 and majority leader in 2003, DeLay raised millions of dollars in funding after consulting with Republicans in the Texas legislature and with Governor Perry on the issue of statewide redistricting.

During the 2003 legislative session, the new Republican majorities that emerged as a result of the *Balderas* map introduced legislation to replace the congressional, but not the state house or senate, districts drawn by the court. Texas Democrats unsuccessfully protested the legislation and eventually decided to walk out of the legislature to prevent a quorum (whereby at least two-thirds of the members of each chamber must be present for a vote) from being achieved. In May 2003 more than fifty Democrats stated that they were boycotting the legislature (Gaddie 2004). Governor Perry visited the House floor as members remained under a "call" that prohibited them from leaving the chamber as the search continued for the missing members (King, Engstrom, and Riddlesperger 2004).[15]

The Republican leadership moved to force Democrats' attendance, directing state law enforcement agencies to locate and return the legislators to Austin, the state's capital (Gaddie 2004). The Democratic legislators were found in Ardmore, Oklahoma, and requests were made to federal government agencies, such as the FBI and the U.S. Marshals, to return them to Texas. On May 16, after four days in Oklahoma, Republicans promised not to readdress redistricting during the regular session of the legislature, and the Democrats voluntarily returned to Austin. In keeping with their agreement, Republicans did not revisit redistricting until Governor Perry called a special session. The Texas House of Representatives approved a new map during the first days of the special session, but it could not be considered because of a longstanding tradition that required support from two-thirds of the members present. Consequently, the special session ended without a new redistricting plan.

Lieutenant Governor David Dewhurst then announced that if a second special session was held, he would dispense with the two-thirds rule for the Texas senate, and within thirty minutes of the end of the first special session a second special session was held. Eleven of the twelve senate Democrats left the state. They were found in Albuquerque, New Mexico, and said they would return only when Dewhurst promised to reinstate the two-thirds rule. During a monthlong standoff, the Democrats filed a lawsuit in the U.S. District Court seeking to prohibit law enforcement agents from arresting them on their return to Texas and challenging the right of the governor to call a special session on redistricting since a valid redistricting plan through 2011 had been created after the 2000 Census. A three-judge panel rejected the suit and held that the federal courts "have a duty . . . to walk gingerly into state issues" (Moritz 2003a). In turn, Republicans asked the Texas Supreme Court to compel the Democrats to return home and to fine them if they ignored the order; the all-Republican supreme court rejected the request without comment (Moritz 2003b). The second special session, too, ended without redistricting changes.

A third special session was called and focused on what a new redistricting map should look like; this brought about intraparty conflict among Republicans on the issue of redistricting in West Texas in which the Speaker preferred a congressional district centered on oil interests and an influential senator wanted a district designed around agricultural interests (Moritz 2003c). The House version of the redistricting bill, which favored the speaker's position, passed almost immediately, and the senate map favoring the interests of West Texas farmers passed soon thereafter. Another major difference between the two bills was that the senate version left U.S. Representative Martin Frost's (D) District 24 largely untouched.[16] The differences in the bills led to gridlock between the Texas house and senate: "Tom DeLay intervened and pushed through a plan that would maximize Republican opportunities to win control of the Texas delegation by splitting the districts of vulnerable Texas Democrats to limit their incumbency advantage in reelection bids" (King, Engstrom, and Riddlesperger 2004: 9–10). Not surprisingly, Democrats said the bill was illegal, and several lawsuits were filed immediately after its passage.

Three cases were consolidated for trial before the U.S. District Court for Eastern Texas. On January 6, 2004, a three-judge panel upheld the redistricting plan that the legislature passed in *Session et al. v. Perry et al.* (Civil Action No. 2:03-CV-354). Further, the U.S. Department of Justice issued a ruling that the congressional redistricting plan enacted in 2003 did not violate the Voting Rights Act of 1965 and could be used in the 2004 congressional elections. Appeals of the redistricting processes continued, as voters, the League of United Latin American Citizens (LULAC), and the G.I. Forum of Texas all filed cases, which were accepted by the U.S. Supreme Court. In *League of United Latin American Citizens v. Perry* (548 U.S. 399 [2006]), the Supreme Court ruled, by a vote of 5–4, that only District 23 of the 2003 Texas redistricting violated the Voting Rights Act. Old District 23 was a qualified protected majority-minority Latino district, while the newly created District 23 was in no shape or form a qualifying Latino district, largely due to moving one hundred thousand Latinos into neighboring District 28.

However, the Court refused to throw out the entire plan, ruling that the plaintiffs failed to state a sufficient claim of partisan gerrymandering. The opinion required lawmakers to adjust congressional district boundaries to comport with the Court's ruling, though the ruling does not threaten Republican gains as a result of the redistricting in Texas. Ordered by the justices to remedy this situation, a federal panel on

August 4, 2006, adjusted the lines of Districts 15, 21, 23, 25, and 28. The congressional district that serves the area northeast of San Antonio, District 21, is held by Lamar Smith (R). In the 2006 election, Lamar Smith was reelected, defeating veteran and college administrator John Courage with 60 percent of the vote. District 23 now runs along the majority of Texas's southwestern border with Mexico; the district is predominantly rural, with no major urban area, although it abuts the El Paso suburbs at its western point and the San Antonio suburbs at its eastern point. In 2007 Henry Bonilla, the Republican representative for District 23, was defeated by Democrat Ciro Rodriguez in a newly 61 percent Hispanic district.

Finally, District 28, which is now represented by Democrat Henry Cuellar, who assumed office in January 2005, serves a strip of land in deep South Texas starting south of San Antonio and ending at the U.S.-Mexico border. I address the other districts below.

Many have argued that the changes made in 2001 and 2003 in Texas were intended to unseat Democratic incumbents, mostly Anglos, and to make it more difficult for white Democratic candidates to win in urban and/or majority-minority areas (Gaddie 2004; King, Engstrom, and Riddlesperger 2004; Lindell 2004; Blum and Thernstrom 2005). Some primary election results may support these allegations. The Democratic primary election in the Ninth Congressional District in Houston serves as an illustration. Chris Bell, a white incumbent who was elected to office in 2002, faced Al Green, a strong black candidate. The campaigns were contentious, and racial voting played a significant role in the election results. In March 2004 Green, former Harris County justice of the peace and former president of Houston's chapter of the NAACP, received 66 percent of the vote to Bell's 31 percent. On receiving the election results Green stated, "We are now beyond the primary, and it is now time to start representing the people" (Hegstrom and Lezon 2004: 16). This quote is telling. Green did not have to gear up for a fight in the general election, where he would face Republican Arlette Molina, because Houston was in a heavily Democratic district, and therefore primary election results largely determine general election outcomes.

Many in the Houston metropolitan area have argued that the Republican redistricting plan, which was created to divide the Democratic Party and its constituents, was successful. Congresswoman Sheila Jackson Lee, a Houston Democrat, called the race a "tragedy" (Hegstrom and Lezon 2004). After the election results were released, Bell agreed with these sentiments and stated that the race was "divisive . . . and in some ways rather ugly," and he decided to take further action (Hegstrom and Lezon 2004). In June 2004, three months after the primary election, Bell filed ethics charged against Tom DeLay for his actions during the Texas redistricting procedures. In October of the same year, the U.S. House Ethics Committee admonished DeLay on two charges and left the third charge for a criminal investigation. A year later, in October 2005, a Texas court issued an arrest warrant for DeLay, requiring him to appear in Texas for booking on state conspiracy and money laundering charges; at that time, DeLay (R-Sugarland) stepped down as U.S. House majority leader (Gamboa 2005). Chris Bell concurrently attempted to build momentum for a gubernatorial campaign in 2006.[17]

Another controversial primary election was the Democratic primary of District 28 in the San Antonio area. Incumbent Ciro Rodriguez and challenger Henry Cuellar campaigned hard against each other and eventually went to court to settle allegations of ballot miscounting. Charges were made on both sides that the candidates were "closet Republicans." While Rodriguez had served as chair of the Hispanic Congressional Caucus, he endorsed Bush during the 2000 presidential election. It was also pointed out that Republican Governor Rick Perry had appointed Cuellar, a former Texas state representative (D-Laredo), to the position of secretary of state in Texas. Both candidates engaged in negative campaigning, which became quite intense and dominated the race. Once campaigning ended and the votes were in, District 28 was in for more controversy.

The first election results released called for a Rodriguez victory. These results were challenged by the Cuellar campaign. After a series of court decisions—and a series of recounts—Cuellar was declared the winner. In brief, Rodriguez won the election with 145 more votes than Cuellar out of a total 49,000 votes on March 9. Based on a recount conducted with votes that had never been counted in Webb and Zapata Counties, Cuellar won the election with 203 more votes than Rodriguez. A third recount was also conducted; it contended that Cuellar was still the winner but with only 58 more votes than Rodriguez (see table 6.3).

Throughout the course of these counts and recounts, forty-two applications for mail-in ballots in the names of deceased voters were found in the San Antonio area. Like Houston, San Antonio is a heavily Democratic district; therefore, despite the mudslinging and controversy of this primary election, the Democratic victor was able to set his sights on governing rather than the general election. In the end, Rodriguez vowed to run again in 2006 (Cortez 2004; Lozada 2004; Fund 2005).[18]

STATE AND LOCAL GENERAL ELECTIONS IN TEXAS

The 2003 redistricting plan also played a role in the general elections across the state. In the First Congressional District, now located solely in northeastern Texas, there was a tough race between incumbent Democrat Max Sandlin and Republican challenger Louie Gohmert. Sandlin, who had served as chief deputy whip for the Democratic Caucus since 1997, was a moderate Democrat running in a redistricted area that had been transformed into a heavily Republican district—major

Table 6.3. Results of Democratic Primary Elections in Competitive, Majority-Minority Areas

District	*Candidate*	*Percent Vote*	*Vote Number*	*Total Turnout*
9	Chris Bell (incumbent)	31.3	8,492	27,133
	Al Green	66.5	18,034	
25	Lloyd Doggett (incumbent)	64.4	40,306	62,611
	Leticia Hinojosa	35.6	22,305	
28	Ciro Rodriguez (incumbent)	49.8	24,448	49,099
	Henry Cuellar	50.2	24,651	

Source: Author's calculations based on Texas elections data.

cities with large numbers of Hispanic voters such as Dallas were moved out of the district. The local papers labeled Sandlin the underdog, although he stated that he had confidence in his ability to win because he was a Blue Dog (fiscally moderate) Democrat. His Republican opponent, former state appeals court judge Louie Gohmert, had the support of Vice President Cheney, who attended fund-raisers on his behalf. Although both candidates spent a great deal of money during their campaigns—Sandlin $1.7 million and Gohmert $1.8 million—Gohmert won with 62 percent of the vote, compared to Sandlin's 38 percent. Because the new district boundaries played such an important role in his defeat, Sandlin hoped that the courts would declare the Texas redistricting map unconstitutional, thereby requiring a special election. In October 2004 the U.S. Supreme Court gave hope to him and other Democrats by requiring the Texas courts to review the plan. Cases moved through the Texas judicial system for the next six months, and on June 10, 2005, a federal panel ruled in favor of the state. The next step was a direct appeal to the U.S. Supreme Court (Cervantez 2004). However, the Court did not rule to change this district.

Another important race was in U.S. House District 2 between Ted Poe (R) and the incumbent Nick Lampson (D) in the Houston metropolitan area. Redistricting, again, played a major role in this race as Lampson's U.S. House District 9 was altered to include the heavily Republican Beaumont area. George H. W. Bush was a constituent in this new district, and the former president endorsed the former felony court judge from Houston, Ted Poe. Although Bush's endorsement of a Republican candidate was not surprising, it changed the context of the debates. Bush commented that Poe would better "support his son," thereby bringing to the fore issues such as the war in Iraq and President G. W. Bush's tax cuts. Social issues also played an important role as Poe clearly stated that he was firmly against abortion and would support a ban on gay marriage. As a result, Lampson, considered the underdog in this redrawn district, was constantly on the defensive—arguing that he supported President Bush on the war in Iraq and on some of the administration's proposed tax cuts. In addition, Poe received financial backing from the National Republican Congressional Committee. While Poe won that seat, Lampson stated that he would challenge Tom DeLay for his seat in the 2006 elections, as 120,000 of his former constituents were moved into DeLay's district under the redistricting plan. Lampson followed through on his word and was the representative in DeLay's old district, District 22, until November 2008, when he was defeated by Republican Pete Olson.

FIGHT FROM START TO FINISH?

Congressional District 25, known by some as the "fajita district," was also redrawn. It encompasses over three hundred miles from Austin to the Rio Grande Valley (RGV) along the Texas-Mexican border. The incumbent of former Congressional District 10, Lloyd Doggett, was a relative unknown in South Texas. He faced RGV district court judge Leticia Hinojosa in the Democratic primary. Although Hinojosa was considered the underdog, she received the endorsement of the Austin Tejano Democrats. Doggett received endorsements from teachers and other unions such as the United Farm Workers. While Doggett had a clear advantage in terms of political and campaigning experience and a war chest of $2.3 million, some were concerned that an Anglo candidate from Austin could not win votes from South Texas Hispanics. In the end, Doggett demonstrated that a grassroots campaign is an effective strategy in the RGV: he won the primary election with 64 percent of the votes (see table 6.3). Doggett then faced Republican Becky Armendariz Klein in the general election in November 2004, another controversial race (see table 6.4).

The Doggett campaign stated publicly that they believed Klein was the "hand-picked candidate" of Karl Rove, a Bush adviser, and Tom DeLay. Klein, former chair of the Texas Public Utility Commission and former policy director for Governor Bush, had a strong showing in the Republican primary, winning 60 percent of the vote in the district. Allegations were made that Klein was running in the general election against Doggett not in order to win but in order to gain favor with the Bush administration and Republicans by pushing Doggett to spend his war chest. In addition, Klein was considered a potential candidate for appointment to the Federal Communications Commission or the Federal Energy Regulatory Commission.[19] While Doggett outraised and outspent Klein almost 3 to 1, it is important to note that utility and communications companies such as SBC Communications and Halliburton provided approximately 60 percent (more than $800,000) of Klein's funding (Labaton 2005). Despite this Latina challenge, Doggett was able to win by a 37-point margin, but his campaign maintained that the redistricting and subsequent Republican efforts were targeted to oust him from office and/or weaken his standing in his district. As a result of the *LULAC* case, this district now serves Central Texas. Doggett won his bid for reelection and continues to serve Texas's District 25 at the time of this writing.

Table 6.4. Results of the 2004 General Elections in Contested, Redistricted U.S. House Districts

District	*Candidate*	*Percent Vote*	*Vote Number*	*Total Turnout*
1	Louie Gohmert (R)	61.5	157,068	255,507
	Max Sandlin (D, incumbent)	37.7	96,281	
2	Ted Poe (R)	55.5	139,951	252,038
	Nick Lampson (D, incumbent)	43.0	108,156	
9	Arlette Molina (R)	26.6	42,132	158,566
	Al Green (D)	72.2	114,462	
17	Arlene Wohlgemuth (R)	47.4	116,049	244,748
	Chet Edwards (D, incumbent)	51.2	125,309	
19	Randy Neugebauer (R, incumbent)	58.3	136,459	233,514
	Charles Stenholm (D, incumbent)	40.1	93,531	
25	Rebecca Armendariz Klein (R)	30.8	49,252	160,217
	Lloyd Doggett (D, incumbent)	67.6	108,309	
28	James F. Hopson (R)	38.6	69,538	180,166
	Henry Cuellar (D)	59.0	106,323	
32	Pete Sessions (R, incumbent)	54.3	109,859	202,236
	Martin Frost (D, incumbent)	44.0	89,030	

Source: Author's calculations based on Texas elections data.

Note: After the redistricting maps were drawn, Districts 19 and 32 included two incumbent candidates from what were previously different districts.

After the 2004 elections, only three of eleven Democrats representing Texas in the U.S. Congress were Anglos. The Texas house had fewer Anglo than Hispanic Democrats, and minority Democrats outnumbered Anglo Democrats in the senate (Blum and Thernstrom 2005).

OPPORTUNITIES FOR HISPANICS CREATED BY HISPANICS

Several Hispanics were elected to local offices for the first time in 2004. For example, Lupe Valdez, a former law enforcement officer, defeated three challengers in the Democratic primary election and then Republican candidate Danny Chandler in the general election to become the first Latina—and the first openly gay—sheriff of Dallas County. Valdez received support from the Gay and Lesbian Victory Fund in Washington, D.C., which caused her Republican opponent and the Eagle Forum to strengthen their opposition to her candidacy (Moreno 2004). In the end, despite the opposition she faced from them and from the sheriff's department unions, Valdez garnered 51 percent of the vote in the general election.

Dallas County also elected its first Hispanic district court judge in the 303rd State Family Court District. Dennise Garcia (D) defeated Beth Maultsby (R) by a margin of 50.54 percent to 49.46 percent. Garcia (2005) stated that she was elected because voters "believed that the Dallas courts should be both qualified and diverse." Garcia's and Valdez's victories are the result, in part, of increases in the Hispanic population in the county and increases in Latino voter turnout (Moreno 2004). This trend of electing local Hispanic officials, or more specifically, Latinas, may continue as the complexion in more counties, especially those that include urban areas, becomes increasingly "brown."

FINAL THOUGHTS

I have discussed three unique general themes of the 2004 elections in Texas. First, Texas was not a "purple" state, and because it was not considered a battleground state, Texas as a whole and Tejanos in particular did not receive much attention from the candidates, campaigns, and parties. As a result, voter turnout was depressed in Latino communities. As has been demonstrated on numerous occasions, Republicans win when voter turnout is low—which is precisely why local Democratic Party affiliates attempted to mobilize voters. The key for Democrats in Texas is getting out the vote, especially in local races, as the cases of Valdez and Garcia reveal.

Second, what little attention was paid to Hispanic voters reached them through a new vehicle, the Catholic Church. Whether this strategy was successful for Bush and the Republicans is still unclear and will likely remain so due to the exit poll data controversies. Future research should ask the following questions: What repercussions or advantages, if any, resulted from this strategy? Will Democrats pursue political mobilization strategies through Catholic churches in Latino communities in the future? In the end, it may be safe to say that the Bush campaign approached Hispanic voters exactly the way it did everybody else, "by reaching out for cultural conservatives, who in this case just happened to be Hispanic" (Johnson 2004). As Johnson (2004) states, "The Kerry campaign sought votes as if Hispanics, as in the past, were reliably Democrat. The advertisements emphasized issues like immigration and economic opportunity and used few attack advertisement techniques, omnipresent on English-language television, to close the deal."

Finally, the saga of redistricting is of particular importance. Many of the most contested districts that were redrawn in 2004 have high numbers and concentrations of Latino residents and voters. The opinions of the U.S. Supreme Court on the Texas redistricting cases will therefore reverberate through other states with similar demographics, and the impact could be long lasting.

Overall, two concerns make the Texas case noteworthy in U.S. politics more generally. First, have Hispanics shifted to the Republican Party in Texas—and in the country as a whole? Andy Hernandez, a political analyst and past president of the SVREP, stated that young Latinos today are growing up with Republicans in political power and they are becoming increasingly Evangelical: "There are now more conservative Christians in the Latino community. . . . Numerically, there has been huge growth over the last 25 years" (Rodriguez 2004). Although major shifts are unlikely, political and cultural socialization could make a difference in future Hispanic voting patterns in Texas.

Finally, one of the most important contemporary national issues is immigration. Texas clearly has a major stake in that debate. While President Bush has advocated guest worker programs and paths to U.S. citizenship for undocumented workers, Republican elected officials in Texas have taken a hard-line stance against those policies and have focused their efforts on border security issues. In spring 2005 approximately 500,000 people in major cities protested against these policies.[20] Will there be a backlash against Republicans as a result of these differences? Texas may serve as a test case for the nation because all statewide and legislative offices will be up for election in 2006. Given that approximately one in five Hispanics in the United States lives in Texas, the electoral response of Hispanics in the state could have a significant impact on national trends.

NOTES

1. The terms *Tejanos* and *Texas Hispanics* are used interchangeably throughout this chapter, as they reflect the preferences of the population being discussed.

2. Redistricting is the process by which the boundaries of elective districts are periodically redrawn to maintain equal representation on the basis of population. Article III, Section 28, of the Texas Constitution requires the Texas legislature to redistrict both houses (the Texas House of Representatives and the state senate) at its first regular session after publication of the federal decennial census. The legislature meets in odd-numbered years. If the legislature fails to adopt a redistricting plan by the end of the legislative session, a Legislative Redistricting Board (LRB) consisting of the lieutenant governor, comptroller of public accounts, Speaker of the House of Representatives, attorney general, and commissioner of the General Land Office shall convene within ninety days of adjournment and adopt a plan within sixty days of convening.

The legislature did not adopt a plan for either the Texas house or senate in 2001. The LRB met on June 6, 2001, for an organizational meeting. On July 25, 2001, the LRB voted on plans for both houses of the legislature. The adopted plans were then submitted to the U.S. Justice Department for approval required under the federal Voting Rights Act. Ultimately, the Justice Department approved the senate plan and objected to the house plan. Subsequently, the courts determined the house plan. In addition to redistricting the Texas house and senate, the legislature must redistrict congressional districts; again this is usually done at the first regular session after publication of the federal census. The legislature failed to adopt a congressional plan during the 77th legislative session in 2001. A plan was finally approved through litigation.

3. Approximately 7.6 million residents; this number and percentage are up slightly from the 2000 data. U.S. Census Factfinder 2005 (http://factfinder.census.gov/).

4. It is important to note that early voting began on February 20, 2004. Also, Texas has 195 pledged and 37 unpledged delegates. Of the 195 pledged delegates, 127 are district-level (based on results of a given district's binding primary), 43 are at-large, and 25 are "party leader and elected official" (PLEO). Of the 37 unpledged delegates, 34 are PLEO delegates and three are add-ons selected at the state Democratic convention on June 19, 2004.

5. Again, there has been some controversy regarding the results of exit poll data and Latino voting in the 2004 elections. The Texas results are especially controversial, and some exit poll data have still not been released. See Leal et al. 2005 for more information.

6. Interviews in the exit poll are conducted with voters as they leave the polling place immediately after voting.

7. SVREP is a national nonprofit, nonpartisan organization committed to the political empowerment of Latino communities through voter registration, voter education, and voter participation. SVREP was established in San Antonio, Texas, in 1974 by the late William C. Velasquez to encourage civic and political participation in Latino and other ethnic communities. Since its inception, SVREP has registered more than 2.2 million Latino voters throughout the Southwest and Florida. SVREP has offices in San Antonio, Los Angeles, Phoenix, and Miami.

8. MAD, a statewide organization of Democrats founded in 1975 to promote the interests of Mexican Americans, represented a shift away from the nationalist politics of the Raza Unida party.

9. The Tejano Democrats came together in 1994, after many of them walked out of the state convention of MAD.

10. Democratic Party insiders stated that since voter registration in the area is relatively high, less time and energy were spent on registration drives and more time was spent on a get-out-the-vote campaign.

11. The Rio Grande Valley is an area located in the southernmost tip of Texas. It lies along the northern bank of the Rio Grande, which separates Mexico from the United States. The region is made up of four counties: Starr, Hidalgo, Willacy, and Cameron. As of January 1, 2007, the Texas State Data Center estimated the population of the Rio Grande Valley at 1,139,581. More than 80 percent of the residents are Hispanic or Latino. The largest city is Brownsville (Cameron County), followed by McAllen (Hidalgo County). Other major cities include Harlingen, Mission, Edinburg, and Pharr.

12. Republican Party officials were contacted for interviews on numerous occasions. No official response was provided.

13. Some have pointed out that the archbishop failed to mention that the Catholic Church also stands against capital punishment and so-called unjust wars.

14. Exit polls in Texas in 2004 have come under tremendous scrutiny (see Teiexeira 2004; Leal et al. 2005).

15. For more, see "Texas House Paralyzed by Democratic Walkout." www.cnn.com/2003/ALLPOLITICS/05/13/texas.legislature/.

16. This is the congressional district that serves a suburban area between Fort Worth and Dallas.

17. While he won the Democratic nomination, he was defeated in a four-candidate race.

18. As indicated earlier, he did return to Congress in 2006 by unseating incumbent Republican Representative Henry Bonilla.

19. It appears that Klein, while seriously considered for these positions, did not receive either appointment. The president nominated Kevin Martin to the FCC in March 2005, and Joseph Kelliher was appointed to FERC in July 2005.

20. Figures range from 439,500 to 593,500 people marching in protest in the following cities: Amarillo, Austin, Bryan, Dallas, El Paso, Fort Worth, Houston, and San Antonio. (Figures from the Rio Grande Valley are not included.)

REFERENCES

Bernstein, Jake. 2004. "Cruelty Thy Name Is Redistricting." *Texas Observer,* February 27. www.texasobserver.org/article.php?aid=1579.

Bishop, Bill. 2004a. "The Great Divide: An Utterly Polarizing U.S. Election." *Austin American-Statesman,* December 4.

———. 2004b. "A Starkly Polarizing U.S. Election; Not Since World War II Has a Presidential Vote So Split the Major Parties, Results Show." *Austin American-Statesman,* December 5, A1.

Blum, Edward, and Abagail Thernstrom. 2005. "Executive Report of the Bullock-Gaddie Expert Report on Texas." American Enterprise Institute for Public Policy, October 10. www.aei.org/include/pub_print.asp. Accessed August 25, 2008.

Castillo, Mariano. 2004. "District 15 Race Could Be Closer than Expected." *San Antonio Express-News,* October 26, 8A.

Cervantez, Jessica. 2004. "Gohmert Defeats Sandlin." Channel 9 KTRE News, November 3. www.ktre.com/Global/story.asp?s=864214. Accessed August 25, 2008.

CNN. 2003. "Texas House Paralyzed by Democratic Walkout: Redistricting at Issue." May 19. www.cnn.com/2003/ALLPOLITICS/05/13/texas.legislature/. Accessed February 9, 2009.

Conn, Joe. 2004. "Watchdog Group Seeks Action from Federal Tax Agency against Westover Hills Church of Christ." www.au.org/site/News2?page=

NewsArticle&id=6520&abbr=pr&security=1002&news_iv_ctrl=1241. Accessed March 12, 2004.

Cortez, Tricia. 2004. "Rodriguez Files Brief with Appeals Court." *Laredo Morning Times,* May 22. http://madmax.lmtonline.com/textarchives/o52204/s4.htm. Accessed August 25, 2008.

Curiel, Carolyn. 2004. "How Hispanics Voted Republican." *New York Times,* November 8.

Dowd, Maureen. 2004. "Vote and Be Damned." *New York Times,* October 17, sec. 4, p. 11.

Feuerherd, Joe. 2004. "Battling the 'Heretics' at the Republican National Convention; Former Corpus Christi Bishop Prays for Bush Victory." *National Catholic Reporter,* September 8. www.nationalcatholicreporter.org/washington/wnb090804.htm.

Fund, John. 2005. "Un Nuevo Día?" *Wall Street Journal,* April 5. www.opinionjournal.com/diary/?id=110004909.

Gaddie, Ronald Keith. 2004. "The Texas Redistricting, Measure for Measure." *Extensions* (Fall): 19–24.

Gamboa, Suzanne. 2005. "Texas Court Issues Warrant for DeLay." Associated Press Online, Washington Dateline, October 19.

Garcia, Dennise. 2004. "A Message from Judge Garcia." Candidate Web site. www.dennisegarcia.com/fromdennise.htm. Accessed December 1, 2005.

Garcia, Guillermo X. 2004. "District 25 Rivals Square Off over E-mails." *San Antonio Express-News,* October 28.

Gimpel, James G. 2003. "Latinos and the 2002 Election: Republicans Do Well When Latinos Stay Home." In-house report, Center for Immigration Studies, January. www.cis.org/articles/2002/back203.html.

———. 2004. "Losing Ground or Staying Even: Republicans and the Politics of the Latino Vote." In-house report, Center for Immigration Studies, October. www.cis.org/articles/2004/back1004.html.

Gómez, Lisa Marie. 2004. "Why Don't Hispanic Polls Seem to Add Up?" *San Antonio Express-News,* November 7, 12A.

Guerra, Fernando J. 1992. "Conditions Not Met: California Elections and the Latino Community." In *From Rhetoric to Reality: Latino Politics in the 1988 Elections,* ed. Rodolfo O. de la Garza and Louis DeSipio, 99–107. Boulder, CO: Westview Press.

Halbfinger, David. 2003. "Across U.S., Redistricting as a Never-Ending Battle." *New York Times,* July 1, 1A.

Hegstrom, Ed, and Dale Lezon. 2004. "Al Green: Green's Supporters Jubilant." *Houston Chronicle,* March 10, 16A.

Johnson, Kirk. 2004. "Hispanic Voters Declared Their Independence." *New York Times,* November 9.

King, James, Richard Engstrom, and James Riddlesperger. 2004. "Redistricting in Texas and Colorado: Questions of Process and Impact." Paper presented at the Annual Meeting of the American Political Science Association, Chicago, IL, September 2–5.

King, Michael. 2004. "Vote for Show, Map for Dough." *Austin Chronicle,* March 10.

Kirkpatrick, David D., and Laurie Goodstein. 2004. "Group of Bishops Using Influence to Oppose Kerry." *New York Times,* October 12, 1A.

Labaton, Stephen. 2005. "Powell Is Stepping Down as Chairman of FCC." *New York Times,* January 21, 1A.

Leal, David, Matt Barreto, Jongho Lee, and Rodolfo de la Garza. 2005. "The Latino Vote in the 2004 Election." *PS: Political Science and Politics* 38: 41–50.

Lindell, Chuck. 2004. "Redistricting's Endgame Is Here." *Austin American-Statesman,* November 2, A5.

Lozada, James. 2004. "District 28 Races Head to Court." News 8 Austin, April 1. http://news8austin.com/content/headlines/?ArID=10253IDSecID=2.

Martinez, Valerie J. 1996. "Unfulfilled Expectations for Political Gains in Texas." In *Ethnic Ironies: Latino Politics in the 1992 Elections,* ed. Rodolfo O. de la Garza and Louis DeSipio, 113–29. Boulder, CO: Westview Press.

Michelson, Melissa. 2006. "Politics at the Grassroots: Mobilizing Latino Voters." In *Black and Latino/a Politics: Issues in Political Development in the United States,* ed. William E. Nelson Jr. and Jessica Lavariega Monforti, 235–48. Miami, FL: Barnhardt and Ashe.

Michelson, Melissa, and Scott J. Susin. 2004. "What's in a Name: The Power of Fusion Politics in a Local Election." *Polity* 36, no. 2 (January): 301–23.

Montoya, Lisa J. 2005. "Still Waiting in the Wings: Latinos in the 2000 Texas Elections." In *Muted Voices: Latinos and the 2000 Elections,* ed. Rodolfo O. de la Garza and Louis DeSipio, 163–72. Lanham, MD: Rowman and Littlefield.

Moreno, Sylvia. 2004. "Democrats Gaining a Foothold in Texas." *Washington Post,* November 10.

Moritz, John. 2003a. "Court Won't Block Redistricting Effort." *Fort Worth Star-Telegram,* September 13, 1, 15A.

———. 2003b. "Texas 11 Win Battle in State's High Court." *Fort Worth Star-Telegram,* August 12, 1, 11A.

———. 2003c. "Remap Strain Shows on GOP." *Fort Worth Star-Telegram,* September 17.

Navarrette, Ruben, Jr. 2004. "Latino Voters Being Targeted All Wrong." *Puerto Rico Herald,* October 4, 1, 4B.

Ovaska, Sarah. 2004. "A Wife's Work: Teresa Heinz Rallies Valley Support for Kerry Campaign." *Monitor,* October 11, 1.

Puzzanghera, Jim. 2004. "Latino Support Helped Bush Sway Election, Analysts Say; GOP Outreach at Churches Aided President with Nationwide Gains." *San Jose Mercury News,* November 4, 7A.

Rodriguez, Ken. 2004. "More Latinos Identifying with Republicans and Independents." *San Antonio Express-News,* May 14, 3A.

Shapiro, Robert Y. 2005. "Introduction: Awaited Voices: Latinos and U.S. Elections." In *Muted Voices: Latinos and the 2000 Elections,* ed. Rodolfo O. de la Garza and Louis DeSipio, 1–12. Lanham, MD: Rowman and Littlefield.

Stutz, Terrence. 2002. "GOP Expecting to Grab House; Redistricting Tilted Several Seats Away from Democrats." *Dallas Morning News,* January 3. www.fairvote.org/redistricting/reports/remanual/txnews5.htm#tilted. Accessed August 25, 2008.

Texas Legislative Council Report. 2004. "County General Election Analysis: 2004 General Election, Spanish Surname Data." RED-M700.

Teiexeira, Ruy. 2004. "44 Percent of Hispanics Voted for Bush?" *AlterNet,* November 24. www.alternet.org/election04/20606/. Accessed February 9, 2009.

Tolson, Mike. 2004. "Latinos' Support for Bush Debated." *Houston Chronicle,* November 6, A4.

Toner, Robin. 2004. "Conservatives Try to Exploit Catholic Democrats' Views." *New York Times,* April 20, 17A.

Chapter Seven

Why California Matters

How California Latinos Influence Presidential Elections

MATT A. BARRETO, RICARDO RAMÍREZ,
LUIS R. FRAGA, AND FERNANDO GUERRA

As was the case in 2000, California was a safe Democratic state in 2004. Although California provides 55, or just over 20 percent, of the 270 Electoral College votes necessary to win the White House, neither George W. Bush nor John Kerry spent much money in the state. In the most expensive presidential election in the nation's history, in which campaigns spent a combined total of more than $600 million, less than $1 million, a mere 2 percent of total campaign advertising expenditures, was spent in the Golden State. Early polls showed Kerry with a fifteen-point margin over Bush (DiCamillo and Field 2004). In comparison, more than $40 million was spent in Ohio, $50 million in Florida, and $60 million in Pennsylvania—all states that were much more competitive. In the end, Kerry handily won California by more than one million votes.

Throughout the campaign, however, California played an important role as both presidential campaigns focused fund-raising efforts there. The Kerry-Edwards campaign raised a full 20 percent of all its contributions from California, a larger proportion than it received from any other state. The Bush-Cheney ticket received 13 percent of all its contributions from California; only Texas provided more money to the Bush campaign than did the nation's most populous state.

One could also make the argument that California was relevant to the 2004 campaign as a target of attack for the GOP, especially the Bush campaign; gay marriage became a pillar of their overall appeal to traditional, so-called family values voters. In San Francisco, Mayor Gavin Newsom used his authority to legalize gay marriage. Pictures of lesbians and gay men standing on the steps of San Francisco City Hall appeared in many newspapers across the nation (CNN.com 2004b). Although the California courts would soon overturn his decision (Case 4265 2005), the episode served as further evidence that on issues related to sexuality, portions of California were different from the majority preferences of voters in many other states. We must remember that eleven states enacted legal bans on gay marriage in popular referendums held at the same time as the 2004 presidential election.

It was not surprising, therefore, when many scholars, pollsters, and pundits stated that 2004 once again demonstrated that Latino voters in California, like the state as a whole, were largely irrelevant in the national election (Helton 2004) and may have suffered because neither fund-raising nor gay marriage were especially relevant to Latinos. Thus to the extent that these issues influenced the state's marginal role in the election and were used to mobilize conservative white voters in other states, Latinos may have been even more marginalized than were other California Democrats.

We argue, however, that it is not accurate to characterize the impact of California Latino voters as limited in the 2004 election in four distinct respects, which we explore in this chapter. First, Latino voters were again critically important contributors to the statewide electoral majority that keeps the largest state in the nation safely Democratic. Continuing a pattern set in the mid-1990s, Latinos have consistently voted at a two-to-one rate in favor of Democrats in major elections. Moreover, the projected growth in the Latino population and its related statewide electoral influence suggest that Latinos are likely to continue to be major contributors to California remaining a safe Democratic state (see Appendix A for overall statistics on the Latino and non-Latino population and electorate in California).

Second, Latino voters in California not only remained loyal Democrats; they also sustained their coethnic representational gains for yet another election cycle. Interestingly, this does not occur among Latinos in both political parties. While elected Anglo Republicans replaced Latino Republicans, Democratic Latino candidates successfully won additional seats and defended most of their incumbent seats at both the congressional and state legislative levels. As a result, California's Latinos have further solidified their influence within the national and state legislative delegations of the Democratic Party. In addition, the Democratic preferences of Latino voters demonstrated in the California 2004 election continue to provide a direct incentive to the Republican Party to consider how it can best integrate more Latinos in its ranks (Nuño 2007). Despite the election of Arnold Schwarzenegger as governor in the recall election of 2003, Republicans are still at a systematic disadvantage relative to Democrats. Latino voters in California serve as a constant reminder to Republicans of the long-term costs of becoming tagged the anti-immigrant, anti-Latino party, whose statewide victory is possible only with a solid white bloc vote.

Third, as a safe Democratic state, California sets fundamental parameters within which all presidential and related national campaigning occurs. Primary among these is setting the baseline strategy for campaign spending in more competitive states. When California is not in play, both political parties can spend substantial sums of money elsewhere, in more competitive states. Interestingly, however, California was still a crucial state to both political parties in national legislative elections. California provides among the largest number of both Democratic and Republican members to the House of Representatives, and California voters still drive the national legislative influence of both political parties in fundamental ways. At present, California sends thirty-three Democrats and twenty Republicans to the House. Only Texas sends more Republicans to the federal lower chamber—twenty-one after the 2003 redistricting process (reduced to nineteen after the 2006 midterm elections).

Finally, we conclude by looking forward to the next two presidential elections in 2008 and 2012. How likely is it that Latino voters will keep California as a solidly blue, Democratic state? How many Latino voters does the Republican Party need to consistently recruit to significantly enhance its statewide competitiveness in the most populous state in the nation? What strategies might be most effective appeals to Latino voters either to maintain their loyalty as Democrats or to provide them incentives to become Republican partisans? The answers to these questions point to the influential role that Latino voters will play in future California and national politics.

THE LATINO VOTE IN CALIFORNIA: 1980–2004

In 2004 Latinos in California voted heavily in favor of Democratic presidential candidate John Kerry over Republican George W. Bush. While the exact results of the Latino vote are not known due to questions surrounding exit polling techniques in 2004 (Olivera 2004; Gómez 2004; see Leal et. al. 2005 for a comparative analysis of polls conducted in 2004), all polls noted a consistent pattern of Kerry support. Comparing four polls of Latinos in this state and conducting an analysis of precinct returns, we estimate that Kerry won the Latino vote in California by a margin of 72 to 27 percent (see table 7.1). Although the state of California and its fifty-five electoral votes went to the Democrats (54 to 45 percent), neither the Latino vote nor the state as a whole was always a sure thing for the Democrats. According to polling data from the Field Poll, California native Ronald Reagan raised his share of the Latino vote in his presidential bids from 35 percent in 1980 to 45 percent in 1984 (when he carried 59 percent of the statewide vote). Since then, Latino partisanship has become markedly more Democratic while their share of the overall state electorate has doubled (Barreto and Ramírez 2004).

After 1996, when Latinos made up more than 10 percent of all voters in the state, more than 70 percent of whom voted Democratic, it is no coincidence that California became an easy win for the Democrats. As Latino voter registration grew in the mid- to late 1990s, the Republican Party continued to emphasize anti-immigrant ballot measures that led new Latino registrants to check the "Democrat" box on their registration cards (Segura, Falcon, and Pachon 1997; Ramírez 2007; Barreto

Table 7.1. California Latino Vote in 2004 Presidential Election

	Kerry	*Bush*	*% of State*
National Exit Poll	63	32	21
Los Angeles Times	68	31	14
Willie C. Velasquez	71	27	19
Tomás Rivera (preelection)	76	23	n/a
Precinct Analysis	74	25	16
Barreto et al. estimate	72	27	17

Source: Results of California polls and authors' analysis.

and Woods 2005). In an analysis of voter registration records in Los Angeles County between 1992 and 1998, Barreto and Woods (2005) found that just 10 percent of new Latino registrants affiliated with the Republican Party as a direct result of the three so-called anti-Latino propositions in California. What is more, the anti-Latino initiatives motivated many new Latinos to vote. Pantoja, Ramírez, and Segura (2001) found that Latinos who naturalized and registered to vote during the 1990s were significantly more likely to turn out to vote than were immigrant Latino voters in other states. The result was more Latinos registering and voting as Democrats than in previous years.

The 2000 election suggested that the anti-Latino era might be over, however. Republican presidential candidate George W. Bush used his closeness to and understanding of Latino voters in Texas to rally support for the Republican ticket in the Latino community—quite the opposite of the Republican strategy during California Governor Pete Wilson's administration from 1991 to 1999 (Nuño 2007). Even as Bush attempted to introduce a new compassionate face to the Republican Party, the California Republican Party had an image problem with Latino voters. A survey conducted by the Tomás Rivera Policy Institute during the 2000 election revealed that 53 percent of Latino voters in California still associated the Republican Party with former Governor Wilson, a chief proponent of the anti-immigrant Proposition 187 (TRPI 2000). The result was strong Latino support for Democrat Al

Gore in 2000, propelling the Democrats to their third straight victory in California after losing the state in 1980, 1984, and 1988. Figure 7.1 illustrates that as the Latino vote grows in influence, California becomes a more Democratic state.

In addition to voting in presidential elections, Latinos in California have also become consistent Democratic voters in other statewide elections since the Reagan era. Statewide results indicate that Latinos voted two-to-one on average in support of Democratic candidates for governor and the U.S. Senate in every election between 1992 and 2002 (Barreto and Ramírez 2004). Although some may view the 2003 Gubernatorial Recall election as a potential shift away from the Democratic Party (Marinucci 2003), most analyses now concur that it is not valid to infer trends from the unique circumstances and context of this election and, further, that the Republican surge was not long lasting (Kousser 2006). The recall election, however, highlights just how important Latino voters are to the Democratic Party in California; in part

Figure 7.1. Percent of California Presidential Vote Won by a Democrat, 1980–2004

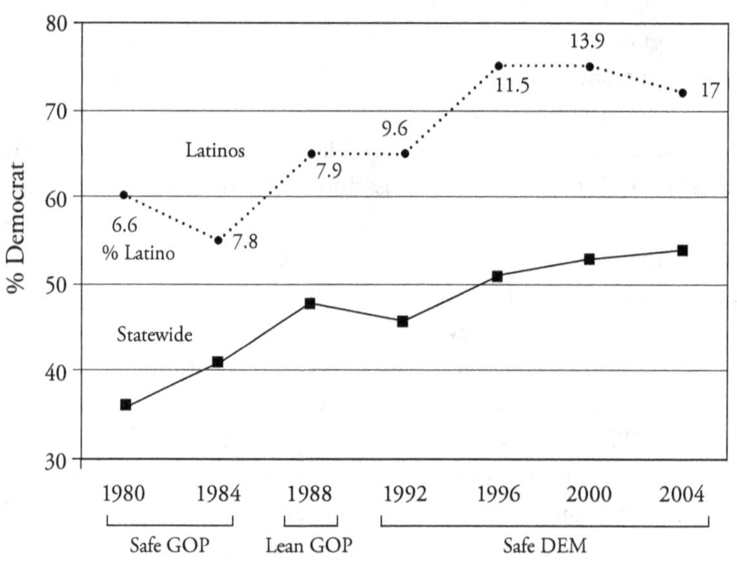

Source: Los Angeles Times exit polls; Tomás Rivera Policy Institute polls.

due to the approximately ten-point drop in Latino support rates for Democratic candidates, Democratic Governor Gray Davis was recalled from office and replaced with Republican candidate Arnold Schwarzenegger (DeSipio and Masuoka 2006). Had Latinos turned out at slightly higher rates and voted at their average support rate for the Democratic candidates, Davis would not have been recalled. While the peculiarities of the 2003 recall election are unlikely ever to be reproduced in a national presidential election, the outcome reveals that Latinos are a key component to Democratic success in California.

THE 2004 ELECTION IN CALIFORNIA

Although California had a new Republican governor, it was never considered in play during the 2004 presidential election given its vast size and expensive media markets. While Schwarzenegger gained office on a surge of anti–Gray Davis sentiment, this did not carry over to national Democratic figures, namely, John Kerry. Instead, it was localized to California and personalized specifically to unfavorable ratings and opinions of Democratic Governor Davis, resulting in his ouster. In August 2004 Republican Governor Schwarzenegger had a 65 percent approval rating, but Republican President Bush had just a 41 percent approval rating (Field Research Corporation 2004). Thus the national Republican Party was hard pressed to mount a reelection campaign for George W. Bush in the Golden State.

On the Democratic side, the chance that California would play an important role was palpable, as the primary election was held in March during the 2004 campaign cycle (although it was moved to June in 2006). With early victories in Iowa, New Hampshire, Arizona, Missouri, and New Mexico, however, John Kerry had virtually wrapped up the Democratic nomination, and his challengers had essentially dropped out of the contest before the California primary. On March 2, 2004, Kerry received 65 percent of the Democratic vote in California versus 20 percent for John Edwards and 4 percent each for Howard Dean and Dennis Kucinich. Among Latinos, Kerry won 74 percent of the primary vote, higher support than among any other group of voters in California. Despite the impressive win, voters in California were not exposed to a significant primary campaign for the Democratic nomination, a trend that continued into the general election in November.

Although the presidential election lacked visibility in California, Senator Barbara Boxer faced a reelection challenge from former Secretary of State Bill Jones, and both candidates spent millions of dollars on radio and television advertisements. Boxer, who had defeated Republican challenger Matt Fong by 10 points in 1998, increased her margin in 2004, defeating Jones by a 20-point margin (58 to 38 percent). Boxer won an estimated 71 percent of the Latino vote versus 23 percent for Jones. Two statewide initiatives concerning the expansion of casino gambling failed, while an initiative to establish a stem cell research fund passed—all by healthy margins. Proposition 72, concerning the expansion of health care coverage, offered the closest election outcome among ballot initiatives; it failed by less than 1 percent, with wide vote differences based on race and ethnicity. The *Los Angeles Times* exit poll estimated that 58 percent of whites voted no on Prop 72, in contrast to 64 percent of Latinos who voted yes. Likewise, a majority of black and Asian voters supported the health care initiative. In the state legislature, Democrats held on to their majority status, 48 to 32 in the assembly and 25 to 15 in the Senate, with only a handful of competitive districts across the state.

In contrast to prior elections, in 2004 no hotly contested or divisive statewide contests mobilized or demobilized Latino voters. Given the history and growth of the Latino vote and Democratic support in California, however, nothing new in 2004 would suggest that voter participation would drop off significantly or that support would shift to Bush.

Ties to the Democratic Party extend beyond vote preference from one election to the next, however. Latinos affiliated with the Democrats hold many key elected and appointed positions. Some are new faces; others have been encouraging Latinos to vote Democratic for more than twenty years. As their ranks grow within the party, Latinos help elect Latinos to office as Democrats, and Democratic Latino elected officials direct resources to registering and mobilizing Latino voters within the Democratic Party, thereby creating a self-sustaining cycle. Although the Republican Party has started to make inroads through the election of Latino Republicans to the state legislature, creating a potential for competition over Latino voters, only Latino Democratic representation has been sustained to date; Latino Republican representation has been ad hoc.

SUSTAINED VERSUS AD HOC REPRESENTATION

For any group, the first step toward representation is the election of its candidate. The next, and perhaps more crucial, step is holding on to that representation. Since 1960 California has witnessed more than 4,000 elections for the state legislature and Congress, and in more than 1,000 cases there was an instance of turnover in which the office changed hands from one representative to another. By this we mean instances in which the incumbent lost, stepped down, or was forced out by term limits. When this vacancy exists, a good measure of institutional influence for any group is the extent to which the newly elected representative is similar to the previous representative. That is, how often can blacks, Latinos, and Asian Americans *sustain their influence* in California politics by retaining control of certain legislative seats? For Latinos, we divide the representatives into Democrats and Republicans. Since 1960, 80 Latino Democrats have been elected to legislative office (state and Congress), and 53 Latino Democratic seats have opened. In these instances of turnover, an outgoing Latino Democrat was replaced by a new Latino Democrat 81 percent of the time. In contrast, a Latino Republican has never replaced a Latino Republican (see table 7.2). Thus, while Latinos have been able to sustain their representation and influence within the Democratic Party, Latino representation in the Republican Party has been pieced together from one district to another in an ad hoc fashion.

Table 7.2 also shows that African American representation has been sustained within the Democratic Party at levels even higher than that of Latino Democrats. Why, then, do many observers see the Latino constituency as more important to the future success of the Democrats? The answer lies in a second necessary component of influence: the relative size and/or growth rate of the black and Latino vote. As table 7.2 indicates, twenty-nine Latino Democrats are currently elected to state legislative and congressional districts, compared to only ten African Americans. On this dimension, it is clear that the Latino vote is not

Table 7.2. Sustainability Rating of Minorities in California Legislature

	Total Black	*Democratic Latino*	*Republican Latino*	*Total Asian*
Total elected	52	80	7	24
Current incumbents	10	29	3	11
Turnover	41	53	5	13
Coethnic elected	35	43	0	0
Sustainability	85.4%	81.1%	0.0%	0.0%

Source: 2004 California State Legislature Member Index.

only larger but also growing steadily. This is not to suggest that African Americans are not important partners in the Democratic coalition—indeed they are. Instead, we argue that only the Latino vote shows signs of solid support for Democratic candidates, sustained representation within the party, and an expanding share of the state electorate.

Table 7.3 reports population growth and voter registration growth in California over the past ten years, broken down by racial and ethnic group. The state grew by nearly 15 percent (or 4.6 million people) overall, almost entirely as a result of growth in the Latino and Asian American populations. Similarly, Latinos and Asian Americans are driving voter registration growth in the Golden State. Between 1994 and 2004 California added an estimated 1.8 million registered voters, of which 66 percent were Latino and 23 percent were Asian; just 11 percent of new voters were either white or black (see figure 7.2). Thus Latinos represent the "key" to sustaining a Democratic majority in California for two main reasons. First, they strongly support the Democratic Party. Second, they are the fastest-growing segment of the California electorate.

To better assess the role of Latino partisan politics in California, a simple matrix can be used (see figure 7.3). For each group in California—Anglos, Latinos, blacks, and Asians—we gauge current political status in two areas: percent of all voters and partisan influence, yielding a simple 2 x 2 table. A group can be either *increasing* or *decreas-*

Table 7.3. Population and Voter Registration Growth, 1994–2004, by Race/Ethnicity

	Total	*Black*	*Latino*	*Asian*	*White*
Population 1994	31,523,000	2,197,155	9,084,787	3,306,782	16,662,672
Population 2004	36,144,000	2,240,928	11,891,376	4,192,704	16,843,104
Growth	4,621,000	43,773	2,806,589	885,922	180,432
Growth rate	14.7%	2.0%	30.9%	26.8%	1.1%
Voter registration 1994	14,723,784	957,046	1,766,854	736,189	11,263,695
Voter registration 2004	16,557,273	993,436	2,980,309	1,159,009	11,424,518
Growth	1,833,489	36,390	1,213,455	422,820	160,824
Growth rate	12.5%	3.8%	68.7%	57.4%	1.4%

Source: California Department of Commerce Population Division; Field Institute 2004 Voter Registration Report.

Figure 7.2. New California Registered Voters, 1994–2004

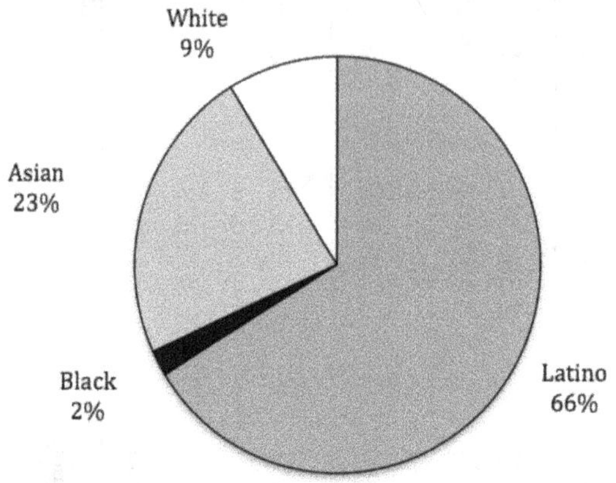

Source: Field Institute (Field Research Corporation) 2004 Voter Registration Report.

ing as a percentage of the electorate, and its partisan influence can be described as *sustained* or *ad hoc.* Thus racial and ethnic groups in California can be divided into four possible quadrants based on the matrix below: (a) growing/sustained, (b) decreasing/sustained, (c) growing/ad hoc, and (d) decreasing/ad hoc. For a group to be an important influence in state presidential-year politics, they need to be in Quadrant A, growing/sustained.

This is not to suggest that Anglos, as the largest voting bloc in the state, do not have important influence but instead that white voters in California are not the reason California is a safe Democratic state. Because white voting patterns and representation are roughly split between the Democratic and Republican Parties, presidential candidates would have to spend millions of dollars, time, and resources campaigning for their votes. Further, despite Anglo dominance in the California legislature, the Democratic majority is in power precisely because of Latinos in the state, and many Latinos have risen to leadership positions in the state assembly and state senate (Pachon, Barreto, and Marquez 2005). As of 2004 Latinos held key posts, such as speaker of the assembly, majority floor leader, and chair of the Budget Committee, which demonstrates their sustained influence within the Democratic Party.

Figure 7.3. Matrix of Influence in California Statewide Politics

		Percent of All Voters	
		Increasing	Decreasing
Partisan Influence	Sustained	(a) *Latino Dems*	(b) Black Dems
	Ad hoc	(c) Latino Republicans Asian American	(d) Anglo

CALIFORNIA AND THE NATIONAL CAMPAIGN STRATEGY

When California is locked up for the Democratic Party, both political parties actually gain. Although the Republican candidate would love to win the 55 electoral votes in California, from a resource perspective, it is better to spend elsewhere. Given the choice of spending tens of millions of dollars and losing California or spending $0 and still losing California, the candidate will always prefer to spend nothing. Just how expensive is California in a presidential race? While it is difficult to know the exact answer, a few good indicators are available. According to campaign finance analysis by California Common Cause (2003), more than $80 million were raised and spent in the October 2003 recall election (Wilson 2003). In 2005, when a special statewide election was called for eight propositions, more than $100 million were spent, and estimates for the 2006 gubernatorial election put spending by the Republican Party alone at over $120 million (Barabak and Finnegan 2006). To be competitive in California in 2004, each candidate (and supporting 527s) probably needed to spend a minimum of $50 million and as much as $100 million, due to airing expensive television commercials and the additional costs of visiting the state and shaking hands from San Diego to San Francisco and everywhere in between.

Data compiled by the Campaign Media Analysis Group (CMAG) for 2004 showed that in the final month of the 2004 campaign, over 250,000 ads were purchased and aired by Kerry, Bush, and their affiliates; not a single ad appeared in the state of California, however. Spending on these ads in some of the most important swing states combined is probably in the range of what competing for votes in California would have cost. For instance, between September 26 and November 2, 2004, more than $47 million was spent in Ohio, $36 million in Pennsylvania, $14 million in Wisconsin, $8 million in New Mexico, and $8 million in Nevada (CNN.com 2004a). Taken together, spending in these states totaled about $115 million, probably a low estimate for campaigning in California in 2004.

We argue that maintaining California as a safe Democratic state frees up money and time that each campaign can better use in other competitive states. Further, as we have demonstrated above through voting patterns and representation trends, Latinos are the key partners in pushing California to the safe Democratic status that it now holds.

LATINOS AND THE CALIFORNIA VOTE IN 2008 AND 2012

The discussion and data presented so far have focused on California politics in 2004 and before. The trends and historical data are informative not just for 2004 but also looking ahead to the presidential elections in 2008 and 2012. At a minimum, the Latino vote in California and, indeed, nationwide is expected to continue to grow, likely leading to more influence and more attention from the media and politicians. Given the growth in the Latino vote over the past decade in California, it is not unreasonable to anticipate that in 2008 one in five voters will be Latino and that in 2012 Latinos may constitute 23 percent of the electorate. At the same time, the white proportion of the electorate will decline and potentially drift toward the Republican Party (a trend already noticeable). As a result, the Latino influence in maintaining California's status as a safe Democratic state will increase even more because they would account for a larger share of the Democratic majority (fig. 7.4).

In table 7.4 we present our projections of the Latino vote and the California vote in 2008 and 2012. Using 2000 and 2004 as a baseline (as well as 1992 and 1996), we estimate that the Latino electorate will

Figure 7.4. Proportion of the Democratic Vote in California (Projections for the 2008 and 2012 Presidential Elections)

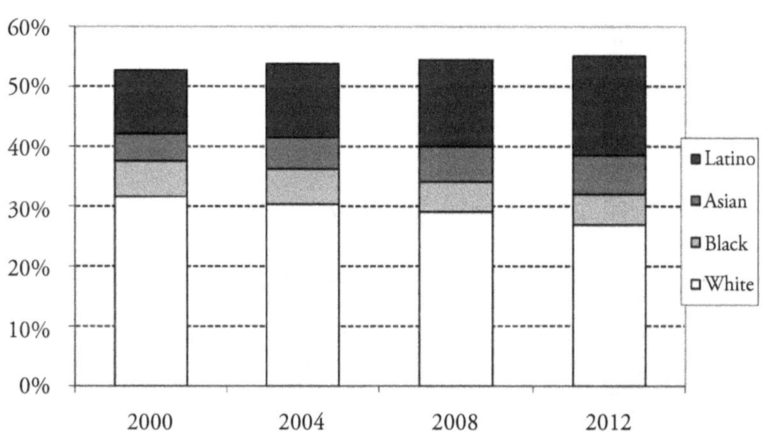

Source: Authors' projections based on previous vote data.

grow from 14 percent in 2000 to 23 percent in 2012 and hold constant the vote for the Democratic candidate at 72 percent. If this is the case, California will become an even easier win for the Democratic Party in the next two presidential elections. In contrast, the Democratic vote of non-Latinos in the state is expected to hover around the 50 percent mark (again based on historical data and trends). In fact, Latinos are likely to be the primary racial/ethnic group keeping California a blue state in 2008 and beyond. While African Americans might vote Democratic at over 80 percent, they account for less than 7 percent of all voters in the state. If these projections become reality, the California and national GOP will be forced to reassess their outreach and recruitment strategies vis-à-vis Latinos.

CONCLUSION

We have focused on why California matters to the national election and how Latino voters are the key component. We presented three reasons for why this is the case. First, at the individual level, Latino voting

Table 7.4. Percent Vote for Democrat by Latino and Non-Latino

Year	*Percent Latino*	*Percent Vote for Democrat*		
		Latino	*Non-Latino*	*State*
2000	14	75	49	53
2004	17	72	50	54
2008	20	72	50	54
2012	23	72	50	55
Year	*Percent Black*	*Percent Vote for Democrat*		
		Black	*Non-Black*	*State*
2000	7	85	51	53
2004	7	85	52	54
2008	6	85	52	54
2012	6	85	53	55
Year	*Percent Asian*	*Percent Vote for Democrat*		
		Asian	*Non-Asian*	*State*
2000	7	65	52	53
2004	8	65	53	54
2008	9	65	53	54
2012	10	65	54	55

Source: Los Angeles Times exit polls and authors' projections.

patterns have remained consistently in favor of Democratic candidates, and their proportion of the electorate continues to grow. Second, Latino influence in California politics is not only on the rise (the fastest-growing segment of the electorate), but Latinos have been able to sustain their representation within the Democratic Party. While elected Anglo Republicans have always replaced Latino Republicans, Latinos have successfully won and defended almost all their Democratic seats, thereby sustaining their influence within the Democratic Party.

Third, even as an uncompetitive state, California has considerable influence on the national election because when the state is out of play, candidates are free to campaign effectively in at least six or seven other states. If California were only a Democratic-*leaning* state, the Democratic Party would surely spend tens of millions of dollars to ensure that it remained Democratic and to win its fifty-five electoral votes, thereby expending money, time, personnel, and other resources that could be used in other, more competitive states. While the lack of a vigorous presidential campaign in California in 2004 may have indicated that the California Latino vote was again irrelevant to the national election, this chapter offers an alternative framework to assess the relevance of Latino voters. We conclude that the growth and marked Democratic partisanship of the Latino electorate in California did influence the national presidential campaign in 2004 and will continue to influence it into the future.

APPENDIX A

Table A.7.1. 2004 California Population by Citizenship and Voting Status

		Latino		*Non-Latino*	
	Total	*Total*	*Percent*	*Total*	*Percent*
Total population	35,583,756	12,590,542	35.4	22,993,214	64.6
Citizen population	29,548,736	8,440,252	28.6	21,108,484	71.4
Citizen VAP (CVAP)	20,692,792	4,432,908	21.4	16,259,885	78.6
Registered voters	14,192,951	2,455,326	17.3	11,737,625	82.7
Voted in 2004	12,806,694	2,081,410	16.3	10,725,284	83.7
Turnout / registered	90.2%	84.8%		91.3%	
Turnout / CVAP	*61.9%*	*47.0%*	*66.0%*		

Source: 2004 Current Population Survey, Voting and Registration Supplement.

REFERENCES

Barabak, Mark, and Michael Finnegan. 2006. "Arnold Has 120 Million Goal for Re-election Campaign." *Los Angeles Times,* February 19, A1.

Barreto, Matt, and Ricardo Ramírez. 2004. "Minority Participation and the California Recall: Latino, Black, and Asian Voting Trends 1990–2003." *PS: Political Science and Politics* 37 (January): 11–14.

Barreto, Matt, and Nathan Woods. 2005. "The Anti-Latino Political Context and Its Impact on GOP Detachment and Increasing Latino Voter Turnout in Los Angeles County." In *Diversity in Democracy: Minority Representation in the United States,* ed. Gary Segura and Shawn Bowler, 148–69. Charlottesville: University Press of Virginia.

California Common Cause. 2003. "Recall Money Line–No. 16–October 10, 2003." RecallMoneyWatch.com. (No current URL, February 9, 2009.)

CNN.com. 2004a. "America Votes 2004: Campaign Ad Buys." www.cnn.com/ELECTION/2004/special/president/campaign.ads/. Accessed August 25, 2008.

———. 2004b. "Mayor Defends Same-Sex Marriages." CNN.com, February 22. www.cnn.com/2004/LAW/02/22/same.sex/index.html?iref=newssearch. Accessed September 9, 2009.

DiCamillo, Mark, and Marvin Field. 2004. "Kerry Has Double Digit Lead over Bush." Field Poll, Release #2114, May 26. Field Research Corporation, San Francisco, CA.

DeSipio, Louis, and Natalie Masuoka. 2006. "Opportunities Lost? Latinos, Cruz Bustamante, and California's Recall." In *Clicker Politics: Essays on the California Recall,* ed. Shaun Bowler and Bruce Cain, 112–27. Upper Saddle River, NJ: Prentice Hall.

Field Research Corporation. 2004. The California Poll. Field Poll 2004, February 24–25. San Francisco, CA.

Fraga, Luis, and Fernando Guerra. 1996. "Theory, Reality, and Perpetual Potential: Latinos in the 1992 California Election." In *Ethnic Ironies: Latino Politics in the 1992 Elections,* ed. Rodolfo O. de la Garza and Louis DeSipio, 131–45. Boulder, CO: Westview Press.

Gómez, Lisa Marie. 2004. "Why Don't Hispanic Polls Seem to Add Up?" *San Antonio Express-News,* November 7.

Helton, John. 2004. "Dems, GOP Assess Latino Impact." CNN.com, March 9. http://www.cnn.com/2004/ALLPOLITICS/03/08/latino.vote/index.html.

Kousser, Thad. 2006. "Recalling the Realignment Literature: Did October 2003 Bring a Critical Election?" In *Clicker Politics: Essays on the California Recall,* ed. Shaun Bowler and Bruce Cain, 52–67. Upper Saddle River, NJ: Prentice Hall.

Leal, David, Matt Barreto, Jongho Lee, and Rodolfo de la Garza. 2005. "The Latino Vote in the 2004 Election." *PS: Political Science and Politics* 38: 41–49.

Marinucci, Carla. 2003. "President Avoids Recall Talk in Visit." *San Francisco Chronicle,* August 15, A19.

Nuño, Stephen. 2007. "Latino Mobilization and Vote Choice in the 2000 Presidential Election." *American Politics Research* 35: 273–93.

Olivera, Mercedes. 2004. "Election's Latino Vote May Reflect New Range of Support." *Dallas Morning News,* November 12, B1.

Pachon, Harry, Matt Barreto, and Frances Marquez. 2005. "Latino Politics Comes of Age in the Golden State." In *Muted Voices: Latino Politics in the 2000 Election,* ed. Rodolfo de la Garza and Louis DeSipio, 84–100. New York: Rowman & Littlefield.

Pantoja, Adrian D., Ricardo Ramírez, and Gary M. Segura. 2001. "Citizens by Choice, Voters by Necessity: Patterns in Political Mobilization by Naturalized Latinos." *Political Research Quarterly* 54 (4): 729–50.

Ramírez, Ricardo. 2007. "Segmented Mobilization: Latino Non-Partisan Get Out the Vote Efforts in the 2000 General Election." *American Politics Research* 35 (March): 155–75.

Segura, Gary M., Denis Falcon, and Harry Pachon. 1997. "Dynamics of Latino Partisanship in California: Immigration, Issue Salience, and Their Implications." *Harvard Journal of Hispanic Politics* 10: 62–80.

Tomás Rivera Policy Institute. 2000. "2000 Primary Election Survey: California Latino Voters." Claremont, CA.

Wilson, Stan. 2003. "Schwarzenegger Leads Money Chase in California Recall." CNN.com/Inside Politics. September 26.

Chapter Eight

New York in 2004

Political Blues for Hispanics

DOUGLAS MUZZIO AND JERONIMO CORTINA

As in previous presidential elections, in 2004 Latinos were the focus of considerable early national media attention. The "Latino vote" was variously characterized as "potent" and "pivotal," and some considered Latinos "swing voters." As late as mid-October 2004, a CNN headline read, "Hispanics Could Hold Key to a Win" (CNN 2004). Also as in previous presidential elections, however, these early high hopes were dashed on Election Day (Leal et al. 2005). While Latinos were sometimes said to be "up for grabs," this was certainly not the case in New York State in 2004 ("Most Hispanics Say" 2002).[1]

A key feature of contemporary U.S. presidential elections—and the 2004 contest in particular—is the "battleground state" dynamic. Some states are solidly blue; that is, they are highly likely to support almost any Democratic presidential candidate. The red states are equally likely to support the Republican nominee. The remaining states are the battleground states—a relatively small number (fifteen or so) that had narrowly gone one way or the other in 2000. These were the electoral targets in 2004; the candidates and their campaigns virtually ignored all others, except for fund-raising, most notably in New York and California.[2]

Latinos were concentrated in several states rich in Electoral College votes, such as California (55), Texas (34), New York (31), Florida (27), and Illinois (21), as well as in Arizona (10) and New Mexico (5). Of these, only Florida and New Mexico were battleground states. California, New York, and Illinois were virtual locks for John Kerry, whereas Texas and Arizona were strongly for President George W. Bush. The claim that Latinos constituted an up-for-grabs swing vote was based in large part on their cultural conservatism and Catholic religious affiliation, which would seem to make them receptive to the GOP message on social issues such as abortion. Also, some local and state elections in both New York City and New York State saw an increasing Latino propensity to support Republican candidates. Latinos in New York City, for instance, had increasingly voted Republican in the four mayoral elections from 1989 to 2001. In 2001 Republican Michael Bloomberg received nearly half the Latino vote. In addition, there was a recognition that growing Latino numbers in New York and nationally made them an increasingly potent constituency—a dominant one in some jurisdictions, and one in New York motivated less by party identification than by ethnicity (Mollenkopf and Miranda 2002).

In 2004, as they had four years earlier, the national Republican and Democratic Parties and the presidential candidates pursued a "Latino southern strategy" that targeted Mexican and Cuban Americans in the Southwest and Southeast. As before, Puerto Ricans, Dominicans, and other Latinos in New York and the Northeast were virtually ignored (Falcon 2005)—but so were whites, blacks, and Asians in these regions. Neither party mounted anything resembling a vigorous campaign in the Empire State. It would have been masochistic for Republicans and a waste of resources for Democrats. John F. Kerry was going to win New York regardless of campaign efforts.

It was not a surprise that neither presidential candidate campaigned in New York State during the 2004 general election. President Bush did fly into New York City in early September to accept his party's nomination in Madison Square Garden, but even this media event was meant to reach television audiences throughout the United States, not New Yorkers in particular. During the fall "campaign," there were no television ads, no 527s,[3] no ballot initiatives, and no discussion of important Latino issues. *Nada.*

What was the effect of Latino voters in New York on the presidential outcome in the state? The same—*nada.* The "Latino wave" (Ramos 2004) was merely part of the Democratic tsunami in New York State and New York City. The statewide election results, however, do not tell the entire story of the impact of Latino voters in New York in 2004. As in California, Latino voters were important contributors to the statewide electoral majority that has kept New York a safe Democratic state, thus affecting Republican and Democratic strategies and spending in more competitive states (see chap. 7, this volume). Also, Latinos expanded their coethnic representation in the state senate and state assembly (by one seat each).

THE 2004 LATINO PRESIDENTIAL VOTE

On November 3, 2004, John Kerry beat George Bush in a landslide in New York State—58 percent to 41 percent. In 2000 Al Gore had buried George W. Bush by 60 percent to 35 percent. In 1996 Bill Clinton won over Bob Dole, 61 percent to 31 percent. The last Republican to get New York's electoral votes was Ronald Reagan in 1984.

The state was Democratic and getting more so. At election time registration rolls statewide numbered 5,535,000 Democrats and 3,209,000 Republicans. Democrats had grown by 290,000 and Republicans by fewer than 40,000 since the 2000 election (CPS 2005).

Latinos in New York State voted overwhelmingly for Democrat Kerry—75 percent versus 24 percent for Bush. Surveys by the Hispanic Federation from 1996 to 2004 found at least seven in ten New York City Latinos registered as Democrats (see table 8.1).

The proportion of the Latino voting age population that voted in New York State increased slightly in 2004 from four years earlier: 31 percent cast a ballot in 2004, up from 29.4 percent of the voting age Latino population in 2000. Latino turnout in New York City grew 4.5 points, to 32.8 percent (CPS 2005). This increased Latino voter turnout seemed to reflect a greater public interest in the Bush/Kerry campaign than the Bush/Gore 2000 contest (Wattenberg 2005). It does not reflect a greater effort by political parties and political action groups to mobilize Latino voters, as the state and the city were safely Democratic in both elections.

Table 8.1. NYC Latino Voter and Party Registration, 1996–2004

		Party Registration	
Year	*% Registered*	*Democrat*	*Republican*
2004	68	73	13
2003	67	74	9
2002	69	74	11
2000	60	69	12
1999	58	76	9
1998	53	71	12
1997	57	73	11
1996	51	70	15

Source: Annual Hispanic Federation surveys.

In 2000 Gore received 81 percent of the state's Latino vote (and 90 percent of New York City's Latino vote), while Bush received 16 percent statewide.[4] Although Bush narrowed the gap in 2004, New York State Latinos still voted for Kerry three to one (rather than the five to one for Gore). Exit polling showed that Latinos constituted 12 percent of Kerry's overall New York State vote and 5 percent of Bush's. The earliest preelection polls predicted Kerry's big win, both overall and among Latinos, which is why the state was not contested.

In 2004 the state's Hispanic voters were in between whites and blacks in their presidential choice. White New York State voters split their ballots—50 percent for Bush, 49 percent for Kerry. Blacks, the most loyal element of the New York City, New York State, and national Democratic "base," gave 90 percent of their votes to Kerry. Again, the presidential preferences of Latinos, whites, and blacks were previewed in the early preelection polls.

In 2000 New York also had been a blue state that was little contested by Gore and Bush. In that year, however, the presidential race was overshadowed by the far more interesting and competitive Clinton/Lazio U.S. Senate election (Falcon 2005). Hillary Rodham Clinton campaigned heavily among Latinos statewide, winning over 80 percent of their votes. In 2004 there was for all practical purposes no U.S. Senate race. Incumbent first-term senior senator, Charles Schumer, was reelected in a historic landslide—71 percent to 25 percent—against unknown and underfunded Republican upstate assemblyman, Howard Mills.[5]

Latinos statewide gave Schumer an even bigger margin—79 versus 19 percent. During his first Senate win in 1998 (against three-term Republican incumbent Alfonse D'Amato), Schumer had vigorously sought the votes of Hispanics, ultimately receiving 86 percent.

Big Democratic/Kerry Win Not in Doubt

Preelection polling largely predicted John Kerry's big win in New York—and even bigger margin among New York State Latinos. The most notable poll was the June 2004 survey conducted by the Hispanic Federation in New York City, where 62 percent of Hispanics who would vote in November resided.[6] John Kerry, the certain Democratic nominee, beat George Bush in a hypothetical horserace by 58 percent to 17 percent. This is a better than 3 to 1 ratio among New York City Hispanics who were registered to vote; only 17 percent were undecided with five months remaining before the election. Among those making a candidate choice, 74 percent of New York City Latinos surveyed by the Hispanic Federation were for Kerry, which is almost exactly what he received in the November election, and 22 percent supported Bush, which is very close to his actual vote count. For New York State generally, a Quinnipiac University Poll conducted from August 3 to 9 found that Kerry would beat Bush 53 percent to 35 percent among registered voters if the election were held then, while 7 percent were undecided; four months earlier (April 5–12), the results were nearly identical: 53 percent Kerry versus 36 percent Bush, with 9 percent undecided.

Anticipating concerns expressed on Election Day, New York City Latinos provided very negative assessments of George Bush in the late spring–early summer Hispanic Federation poll. Two-thirds characterized his overall job performance as either "poor" (32 percent) or "not so good" (34 percent). Bush did even worse among Latino New Yorkers in regard to how he had served the Hispanic community. Fully 7 in 10 called his service to Latinos either "poor" (38 percent) or "not so good" (32 percent).

The survey also revealed that the economy and jobs and the Iraq war and national security were the top two issues that New York City Latinos said would determine their presidential vote choices. They felt that Bush was mishandling both: fully three-fourths disapproved of Bush's handling of the war, and 7 in 10 disapproved of Bush's stewardship of the economy. These sentiments are similar to those Latinos expressed when they voted in the November election.

2004 Latino New Yorker Voter

On Election Day 2004 the National Election Pool (NEP)—a consortium comprising ABC, AP, CBS, CNN, Fox, and NBC—surveyed 1,452 New York State voters, including 148 self-described Hispanics, as they left the polls. Because the Latino subsample is small, the maximum error margin is large (+/–8 percent); consequently, the analysis that follows is meant to be evocative, certainly not exact.[7] It is true that the sample of Latinos is frustratingly small, but we feel, even with its deficiencies, the 2004 NEP exit poll is useful.

In terms of vote share, the NEP found that Hispanics constituted 9 percent of the 2004 New York State presidential election voters (with a maximal error margin of +/–3 percent, or approximately 620,000 voters. These results essentially reflect the U.S. Census Bureau's November 2004 "Voting and Registration Supplement to the Current Population Survey," which estimated 613,000 Latino voters with a margin of error of +/–4.6 percent (CPS 2005). In 2000, according to exit polls, Hispanics made up 8 percent of the state electorate, or about 545,000 voters.

Geographically, Latino voters primarily lived downstate in the New York City metropolitan area. Sixty-two percent of those exit polled lived in New York City (75.3 percent of New York State Latinos lived in the city [U.S. Census 2001]), 21 percent in Nassau and Suffolk Counties on Long Island, and 12 percent in the Lower Hudson Valley, which consists of Westchester, Rockland, Putnam, Orange, Dutchess, Ulster, and Sullivan Counties. Only 1 in 20 New York State Latino voters lived in upstate urban and rural areas.

THE 2001 NEW YORK CITY MAYORAL ELECTION

The most important factor in increased Latino turnout was the energizing and mobilizing effect of the 2001 New York City mayoral campaign of Fernando Ferrer, the former Bronx borough president. Around the time of the 2004 election, it was widely assumed that Ferrer would run for mayor in 2005. He was the Democratic frontrunner, leading incumbent Republican Mayor Michael Bloomberg in the polls.[8]

Ferrer's candidacy resulted in a record Latino turnout, bringing tens of thousands of Latinos to the polls for the first time and registering additional tens of thousands of others. His was the strongest mayoral campaign by a Latino since then-Bronx congressman and former Bronx borough president Herman Badillo's losing mayoral runoff against Abraham Beame in 1973 (McNickle 1993). Indeed, among the conditions that have been found to stimulate heightened political attention and involvement among Latinos is the presence of a Latino candidate (Barreto 2007; Cruz 2005).

Ferrer was a product of the Bronx County Democratic organization and a protégé of the Bronx County Democratic chair, assemblyman Roberto Ramirez. In 2004 the political center of Latino politics in New York City remained in the South Bronx, with Puerto Ricans such as Ferrer and Ramirez still chief Latino players in New York City politics (Falcon 2005).

In the September 25 Democratic mayoral primary (moved back two weeks after the originally scheduled 9/11 primary was canceled), Hispanics were a historically high 23 percent share of the vote. They cast 72 percent of their ballots for Ferrer against three opponents. Ferrer, somewhat surprisingly, came in first overall with 35.6 percent of the vote. Public Advocate Mark Green came in second with 31 percent, followed by New York City Council Speaker Peter Vallone with 19.8 percent, and New York City Comptroller Alan Hevesi with 12.1 percent.

Ferrer did not reach the 40 percent threshold necessary to avoid a runoff with second-place finisher Green. In the October 11 runoff, Latinos were 24 percent of a slightly larger electorate (787,000 vs. 781,000), with Ferrer receiving 84 percent of the Latino vote and Green 16 percent. The Hispanic Federation's *Latino Political Participation* report (Mollenkopf and Miranda 2002) documented the overwhelming support that Ferrer received in predominantly Hispanic election districts (EDs), receiving 71 percent in the first primary and increasing to 82 percent in the runoff.

Green beat Ferrer 51 percent to 49 percent overall, however. In the general election between Green and billionaire businessman Bloomberg,

Latinos made up 18 percent of the electorate and essentially split their vote—47 percent for Bloomberg, 49 percent for Green. The *New York Times* headline read, "City's Hispanic Shift, Moving Toward the G.O.P" (Ojita 2004).

Perhaps less a move to the Republicans than a sign of their displeasure with the conduct and outcome of the runoff, Latino voters either stayed home or voted for Bloomberg in response to what they saw as an ethnically/racially charged Green runoff campaign (Ojito 2004). The Green campaign had distributed literature showing a *New York Post* cartoon portraying Ferrer kissing Al Sharpton's posterior.

The hostilities between the Ferrer and Green camps were damaging to both candidates only weeks before the general election. The conflict precipitated a meeting of local state and national Democratic leaders, including the Democratic national chairman, Terry McAuliffe, to call a ceasefire. At that meeting, Green stated that although he needed Hispanics to govern the city, he did not need them to win an election against Bloomberg. Latino leaders were incensed and left determined to prove the second part of Green's proposition wrong.[9]

General election turnout in majority-Hispanic election districts sagged heavily, most notably in the Bronx, where it appears that the Latino-dominated Bronx County Democratic organization (out of which Ferrer had come) sat on their hands on Election Day. Thus, while turnout in majority-Hispanic election districts was 1.1 percentage points above the citywide average in the runoff, it was 12 points below the citywide average in the general election.

The 2001 Democratic mayoral primary elections were, according to Mollenkopf and Miranda (2002: 16), "a watershed for closing the gap between turnout among Latinos and the overall turnout rate." The effect proved short-lived, as it collapsed in the general election, with falloff universal but varying across Latino neighborhoods. Had Ferrer been the Democratic nominee, it is almost certain that Hispanics would have turned out in record numbers. The 2001 Democratic mayoral primary, runoff, and general election support the notion that "shared ethnicity directly influences Latino vote choice" (Barreto 2007: 438). Latinos in New York City, like Latinos in other American cities, are unlikely to have high levels of turnout when no Latino candidate is running. "The presence of a viable Latino candidate uniformly results in increased voter turnout in Latino precincts" (Barreto 2007: 439). There may be a downside of this upsurge—a backlash in response to the Latino candidate. Turnout in majority white districts increased in the runoff election (Mollenkopf and Miranda 2002: 15); white voters may have turned out to vote against Ferrer.

The ethnic composition of Ferrer's support among Latinos ran counter to the belief of some analysts, including Latinos, that Ferrer, a Puerto Rican, faced a challenge in assembling a coalition across the many Latino nationality groups. The Hispanic Federation's 2001 annual survey had suggested otherwise.[10] In spring 2001 Ferrer's 74 percent support among Dominicans, for instance, was higher than that among any other Latino group, including Puerto Ricans (62 percent) and "other Hispanics" (61 percent).

The outpouring of support for Ferrer by Hispanics and the splitting of Latino ballots between Republican Bloomberg and Democrat Green suggested that Latinos had emerged as a potent and pivotal actor in New York City politics. Indeed, from 1989 to 1997, ABC News exit poll data show that the Latino share of the total New York City electorate grew from 8 percent in 1989 to 13 percent in 1993 to 21 percent in 1997, then fell, as noted, to 18 percent in the 2001 general election (table 8.2).

Furthermore, the proportion of Latinos voting for a Republican candidate—Rudy Giuliani in 1989, 1993, and 1997 and Michael Bloomberg in 2001—steadily rose from about one-fourth in 1989, according to ABC News, to nearly one-half in 2001. The Republican candidate received an increasing share of the Hispanic vote with each succeeding election. Such figures help to explain the perception that the Hispanic vote was up for grabs.

THE 2002 STATE ELECTIONS

According to a 2002 series in *Newsday,* Latino voters held "the potential to swing statewide and local races" (Metz 2002; Rau 2002a; see also Rau 2002b). Republican Governor George Pataki assiduously courted Latinos in his 2002 reelection campaign, supported by Amigos for Pataki in the state. Four years earlier, Pataki had received 24 percent of

Table 8.2. Latino Voting in NYC Mayoral General Elections, 1989–2001

Election	*Percent of Latino Share (Source)*	*No. of Latino Voters / Total No. of Voters*	*Vote Choices and Percent of Latino Vote*	
1989	8 (ABC)	152,000 / 1,899,845	Dinkins	73
			Giuliani	26
1993	13 (VNS)	245,570 / 1,889,003	Dinkins	60
			Giuliani	38
1997	21 (VNS)	285,000 / 1,357,249	Messinger	57
			Giuliani	42
2001	18 (EMR)	267,000 / 1,480,914	Green	49
			Bloomberg	47

Sources: "Hispanic Share" and "Vote Choices" drawn from exit polls conducted by ABC News and CBS/New York Times, Voter News Service, and Edison Media Research; "No. of Latino Voters" computed by multiplying the Latino share by the certified vote count of the New York City Board of Elections and rounded to nearest 1,000.

the Latino vote in his second campaign, defeating Democrat Peter Vallone 54 percent to 33 percent. In 2002 Pataki tapped into the number one concern of Latinos in the state, education, and ran the Spanish-language ad "Governor Pataki Cares about Our Children." Pataki beat Democrat Carl McCall 49 percent to 34 percent that year.

There were no exit polls for the gubernatorial race, but available voting data suggest that Pataki increased his share of the state Latino vote. Pataki's share of the vote in the assembly districts represented by Latino assembly members from 1998 to 2002 shows a sizable increase. In the eight assembly districts with Latino legislators in 1998, Pataki received 16 percent of the vote. In 2002 (after redistricting) there were ten Latino-represented assembly districts; Pataki doubled his portion of the vote to 32 percent. Also, it appears that Pataki did better among non-Puerto Ricans. In the then-new Thirty-ninth Assembly District in Queens, the Latino district with the lowest number of Puerto Ricans,

Pataki received 51 percent of the vote. In the Seventy-second Assembly District in Washington Heights, the capital of New York City's Dominican community (where Pataki campaigned hardest), his share of the vote more than doubled: to 36 percent from 17 percent four years earlier (PrimeNY 2002).[11]

In an attempt to attract more Latino voters, the GOP nominated the first Latino statewide major party candidate, former judge Dora Irizarry (who also ran on the line of the Conservative Party in the New York State multiple-line fusion system). In her run against incumbent Democratic Attorney General Eliot Spitzer (who ran also as the candidate of the Independence, Liberal, and Working Families Parties), she was soundly defeated, winning only 29.8 percent against Spitzer's 66.4 percent.

2003–2004: NEW YORK CITY AND BEYOND

Most Latino elected officials have come from New York City because most of the state's Hispanic population has traditionally been concentrated there. Nonetheless, in 2004 more than 700,000 Latinos resided outside the city, with the largest number in the Long Island counties of Nassau and Suffolk, followed by the Rochester, Buffalo-Niagara Falls, and Albany-Schenectady-Troy metropolitan statistical areas (U.S. Census Bureau 2003). As the state's Hispanic population outside the city has grown, so too has the number of Hispanic public officials. In 2003, 24 percent of Latino state elected officials represented jurisdictions outside the city. Overall, the state had 89 Latino officials in 2003, including 2 U.S. representatives, 15 state legislators, and 72 local elected officials. Four years earlier, in 2000, there were 73 Latino elected officials in the state; in 1973 there were just 10 Spanish-surnamed persons elected to any level of government in New York (NALEO 2003; Barreto 2007).

In Rochester, the state's third largest city, Latinos constituted 13 percent of the total population of more than two hundred thousand in 2002. Hispanics were elected to the positions of councilwoman, county legislator, school board member, and judge. In Syracuse, voters elected a Latino city councilwoman and a school board member (Metz 2002).

2004 NEW YORK STATE LEGISLATIVE AND CONGRESSIONAL RACES

In the 2004 elections both Latino U.S. representatives (Democrats from New York City, Nydia Valasquez of Brooklyn and Jose Serrano of the Bronx) and fourteen of fifteen incumbent state legislators (four state senators and eleven assembly members)—all of them Democrats except for the party-switching Senator Olga Mendez (who was defeated, see below) and all but one of them from New York City—were comfortably reelected. A nonincumbent Latina won an assembly seat in the Bronx vacated by a non-Latino. Thus Latino representation grew by one member in each house (with the Mendez seat becoming Democratic again). Hispanic challengers on Long Island—one Democrat and two Republicans—were defeated. Non-Latino incumbents defeated the Democrat and one Republican. The second Republican lost to an incumbent Latino, the only Latino state legislator to represent a district wholly outside New York City, Suffolk County's Sixth Assembly District.

El Barrio: Bellweather? No!

One New York race that received a great deal of attention in 2004 was for senate District 28, which covered East Harlem's El Barrio and the South Bronx. The election featured the twenty-six-year incumbent state senator, Olga Mendez, the first Puerto Rican woman elected to a state legislature on the U.S. mainland and the longest-serving member of any state legislature, who defected to the GOP a month after her 2002 victory as a Democrat. She had supported incumbent Republican governor, George Pataki, for reelection in 2002 and was widely criticized by her Democratic colleagues. She knew there would be consequences. "I know when I'm not wanted," she reasoned (Jordan 2003). She justified the switch by arguing that she had a better chance of passing legislation and receiving money for her district if she were a member of the senate majority. Critics contended that her motives were more personal, that she would receive an extra $12,500 as a committee chair (her reward for defecting). Indeed, in June 2004 Mendez became the first woman to chair the senate Labor Committee (Ramirez 2004).

Her challenger was Democratic City Councilman Jose Serrano Jr., son of a U.S. congressman representing a Bronx district. Observers saw the race as a possible harbinger of Republican electoral inroads into the Hispanic community (Chernikoff and Dougherty 2005).

El Barrio is New York City's quintessential Latino neighborhood; Latinos make up 52.1 percent of the total population and 50.2 percent of the voting age population. The neighborhood is "the cradle of the Puerto Rican community" in the United States and a point of entry for many new arrivals (Goris and Pedraza 1994). Recently, El Barrio has become home to the second largest Mexican immigrant community in the city, approximately eight thousand persons (Department of City Planning 2004), who have been arriving in the neighborhood at a steady pace since the mid-1990s. El Barrio is one of the poorest neighborhoods in Manhattan and getting poorer. In 2000 almost 37 percent of its total population received income support such as Temporary Assistance for Needy Families (TANF), Supplemental Security Income, and Medicaid; in 2004 almost 49 percent of the population received such aid.

Republicans believed that the Mendez/Serrano contest provided an opportunity for residents and civic leaders in El Barrio to act on a presumed frustration with the Democratic Party and support Mendez. Invoking El Barrio's needs, she justified her defection by saying her constituents would benefit from having a representative in the majority. She similarly highlighted the likely difficulties that Serrano would face as a Democratic newcomer in a Republican-dominated senate.

According to the New York State Board of Elections Financial Disclosure Report, the committee to reelect state senator Olga Mendez received $100,000 from the state senate Republican Campaign Committee. In contrast, the senate Democratic Campaign Committee gave only $15,000 to Serrano. The large difference between each party's contributions to its candidates may be indicative of the commitment of the GOP to win one of the city's historic Latino Democratic bastions (and the Democrats' belief that the district would vote overwhelmingly for Serrano). Such financial support might have seemed like a good bet for the GOP given her past electoral performance. Mendez had an impressive electoral record, having won eleven previous elections, never polling less than 89 percent, and winning 95 percent of the vote in 2002

(Chernikoff and Dougherty 2005). To win in 2004, however, Mendez would have had to convince thousands of Democrats to cross party lines. In senate District 28, there were 77,881 voters registered as Democrats in the Bronx and 55,361 in Manhattan; there were only 12,691 registered Republicans in the entire district. Mendez's situation was made worse by district boundaries redrawn in 2002 that put 60 percent of the district's voters in the Bronx, where Serrano's family name and his work as a council member would have greater effect on voters.

When the ballots were counted, voters in District 28 remained loyal to the Democratic Party, as Serrano crushed Mendez 82 percent to 18 percent. Latino registered voter turnout was estimated at 26 percent, almost 7 percent lower than the average citywide Latino turnout. The district's low turnout rate may be attributable to the disappearance of community organizations in El Barrio (de la Garza and DeSipio 1994), the lack of competitive races at the local and state levels, and elected officials' complacency in taking their constituents for granted, in addition to the widely held expectation that Serrano would win easily. Whatever the reasons for the low turnout, those who voted were Democrats; Kerry received 97 percent and Bush received 2 percent of the Latino vote in the district.

The 2004 Election Season

The 2004 election season in New York began in the weeks preceding the March 2 Democratic presidential primary (President Bush was unopposed in the Republican primary), followed by the Republican National Convention held in New York City from August 30 to September 2. On September 14 Democratic and Republican primaries were held for U.S. senator, both houses of the state legislature, and hundreds of local offices. The general election was on November 2.

The story on the Republican side began in July 2003, when Republican National Chairman Marc Racicot, along with top Republican National Committee officials and Republican Governor George Pataki, opened, to much fanfare, an office in Washington Heights, located in northern Manhattan and the political center of Dominican politics. The Hispanic Outreach Center, a branch of the New York Republican Committee, was meant to signal Republican seriousness in courting the Latino vote (Sargent 2003).

The date of the presidential primary was moved up to enhance the state's role in selecting the major party nominees. New York offered the largest delegate pool of the ten Super Tuesday states that were holding presidential contests that day. John Kerry, with his wins in Iowa and New Hampshire, went on to win all but two of the next primary contests and entered New York with a commanding lead among delegates and in the polls. Kerry's only real competition came from U.S Senator John Edwards (D-NC), who had never registered above 3 percent in New York statewide polls before February 2004. The black activist Al Sharpton also campaigned actively, focusing on New York City.

On primary day Kerry decisively defeated Edwards, 61 percent to 24 percent, with Sharpton garnering 8 percent. According to exit polls, Kerry won every major demographic and ideological group. He did especially well among voters over sixty-five, Jewish voters, and Latino voters. Kerry won 71 percent of the Latino vote, 62 percent of the white vote, and 54 percent of the black vote. One-third of blacks voted for Sharpton.

Latino leaders and public officials split in their support of Kerry and Sharpton. Al Sharpton was one of the leaders of the "black-Hispanic coalition" in New York City, and he actively supported and was embraced by Fernando Ferrer in the 2001 New York City Democratic mayoral primary and runoff. Ferrer and most Latino elected officials supported Kerry (after some had backed Howard Dean).[12] Assemblyman Jose Rivera, the Bronx Democratic Party chair, U.S. Representative Jose Serrano, and Assemblyman Ruben Diaz Jr., both also of the Bronx, backed Sharpton.

The New York primary was, as the *New York Times* characterized it, a "make or break contest" for Edwards (Slackman 2004). Kerry's big win in New York, coupled with eight of nine Super Tuesday victories, drove Edwards out of the race the next day. The rest of the primary season was a prelude to Kerry's nomination at the Democratic National Convention in Boston in July. New York Latino leaders and officials actively campaigned outside of New York for Kerry both before and after his nomination.

At the convention, two Latinos played prominent roles. Governor Bill Richardson of New Mexico was the first Latino national convention chairman, and Congressman Robert Menéndez, chair of the House Democratic Caucus, addressed the convention on opening night, partly in Spanish. Latinos made up about 11 percent of the nearly 4,300 convention delegates in Boston. Ferrer addressed the convention on its third day. Did Latinos flex the political muscle many had forecast? No. Furthermore, no compelling Latino figure emerged at the convention in the manner of Barack Obama of Illinois.

The Republican National Convention in New York did not dance to salsa either. Indeed, the Latino Coalition's featured politician was Senator John McCain (R-AZ). No Hispanic politicians or officials were included in the prominent portions of the formal program (Tejeda 2004). Theresa Santiago, chair of the New York State Consumer Protection Board, who had headed Amigos for Pataki in the 2002 gubernatorial campaign, led the delegation. About 6 percent of the more than 4,800 delegates were Latino, a single percentage point more than at the 2000 convention. Latinos did provide benedictions and music, however. The only New York Latino to address the Republican faithful was Fernando Mateo, president of Hispanics Across America and head of the New York City taxi drivers' union.

One of the obstacles for New York City Latinos in translating population percentages into political power (most notably, to achieve greater coethnic representation) is that, unlike other U.S. cities, they are "more dispersed and politically complex for institutional and demographic reasons" (Falcon 2005: 205; Cruz 2005).

Latino voting in 2004 in New York City suggests a "concentration effect": the greater the proportion of Latinos in an election district (the equivalent of a precinct in other states) with at least one hundred voters, the better Kerry did against Bush.[13] Such concentration effects have been noted by Cruz, Ferradino, and Friedman (2006), who found, using ecological inference techniques (King 1997) on 2004 voting data for the 150 districts composing the New York state assembly, that the proportion of Latinos voting Democratic declined where Latinos were less concentrated.[14] A 1 percent increase in the proportion of Latino voters is associated with a 0.27 percent increase in the Democratic vote and a statistically significant decrease of 0.34 percent in the Republican vote (Cruz, Ferradino, and Friedman 2006).

What are the consequences of such a finding? It depends on several factors, including, most notably, how competitive the election is and the relative turnout of other racial or ethnic groups in comparison to that of Latinos.

Hispanics leaving the polls in New York 2004 overwhelmingly described themselves as Democrats—68 percent versus the 16 percent who "usually think of themselves" as Republicans—similar to the Hispanic Federation poll results in June. Twelve percent thought of themselves as Independents. Ideologically, nearly half (47 percent) of New York State Latinos considered themselves moderates, 31 percent said they were liberals, and 24 percent called themselves conservatives. Even considering the large error margins, Latinos were decidedly Democratic in their presidential vote and liberal-to-moderate in their political ideology.

In terms of gender, Latinas made up 60 percent of New York State Latino voters in November 2004 (63 percent four years earlier). Thus, even with the large margin of error (+/–8 percent), Latinas made up a majority of the Latino electorate. Women made up the same proportions of white and black voters in the NEP exit poll, while Asian voters were about evenly divided by gender.

About one in four (26 percent) Latino voters were casting a ballot for the first time in 2004—three times the percentage of whites (8 percent) and blacks (7 percent). Latinos, except for Puerto Ricans, are a "newer" electorate, reflecting their immigrant status and younger than average age in comparison to the typical New Yorker.

The NEP also asked a few questions about President Bush and key policy issues. New York State Latino voters were quite negative in their assessments of his presidency. Fully two-thirds (67 percent) disapproved of his overall job performance, and the same number disapproved of his handling of the Iraq war (and with a near-majority strongly disapproving). Sixty-one percent said the war was a mistake, and 60 percent said the economy was in bad shape and that their financial situation had worsened. Again, even given the large error margin, it is clear that sizable and sometimes overwhelming majorities of Latinos disapproved of George Bush's job performance and the war in Iraq.

LATINO POTENTIAL AND ACTUAL ELECTORATES IN NEW YORK

It has become a cliché that Latinos nationally, including those in New York, register and turn out in lower proportions than whites, blacks, or Asians (DeSipio 1996; Pachon 1999; Cruz 2005; Barreto 2007). In

New York City, 32 percent of Latinos reported not being registered to vote (Hispanic Federation 2004). It follows that should Latinos register and vote, they will play increasingly influential and sometimes decisive roles in New York City, New York State, and national politics. What, then, are the actual and potential Latino electorates in New York?

Age, citizenship, and registration are the legal gates to electoral participation. Adult citizens must be registered, and these potential voters must actually cast a ballot. Thus four population categories represent different levels of political potential (see Pew 2005): (1) the *overall population,* which includes people of all ages and citizenship statuses; (2) the *electorate,* which constitutes individuals who are eligible to vote—those at least eighteen years old and having U.S. citizenship; (3) *registered voters,* constituting those who are eligible and officially enrolled; and (4) *actual voters,* that is, individuals who are eligible to vote, registered, and actually cast a ballot. Like Latinos nationally, population growth in New York City and New York State through immigration and high birthrates "yields increases in the number of eligible voters at a slower and potentially diminished rate compared to other groups" (Pew 2005: 2).

Overall Population

The 2000 census found 2,868,000 Latinos residing in New York State, or 15.1 percent of the state's population of 18,980,000. This was a 12 percent increase from 1990. New York was home to the third largest Latino population in the United States (following California and Texas) and was the eighth largest in terms of percent of the state Latino population. Latinos made up 66 percent of total state population growth from 1990 to 2000. During that decade, the total state population rose 5.5 percent, and the Latino population grew by 29.5 percent.

In New York City, 2,161,000 residents (27 percent of the 8,008,000 New Yorkers) characterized themselves as "Hispanic" in the 2000 census, up from 1,783,511 individuals in 1990 (24.4 percent).[15] By 2004 the population grew to 2,219,000 people of the 7,919,000 total, or 28 percent of the city (U.S. Census Bureau 2004). In addition, according to estimates from the 2004 American Community Survey, the statewide Hispanic population had grown to 3,034,000 individuals of the 18,634,000 total New Yorkers, or 16 percent of the state.

Not only did the number of Latinos increase in the state and in New York City, but so did the national-origin diversity of this population. Most important, Puerto Ricans continued their decline as a proportion of the overall Latino population: in New York City, from 1990 to 2000, by 12.2 percent (108,000 fewer individuals, for a new total of 790,000); in New York State, from 49 percent in 1990 to 38 percent in 2000. By contrast, Dominicans and Mexicans dramatically increased in numbers (to 2 percent and 9 percent, respectively, by 2003), and Central and South Americans grew to 25 percent of all New York State Hispanics.

The Electorate

Latino voter eligibility continues to lag overall Latino population growth in both New York City and New York State. While Latinos make up 15 percent of the total state population, they constitute 14 percent of the voting age population (VAP). In New York City, Latinos similarly make up 27 percent of the general population but 25 percent of the VAP.

Because many adult Latinos are not citizens (32 percent), the VAP of Hispanic citizens is lower still. During the 1990s and into 2004, while the overall Hispanic population grew substantially, the growth of the VAP was much smaller. This was due to increased immigration and the aging and emigration of Puerto Ricans, although these factors were partially offset by the surge in naturalization of adult immigrants since 1996, which greatly expanded the pool of potential Hispanic voters (Mollenkopf and Miranda 2002). Though the Hispanic citizen VAP only grew slowly, the city's overall eligible electorate actually declined, thus increasing the relative Hispanic share.

Registered Voters

According to the U.S. Census Bureau, about 754,000 Hispanic New York State residents were registered to vote in 2004—only 56 percent of those eligible. White and black New York eligible voters were more likely to register—62 percent and 71 percent, respectively. Only eligible Asian American citizens registered at a lower rate, 47 percent.

Nonetheless, the sheer number of Latinos registered to vote grew substantially in both the state and the city. In New York City, the number of Latino registrants increased by 46 percent, from 450,000 in 1990 to more than 657,000 in 2004. In fact, Latino registration accounted for about a third of the overall growth in registered voters in New York City during the decade. Latino voter registration increased in all boroughs, with the most growth in the Bronx and Queens. In terms of partisanship, approximately 518,000 were registered as Democrats, compared to 57,000 registered as Republicans in 2002. The just over one hundred thousand Independents outnumbered the combined registration of Latinos in all minor parties (Mollenkopf and Miranda 2002).

In 2004 two-thirds (68 percent) of eligible New York City Latinos reported that they had registered to vote.[16] They have reported higher registration levels over the past several years, according to the Hispanic Federation's annual surveys (see fig. 8.1). Indeed, from 1996 to 2004 the proportion of registered Latinos increased by 17 points, or by fully one-third. The proportion of Puerto Ricans, Dominicans, and other Latinos among all registered Latino New Yorkers has been fairly stable over the past few years of the Hispanic Federation surveys.

Why are Hispanic New Yorkers not registered to vote? The 2004 Hispanic Federation Survey found that among those not registered, 40 percent were not citizens, and 18 percent said they intended to register but had not yet done so.

Before the 2004 election, the National Association of Social Workers (NASW) NYC Chapter and the Human Services Council (HSC) of NYC, Inc.,[17] launched a nonpartisan voter registration project that enrolled more than 23,000 new potential voters. The NASW-HSC project was a citywide effort and targeted a wide number of zip codes where Latinos make up a large component of the population, such as the southern Bronx and the Upper East Side of Manhattan (see fig. 8.1).

This project was one of the few that actively registered new Latino voters. None of the most important national registration and mobilization campaigns that target Latinos—such as those conducted by the Southwest Voter Registration Education Project (SVREP) and the New Democrat Network (NDN)—had a significant or strong presence in New York. To some extent, this may explain the low turnout rates experienced in the city, since these campaigns are a direct way of increasing

Latino turnout (de la Garza 2004). In contrast, the Hispanic Federation of New York ran a successful Latino voter registration effort in the New York metropolitan area, registering 15,000 Latinos in New York, New Jersey, and Connecticut, in the three months before the registration deadlines in those states.

Although registration efforts do not increase Latino turnout automatically, registration drives may have other important political effects. For instance, registering new voters may change the nationality/ancestry voter distribution in a particular area. Elected officials would likely be attentive to this demographic change since it has the potential to alter the political alignments in their districts.

According to the 2005 Hispanic Federation Survey, fewer than half (46 percent) of New York City Latinos eligible to vote actually cast ballots in 2004. Among those who were registered, the reported turnout rate was 81 percent. White and black New Yorkers had higher rates of participation: among whites, 65 percent of eligible voters and

Figure 8.1. Total Number of Newly Registered Voters by Zip Code

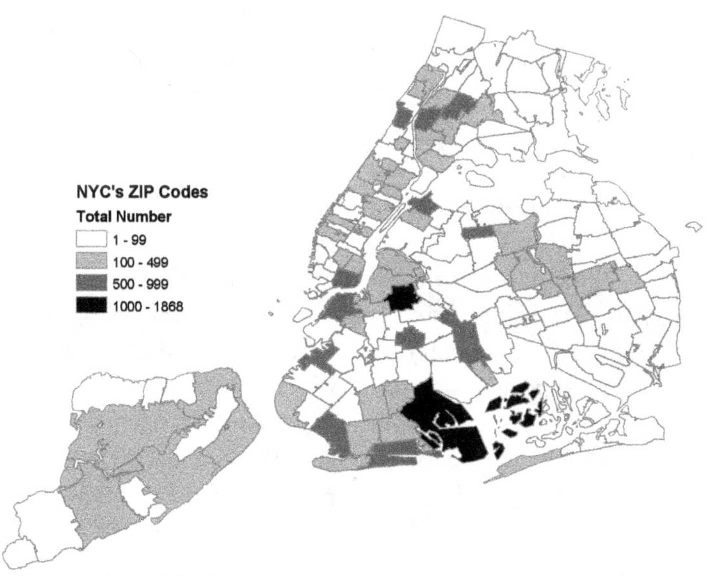

Source: Authors with data from Human Services Non-Partisan Registration Project.

91 percent of registered voters voted; among blacks, the numbers were 62 percent and 88 percent, respectively. Asian American participation was most similar to that of Hispanics, as only 39 percent of Asian American eligible voters and 84 percent of registered voters cast a ballot.

Impact of Increased Diversity

Increased diversity of nationality/ancestry appears to affect Latinos' diversity of participation and partisanship. As the diversity of nationality/ancestry increases, new political, economic, and social circumstances confront Latinos that may affect not only their political participation but also their policy perspectives. In addition, more diverse neighborhoods will increase the likelihood that Latinos socialize with neighbors that have different political allegiances and preferences, thus affecting how they participate and identify politically (Brown 1981; de la Garza and Cortina 2007; Gimpel 1999).

In areas of New York City with sizable immigrant populations, Latino turnout rates and support for Kerry and Bush among registered voters varied. Districts with higher concentrations of specific immigrant groups (e.g., immigrants from the Dominican Republic in senate District 31 and immigrants from Colombia and Ecuador in senate District 13)[18] have turnout rates above the Latino citywide average turnout (45 percent and 42 percent, respectively). In contrast, Latino registered voter turnout among those who live in the northern Bronx, where a number of non-Latino Jamaican immigrants live, was around 36 percent.

Similarly, ethnicity/nationality/ancestry appears to have influenced the voting partisanship of Latino subgroups. For instance, approximately 92 percent of Latino voters in the largely Dominican Washington Heights area supported John Kerry while only 4 percent voted for George Bush. Latino registered voters who lived in Jackson Heights, Corona, and Elmhurst, where there was a sizable population of immigrants from Colombia, Ecuador, the Dominican Republic, and Mexico, also voted overwhelmingly for Kerry—88 percent, versus 11 percent for Bush.

According to the Hispanic Federation Survey, national-origin group affiliation also affected Latino voter registration rates in 2004. Eighty-nine percent of Puerto Ricans, who are native-born citizens and the longest and most widely settled Latino group, reported being registered to vote, in comparison to 61 percent of Dominicans and 55 percent of all other Hispanics. These figures are all slight improvements over 2001, which saw 86 percent of Puerto Ricans, 56 percent of Dominicans, and 48 percent of other Latinos reporting voter registration.

Voter registration figures also show that registered Puerto Ricans and Dominicans are more Democratic (76 percent and 79 percent, respectively) than are other Latinos (67 percent). These "other Latinos" are not more Republican, however, but more likely to be unaffiliated (11 percent for other Hispanics vs. 5 percent for Puerto Ricans and 4 percent for Dominicans). The Hispanic Federation Survey shows that the overwhelming majority among all Hispanic income groups are Democrats, even among the most affluent ($40,000+); 68 percent identified as Democrats versus 19 percent as Republicans (this is in line with previous research by Gimpel and Kaufmann [2001]).

The increasing number and diversity of the city's Latino population has sometimes produced conflict and electoral competition among Latino subgroups. This is especially the case between the more established Puerto Rican population and the growing number of Dominicans, Central and South Americans, and Mexicans, such as in City Council District 21 in Queens. South and Central Americans tend to be more conservative and somewhat more Republican (though still substantially Democratic). They tend to be somewhat more middle class, with higher income, and more likely to own rather than rent their residences.

Last, as the political science literature would predict, Latino voter registration rates increased with the number of years residing in New York, education, income levels, and age. The registration rate for Latinos making less than $10,000 is 55 percent, but for those making over $40,000 it is 85 percent. Fifty-nine percent of the youngest age group (18 to 24) are registered versus 83 percent of the oldest (65+).[19]

FINAL THOUGHTS

The politics of New York City (and New York State) has and will always be shaped by demography—race, ethnicity, and country of origin or ancestry. These demographic factors do not immediately translate into political destiny, however. General population numbers do not necessarily mean a greater number of voters or additional representation in legislative or executive offices. Socioeconomic status, citizenship status, national origin, length of residency, generation, gender, and age will powerfully affect who votes (and for whom). Decennial redistricting, Voting Rights Act requirements, local term limits, the personalities and issue appeals of candidates, the role of parties, emerging ethnic group leadership, and the idiosyncratic and unpredictable factors that haunt all elections are also important variables.

Historically, shifts in New York's political topography have been tectonic, not catastrophic—gradual but inexorable. The political landscape of New York City and New York State presents different levels: local (city council and state legislature), boroughwide/countywide, citywide, and statewide. In New York City, other immigrant groups such as the Irish, Jews, and Italians took a generation or two between their arrival in force and their climb to political power. African Americans followed a similar course. So, too, have Latinos, though the specific political contours differ.

While the share of votes cast by Latinos in New York State and New York City general elections is still much lower than their share of the respective population, the voting potential of Latinos is remarkable given that so many (29 percent in the city) were not registered to vote. In addition, the old and new immigrants have produced a large second generation that is now approaching voting age. Like young people from all ethnic and racial backgrounds, however, Latino young adults are less likely to vote than their elders. Only as more of those of voting age, both current citizens and those who will become naturalized, register to vote and then actually cast ballots will the latent power of Latino voters become manifest.

As for the 2004 presidential election, the Latino presence in the state electorate had no discernible influence on the issues raised and emphasized by the campaigns of the Republican and Democratic Parties (or in the U.S. Senate race). The campaigns conducted virtually no meaningful Latino-specific outreach. Nor did the churches or 527s have a discernible effect on Latino voting in New York.

In sum, the 2004 presidential, U.S. Senate, and local elections were "status quo" elections for New York State Latinos. Whether Latinos are an emerging "swing vote" or still a Democratic "hip pocket" group remained unanswered. In 2004 Latinos did not influence the presidential outcome in New York State. They were strongly Democratic voters in a solidly Democratic state. They could be safely ignored by both parties.

Latino voters in New York, while making up a similar proportion of the national electorate, were far more likely to vote for Democrat John Kerry than were Latinos nationally (75 percent to 24 percent for Bush in New York vs. 59 percent to 40 percent nationally). Latinos in New York and throughout the nation have changed U.S. economic, social, cultural, and political life, but they have not had "much political influence in presidential politics" (Shapiro 2005). They did not in New York in 2004.

NOTES

1. Although this chapter generally and much of the literature talks about a "Latino vote," Latinos, specifically in New York, are not monolithic; they are divided by nativity (U.S. born or not), class, national origin, and geography. There are distinct cultural and historical differences among Latinos. The Latino electorate in New York City is changing, with Puerto Ricans, the longest-residing Latino New Yorkers, declining both in absolute numbers as they move out of the city and proportionately as the number of Dominicans and "other" Latinos grow.

2. "Red" and "blue" classifications cannot capture the myriad and complex political dynamics in most states. For example, some states labeled "red" by the media have one or more Democratic statewide officeholders, and some "blue" states do not shy away from electing GOP senators or governors, including three terms for New York Governor George Pataki.

3. The 527 groups are tax-exempt, organized under section 527 of the Internal Revenue Code to raise money for political activities, such as voter mobilization efforts and issue advocacy.

4. New York City Latinos gave 78 percent of their votes to Michael Dukakis in 1988, 77 percent to Bill Clinton in 1992, and 90 percent to Clinton in 1996 (Falcon 2005).

5. Schumer bested the 69 percent that Daniel Patrick Moynihan garnered in his 1988 U.S. Senate reelection bid against Robert R. McMillan.

6. The survey was conducted by Mirram Global, June 9–30, 2004. The survey reached 800 Hispanic adults living in New York City, with a maximum error margin of +/–3.5 percent at the 95 percent confidence level. Muzzio assisted in the development of the questionnaire and with the analysis and reporting of the data.

7. The nationwide NEP poll had George Bush garnering 44 percent of the Latino vote; the result was widely reported but challenged (e.g., Fears 2004). Teixeira's (2004) and National Council of La Raza's 2004–5 analyses suggest 39 percent, which has been adopted by other analysts (see Leal et al. 2005 for a detailed discussion of the issue). There is no evidence that the final exit poll did not represent New York State voters, including Latinos.

8. Ferrer did indeed win the Democratic nomination for mayor in 2005 but lost to incumbent Republican Mayor Mike Bloomberg in a 59–39 percent landslide. An Election Day (Nov. 8) telephone survey among 1,105 registered voters who reported having voted that day in New York City conducted by Pace University (error margin of +/–2.9 percent) suggests that Bloomberg got a sizable proportion of the Latino vote—34 percent—against the city's first Latino mayoral candidate (Trichter and Paige 2005).

9. Muzzio conversation with Fernando Ferrer, Congressman Charles Rangel, and two other participants in the meeting.

10. The survey was conducted by Blum and Weprin Associates between April 22 and May 2001. The survey interviewed 1,001 Hispanic adults living in New York City, with a maximum error margin of +/–3 percent at the 95 percent confidence level. Muzzio assisted in the development of the questionnaire and with the analysis and reporting of the data.

11. Such data are limited because (1) the assembly districts are not exclusively Hispanic and (2) Hispanics living in other parts of the city are excluded.

12. Dean had been endorsed by U.S. Representative Nydia Velazquez (D-Brooklyn) and four New York City Council members.

13. The Latino vote for each candidate was estimated using New York City's voter list and the electoral returns for each electoral district. We follow standard approaches of ecological inference following the methodology outlined in King (1997) and King, Rosen, and Tanner (2004).

14. Cruz, Ferradino, and Friedman (2006) also found that the proportion of Latinos voting Democratic declined in areas outside New York City as well as where there are lower concentrations of Latinos (there is overlap). The authors "suggest that when thinking about Latino politics in New York it is inappropriate to see New York State as simply New York City writ large" (1).

15. Changing census definitions of "Hispanic" make strict comparability difficult. In the 2000 census, people of Spanish-Hispanic-Latino origin could identify as Mexican, Puerto Rican, Cuban, or other Spanish-Hispanic-Latino. "Latino" appeared on the census form for the first time in 2000 (U.S. Census Bureau 2001).

16. Reported registration grew to 77 percent of New York City Latinos in summer 2005, according to the 2005 Hispanic Federation survey. This was the largest one-year increase in the thirteen years that the Hispanic Federation has conducted surveys.

17. The authors would like to thank Allison Sesso, associate director of the Human Services Council of New York, for providing registration data.

18. As suggested by Mollenkopf, Olson, and Ross 2001.

19. See Mollenkopf and Miranda 2002: table 1 for minor party registration figures.

REFERENCES

Barreto, Matt. 2007. "¡Sí Se Puede! Latino Candidates and the Mobilization of Latino Voters." *American Political Science Review* 101 (3): 425–41.

Brown, Thad A. 1981. "On Contextual Change and Partisan Attitudes." *British Journal of Political Science* 11 (4): 427–47.

Chernikoff, Helen, and Kelly Dougherty. 2005. *The Latino Vote 2004: Partisanship vs. Personalities in El Barrio.* New York: Columbia University Press.

CNN 2004. "Hispanics Could Hold Key to a Win." www.cnn.com/2004/ALL POLITICS/10/18/latino.vote/index. Accessed May 8, 2008.

Cruz, Jose E., and Efrain Escobedo. 2005. *Looking Backward, Looking Forward: The 2005 New York City Mayoral Race.* Albany: State University of New York Press.

Cruz, Jose, Cecilia Ferradino, and Sally Friedman. 2006. *Latino Voting in the 2004 Election: The Case of New York.* Albany, NY: NYLARNet.

Current Population Survey (CPS). 2005. "Voting and Registration in the Election of November 2004." U.S. Bureau of the Census, Washington, DC.

Department of City Planning. 2004. "The Newest New Yorkers." City of New York.

de la Garza, Rodolfo. 2004. "Latino Politics." *Annual Review of Political Science and Politics* 7: 91–123.

de la Garza, Rodolfo, and Jeronimo Cortina. 2007. "Are Latinos Republicans but Just Don't Know It?" *American Politics Research* 35 (2): 202–23.

de la Garza, Rodolfo, and Louis DeSipio. 1994. "Overview: The Link between Individuals and Electoral Institutions in Five Latino Neighborhoods." In *Barrio Ballots: Latino Politics in the 1990 Elections,* ed. Rodolfo de la Garza, Marta Menchaca, and Louis DeSipio, 1–42. Boulder, CO: Westview Press.

Falcon, Angelo. 2005. "Pues, at Least We Had Hillary: Latino New York City, the 2000 Elections, and the Limits of Party Loyalty." In *Muted Voices: Latinos and the 2000 Elections,* ed. Rodolfo O. de la Garza and Louis DeSipio. Lanham, MD: Rowman and Littlefield.

Fears, Darryl. 2004. "Pollsters Debate Hispanics' Presidential Voting: Discrepancy in Estimates vs. Results Examined." *Washington Post,* November 26.

Gimpel, James G. 1999. *Separate Destinations: Migration, Immigration, and the Politics of Places.* Ann Arbor: University of Michigan Press.

Gimpel, James G., and Karen Kaufmann. 2001. "Impossible Dream or Distant Reality? Republican Efforts to Attract Latino Voters." Center for Immigration Studies, Washington, DC. *Backgrounder,* August. Available at www.cis.org/articles/2001/back901.html.

Goris, Anneris, and Pedro Pedraza. 1994. "Puerto Rican Politics in East Harlem's 'El Barrio.'" In *Barrio Ballots: Latino Politics in the 1990 Elections,* ed. Rodolfo O. de la Garza, M. Menchaca, and Louis DeSipio, 65–82. Boulder, CO: Westview Press.

Hispanic Federation. 2004. "Hispanic Nueva Yorkers on Nueva York." Hispanic Federation's 12th Annual Survey, New York.

Jordan, Howard. 2003. "A Puerto Rican Loses Sight of Her People." *Puerto Rico Herald,* January 7.

King, Gary. 1997. *A Solution to the Ecological Inference Problem: Reconstructing Individual Behavior from Aggregate Data.* Princeton, NJ: Princeton University Press.

King, Gary, Ori Rosen, and Martin A. Tanner, eds. 2004. *Ecological Inference: New Methodological Strategies.* New York: Cambridge University Press.

Leal, David L., Matt A. Barreto, Jongho Lee, and Rodolfo O. de la Garza. 2005. "The Latino Vote in the 2004 Election." *PS: Political Science and Politics* 38 (1): 41–49.

McNickle, Chris. 1993. *To Be Mayor of New York: Ethnic Politics in the City.* New York: Columbia University Press.

Metz, Andrew. 2002. "Emerging Political Power: Hispanics Make their Mark Upstate." *Newsday,* August 27.

Mollenkopf, John, and Luis A Miranda Jr. 2002. *Latino Political Participation in New York City: A Report to the Hispanic Federation.* New York: Hispanic Federation.

Mollenkopf, John, David Olson, and Timothy Ross. 2001. "Immigrant Political Participation in New York and Los Angeles." In *Governing American Cities: Interethnic Coalitions, Competition, and Conflict,* ed. M. Jones-Correa. New York: Russell Sage Foundation.

"Most Hispanics Say They're Democrats: Those Polled Also Show Some Ambivalence." 2002. *Washington Post,* October 2.

National Association of Latino Elected and Appointed Officials (NALEO). 2003. *National Directory of Latino Elected Officials.* Los Angeles: NALEO Educational Fund.

Ojita, Mirta. 2004. "City's Hispanics Shift, Moving toward G.O.P." *New York Times,* November 8.

Pachon, Harry. 1999. "California Latino Politics and the 1996 Election: From Potential to Reality." In *Awash in the Mainstream: Latino Politics in the 1996 Elections,* ed. Rodolfo O. de la Garza and Louis DeSipio, 167–90. Boulder, CO: Westview Press.

PrimeNY. 2002. E-mail communication with Douglas Muzzio. New York.

Ramirez, Elva. 2004. "Mendez Ends Longest Senate Career by a Puerto Rican 2004." http://web.jrn.columbia.edu/studentwork/election/2004/ny_state_ramirez01.asp. Accessed May 8, 2008.

Ramos, Jorge. 2004. *The Latino Wave: How Hispanics Will Choose the Next President.* New York: HarperCollins.

Rau, Jordan. 2002a. "The Vote to Watch: Latinos Hold Potential to Swing Statewide and Local Elections." *Newsday,* August 25.

———. 2002b. "The Dominican Factor: Group Struggles with Political Growing Pains." *Newsday,* August 26.

Sargent, Greg. 2003. "GOPs Chair Remaking NY in Bush Image." *New York Observer,* July 27. Available at www.observer.com/node/47853.

Shapiro, Robert Y. 2005. "Awaited Voices: Latinos and U.S. Elections." In *Muted Voices: Latinos and the 2000 Elections,* ed. Rodolfo O. de la Garza and Louis DeSipio, 1–12. Lanham, MD: Rowman and Littlefield.

Slackman, Michael. 2004. "Kerry and Edwards Scrambling for Support in New York Vote." *New York Times,* February 24, B2.

Suro, Roberto, Richard Fry, and Jeffrey Passel. 2005. *Hispanics and the 2004 Election: Population, Electorate and Voters.* Washington, DC: Pew Hispanic Center.

Teixeira, Ruy. 2004. "44 Percent of Hispanics Voted for Bush." AlterNet 2004. http://www.alternet.org/election04/20606/. Accessed May 8, 2008.

Tejeda, Gregory. 2004. "Commentary: GOP Uses Hispanics for Show." *Washington Times,* August 24.

Trichter, Jonathan, and Chris Paige. 2005. "New York City Mayoral Election Study: General Election Telephone Exit Poll." Pace University Poll. Available at www.pace.edu/page.cfm?doc_id=10380.

U.S. Census Bureau. 2000. Summary File 1 (SF 1) 100-Percent Data.

———. 2001. "The Hispanic Population: Census 2000 Brief." May.

———. 2004. "Current Population Survey, Voting and Registration in the Election of November 2004." Table 4a, Reported Voting of the Total Voting-Age Population, by Sex, Race and Hispanic Origin, for States. November.

Wattenberg, Martin P. 2005. "Elections: Turnout in the 2004 Presidential Elections." *Presidential Studies Quarterly* 35 (1): 138–46.

Chapter Nine

The Hispanic Vote in Florida

DARIO MORENO, MARIA ILCHEVA, AND JUAN CARLOS FLORES

Florida's twenty-seven Electoral College votes and the state's status as a pivotal swing state ensure its continued importance in national politics. The 2000 presidential election, despite all the irregularities and mistakes, was Florida's coming-out party as a critical player in American presidential politics. This role was repeated in the 2004 election, as both major political parties poured money, personal time, and other resources into the state. Political pundits repeated the mantra throughout the 2004 election that the road to the White House went through Florida and Ohio. Because of continuous rapid population growth, Florida is projected to surpass New York by 2010 as the nation's third most populous state. This will heighten the importance of Florida as a battleground state as well as the importance of its Hispanic vote.

The 2004 presidential election saw the continuation of the growth and diversification of the Hispanic vote in the Sunshine State. Hispanic voters now constitute 15 percent of the Florida electorate, nearly equaling the number of African American voters, who have traditionally been the most politically important minority in the state.[1] The growth in the Hispanic electorate is remarkable considering that as late as 1998 Hispanics constituted only 9 percent of the state's voters. In addition to having one of the largest Hispanic communities in the United States, Florida has the most diverse Hispanic population. The once-dominant Cuban Americans make up only 50 percent of the Hispanic vote; Puerto Ricans now make up roughly 30 percent, and the remaining 20 percent consists primarily of Colombians, Nicaraguans, Mexicans, Venezuelans, Peruvians, and Salvadorans.

Current demographic trends confirm Hispanic confidence in their growing influence in state politics. Hispanics are now the largest minority group in Florida. According to the 2000 census, they accounted for 16.8 percent (2,682,715 individuals) of its population. This is remarkable growth considering that there were only 860,000 Latinos (8.9 percent of the population) in Florida in 1980. The 1990 census showed a ten-year 83 percent growth in the Hispanic population to 1,574,000, or 12.1 percent of the state total. The Hispanic population then grew by an impressive 70.4 percent from 1990 to 2000. More recent U.S. Census Bureau estimates from the 2003 American Community Survey put the Hispanic population of Florida at 3,108,578, or 18.7 percent of the state's population. Given the rapid pace of population growth, Hispanic political power in Florida should continue to grow for the foreseeable future.

Cuban Americans, accounting for just one-third of Hispanics in Florida, remain the dominant Hispanic national-origin group in that state. Over two-thirds of all Cubans in the United States live in Florida, and this extraordinary concentration has been a critical factor in Cuban political influence generally. Cuban Americans comprise eight percent of Florida's electorate,[2] and Florida's close partisan divide allowed Cuban Americans to be the decisive voters in at least three statewide elections. Overwhelming Cuban support for Connie Mack (R-FL) was instrumental in his narrow 1988 U.S. Senate election victory. Mack edged out Buddy McKay by only 33,612 votes of the more than four million cast. Similarly, Cuban Americans provided the critical margin of victory for George H. W. Bush in Florida in 1992 and for George W. Bush (and thereby in the Electoral College) in the controversial 2000 election.

In the Sunshine State, Cubans number 833,120, and a remarkable 650,601 reside in Miami-Dade County. In other words, over half of all Cubans in the United States (52 percent) and over three-fourths (78 percent) of all Cubans in Florida live in just one county. This makes Miami-Dade the epicenter of Hispanic politics in Florida (Moreno 2004: 84). It is also the only Florida county that is majority Hispanic, with a total Latino population of 1,291,737 individuals, or 58 percent. Nearly half (48.1 percent) of all Hispanics in Florida live in Miami-Dade County. Neighboring Broward County has the second-largest Hispanic population in the state. Combined, 55.2 percent of the total Florida Hispanic population resides in these two southeastern Florida counties. Not surprisingly, Hispanics control nearly every major political institution in Miami-Dade County. At the time of this writing, the county mayor is Cuban American, as are seven of the thirteen members of the county commission, five out of the nine school board members, and the state attorney.

The rapid growth of the Puerto Rican population in Central Florida has supplemented this heavy concentration of Hispanics in South Florida. Florida has replaced New Jersey as the state with the second-largest concentration of Puerto Ricans and is now only behind New York (U.S. Census Bureau 2001). More than two hundred thousand Puerto Ricans have settled in the Orlando area of Central Florida, comprising Orange, Osceola, Volusia, Seminole, and Polk Counties. Another 97,800 Latinos reside in Tampa Bay, down the I-4 corridor from Orlando. More important for future trends, Orange and Osceola Counties have displaced the Bronx as the top destination for Puerto Rican newcomers. While 9,240 newcomers left the island to settle in Orange County and 7,000 more moved to neighboring Osceola County, only 5,319 went to the Bronx (Ramos 2005).

These figures show that the Puerto Rican population of Central Florida is far more dispersed than the Cuban community in Miami. Whereas Cuban Americans are concentrated mostly in one county, Puerto Ricans are spread out over seven Florida counties that straddle Interstate 4. This settlement pattern means that electing Hispanic leaders is far more difficult in Central Florida than in South Florida. It was not until 2002 that a Central Florida Puerto Rican was elected to the state legislature, and in 2004 Mildred Fernandez became the first Puerto Rican county commissioner in Orange County.

FLORIDA AS A BATTLEGROUND STATE

Florida has not always been a battleground state. It was historically part of the Democratic "solid South," and it then became one of the most Republican states in the South. In 1998 it became the first southern state in which the GOP was able to establish control over the governor's mansion and both houses of the state legislature. Locally, the Republican Party has become dominant. In the state legislature, near-hegemonic control of the Florida house and senate by the Democrats has given way to Republican domination. In 1976 Republicans controlled only 29 out of 120 seats in the Florida house and 9 of the 40 seats in the senate. By 2004 Republicans controlled 83 of the 120 seats in the house and 26 of the 40 seats in the senate. During the same period, the Republicans swept every major statewide office except the U.S. Senate seat currently held by Democrat Bill Nelson.

Since 1952 Florida has voted for Republican presidential candidates in all but three elections: 1964, 1976, and 1996. The rising number of Independent voters has mitigated the Republican dominance of Florida politics, however. While in 1994 only 8 percent of Florida's registered voters were Independents (no party affiliation), the number of Independents had mushroomed to 18.3 percent by the 2004 presidential election. Democratic registration fell from 49.4 percent to 41.3 percent, while Republican registration declined from 41.8 percent to 37.7 percent. This Independent streak among Florida voters helps to explain Ross Perot's strong showing, both in 1992 when he received 19.8 percent of the vote and in 1996 when he obtained 9.1 percent (Florida Department of State 2005). This is slightly better than Perot's nationwide performance of 18.9 percent and 8.4 percent, respectively. Independent-minded voters have increasingly become a critical swing vote in Florida elections.

The gains made by the Republican Party and the increases in Independent voters have come at the inevitable expense of the Democratic Party. Although Democrats hold a slim 368,757 lead among registered voters, their victories have become more sporadic. Tracking partisan changes in Florida, the political scientist Stephen Craig (1998: 31) concludes, "At the very least, it is clear that the Democrats' stranglehold of voter loyalties is a thing of the past." Some political analysts argue that the right candidate can put Florida back into the Democratic column, however. For example, Susan MacManus (2004: 15) contends that "the right candidate tends to be a moderate, a centrist." It is no coincidence that the only three Democratic presidential candidates to carry the Sunshine State in recent history all ran as moderates from the South: Lyndon Johnson, Jimmy Carter, and Bill Clinton.

Hispanics have played a crucial role in the transformation of Florida politics. Cuban Americans in particular were instrumental in the ascendancy of the Florida GOP. They made their political debut during the 1980 presidential election, when Ronald Reagan became the first presidential candidate to openly court their votes. He was rewarded with over 80 percent Cuban support in 1980 and 88 percent in his 1984 reelection campaign (Moreno and Warren 1992: 127). The process of Cuban American empowerment was accelerated by the 1980 reappointments and Florida's shift from multimember to single-member state house and senate districts. In 1982 three Cuban Republicans defeated three Democratic Anglo incumbents in state house races in Miami. This initiated a political transformation of the South Florida delegation to the state legislature in which Cuban Republicans replaced Anglo Democrats in Tallahassee, facilitating the Republican takeover of the Florida legislature.

Cuban Americans reaffirmed their strong ties to the Republican Party in the 1988 presidential election. Republican George H. W. Bush carried the Hispanic precincts of Miami-Dade County with approximately 85 percent, and conservative GOP Senate candidate Connie Mack carried those same precincts with 80 percent of the vote (Moreno and Warren 1992: 127). Cuban American Republicans continued to make impressive gains in the state legislature, capturing two additional seats in the senate. By 1990 they represented seven districts in the Florida house, three districts in the state senate, and one U.S. House seat, all seats previously held by Anglo Democrats.

The 1992 presidential election marked the first time a Democratic nominee for president campaigned among Florida's Hispanic voters. Democrats believed that their ticket of Bill Clinton and Al Gore, both moderate southern Democrats, had a real opportunity to win in Florida. Given Clinton's relatively secure status in most of his must-win states, the Democratic strategy in Florida was to keep President Bush pinned down trying to protect his own base. One political pundit described it as "the political equivalent of a full court press, of in-your-face campaigning going after the other guy's strength" (Fiedler 1992). Part of this strategy was wooing Republican Cuban American voters. Clinton surprised the Bush administration by endorsing the Cuban Democracy Act (also known as the Torricelli bill) in April 1992 at a Little Havana fund-raiser in Miami (Moreno and Warren 1996: 175). The Bush administration had been reluctant to support the bill because it contained provisions that imposed U.S. laws beyond its borders. In part due to this pressure, President Bush finally endorsed the bill in summer 1992.

In addition to his early support for the Torricelli bill, Clinton spoke out against Fidel Castro in ways that distinguished him from previous Democratic candidates. He based his Miami strategy on reassuring Cuban Americans that he would not lift the economic embargo against Cuba (Moreno and Warren 1996: 176). This allowed him to make inroads among Cubans, especially at the elite level. He raised $275,000 in two Little Havana fund-raisers, one of which was attended by the president of the influential Cuban American National Foundation (CANF), Jorge Mas Canosa. Hillary Clinton and Tipper Gore made several follow-up visits that were considered successful. Democrats hoped that Clinton's campaign would lay the groundwork for reversing some of the bitterness and distrust toward Democrats that still lingered among many Cuban American voters, stemming from Kennedy's Bay of Pigs fiasco in 1961 and Carter's controversial dialogue with the Castro regime in 1977.

Clinton's strategy did make modest inroads among Cuban American voters. Bush received 70 percent of the vote in the Hispanic precincts of Miami-Dade County, whereas he had received 85 percent in the same precincts four years earlier (Moreno and Warren 1996: 177). Bush's margin of victory in Florida was only 86,000 votes, a dramatic reduction of his almost one-million-vote margin in 1988. Although Clinton received only 22 percent of the Cuban American vote in 1992 and fell short of Democratic higher expectations, it was still a high-water mark for a Democratic presidential nominee. The fact that gains had been realized also demonstrated that some Cuban American voters could be drawn to the Democratic column by a pledge to maintain the U.S. economic embargo on Cuba. More important, Clinton's outreach to the CANF and Jorge Mas Canosa created new opportunities for the Democrats among the Cuban American leadership.

Clinton used the groundwork he laid in the 1992 presidential election to achieve a remarkable victory in the 1996 election. Florida became the largest state to join the Democratic "win" column, only the third time that the Democrats were victorious in the state since 1952. Clinton's margin of victory, 302,000 votes, was notable given past Republican landslides. Of the constituencies targeted by the 1996 Clinton reelection campaign, no results offered a bigger surprise than the Cuban American vote (Moreno and Warren 1999: 219). For the first time, Cuban American voters gave the Democratic nominee a significant portion of their support, with more than a third voting for Clinton. Exit polls showed that only 46 percent of Florida's overall Hispanic population voted for the Republican nominee. President Clinton's 42 percent of the Hispanic vote represented a 91 percent increase over the 1992 benchmark results (Fiedler 1996).

Bob Dole's poor performance among Hispanic voters was underscored by his weak showing in Miami-Dade County. A review of the predominantly Cuban American precincts reveals how disastrous the 1996 election was for the Republicans. Even in the most lopsided Republican precincts, Hialeah and Little Havana, precincts that Bush and Reagan had carried by a margin of nine to one, Dole barely received 60 percent of the vote (Moreno and Warren 1999: 220). In the more middle class Hispanic neighborhoods of Concord and West Kendall, Clinton either cut further into or turned the Dole lead on its head (Moreno and Warren 1999: 220). Beyond wining votes, Clinton's 1996 campaign demonstrated the ability to build an organization within the Cuban community, court elite support, mute vocal opposition, and raise money. The election of a Cuban American Democrat as mayor of Miami-Dade County, Alex Penelas, reinforced the Democratic hope of building a firm toehold among Cuban Americans.

The hard work of Bill Clinton and the Democratic Party in building support in Miami's Cuban community came to an abrupt end with the Elian Gonzalez affair. Attorney General Janet Reno's decision to send the boy back to his father in Cuba set off a firestorm of protests among Cuban Americans against the Clinton administration and the

Democratic nominee, Vice President Al Gore. Many Cubans viewed the Elian case as yet another Democratic presidential betrayal in their anti-Castro struggle. Many felt that Clinton betrayed the exile community in the same way that Kennedy and Carter had done. The Elian Gonzalez affair deeply affected the Florida Hispanic campaign of both parties (Hill and Moreno 2005: 219). Vice President Gore was forced to abandon his 2000 campaign among Miami's Cuban Americans. In fact, Gore could not venture into Cuban parts of Miami for fear of massive protests over the Clinton administration's handling of the Elian case. Few prominent Cuban American Democrats, with the exception of Hialeah Mayor Raul Martinez, campaigned with the Democratic nominee. Mayor Penelas, who had publicly chastised the Clinton administration for its decision in the Elian case, concentrated instead on his own reelection. After his first-round victory in the mayoral election in September 2000, he took an extended vacation in Spain. Dispirited Cuban Democrats were left leaderless and without resources as Cuban Republicans were energized by prospects of punishing the Democrats.

Given the realities of Cuban American Miami, the Gore campaign concentrated its efforts to read the Hispanic community in Central Florida. Its strategy was to concede the Cuban vote and instead attract the rapidly growing non-Cuban Hispanic vote along the I-4 corridor between Tampa Bay and Orlando (Hill and Moreno 2005: 219). As expected, Bush did exceptionally well among Florida's Cuban Americans, taking nearly 75 percent of the vote, while Gore edged out a 53 percent victory with non-Cuban Hispanics (Hill and Moreno 2005: 221). The razor-thin Bush victory (537 votes made the difference in Florida) would not have been possible without Cuban American support, although it should be noted that many groups can claim responsibility when outcomes are so close.

THE 2004 CAMPAIGN

The narrow Republican victory in 2000 guaranteed that Florida would again be a battleground state in the 2004 presidential election. Moreover, the heavy concentration of Hispanics in a vital presidential swing state led both parties to mount aggressive campaigns to woo this disparate group.

The Democrats, in sharp contrast to the 2000 election, committed themselves to compete for votes among Miami's Cuban Americans. Party strategists borrowed a play from Clinton's successful 1992 playbook, reasoning that campaigning in the Cuban American community would force the Republicans to expend resources and time in an area where they were relatively strong. The Democrats hoped to take advantage of some important changes that had occurred in Miami in the aftermath of the Elian Gonzalez saga. Many members of the Cuban American elite believed that the outpouring of passions and emotions in the wake of the child's forceful removal had made Cuban Americans look like extremists and had given the community a black eye. Joe Garcia, then director of CANF, and prominent businessmen such as Carlos de la Cruz and Carlos Saladrigas were the most vocal proponents of this view.

Moreover, the lack of attention paid to the Cuba issue by the Bush administration disappointed many hard-line Cuban Americans. In August 2003 the entire Republican Hispanic caucus of the Florida House of Representatives sent President Bush a letter warning him that Cuban American support might suffer if he did not get tougher on Cuba. In May 2004 the administration imposed new restrictions on travel and remittances to Cuba in part as a result of these complaints. The new restrictions drew sharp criticism from some Cuban Americans (mostly recent arrivals) who argued that the new policy made it more difficult for them to aid their families in Cuba (de Valle and de Vise 2004). A poll conducted by the William Velasquez Institute and the MirRam Group indicated that support for President Bush among Cuban American registered or eligible voters had slipped to 66 percent, down from 82 percent in 2000 (Diaz 2004).

The Democrats developed a three-prong strategy to improve their showing among Hispanics in the Sunshine State. First, they invested considerable resources to replicate Gore's strong showing among Hispanics in Central Florida and in Hillsborough County. With a population of more than one million residents of which approximately 18 percent are Latino, Hillsborough is the largest county in the Tampa-St. Petersburg-Clearwater Metropolitan Statistical Area. In Hillsborough, as well as in Orange, Osceola, and Seminole Counties to the east along the I-4 corridor, the Democratic Party relied on myriad 527 groups to organize registration and get-out-the-vote (GOTV) drives among the mostly non-Cuban Latinos.

Second, spearheaded by the New Democrat Network, the party invested heavily in trying to reduce the significant Cuban American support for the Republican ticket. Democrats hired two experts on the Cuban community, former CANF executive director Joe Garcia and pollster Sergio Bendixen, to court the Cuban vote. Democrats also opened campaign headquarters in Little Havana in order to establish a physical presence in the Cuban community. Their message to Cuban Americans was simply that Republican promises to liberate Cuba were nothing more than demagoguery; what really matters to Hispanics in Miami are domestic issues such as access to health insurance, cheaper prescription drugs, and expanding Medicare (Noticias.Info 2004). The ads steered clear of the president's controversial crackdown on travel to Cuba, instead arguing that Democrats are better suited to deliver health care and jobs. "We're keeping to the economy and health care because those are the issues we've framed for our campaign, across the board," said Maria Cardona, who directed the New Democrat Network Hispanic outreach effort (Ovalle, Corral, and Clark 2004).

Third, the Democrats ran young Latino candidates for state legislative seats. Barbara Herrera-Hill in Broward, Susan Bucher in Palm Beach, and Israel Mercado in Orange County were viewed as the future of the Democratic Party among the state's Hispanics. Herrera-Hill, the only Cuban American female city commissioner in Broward County, competed against Susan Goldstein for the seat vacated by Democrat Nan Rich. Bucher, the Mexican American Democratic incumbent from Palm Beach, was challenged by Ed Heeney, a candidate without political experience. Israel Mercado, a pastor and college instructor of Puerto Rican descent, ran against incumbent John Quinones, the first Republican Puerto Rican to be elected to the Florida legislature in 2002.

The Republican campaign countered with a two-prong strategy of its own. First, Republicans touted political and policy goals. They reminded Cuban voters that President Bush was pursuing a robust strategy to hasten Cuban democratization, including toughened travel restrictions to the island and a restricted amount of remittances that exiles can send. The Bush campaign also stressed the administration's policy of spending money to help organizations that protect Cuban dissidents and promote human rights. Republicans organized a strong GOTV campaign in the traditional Cuban neighborhoods of Miami-Dade County. Second, they promoted Republican candidates in various other races. In particular, the president encouraged the U.S. Senate candidacy and nomination of Mel Martinez, his former housing secretary. As a Cuban American, Martinez was expected to mobilize a historic turnout among his co-nationals in Miami-Dade County. As the former mayor of Orange County, Martinez might also encourage his former Latino constituents in Central Florida to vote for the Republican ticket. Republican strategists hoped that Martinez's candidacy would not only aid the president's reelection effort in Florida but also help Republicans regain control of the U.S. Senate. If elected, Martinez would replace the retiring Bob Graham, a Democrat.

Although Bush did not give Martinez an "official" endorsement, support from the White House was construed from his position as a former cabinet member and the perception that he could increase Republican gains in the Sunshine State as a Cuban American (Yardley 2004). Martinez's main obstacle was to prove to the conservative Republican base that he would uphold core conservative values. This was especially critical in the Republican primary, as his opponent, former U.S. Representative Bill McCollum, had been one of the leaders in the Republican efforts to impeach President Clinton and was very popular among Florida's conservatives. He was leading the race in the early months of the campaign but started to trail as the Martinez ads questioned his conservative credentials. McCollum was branded "anti-family" for supporting stem cell research and a hate crimes law that strengthened protections for gays and lesbians. Martinez also took positions to the right of the conservative former congressman on social issues. Moreover, he retreated from his early endorsement of the Varela project, an effort by Cuban dissidents to hold a referendum on Cuban dictator Fidel Castro, in order to reassure his anti-Castro Cuban American supporters; many Cuban exiles opposed this policy because they feared it might legitimize the current Cuban constitution. Martinez also referred to the federal agents who seized Elian Gonzalez as "thugs."

The campaign leading to the Republican primary became so acrimonious that Governor Jeb Bush asked the two opponents to tone down their attacks. Days before the primary, in response to an accusation that Martinez had mismanaged government funds as secretary of Housing and Urban Development (HUD), a White House spokesman asserted, "Mel Martinez was an outstanding secretary. . . . The President appreciates Mel Martinez's service, to his administration and to his country" (Bousquet and Krueger 2004). Martinez's strategy paid off as he easily beat McCollum in the Republican primary by over 160,000 votes. Martinez trounced McCollum in heavily Hispanic Miami-Dade County by over 90,000 votes (102,441 to 10,372).

The Democratic campaign among Florida Hispanics was haunted by the specter of the Elian Gonzalez affair, which became an issue in the contest for the U.S. Senate. Alex Penelas, mayor of Miami-Dade County, who had been one of the protagonists in the saga, announced that he was running for the U.S. Senate seat being vacated by Graham. He faced Broward Congressman Peter Deutsch and the former president of the University of South Florida, Betty Castor, in the Democratic primary. The Democratic opponents of Penelas questioned his behavior during the Elian Gonzales affair and its aftermath in the campaign. Penelas had stunned his non-Cuban constituents in March 2000 by condemning the Clinton administration for its handling of the Elian affair and by suggesting that local law enforcement agencies would not cooperate with federal officials to seize the boy. Penelas also warned that any violence resulting from the seizure of Elian Gonzalez would be the fault of federal officials.

Penelas was so upset with the Clinton administration that he conveniently went on vacation in September and thus avoided having to make any campaign appearances with Al Gore. Moreover, he was not helpful in Gore's efforts to secure a recount of Miami-Dade's ballots during the 2000 postelection. Because of such behavior, Gore called Penelas "the single most treacherous and dishonest person I dealt with during the campaign anywhere in America" (Reinhard 2004: 1B). Penelas's opponents in the 2004 Senate Democratic primary accused the mayor of being disloyal to his party in the 2000 election. Peter Deutsh was especially harsh, accusing the mayor of abandoning Gore during the 2000 presidential race. Even his hometown newspaper, the *Miami Herald,* pointed out in its editorial endorsing Betty Castor that Penelas "does not enjoy his party's favor, given his less than enthusiastic support for the ticket in 2000" (*Miami Herald* 2004: 4L). Penelas finished a poor third in the Democratic primary, receiving only 10.1 percent of the vote. Penelas's coethnic, Mel Martinez, had a much easier path to the Republican nomination for the U.S. Senate.

The results of the primaries in the race for the U.S. Senate put Republicans at a considerable advantage among Florida's Hispanics. Not only had the Republicans nominated a Cuban American to head their statewide ticket, but the Democrats had accused the only Hispanic seeking their nomination of disloyalty to the party. It was not surprising that the president enjoyed a comfortable 53 percent to 32.3 percent lead over Kerry among Florida Hispanics and that Martinez had a stronger 52.6 percent to 28.3 percent lead among his coethnics over Betty Castor, the Democratic nominee (*Washington Post,* Univision, and TRPI 2004).

Martinez was also able to gain considerable support among Puerto Rican Democrats in Central Florida. Non-Cuban Hispanic voters felt that Martinez had ably represented them when he was mayor of Orange County. Mildred Fernandez, a staunch Democrat who was running for the Orange County Commission, best articulated this feeling: "That man [Martinez] has always helped me without looking at nationalities" (Mathers and Elias 2004). Among Cuban Americans, the margins were even more dramatic, with the president enjoying a 77.5 percent to 18.4 percent lead over Senator Kerry and Martinez trouncing Castor 76.4 percent to 15 percent (Campaign Data 2004). President Bush's strong showing among Florida Hispanics was important given that most statewide polls showed a dead heat in Florida during the final month of the election. For example, a Washington Post poll estimated that Bush had only a three-percentage point lead going into the final month of the campaign (*Washington Post* 2004).

Both presidential candidates visited Florida on a regular basis, at least once or twice a week during the last six weeks of the election. Both campaigns made major efforts in the Hispanic media, and Senator Kerry became the first Democratic presidential candidate to advertise on Cuban American Miami radio. President Bush held two major rallies in Miami that focused on Hispanic themes, but both campaigns were also eager to court the undecided Anglo swing voters along Central Florida's I-4 corridor. The Democrats concentrated on their core constituents, African American and Jewish voters, but tailored messages to Hispanic voters as well. They spent $6 million on ads focusing on issues such as education, health care, the economy, and the Republicans' "demagoguery about Cuba," which were broadcast in both Spanish and English. The Kerry campaign relied mostly on out-of-state surrogates like Bob Menéndez, Bill Richardson, and Loretta Sanchez for their Florida Hispanic campaign.

THE RESULTS

The Republican strategy was ultimately a success, as Bush carried the Sunshine State by a 380,978-vote margin. This was the largest Republican victory in Florida since the 1988 presidential election, when the GOP won the state by nearly a million votes. Hispanic voters were an important segment of the president's winning coalition. Bush not only improved his showing from the 2000 presidential election among Florida's Hispanic voters but also led a Republican ticket that did relatively well across the state's diverse Hispanic communities.

An MSNBC exit poll in 2004 showed that 56 percent of Florida's Hispanics supported Bush, compared to 49 percent in 2000. The GOP candidate for the U.S. Senate, Mel Martinez, received over 70 percent of the state's Hispanic vote. The election of Martinez demonstrates the continuing close alliance between Florida's Hispanic voters and the state's Republican Party. Martinez's presence on the Republican ticket not only likely improved Bush's performance in Florida's Hispanic neighborhoods but also continued the rapid political empowerment of the state's Cuban Americans.

Despite the best efforts of the Kerry campaign and the New Democrat Network (NDN), Cuban Americans supported President Bush nearly three to one. Although Cuban American support for Bush dropped from 82 percent in 2000 to 72 percent in 2004, this decline can be attributed to the unusual anti-Democratic sentiment and mobilization in Miami after the Elian Gonzalez affair in 2000.

Senator Kerry was victorious in Florida's only majority Hispanic county. Miami-Dade voters gave the Democratic nominee a 47,293-vote plurality. This is a slight improvement over the 39,275-vote plurality they gave Vice President Al Gore in 2000, but it is far below the convincing 107,744 vote margin that President Clinton scored in Miami-Dade County in 1996. In Miami-Dade's Hispanic precincts, Kerry outperformed Gore by 6 percent. Kerry received 31.5 percent of the vote in Miami's Hispanic neighborhoods, compared to 25 percent for Gore in 2000 and 38 percent for Clinton in those same precincts in 1996 (table 9.1).

Miami-Dade voters gave Mel Martinez a narrow 3,000-vote victory over Betty Castor. Martinez ran significantly ahead of the president in that county. In the raw vote, Martinez outperformed Bush by 49,893 votes. Martinez's victory in Miami-Dade can be attributed to his extraordinary performance in the county's Hispanic neighborhoods. In Miami-Dade's Hispanic precincts, Martinez ran seven percentage points ahead of the president: 75.6 percent compared to 68.5 percent.

While President Bush did slightly worse among Miami-Dade Hispanics in the 2004 presidential election than he did four years earlier, he improved his showing elsewhere in the state. In Central Florida, Bush almost exactly split the Hispanic vote with Kerry in those counties with significant Hispanic registered voters. For example, in Orange County, Bush lost by only 800 votes in 2004, compared to 5,800 votes in 2000. Similarly, in neighboring Osceola County, where he had lost by nearly 2,000 votes in 2000, Bush won by over 4,500 votes in 2004. This pattern repeated itself in Hillsborough County, where the president dramatically increased his margin from 11,000 votes in 2000 to 31,000 votes in 2004.

Table 9.1. Historical Presidential Election Voting Patterns in Hispanic Precincts, Miami-Dade County, 1980–2004 (percent)

	1980	*1984*	*1988*	*1992*	*1996*	*2000*	*2004*
Republican	80	88	85	70	62	75	69
Democratic	20	12	15	22	38	25	31

Source: Authors' calculations based on Miami-Dade County electoral data.

The president's improved showing in Central Florida can be attributed in part to his increasing support among Florida's non-Cuban Hispanics. In 2000 exit polls indicated that Bush won only about 40 percent of these voters. In 2004 the polls showed a very narrow gap between Bush and Kerry among Florida's non-Cuban Hispanics. For example, preelection polls showed that Puerto Ricans, the largest Hispanic group in Central Florida, supported Kerry by only a 43 percent to 40 percent margin (*Washington Post,* Univision, and TRPI 2004). Among South and Central Americans, on the other hand, Bush enjoyed a slight edge over Kerry of 43.8 percent to 40.9 percent (*Washington Post,* Univision, and TRPI 2004).

The results from two state house seats with the largest number of non-Cuban Hispanics confirmed the Washington Post-Univision-TRPI preelection polls indicating that Bush would improve his performance among non-Cuban Hispanics. In Central Florida, Bush barely lost, 49 percent to 51 percent, in state house District 47, which is 33 percent Hispanic (mostly Puerto Rican) and which he lost by over 19 percent in the 2000 presidential election. Similarly, in Broward County the president dramatically improved his performance in state house District 97, which he lost by 16 percent in 2000 but only by 4 percent in 2004.

Moreover, two of the three Hispanic Democratic hopefuls for house seats lost, although by narrow margins. In District 97 Cuban American Barbara Herrera-Hill lost with 48.8 to 51.2 percent to Susan Goldstein. In District 49 incumbent John Quinones defeated Democrat Israel Mercado 52.4 to 47.6 percent. Only the incumbent in Palm Beach, Susan Bucher, secured a comfortable victory over the Republican candidate, Ed Heeney.

CONCLUSION AND OUTLOOK

Florida Hispanics continued to be more Republican than their Hispanic counterparts in the rest of the nation. This is due in part to the Cuban community in Miami that has dominated Florida's Hispanic politics for the past three decades. The election of Mel Martinez to the U.S. Senate underscores the continuation of this process of political empowerment. The selection of Carlos Gutierrez as U.S. commerce secretary also serves to strengthen Republican ties with Miami's Cuban community.

Miami-Dade County, which used to be a Democratic bastion, now has a Republican Cuban American mayor, a Republican Hispanic majority in the county commission, and a Republican Hispanic majority on the school board. This pattern of Republican domination is visible throughout the Sunshine State. Almost all elected Hispanic officials in Florida are Republicans—all three Hispanic U.S. representatives are Republican, as well as the three Hispanic state senators and twelve out of the fourteen Hispanic Florida house members. Two of the Republican house members are non-Cuban Hispanics: Juan Carlos Zapata of Miami and John Quinones of Orlando. The two Hispanic Democrats are Cuban American Bob Henriquez, representing the traditional Hispanic neighborhoods of West Tampa, and Mexican American Susan Bucher, representing an Anglo district in Palm Beach County. Besides Bucher and Henriquez, the only other prominent Democratic Hispanic leaders are Hialeah Mayor Raul Martinez, Miami-Dade State Attorney Katherine Fernandez-Rundle, and Orange County Commissioner Mildred Fernandez.

Despite Republican domination of Florida Hispanic politics, Democrats have reasons to be hopeful in Florida. The dramatic increase of Puerto Rican voters in Central Florida makes it highly unlikely that any Republican presidential nominee can again capture 80 percent of Florida's Hispanic vote, as did Reagan and Bush in 1980, 1984, and 1988. Those days are long gone. Moreover, the election of Mildred Fernandez in Orange County and a federal lawsuit to reimpose single-member districts in Osceola County show evidence that strong Puerto Rican Democratic organizations are becoming established in those two Central Florida counties.

Florida's critical role in U.S. national politics as the largest of the so-called swing states magnifies the importance of its Hispanics voters. The rapid growth and the diversity of its Hispanic population has become an important characteristic of its politics. Although Republicans should continue to dominate Hispanic politics for the foreseeable future, the shifting demographic profile of Florida Hispanics (increasingly non-Cubans) favors the Democrats.

NOTES

1. African Americans constitute approximately 16 percent of the Florida electorate.

2. It should be noted that 85.8 percent of the Cuban vote, 28.8 percent of the Puerto Rican vote, 73.2 percent of the Colombian vote, 92.2 percent of the Nicaraguan vote, and 24 percent of the Mexican vote are concentrated in South Florida.

REFERENCES

Bousquet, Steve, and Curtis Krueger. 2004. "Martinez Pulls Plug on Attack Ad." *St. Petersburg Times,* August 29.

Campaign Data, Inc. 2004. Unpublished poll, October 31.

Craig, Stephen. 1998. "Elections and Partisan Change." In *Government and Politics in Florida,* 2nd ed., ed. Robert J. Hunkshorn, 30–65. Gainesville: University of Florida Press.

de la Garza, Rodolfo O. and Louis DeSipio, eds. 1992. *From Rhetoric to Reality: Latino Politics in the 1988 Elections.* Boulder, CO: Westview Press.

———. 1996. *Ethnic Ironies: Latino Politics in the 1992 Election.* Boulder, CO: Westview Press.

———. 1999. *Awash in the Mainstream: Latino Politics in the 1996 Election.* Boulder, CO: Westview Press.

———. 2005. *Muted Voices: Latinos and the 2000 Election.* Lanham, MD: Rowman and Littlefield.

de Valle, Elaine, and Daniel de Vise. 2004. "Cuba Sanctions Hit Home for Families in Miami." *Miami Herald,* July 1.

Diaz, Madeline Baró. 2004. "Poll: Bush Support Slips among Cubans." *South Florida Sun-Sentinel,* July 10.

Fiedler, Tom. 1992. "Clinton Clearly Fights for the Florida Vote." *Miami Herald,* September 13.

———. 1996. "Rewriting the Book on Florida." *Miami Herald,* November 6.

Florida Department of State. 2005. Registration Statistics. http://election.dos.state.fl.us/.

Hill, Kevin, and Dario Moreno. 2005. "Battleground Florida." In *Muted Voices: Latinos and the 2000 Election,* ed. Rodolfo O. de la Garza and Louis DeSipio, 213–27. Lanham, MD: Rowman and Littlefield.

Hill, Kevin, Susan MacManus, and Dario Moreno, eds. 2004. *Florida Politics: Ten Media Markets, One Powerful State.* Tallahassee: Florida Institute of Government.

Hunkshorn, Robert J., ed. 1998. *Government and Politics in Florida.* 2nd ed. Gainesville: University of Florida Press.

MacManus, Susan. 2004. "Florida Overview: Ten Media Markets, One Powerful State." In *Florida Politics: Ten Media Markets, One Powerful State,* ed. Kevin Hill, Susan MacManus, and Dario Moreno, 1–64. Tallahassee: Florida Institute of Government.

Mathers, Sandra, and Cristina Elias. 2004. "Senate Hopefuls Promote Visions: Courting Hispanics, Mel Martinez and Betty Castor Pitch their Dream." *Orlando Sentinel,* September 19.

Miami Herald. 2004. "Our Opinion: For U.S. Senate, Democratic Primary." August 9.

Moreno, Dario. 2004. "Florida Hispanic Voters: Growth, Immigration, and Political Clout." In *Florida Politics: Ten Media Markets, One Powerful State,* ed. Kevin Hill, Susan MacManus, and Dario Moreno, 83–99. Tallahassee: Florida Institute of Government.

Moreno, Dario, and Christopher Warren. 1992. "The Conservative Enclave: Cubans in Florida." In *From Rhetoric to Reality: Latino Politics in the 1988 Elections,* ed. Rodolfo O. de la Garza and Louis DeSipio, 127–45. Boulder, CO: Westview Press.

———. 1996. "The Conservative Enclave Revisited: Cuban Americans in Florida." In *Ethnic Ironies: Latino Politics in the 1992 Election,* ed. Rodolfo de la Garza and Louis DeSipio, 169–84. Boulder, CO: Westview Press.

———. 1999. "Pragmatism and Strategic Realignment in the 1996 Election." In *Awash in the Mainstream: Latino Politics in the 1996 Election,* ed. Rodolfo de la Garza and Louis DeSipio, 211–37. Boulder, CO: Westview Press.

Noticias.Info. 2004. "New Democrat Network Ad: Cuban Woman." www.noticias.info/Archivo/2004. Accessed February 9, 2009.

Ovalle, David, Oscar Corral, and Lesley Clark. 2004. "Campaigns Are Wooing Florida Hispanics: Both Parties Are Vigorously Pursuing Hispanic Voters. A UM Forum Today Will Look at What Hispanics Want in Their Candidate." *Miami Herald,* September 29.

Ramos, Victor Manuel. 2005. "Puertoricanization of Central Florida: Central Florida Top Region for Puerto Ricans." *Orlando Sentinel,* October 4.

Reinhard, Beth. 2004. "Harsh Words, Surprise Moves, 2004 Had It All." *Miami Herald,* December 25, 1B.

U.S. Census Bureau. 2001. "DP-1 Profiles of Demographic Characteristics: National Summary." www.census.gov/PressRelease/www/2001/demoprovile.html. Accessed September 25, 2007.

Washington Post. 2004. "Florida Poll." October 10.

Washington Post, Univision, and Tomás Rivera Policy Institute (TRPI). 2004. "Election Survey of Registered Latino Voters, Florida." October 5.

Yardley, William. 2004. "Both Parties Pin Hopes on Florida Senate Race." *New York Times,* October 30, A10, 1.

Chapter Ten

Illinois Latinos in the 2004 Election

The Waiting Game Continues

JAIME DOMÍNGUEZ

Latino political influence in Chicago has been steadily climbing since the historic election of Harold Washington as mayor in 1983 and 1987. With the support of more than three-fourths of Latino voters, these elections set the foundation for a new era of Latino participation in electoral politics and a new form of independent politics. More important, they signaled a break with the old era of machine domination of predominantly Latino electoral districts and an end to the patronage system known as "hacienda" or "plantation" politics. In addition, they marked the beginning of the Latino-black electoral alliance that would carry over into governance and eventually pave the way for greater Latino representation via the creation of new Latino-majority wards.

Faced with resistance on redistricting, Latinos, with the aid of the Mexican American Legal Defense and Educational Fund, resorted to the courts to ensure fair representation. In the end, the successful court battles to redraw ward boundaries in 1986, 1998, and 2001 significantly altered Chicago's political map and provided a favorable landscape for

Latinos to pursue their interests. In the period 1986–2001 the number of Latino-majority wards grew from four to eleven. For Latinos, the decision by then twenty-sixth ward alderman, Luis Gutierrez, to support Richard M. Daley in 1989 for mayor set in motion events that would redefine political partnerships as well as the position of Mexicans and Puerto Ricans in the electoral and governing coalition in the new Daley administration.

The decision by its elected leadership marked a major break in the black-white paradigm and the traditional political alliances that dominated Chicago politics before 1989. And it signified the beginning of a new Daley-Latino political alliance. Securing the loyalty of the Latino electorate has encouraged Daley to recruit and incorporate Latinos into his governing coalition. In return, Mayor Daley has enjoyed overwhelming Latino electoral support. In his last reelection in 2003, he captured a whopping 91.3 percent of the Latino vote. For Latinos, the increase in political value and viability as coalition partners has put the local and political establishment on notice that Latinos will no longer be ignored in future elections. The 2004 presidential and Senate races are the first to occur fully in this new era of Chicago Latino politics.

Despite the rich political history of Illinois, the voters in this state—including Latino voters—have not played a decisive role in presidential politics in many years. This pattern continued in 2004. Despite a hotly contested national battle between President George W. Bush and Senator John F. Kerry, the two campaigns were focused on attracting and mobilizing voters in battleground states such as Wisconsin, Ohio, Pennsylvania, Florida, and New Mexico. This effort to attract voters in swing states pushed the Republican and Democratic Party establishments to direct financial and other resources to these states and led to little investment in so-called red and blue states such as Illinois where the outcome was considered preordained. While tight competition might have given Latinos (1) a reason to vote, (2) an incentive for the campaigns to mobilize them, and (3) an opportunity to influence the outcome, the Illinois presidential campaign saw none of the above factors at work.

As was the case in 2000, very little effort was made to mobilize the Latino vote in Illinois. None of the presidential candidates in the primaries or the general elections targeted their vote. This is because Kerry had already secured the Democratic nomination before the Illinois primary, and Bush was not challenged in the Republican primary. In the general election, the Bush campaign largely conceded Illinois and its twenty-one Electoral College votes to Senator Kerry early in the campaign. In addition, the Democratic Party did little to recruit Latino candidates, which gave Latino elected leaders even less incentive to mobilize voters in their communities. In the end, Latinos were largely irrelevant to the outcome of the presidential election.

Although Latinos played little role in the race for the White House, the contest to replace retiring U.S. Senator Peter Fitzgerald had a different dynamic. Compared to previous statewide races, this one drew significant national and local attention and generated a high degree of enthusiasm and interest among voters in Illinois. For the Democratic Party, the opportunity to win this seat and thereby possibly tilt the balance of power in the U.S. Senate raised the stakes.

Unlike the presidential election, the various Democratic candidates seeking to replace Senator Fitzgerald made an effort to attract the Latino vote. While some made the decision to more aggressively court the Latino vote than did others, these efforts in turn elicited a response from various actors in the Latino political community. With the Latino vote up for grabs, several Latino elected leaders were courted and recruited to assist in the efforts to win the Democratic Senate primary. This competition led a number of Latino aldermen and state legislators to make endorsements and hit the campaign trail. However, even with former Chicago School Board President Gery Chico running as the first Latino candidate for U.S. Senate in Illinois, there was no consensus candidate among Latino leaders. In fact, these leaders split their endorsements among Chico, state senator Barack Obama, state comptroller Dan Hynes, and entrepreneur Blair Hull. This reflected the heterogeneity, diversity, and varying political allegiances of Chicago's Latino population. Overall, the Democratic primary for the U.S. Senate seat was one of the most competitive and highly anticipated campaigns seen in Illinois in recent years.

Compared to other urban areas with high-density Latino populations, Chicago has one of the most diverse in the nation (Fraga 1992; Gills and Betancur 2000; Rey 1996; Torres 1988), which has political implications in the areas of participation, coalition building, and mobilization. While Latinos in Illinois constitute less than 4 percent of the voting electorate, the nature of electoral competition determines the degree to which their votes will influence election outcomes. Several studies (see Fraga 1992) have shown that the political capital of Latinos in Illinois is conditioned by (1) the relative balance between the Democratic and the Republican parties, (2) the Latino concentration in the city of Chicago, and (3) the divisions between the white and African American communities.

For example, efforts to mobilize and target Latino voters proved instrumental in electing Harold Washington to mayoral office in 1983 and 1987 (DeSipio 2005; Gills and Betancur 2000; Simpson 2003; Torres 1991). More often than not, the recurring scenario for Latinos is that they are not the focus or target of candidate or party competition, which means their potential to act as a decisive vote is less likely to be realized. This has relegated Latinos to the margins of Illinois party politics by contributing to low levels of voter participation and a resulting lack of influence on election outcomes (DeSipio 1999, 2005; Rey 1996; Valadez 1994). Furthermore, the Washington example suggests that if Latinos are to expand their role in future Illinois elections, the preconditions may include not only competitive elections but also coalition building with non-Latino groups and a Latino bloc vote that largely benefits one candidate.

The Washington mayoralty was a crucial event for the Latino community in Chicago. It provided the impetus and political backing for Latinos to challenge the redistricting map that short-circuited Latino representation in the city council in 1986. Their successful legal challenge resulted in the redrawing of the ward map, as a judicial order forced the city to draw new boundaries and hold special aldermanic elections in seven wards (Latino Institute 1986; Rey 1996; Torres 1991). These elections proved pivotal for the overall progressive political movement in Chicago. It created two new majority-Latino wards: the predominantly Mexican twenty-second ward and the predominantly Puerto Rican twenty-sixth ward. In addition, the Washington election gave birth to the Latino-black political alliance that characterized Latino politics in Chicago until the early 1990s. Furthermore, the 1983 mayoral elections marked the beginning of a period in which Latino independent candidates would mount real challenges against machine-supported candidates. These elections brought a new era of political opportunities for Chicago's Latino communities and laid a solid foundation for the development of strong independent politics outside of the traditional Democratic machine.

DEMOGRAPHIC CONSIDERATIONS

The 2000 U.S. Census revealed a growing Latino population at the national, state, metropolitan, county, and city levels. These changes were also evident in Illinois, in particular in the larger Chicago metropolitan area. This growth was phenomenal in both absolute and relative terms. Latinos in Illinois increased their numbers from 904,446 in 1990 to 1,530,262 in 2000—an increase of 69.2 percent. Whereas Latinos were 7.9 percent of the state population in 1990, they constituted 12.3 percent at the end of the twentieth century. Comparisons with data for the Anglo and African Americans populations of Illinois further illustrate the magnitude of this growth. Between 1990 and 2000, the African American population increased by 12 percent and the Latino population by 74.1 percent, while the Anglo population only grew by 6.5 percent. Latinos and African Americans accounted for over half of the state's population increase over the decade.

Latino population growth is nowhere more evident than in Cook County and the city of Chicago. For example, the 2000 census figures show that the population explosion of Latinos in Chicago led to the city's first overall population increase since 1950. According to that census, Chicago's official population was 2,896,016, approximately 4 percent higher than in 1990. While the number of Latinos increased by nearly 210,000—Latinos now represent one of every four Chicagoans—Anglos declined by 150,000 and African Americans by 20,000.

The increase in the Latino population has been profound since the 1970s. Unlike the gradual decline in the city's white and black populations, Latinos grew by triple-digit margins. For example, the Latino population in Chicago increased from 7.3 percent in 1970 to 26.1 percent in 2000. This is a 205 percent increase over three decades. The decline in the white population is indicative of a national urban demographic trend whereby the growth of minority populations, especially

Latinos, is offsetting the loss of the white population. In terms of national-origin groups, Mexicans constitute 70 percent, Puerto Ricans 15 percent, and other groups (i.e., Cubans, Central and South Americans) are the remaining 15 percent.

Many other counties in the state also feel the Latino population surge, including the counties adjacent to Cook: DuPage, Lake, Will, and Kane. Minorities, most prominently Hispanics, are now 32 percent of Kane County residents, 27 percent of Lake County, 23 percent of Will County, and 21 percent of DuPage County, illustrating the significant growth of the Latino population in the region. Furthermore, established Latino communities in places like Waukegan (in Lake County) are now starting to run Latino candidates for local offices. This was not the case a decade ago, and it is likely the start of a phenomenon that will reverberate throughout the region in the years to come.

The explosion in the Latino population in Illinois and in the city of Chicago has a variety of political implications. First, from a policy perspective, it means that legislators and government institutions must begin to be more responsive to the socioeconomic interests and needs of this burgeoning and young population. Among the many issues that are salient and resonate with Latinos are education, employment opportunities and workforce development in the private and public sectors, health care, and social services delivery.

Second, the increase in the Latino population coupled with the decline in the number of whites resulted in the redrawing of local and statewide political districts. At the local level, Latino growth helped to alter the demographic balance in at least four historically white-majority Chicago wards. Despite the call from Latino leaders and community organizations to create five new Latino supermajority wards to reflect their population in the city, this did not happen. In an attempt to avoid the expensive and contentious redistricting litigation of the 1990s, which took eight years to resolve, a political compromise was reached between Latino aldermen, Mayor Daley, and the city council (Neal 2001).

This compromise created four new supermajority Latino wards: the fourteeth ward on the Southwest Side represented by Alderman Edward Burke; the tenth ward on the Southeast Side represented by Alderman John Pope; the traditionally Polish American thirtieth ward on the

Northwest Side represented by Alderman Micheal Wojcik; and the thirty-third ward on the Northwest Side represented by Alderman Richard Mell. In the eleventh ward, the Daley family's historic political turf, which is represented by Alderman James Balcer, Latinos are now a plurality. The most lopsided demographic change occurred in the fourteenth ward, where Latinos now outnumber whites 58,000 to 14,000. Latinos are currently represented in Wards 14 and 33 by two of the longest-serving and most powerful white aldermen on the council, Burke and Mell, but the issue of representation is no longer a legal matter but a political one. As such, it is Latino voters in these wards who must decide who can best represent them.

In 2005, of the fifty wards represented in the city council, nineteen were majority white, twenty were majority black, and eleven were supermajority Latino. It should be noted that several Latino elected leaders and Latino advocacy organizations had called for a reduction in the number of majority-black wards because the black population had drastically declined. The sharpest decline in the black population occurred in Ward 3. While blacks were able to sustain twenty wards in which they were the majority in 2000, it will become increasingly difficult for the black community and its elected leaders to maintain their current level of representation in the city council after the next decennial redistricting.

At the state level, redistricting resulted in the expansion of Latino representation in the state legislature and created the conditions for Latino communities to elect candidates of their choice in the November 2002 election. This led to three additional Latino seats in the General Assembly and two in the state senate (NALEO 2004). Between 1996 and 2000, six Latinos served in the state legislature. In 2004 twelve Latinos, four state senators, and eight state representatives served in the state legislature. At the federal level, the fourth congressional district, created via the provisions of the Voting Rights Act, was kept intact.

While population numbers are important in creating greater electoral opportunities, other demographic factors, including age, legal status, and education, condition the political empowerment of Latinos. The Latino population in Illinois is one of the youngest and poorest in the nation (U.S. Census Bureau 2000). In terms of educational attainment, Latinos do not fare well compared to other groups. According to the 2000 census, more than 53.4 percent of the Latino adult population dropped out of school before the twelfth grade. Of those who do graduate from high school, only 5.6 percent will earn a bachelor's degree. This low educational attainment is important to highlight given the central relationship between education and political mobilization (Wolfinger and Rosenstone 1980). The legal status of this community further exacerbates depressed Latino electoral participation levels; the 2000 census revealed that 32.9 percent of Chicago Latinos were not U.S. citizens, 54.4 percent were U.S. born, and 12.6 were naturalized citizens.

THE LATINO ELECTORATE

Despite the demographic factors that limit the potential influence of the Latino vote, Latinos have constituted a growing share of the state electorate in every presidential and congressional election since 1992. In 1992 Latino voters were only 3 percent of the state electorate. In 2000 they were 4.3 percent of the state electorate. This share rose slightly, to approximately 5 percent of the electorate, in 2004 (U.S. Census Bureau 2004). In the period 1996–2000 the number of Latino voting age citizens, registered voters, and actual voters grew substantially. Latino voting-age citizens grew by more than 50 percent, and the number of Latino registered voters and actual voters increased at faster rates—72 percent and 71 percent, respectively (NALEO 2004). Nevertheless, about 46 percent of eligible Latino voters in 2000 (182,000) did not vote in the presidential election. According to the Hispanic Leadership Institute, approximately 48 percent did not cast a ballot in 2004.

The 2004 general election also revealed a statewide increase in the Latino share of registered voters. Whereas 262,000 Latinos were registered to vote in 2000, 343,000 were registered in 2004—a 30.9 percent increase. Nevertheless, in terms of overall percent registered, the Latino share slightly dropped from 34 percent in 2000 to 33.2 percent in 2004 (U.S. Census Bureau 2004). In addition, Latino turnout statewide increased between 2000 and 2004. For example, 294,000 Latinos voted in 2004, an increase of 34.8 percent from the 218,000 who voted in

2000 (U.S. Census Bureau 2004). While not as dramatic as the increase between 1996 and 2000 (71 percent), the figures suggest that large numbers of new Latino voters are arriving at the polls every presidential election year.

Such numbers should be viewed with some caution, however. As is the case with exit polling involving Latinos, they can be prone to large sampling errors. DeSipio (1999, 2005) documented this problem by noting that the source, the Current Population Survey, is based on self-reported assessments and is therefore susceptible to large or small estimates.

THE 2004 PRESIDENTIAL ELECTION

As stated earlier, the presidential campaigns of Senator Kerry and President Bush did not target Illinois. As in many other states, Latinos in Illinois did not play an influential role in the 2004 presidential election. Even if no Latino had voted, the results would have been the same: Kerry would have carried approximately 55 percent of the statewide vote. Their lack of influence can be attributed to three factors. First, Illinois was not considered a swing state, so the presidential campaigns made little effort to compete for votes—Latino or otherwise. Second, the Democratic Party failed to recruit Latino candidates. Third, the parties did very little to support Latino organizations in their efforts to recruit volunteers for the campaigns or to register voters (Andrade 2005). The cumulative effect of these factors created little incentive for Latinos to get excited about the 2004 elections, and their low turnout at the polls reflected their disinterest.

The Primary Campaign

By the time the primaries reached Illinois in March, Senator Kerry had already defeated his opponents and was on his way to being declared the Democratic presidential nominee. The enthusiasm to get out the vote normally seen in competitive races was absent, and little effort was being made by Election Day to attract the Latino vote. Kerry's victory signaled the end of the primary season, as he won enough delegates in the Illinois primary to secure the Democratic nomination. The situation was not very different in 2000, when Gore defeated Bradley 84 percent to 14 percent and was more concerned at that point with unifying the party than winning additional convention delegates. On the Republican side, President Bush was not facing any serious challenge to his renomination, so it is not surprising that little transpired in the Illinois GOP presidential primary.

The 2004 Illinois presidential primary drew little interest from mainstream or Spanish-language media. While Chicago's major Spanish-language news outlets (Univision, Telemundo, and Galavision), ran one to two Kerry commercials on average in the evening, not one featured a Latino elected official asking Latino voters to support Kerry in November (Hernandez-Gomez 2005). The ads were quite generic and seemingly did little to generate any excitement among potential Latino voters.

The few efforts to capture the attention of Latino voters were associated with the contest to replace retiring U.S. Senator Peter Fitzgerald, not the presidential election. This election meant that Illinois might decide the balance of power in the Senate, and it received a great deal of local and even national attention. For the Democratic Party, the slew of candidates who entered the primary was a testimony to the interest in this office. The contest captured the interest of Illinois voters, including some segments of the Latino community, which is discussed later.

The General Election Campaign

While the general election generated slightly more interest than the primary, it was clear that President Bush had little if any chance of capturing the twenty-one Electoral College votes of this historically blue state. For instance, a *Chicago Tribune*/WGN-TV poll revealed that Kerry had an insurmountable lead over Bush weeks before the election (*Daily Chronicle* 2004), and Kerry did not open any campaign offices in the Chicagoland area. Similarly, from the outset of the election the GOP put very little effort into winning Illinois. By mid-March it became evident that the Bush team was going to concede Illinois to Kerry.

The Bush and Kerry campaigns instead focused on targeting voters in neighboring swing states, such as Wisconsin and Minnesota. The

Kerry campaign's strategy to leave Illinois so as to compete for new voters in battleground states was a mirror image of the Gore strategy in 2000 (DeSipio 2005). The bipartisan neglect of Illinois Latino voters clearly shows that even in states with sizable Latino populations, they will be ignored without competitive elections.

On November 2, 2004, Senator Kerry carried the state of Illinois with nearly 55 percent of the vote. According to the CNN national exit poll, Kerry did much better than Bush among Latino voters, gaining 76 percent of the Illinois Latino vote versus Bush's 23 percent. In terms of their share of the statewide electorate, Latinos made up 8 percent. This was the first time a national exit poll contained a sufficiently large sample of Latinos to allow for the reliable analysis of Latino voting preferences and turnout. As DeSipio (1999, 2005) documented in 1996 and 2000, no exit poll data were available because the Voter News Service consortium did not interview enough Latinos to report reliable results.

Table 10.1 provides a snapshot of Latino voting preferences and turnout in Chicago, revealing overwhelming Latino support for Kerry and the Democratic Party. Based on the share of the vote Kerry received in Latino supermajority precincts in Chicago, he captured approximately 81 percent of the Latino vote in the city (as these precincts include some non-Latinos, 81 percent may be an under- or overestimation of the Latino vote).

As stated earlier, Latinos in Illinois increased their registered voter and voter turnout shares in 2004. If we examine these trends in Chicago, especially in precincts with a high concentration of Latinos, we uncover a different phenomenon. For example, we find a precipitous decline in voter registration in nine of the eleven predominantly Latino wards from 2000 to 2004. Voter registration increased only in the twenty-fifth and thirty-fifth wards (by 15.8 percent and 5.8 percent, respectively). If one considers all wards, Latino voter registration fell by 8.9 percent since the 2000 presidential election. These estimates suggest that Latinos in Chicago are not being targeted for mobilization at either the individual or the community level. In terms of turnout, the picture is not much better. In high-concentration Latino precincts, turnout declined by 4.2 percent between 2000 and 2004.

Table 10.1. Latino Voter Registration and Votes Cast in Highly Concentrated Latino Wards, 2000 and 2004

	Registered Voters			
Ward	*% Latino*	*2000*	*2004*	*% Change*
1	67	24,723	28,493	+13.2
10	62	30,434	27,019	-12.6
12	72	14,677	12,594	-16.5
14	71	19,928	12,255	-62.6
22	77	18,490	15,564	-18.8
25	74	17,810	21,159	+15.8
26	68	25,558	21,726	-17.6
30	67	24,088	20,290	-18.7
31	68	22,394	20,251	-10.6
33	65	19,646	17,533	-12.1
35	64	22,009	23,360	+5.8
Total		239,757	220,244	-8.9

	Votes Cast					
Ward	*2000*	*2004*	*% Change*	*Kerry*	*Bush*	*Other*
1	15,494	20,917	+26.0	79.9	19.5	0.6
10	18,607	16,917	-10.0	76.4	23.0	0.6
12	7,127	6,873	-3.7	79.2	20.1	0.7
14	14,993	10,104	-48.4	78.3	21.4	0.3
22	10,195	8,042	-26.8	87.2	12.4	0.4
25	10,819	13,055	+17.1	79.7	19.5	0.8
26	14,853	14,819	-0.3	81.8	17.5	0.7
30	15,343	11,905	-28.9	74.8	24.6	0.6
31	12,762	12,018	-6.2	74.3	25.1	0.6
33	16,084	13,935	-15.4	77.6	21.6	0.8
35	13,818	15,449	+10.6	79.4	19.7	0.9
Total	150,095	144,034	-4.2	—	—	—

Source: Chicago Board of Election Commissioners, 2004.

In Latino supermajority precincts in Chicago, we previously estimated that Kerry won about 81 percent of the vote. While precinct-level data suggest that Bush fared better in these areas than he did four years earlier, this does not suggest Latinos in Chicago will be switching party allegiances. For example, Bush was able to garner more than 20 percent of the vote in six of the eleven supermajority Latino wards in 2004. In 2000 Bush did not capture more than 18.7 percent in any of the wards in which Latinos were a majority. While this was an improvement, it still suggests a relatively low baseline of support for GOP presidential candidates. Unlike any other city in the United States, Chicago's Democratic Party is one of the strongest, with more than 90 percent of Latino voters in Chicago registered as Democrats.

The U.S. Senate Election

While several races took place at the state level, none was more interesting and eventful than the race for the open U.S. Senate seat. As expected in Democratic and Republican circles, U.S. Senator Peter Fitzgerald announced early in 2004 that he would not seek reelection. A number of candidates sought their party's nomination, but the battle was the most heated in the Democratic primary. The four candidates with the strongest appeal and name recognition were Barack Obama, Dan Hynes, Gery Chico, and Blair Hull. For the first time in Illinois politics, a candidate of Latino ancestry was running for the U.S. Senate. As the Chico campaign and his supporters would soon find out, however, translating shared ethnicity into support at the polls proved quite challenging and elusive.

Barack Obama was a Harvard-educated and charismatic state senator from Hyde Park. As a state senator, Obama had established himself as a champion of civil rights and labor. As the second African American in Illinois to seek this office (Carol Mosley-Braun was the first in 1992), his candidacy received significant media attention, and his support transcended ethnic, racial, and class lines. Obama downplayed the significance of race in an effort to appeal to a wide range of Illinois voters. This strategy was especially helpful in winning the support of voters downstate, where minority and progressive Democratic candidates have historically had a difficult time attracting white voters (Hernández-Gómez 2005).

Early in his campaign, Obama received endorsements from almost every major political organization in the black community, including the Rainbow/PUSH Coalition, the Illinois Legislative Black Caucus, and the Illinois black congressional delegation, which included Jesse Jackson Jr., Danny Davis, and Bobby Rush. His reputation as a consensus builder in the state senate and his inclination to support progressive legislation won him the endorsements of other sectors of the electorate.

Despite the candidacy of Chico, Obama also received support from some segments of the Latino community. As a staunch supporter of Latino redistricting issues such as the expansion of Latino representation in the assembly and the city council, Obama won the endorsements of several members of the Latino caucus. These individuals included two of the state's longest-serving representatives in Springfield—Representative William Delgado and Senator Miguel Del Valle (Hernández-Gómez 2005). For them (and other segments of the Latino community), Obama's strong support for the Dream Act—in particular the provision that would have allowed Latino students to pay in-state tuition at public universities without regard to immigration status—was the deciding factor (Delgado 2004).

Early in the campaign, Obama made it a priority to court the Latino vote, despite the perception that Gery Chico would more easily appeal to the Latino electorate (Andrade 2005). In fact, Obama was very successful in capitalizing on the political networks of elected officials. For example, he and his staff went out of their way to appeal to Latinos by holding several public and private forums with heads of select Latino community organizations, including the Resurrection Project, Latinos United, Pilsen Neighbors, and the Little Village Chamber of Commerce (Torres 2004). The goal was to convince them that he, not Chico, had the resources and pedigree to win in the November general election. Others who attended these forums were intellectuals from the University of Illinois-Champaign, DePaul University, and the University of Chicago. In addition, he was able to bring some Latino elected officials who had already pledged their support, albeit a soft one, to Chico (Torres 2004).

Under most circumstances, studies have shown that ethnicity is a strong predictor for vote choice (Barreto 2004; Stokes-Brown 2003;

García-Bedolla 2005). Ethnicity is a multidimensional social identity that has a powerful influence on the sociopolitical behavior of Latinos (e.g., de la Garza et al. 1992; DeSipio 1999; Padilla 1985). Ethnicity is defined by common cultural practices and shared historical experience (DeSipio 1996, 1999; García-Bedolla 2005). In terms of electoral politics, ethnicity has played a useful role in influencing the political interest of and in mobilizing, organizing, and turning out the vote in both the informal and formal electoral contexts.

Studies have shown that when Latinos have an option to choose a coethnic candidate, more often than not they will do so (Cain 1991; Leighley 2001). Graves and Lee (2000) confirm this phenomenon. In their study of the 1996 U.S. Senate election in Texas, they show that when asked to choose between a Hispanic and a non-Hispanic candidate, 77 percent supported the former. The presence of a coethnic candidate has also been found to be a mobilizing force for Latinos (Barreto and Masuoka 2004; Barreto, Villareal, and Woods 2005).

So why did Chico make such a poor showing among Latino voters? First, there was growing sentiment in Latino political circles that Chico was exploiting his ethnic identity without having any substantive ties to Chicago's Latino communities, in particular, to Mexican Americans. Second, many felt he did not do much to address the needs of the community while serving as the second-in-command on the Chicago School Board, such as ensuring greater funding for extracurricular activities, hiring more Latino teachers and administrators, or building new schools at the high school level. Third, the mayor did not endorse his candidacy. The absence of a mayoral endorsement reaffirmed suspicions that outside of being a second-generation Mexican American, there was not much there. Fourth, he was hampered by an inability to secure endorsements from important Latino political figures.

In the end, Obama's efforts to convince segments of the Latino electorate to support his candidacy paid dividends. Most impressive was Obama's ability to capture more than 40 percent of the vote in four of the city's eleven supermajority Latino wards (1, 26, 33, and 35). In four others wards (22, 25, 30, and 31), he was able to garner at least 30 percent of the vote. Gery Chico, by contrast, was only able to win a majority in one such ward (see table 10.2).

Table 10.2. Candidate Percent Share of the Vote in the U.S. Senate Democratic Primary in High-Density Latino Wards, March 2004

Ward	*Obama*	*Hynes*	*Chico*	*Pappas*	*Hull*
1	58.5	8.4	13.8	7.4	10.3
10	28.8	26.7	28.7	8.8	5.9
12	17.6	22.1	38.0	6.5	4.1
14	12.6	10.9	60.7	8.6	6.5
22	36.4	5.3	39.7	6.1	11.3
25	35.1	20.6	27.7	7.0	8.43
26	49.9	5.9	23.5	6.7	11.8
30	30.5	25.6	21.8	10.1	10.5
31	30.0	13.8	31.5	12.5	10.5
33	45.4	9.1	10.9	7.4	10.7
35	56.8	7.3	16.2	7.6	10.7

Source: Chicago Board of Election Commissioners, 2004.

In addition to endorsements by Latino elected officials, Obama secured many labor endorsements. While Dan Hynes received support from various labor unions, including the powerful AFL-CIO, teamsters, building trades carpenters, and operating engineers, Obama's candidacy received a significant boost when he won the endorsement of the largest labor union in the state, the SEIU–Service Employees and International Union (Neal 2004). The breaking of ranks by the SEIU led another prominent labor union to do the same. In early January, Obama won the endorsement of the state's American Federation of State, County and Municipal Employees (AFSCME). AFSCME Council 31 represents about one hundred thousand active and retired public service workers throughout Illinois, making it the second largest union in the state. By early February, most polls in Illinois and Chicago showed that Obama was on his way to victory, as more than 60 percent of Illinois voters supported his candidacy.

State Comptroller Dan Hynes was considered the darling of the Democratic Party and, in particular, of the Chicago political machine.

He had deep political roots in Illinois politics, as his father, Pat Hynes, was president of the state senate in the early 1990s. Many saw Hynes as the strongest challenger to Obama in the Democratic primary.

Unlike his competition, Hynes benefited from his family's political network. Though he was not publicly endorsed by Mayor Daley, it was clear in political circles that Hynes was his candidate (Hernández-Gómez 2004). The Hynes campaign also received support from some Latinos. While publicly endorsed by Latino representatives such as state senators Martin Sandoval and Tony Munoz as well as aldermen Danny Solis and Ray Suarez (who were close allies of Mayor Daley), the most important endorsement came from the Hispanic Democratic Organization (HDO). For many, the support of HDO and its reputation for helping elect Latino candidates to seats on the city council and state legislature figured to play a critical role in galvanizing Latino voters to support Hynes' candidacy. Victor Reyes, a close ally of Mayor Daley, founder of HDO, and executive director of the Mayor's Office of Intergovernmental Affairs, made HDO's intent to support Hynes clear from the outset. This endorsement led Hynes to believe that he could compete for Latino voters despite the perception that Gery Chico would receive the lion's share (Betancur 2005).

On Election Day the Latino vote split three ways but most strongly went for Obama. In terms of the Latino vote, Hynes was only able to garner about 20 percent of the vote in four supermajority Latino wards (10, 12, 25, and 30). It is not surprising that he fared relatively well in these wards given that they are considered political strongholds for the HDO. In fact, twenty-fifth ward alderman Danny Solis (president pro-tem of the city council and the strongest Latino ally of Mayor Daley) and twelfth ward alderman George Cardenas campaigned heavily on behalf of Hynes throughout the primary, but Obama's appeal was too much to overcome.

Although considered the strongest Latino political organization in Chicago politics, HDO's get-out-the-vote (GOTV) efforts for Hynes seemed to have relatively little influence on the Latino vote. On the other hand, the Chico candidacy and Obama's outreach to the Latino community created a dynamic whereby the candidates aggressively competed for Latino votes. In the end, the split in the Latino vote revealed not only the diversity of the Latino electorate but also and more important its mixed political allegiances.

As the first candidate of Latino ancestry to run for the U.S. Senate in Illinois, Gery Chico was seen by many as a breakthrough for Latino politics. A former president of the Chicago School Board, Chico was credited with turning around the Chicago public schools. In an effort to connect with Latino voters, he made it a point to highlight his Mexican ancestry. Chico also received endorsements from several Latino state representatives, including Susana Mendoza, Cynthia Soto, Ed Acevedo, and Iris Martinez, and aldermen Burke, Munoz, and Sanchez. However, many Latinos thought that Chico had previously and repeatedly downplayed his Mexican ancestry, which some sectors of Chicago's Latino community resented.

In the end, minimal support from Latino voters coupled with the inability to raise sufficient campaign funds led to his crushing defeat in the March primary. Chico captured less than 25 percent of the vote in five supermajority Latino wards (1, 26, 30, 33, and 35). In addition, he received the majority of the vote in only one such ward (14) and a plurality of the vote in three other wards (12, 22, and 31). One might conclude that Chico's reliance on his Mexican ancestry to appeal to Latino voters did not work as planned.

The fourth candidate in the Democratic primary, Blair Hull, was a self-made multimillionaire entrepreneur. To the surprise of many, he was endorsed by Representative Luis Gutierrez of the fourth congressional district, the most visible and powerful Latino elected official in Illinois. No one predicted this endorsement, as most expected Gutierrez to support either Chico or Obama.

Why did Gutierrez support Hull? For one thing, Hull had made financial contributions to his reelection campaigns. Perhaps more important, Chico was seen as having close ties to the HDO, a pro-Daley Latino group that mobilizes voters on Election Day to support the mayor's candidates. To endorse Chico would therefore undercut Gutierrez's appeal as an independent and political maverick. Furthermore, it was difficult for Gutierrez, who had significant appeal in the Latino community, to endorse Chico, who many perceived as disconnected from Latinos at the grassroots level.

Early in the primary Hull launched a media blitz to elevate his name recognition and profile among Illinois voters, and the Gutierrez endorsement was key to his Latino outreach. He ran advertisements in major Spanish media outlets, including Univision, Telefuturo, and Galavision. The ads featured Gutierrez embracing Hull and asking Latinos to support his Senate candidacy. This effort did not appear to gain Hull significant support among Latino voters, however, as his best showing in the eleven supermajority precincts was only 11.8 percent. On the other hand, the low level of Latino support for Chico helps to debunk the myth that the Latino community will support any Latino candidate who happens to run for office in Chicago. It appears that Latinos will make up their own minds, regardless of the ethnicity of the candidate or the endorser.

CONCLUSION

For the fifth straight presidential election cycle, Latinos in Illinois did not play an influential role in the primary or general elections. The 2004 contest illustrates how the lack of competitive elections means that Latino votes are not heard, Latino voters are not mobilized, and Latino votes are not decisive. Without competitive elections, the Republican and Democratic Party establishments can safely ignore Latinos, despite their rising share of eligible and actual voters. A lack of internal and external mobilization efforts also contributes to relatively low rates of Latino turnout, which also works to diminish Latino political influence. As in previous presidential elections, those in 2004 revealed that electoral institutions continue to neglect Latino voters in Illinois.

On the other hand, the 2004 Senate race showed that when candidates target and recruit Latino voters, these efforts can create new levels of excitement and optimism in Latino communities. In addition, the tripartite split in the Latino vote in the Senate Democratic primary revealed that the Latino vote is not homogeneous but reflects the increasing diversity of the Latino electorate.

Latino population growth did lead to the expansion of Latino representation at both the state and city levels. Redistricting created two more state senate and three state legislative seats. In addition, Chicago gained four new supermajority Latino wards. Given the continuing growth in the Latino population, we might expect to see additional Latino districts created after the next decennial redistricting.

Although numbers are important, there is still a large disconnect between population gains and the growth in the share of the Latino electorate. This reflects the reality that Latino population growth has not been matched by similar gains in the Latino adult citizen population, reducing the ability of Latinos to influence current and future elections. And the lack of competitive elections at all levels of government only exacerbates this problem.

Without higher levels of competition between the two parties, few opportunities will arise for Latinos to wield much power in statewide and national politics. As long as Illinois politics continues to offer a significant advantage to one party, the voice of the Latino community will remain muted.

REFERENCES

Andrade, Juan. 2005. President of the United States Hispanic Leadership Institute. Interview by Jaime Domínguez, April 15.

Barreto, M. A. 2004. "Ethnic Cues: The Role of Shared Ethnicity in Latino Vote Choice." Paper presented at the annual meeting of the American Political Science Association, Chicago, September.

Barretto, M. A., and N. Masuoka. 2004. "Do Co-Ethnic Candidates Change the Stakes for Latino and Asian American Voters? Voter Turnout in 2002." Paper presented at the annual meeting of the American Political Science Association, Chicago, September.

Barreto, M. A., M. Villareal, and N. D. Woods. 2005. "Metropolitan Latino Political Behavior: Voter Turnout and Candidate Preference in Los Angeles." *Journal of Urban Affairs* 27: 71–91.

Betancourt, John. 2005. Interview by Jaime Domínguez.

Cain, Bruce. 1991. "The Contemporary Context of Racial and Ethnic Politics in California." In *Racial and Ethnic Politics in California,* ed. Bryan O. Jackson and Michael Preston. Berkeley: Institute for Governmental Studies Press.

City of Chicago, Board of Elections Commissioners. 2004. "General Elections Results for U.S. Senate Race." www.chicagoelections.com/election3.asp.

CNN. 2004. "Final Returns: A State-by-State Analysis, Illinois." www.cnn.com/ELECTION/2004//pages/results/states/IL/index.html. Accessed February 9, 2009.

Daily Chronicle. 2004. "Poll: Kerry's Lead in Illinois Narrows." October 27, 2004.

de la Garza, Rodolfo, and Louis DeSipio. 1992. *From Rhetoric to Reality: Latino Politics in the 1988 Elections.* Boulder, CO: Westview Press.

Delgado, Willie. 2004. State representative. Interview by author, December.
DeSipio, Louis. 1996. *Counting on the Latino Vote: Latinos as a New Electorate.* Charlottesville: University Press of Virginia.
———. 1999. "Election? What Election? Illinois Latinos and the 1996 Election." In *Awash in the Mainstream: Latino Politics in the 1996 Elections,* ed. Rodolfo de la Garza and Louis DeSipio, 193–210. Boulder, CO: Westview Press.
———. 2005. "Electoral College Dropouts: Illinois Latinos in the 2000 Presidential Election." In *Muted Voices: Latinos and the 2000 Elections,* ed. Rodolfo de la Garza and Louis DeSipio, 228–44. Lanham, MD: Rowman and Littlefield.
Fraga, Luis. R. 1992. "Prototype from the Midwest: Latinos in Illinois." In *From Rhetoric to Reality: Latino Politics in the 1988 Elections,* ed. Rodolfo de la Garza and Louis DeSipio, 111–26. Boulder, CO: Westview Press.
García-Bedolla, Lisa. 2005. *Fluid Borders: Latino Power, Identity, and Politics in Los Angeles.* Berkeley: University of California Press.
Gills, Doug, and John Betancur. 2000. *The Collaborative City: Opportunities and Struggles for Blacks and Latinos in U.S. Cities.* New York: Garland.
Graves, S., and J. Lee. "Ethnic Underpinnings of Voting Preference: Latinos and the 1996 U.S. Senate Election in Texas." *Social Science Quarterly* 81: 226–36.
Hernández-Gómez, Carlos. 2001. "Latino Leadership: Population Soars but Political Power Lags." *Chicago Reporter,* September–October.
———. 2005. Journalist. Interview by Jaime Domínguez, March 21.
Latino Institute. 1986. *Al Filo: The Empowerment of Chicago's Latino Electorate.* Chicago: Latino Institute.
Leighley, Jan. 2001. *Strength in Numbers? The Political Mobilization of Racial and Ethnic Minorities.* Princeton, NJ: Princeton University Press.
Longoria, Thomas, Jr. 2000. "Context, Identity, and Incorporation: Are Latinos in the Midwest Different?" In *Minority Politics at the Millennium,* ed. Richard A. Keiser and Katherine Underwood, 179–202. New York: Garland.
National Association of Latino Elected Officials (NALEO). 2004. "Primary Election Profiles: Illinois State Primary." March 16. www.naleo.org/electoralprofiles.html.
Neal, Steve. 2001. "Map Can't Hide Hispanics." *Chicago Sun-Times,* March 23, 30.
Padilla, Felix. 1985. *Latino Ethnic Consciousness: The Case of Mexican Americans and Puerto Ricans in Chicago.* Notre Dame, IN: University of Notre Dame Press.
Rey, Roberto. 1996. "Leverage without Influence: Illinois Latino Politics in 1992." In *Ethnic Ironies: Latino Politics in the 1992 Elections,* ed. Rodolfo de la Garza and Louis DeSipio, 149–68. Boulder, CO: Westview Press.
Simpson, Dick. 2003. *Rogues, Rebels, and Rubber Stamp: The Politics of the Chicago City Council from 1863 to the Present.* Boulder, CO: Westview Press.

Stokes-Brown, A. K. 2003. "Latino Group Consciousness and Political Participation." *American Politics Research* 31: 361–78.

Torres, Maria de los Angeles. 1988. "From Exiles to Minorities: The Politics of Cuban-Americans." In *Latinos and the U.S. Political System,* ed. F. Chris Garcia, 81–98. Notre Dame, IN: University of Notre Dame Press.

———. 1991. "The Commission on Latino Affairs: A Case Study of Community Empowerment." In *Harold Washington and the Neighborhoods: Progressive City Government in Chicago, 1983–1987,* ed. Pierre Clavel and Wim Wiewel, 165–87. New Brunswick, NJ: Rutgers University Press.

———. 2004. Interview with Jaime Domínguez, November 15.

U.S. Census Bureau. 2000. "Census 2000." www.census.gov.

———. 2004. "Census Summary File-3, 2004." www.census.gov.

Valadez, John. 1994. "Latino Politics in Chicago: Pilsen in the 1990 General Election." In *Barrio Ballots: Latino Politics in the 1990 Elections,* ed. Rodolfo de la Garza, Martha Menchaca, and Louis DeSipio, 115–36. Boulder, CO: Westview Press.

Wolfinger, Raymond, and Steven Rosenstone. 1980. *Who Votes?* New Haven, CT: Yale University Press.

Chapter Eleven

El Estado del Jardín

New Jersey Latinos in the 2004 Election

JASON P. CASELLAS

Due in large part to its proximity to the major metropolitan centers of the Northeast, New Jersey has become a more diverse state in recent years. According to the 1990 U.S. Census, Hispanics made up approximately 10 percent of the state's population. By 2000 this number had increased to 13 percent. New Jersey's Latinos themselves are a diverse group. The census reports that the designation "Other Hispanic" outnumbers Cubans, Puerto Ricans, and Mexicans. Puerto Ricans, however, remain the largest subgroup, followed by Mexican Americans and Cuban Americans. While Latinos constituted 5 percent of the state's registered voters in 1992, they had reached 8 percent by 2003. This growing Latino voting population has also spilled over to elected offices. In 2001, 77 Latinos were elected to public office in New Jersey. Currently, 102 elected officials serve the state. Following Governor James E. McGreevey's election in 2001 and the Democratic takeover of the General Assembly, Albio Sires, a Cuban-born Democrat from West New York, became Speaker of the General Assembly, a first in New Jersey politics.

WHY NEW JERSEY MIGHT HAVE GONE RED IN 2004

While Al Gore comfortably won New Jersey in 2000, public opinion polls released in the summer and fall prior to the November 2004 election indicated a surprisingly close presidential race. For this reason alone, we should carefully consider the role of Latinos in New Jersey politics. In addition, former Governor McGreevey, a Democrat, angered many Latinos in 2003 because of his "actions against the interests of the Latino community" (Pérez, quoted in Stainton 2003). In April 2003 the Latino Leadership Alliance of New Jersey, an umbrella organization of Latinos in the state that mostly endorses Democratic candidates, issued a harsh statement accusing the McGreevey administration of failing to appoint Latinos to key cabinet posts, proposing draconian budget cuts in social service agencies, and failing to adequately fund education for poor districts. The alliance went on to warn elected politicians, "If you seek the support of the Latino community, we will hold you accountable and you shall reap what you sow" (Pérez, quoted in Stainton 2003). To make matters worse, McGreevey announced his resignation in August 2004 after the appointment of his lover as director of State Homeland Security. Because of his scandal-ridden administration, many pundits believed that his actions could hurt other Democrats in the general election, including Senator John Kerry. Others speculated that the events of September 11, 2001, especially affected New Jersey and thus resulted in more voters opting to trust President Bush's handling of terrorism. For all these reasons, it was possible on the eve of Election 2004 that Bush could score a narrow victory over Kerry.

Kerry beat Bush in the general election, but the margin of victory was much closer than Gore's 16-point blowout over President Bush in 2000. Statewide, Kerry received 53 percent of the vote and Bush received 46 percent. This narrower margin of victory can be attributed largely to the September 11 effect, as well as to a marginal increase in the Latino vote for President Bush. Kerry's victory was solidified by a strong performance in the northeastern corner of the state, as well as in parts of central New Jersey along the Northeast Corridor and the areas surrounding Camden across the river from Philadelphia, Pennsylvania. Bush's numbers were strongest in the rural areas of northwestern New Jersey and on parts of the Jersey Shore.

The Congressional Hispanic Caucus, however, issued a warning that New Jersey, New York, and California could become competitive states if Democrats ignored the Latino community (Duran 2005). Whether this is a sign of real concern among Latino Democratic leaders or merely an effort to raise awareness among the base, there is no question that Hispanic voters are less strongly Democratic than are African American voters. This has not made a difference in the outcome of the election in New Jersey up to this point and probably will not in the near future either. While this chapter ultimately argues that the Latino vote made little difference in the outcome of the election in the state, it is nonetheless crucial to examine any possible idiosyncratic or atypical behavior of Latino voters.

The chapter proceeds as follows. The first section explores the context of Latino voting and elite officeholding in New Jersey in recent years. Next, Republican efforts to appeal to voters in New Jersey, especially Latino voters, are discussed, along with corresponding Democratic and nonpartisan efforts to appeal to New Jersey voters. Finally, polling data and election outcomes are compared to determine the extent to which campaign efforts effectively translated into votes.

THE CONTEXT: LATINOS IN NEW JERSEY

The influx of Latinos into New Jersey is a relatively recent phenomenon. In 1970 Latinos numbered 4 percent of the population, while in 2000 they totaled 13 percent, giving New Jersey the sixth-largest percentage of Latinos in the population (Salmore and Salmore 1998). The growing number of immigrants from Mexico and Central America seeking better economic opportunities in the New York–Philadelphia region explains much of this increase. At the same time, the Puerto Rican and Cuban American communities in the state are large and more long standing. Puerto Ricans first began to arrive in New Jersey in the 1950s; Cubans followed in the 1960s and 1970s (Connors and Dunham 1993).

As table 11.1 illustrates, Puerto Ricans constitute 41 percent of Latino voters in the state, and Cuban Americans constitute 12 percent. Both groups have established themselves in New Jersey politics, and the few Latino elected officials that do serve are either Puerto Rican or

Cuban American. At the same time, Dominicans now make up 9 percent of Latino voters in the state, while Mexican Americans comprise 4 percent of Latino voters.

The growth in these populations has not directly translated into growth in voting behavior, however. In 2000 the Latino voting age population (VAP) stood at 13 percent of the total state VAP, while the Latino citizen VAP stood at 9.4 percent of that total (U.S. Census Bureau 2000). In 2000, while 14 percent of the total New Jersey population could claim Latino heritage, approximately 5 percent of the total (including documented and undocumented workers) were not U.S. citizens (U.S. Census Bureau 2000), thereby reducing their eligibility as a group to vote.

Fifty-five percent of New Jersey's Latino voters are Democrats, but many have crossed party lines to support Republicans such as Bret Schundler, mayor of Jersey City in the 1990s, and former Governor Thomas H. Kean. Although 26 percent of Latino voters in New Jersey say they are Republican (almost three times more than in neighboring New York), even Cuban American voters in New Jersey still prefer

Table 11.1. Profile of New Jersey Latino Voters

Country of Origin	*Percentage*
Puerto Rican	41
Dominican	9
Mexican	4
Cuban	12
Democrat	55
Republican	26
Other	19
U.S. born	40
Puerto Rico born	15
Born elsewhere	45

Source: Hispanic Federation 12th Annual Survey, July 2004.

Democratic candidates such as Robert Menéndez, former chair of the House Democratic Caucus and current junior senator of the state.

Unlike other states, New Jersey does not have a lieutenant governor, and the governorship is the only statewide elected official (excluding U.S. senators, of course). This gives the governor strong powers to appoint his or her cabinet. No political party has dominated the New Jersey legislature in the past twenty years. The Democrats won control of both houses in 1989 during Governor Jim Florio's landslide, but four years later Republican Christie Todd Whitman defeated Florio in the gubernatorial election, and the Republicans gained control of both houses. Once Whitman left New Jersey to run the Environmental Protection Agency, Acting Governor Donald T. DiFrancesco, a Republican, was dogged by ethics problems and did not run for the 2001 election. Bret Schundler, a conservative Republican, lost in the general election to McGreevey that year as Democrats regained control of both houses of the legislature. The Democrats solidified their gains in 2003. Because elections for state offices, such as the legislature and governor, are held in "off years," the presidential race and the U.S. congressional races, none of which were competitive, were basically the only items on the 2004 ballot. Acting Governor Richard Codey, a Democrat, was up for election in 2005 and decided to opt out of the race rather than face U.S. Senator Jon Corzine after the latter announced he would run for governor. Political insiders correctly predicted that should Corzine be elected governor, he would appoint Menéndez to complete his term in the U.S. Senate, giving New Jersey its first ever Latino U.S. senator.

PRO-REPUBLICAN EFFORTS IN THE PRIMARY AND GENERAL ELECTIONS

No one opposed President Bush in the June 8, 2004, primary in New Jersey, or anywhere else for that matter. Not surprisingly, Bush won 100 percent of the vote. More important, however, were the state delegates chosen for the GOP convention to be held in New York City in August. Four Latinos were chosen among the thirty-nine delegates.[1] In fact, one of the delegates, Cuban-born Mariella Morales, was touted on the convention Web site and was one of two New Jersey delegates photographed.

Given Gore's clear victory over Bush in 2000, many thought that Karl Rove and the Republican National Committee (RNC) would ignore New Jersey and its fifteen electoral votes. As the campaign progressed, however, New Jersey's poll numbers showed a close race within the margin of error. RNC chair Ed Gillespie, himself a New Jersey native, eventually convinced Rudolph Giuliani, Vice President Dick Cheney, and First Lady Laura Bush to make trips to New Jersey just one month before the election.

Giuliani led a rally in Bergen County, a wealthy suburb of New York City, many of whose residents perished in the terrorist attacks of September 11, 2001. The vice president visited South Jersey on October 11, 2004, and touted the president's policies on Iraq and terrorism, along with Department of Homeland Security Secretary nominee Bernard Kerik and state GOP chair Joseph Kyrillos. They were well received at this rally in large part because Kerry had recently made his comment that terrorism should be considered a "nuisance" rather than a focus of U.S. foreign policy. This visit also received attention in the Philadelphia media market, which was a crucial battleground area in the election (Mulvihill 2004). The First Lady visited Hamilton, a suburb of Trenton, on September 16, 2004. Like Cheney's visit to Burlington County, this well-timed visit was also important because the Philadelphia media planned to cover an event in the next-door battleground state of Pennsylvania. In her speech, the First Lady barely mentioned terrorism. She emphasized the president's domestic policies in detail while also touting his efforts to lower health care costs and end frivolous lawsuits. On October 18, 2004, the president himself visited South Jersey, which again was not much of a detour since his visit coincided with one of his almost quotidian visits to Pennsylvania.

None of these high-profile visits targeted Latino voters in any clear way, however. Burlington, Mercer, and Bergen Counties are hardly areas of strong Latino concentration. Trenton in Mercer County has a sizable Latino community, but the bedroom community of Hamilton is primarily a typical white suburb. Although the GOP spent $300,000 in the state for its well-orchestrated get-out-the-vote (GOTV) effort (Donahue and Marsico 2004), this effort targeted registered Republicans regardless of race or ethnicity. Unlike the Democrats, however, Republicans relied on more than twenty thousand volunteers to knock on doors and make telephone calls to registered Republicans. Despite its clear effect on the margin, this effort did not make a difference in this "blue" state.

Coinciding with the high-level visits, Luis Linares led a concerted effort for the state GOP to mobilize Latinos inclined to support the president's reelection. Linares assembled Latino leaders from each New Jersey county united under a clear twelve-point plan to identify Latino voters and turn them out on Election Day. In addition, members of the Republican Hispanic Leadership Council identified Latinos to run for local and state offices.

The Catholic Bishops of New Jersey, who strongly condemned John Kerry's pro-abortion stance, may have influenced Latino voters. Given that 39 percent of the state's population is Roman Catholic, it is not unreasonable to expect that the bishops could have a marginal influence. New Jersey's Catholic bishops, however, are much more conservative than the rank and file. Bishop John Smith of Trenton condemned then-Governor McGreevey for his stance on abortion, leading the governor to agree not to receive communion. Archbishop John J. Myers of Newark also made headlines by claiming it would be "dishonest" for any Catholic politician to receive communion if he or she supported abortion rights. His apostolic letter urged Catholics to vote for pro-life candidates or risk separation from God: "I ask and urge that Catholic voters and Catholics in public life carefully consider their position if they find themselves in opposition to Church teaching in these matters [abortion]. Sadly, I must point out that to continue down this road places them in danger of distancing themselves even more from Jesus Christ and from His Church" (Kocienieweski 2004). The letter was read at all masses in the Newark archdiocese, where a large percentage of practicing Catholics are Latino. For devout Latino Catholics, the archbishop's message was clear: a vote for pro-choice Senator Kerry was not morally permissible.

The Reverend Arturo Soto, president of the Protestant Hispanic Clergy Association of New Jersey, also pointedly attacked Kerry's record:

> John Kerry says that he represents Hispanic values, but his record shows the opposite. . . . Hispanic values are based on the strength of our families, and John Kerry's record in the U.S. Senate has not been pro-family. He has consistently voted against requiring that parents be notified before

> their teenage daughters have an abortion. He was one of the only 14 Senators who voted against the Defense of Marriage Act, signed by President Clinton, which defined marriage as only the union between a man and a woman. He opposed giving parents the choice to select the best school for their children and voted against tax relief for married couples with underage children. This is not the record of a politician that represents Hispanic values. (Latino Coalition 2004)

Because Republicans did not consider New Jersey a top target, few advertisements targeting Latino voters appeared in the state. However, some national advertisements were broadcast on cable television and published in Spanish-language media.

PRO-DEMOCRATIC EFFORTS FROM THE PRIMARY TO THE GENERAL ELECTION

Since the Democratic primary in New Jersey is held so late in the primary process, the major candidates were not very active in the state. Senator Joe Lieberman (D-CT) had early leads in the polls, but this was before the Howard Dean surge and the ultimate Kerry victory in Iowa. By the New Jersey June 8, 2004, primary, the state's Democrats overwhelmingly backed Kerry, with 92 percent of the vote. Supporters included then-Governor McGreevey, who had earlier backed Dean during his period of popularity. By this date Dean had dropped out, but Representative Dennis Kucinich (D-OH) stubbornly refused to concede and won 4 percent of the vote. Perennial candidate Lyndon LaRouche received about 2 percent of the vote. Of New Jersey's 128 national delegates, 107 were allocated as a result of the party's primary. The twenty-one remaining delegates consisted of elected officials and prominent Democratic National Committee members who were considered officially "unpledged" delegates, although most had already endorsed Kerry.

Unlike most other states, New Jersey allocates its delegates by delegate district rather than congressional district. That is to say, the delegates are chosen by state legislative district, for a total of 70 delegates. The remaining 37 delegates are allocated based on the statewide primary vote. Sixteen of the 128 delegates to the Democratic convention were Latinos (13 percent), slightly below the 14 percent Latino population in the state. Suffice it to say that the New Jersey Democratic Party did ensure that Latinos were represented at its convention.

Senator Kerry visited the state five times before winning the Democratic nomination, and he sent Senator John Edwards, his vice presidential running mate, to New Jersey to rally the base on October 8, 2004. Edwards's October visit to New Jersey was necessary in order to respond to encroachments on the Garden State by Giuliani, Cheney, and Laura Bush. Edwards appeared in Bayonne in Hudson County—an area with a high concentration of minorities, including Latinos. His speech, however, focused entirely on the Bush administration's failures in Iraq and the lack of funding earmarked for homeland security, especially port security (Kidd 2004).

The national Democratic Party did not spend any money campaigning in New Jersey. The state party spent $1 million, mostly to mobilize voters through GOTV efforts (Donahue and Marsico 2004). That is, they emphasized the mobilization of minority voters. In the end, this strategy paid off as it put Kerry over the top in the general election. In fact, the electorate in 2004 was 70 percent white, down ten percentage points from 2000. Kerry's total, thus, could not have been reached without some mobilization of minority voters (Donahue and Marsico 2004). To that end, the Kerry-Edwards campaign sought to appeal to Latino voters nationwide by touting the endorsement of U.S. Representative Robert Menéndez (D-NJ), the highest-ranking Latino in Congress. Menéndez stated that he "supports John Kerry because he is a leader that knows our community and will help us to make progress" (Segal 2004). Given that Menéndez is Cuban, however, his endorsement probably was meant to appeal to Latinos in the battleground state of Florida as much as it was to mobilize Latinos in New Jersey.

NONPARTISAN REGISTRATION EFFORTS

The Puerto Rico Federal Affairs Administration (PRFAA) registered more than 300,000 Puerto Rican and other Latino voters in New Jersey, as well as six other states. While not explicitly partisan, these efforts undoubtedly benefited Kerry because they targeted northeastern states with large Puerto Rican populations such as Rhode Island, New York, Florida, New Jersey, Pennsylvania, and Massachusetts.

Likewise, the Dominican American Council of New Jersey launched a registration drive in July 2004 to register Latino voters of all national-origin groups. Touting the fact that New Jersey is "home to eight of the ten cities nationwide with the highest concentration of Dominican Americans," the council president kicked off this campaign in Paterson, New Jersey, which employs a large number of Dominican American women in its substantial sewing industry (Faruque 2004). On the other hand, groups such as America Coming Together (ACT) and MoveOn .org did not focus their efforts on New Jersey. Instead, ACT and MoveOn.org were very active in Pennsylvania, the swing state adjacent to New Jersey. Much of the state, nonetheless, benefited from national campaigning because 527 political groups targeted Pennsylvania. For example, Swift Boat Veterans for Truth advertisements aired in southern and central portions of the state. Some cable subscribers also were exposed to these nationwide advertisements.

ELECTION RESULTS

Most of the public opinion polls released in the months leading up to the election showed Kerry in the lead (fig. 11.1, table 11.2). An early poll in April showed Bush with a four-point lead, but that changed once Kerry became the clear nominee of the Democratic Party. After April, however, all but four of the polls on the list showed Kerry with a lead. Three polls showed the candidates tied; one had Bush in the lead. Two polls taken in late September reported that the candidates were tied, which can be explained by the residual effects of September 11, and one poll gave Bush a four-point lead. As the election drew nearer, two October polls showed that the candidates were tied. An average of polls taken between October 27 and 31 indicated that Kerry had a seven-point lead. The average turned out to be remarkably accurate in that he won the state by seven points, signifying that the undecided voters did not break heavily in either direction.

Figure 11.1. New Jersey Public Polls from June 2004 through Election Day

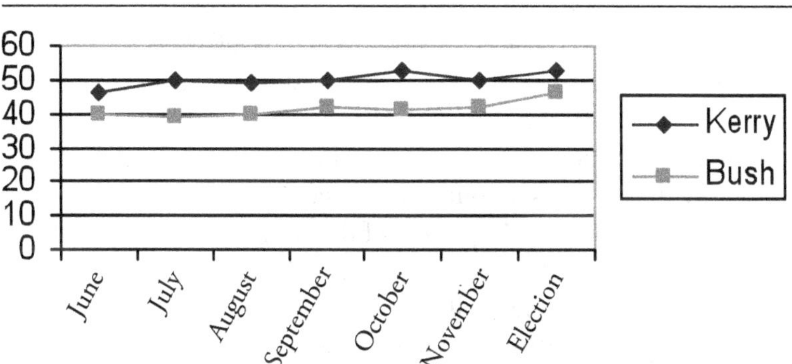

Source: June, Eagleton Poll; July, Research 2000 Poll; August, Strategic Vision Poll; September, American Research Group Poll; October, Rasmussen Poll; November, average of all polls at that point; Election, actual result.

Figure 11.1 shows many of these same polls in graphic form. Notice that beginning in June, Kerry held a modest lead over Bush. Between July and September Kerry had opened up a comfortable lead over Bush. After the Republican National Convention in New York City and the corresponding September 11 anniversary, the race became much tighter. This led RNC chair Ed Gillespie to flirt with the idea of spending resources in New Jersey. The tight race continued throughout the month of October, but Kerry broke away in late October and early November to capture New Jersey's fifteen electoral votes.

Table 11.2 shows a snapshot of several of the same New Jersey polls for Latino voters in the state. According to the ABC exit poll during the 2000 elections, 35 percent of Latinos and 41 percent of the general electorate voted for Bush. In 2004 the ABC exit poll shows that 43 percent of Latinos voted for Bush, yielding an eight-point increase over the previous election. These results should be interpreted with caution, however, given the well-documented errors in the exit polls during the 2004 election and disputes regarding precisely how Latinos voted, with nationwide estimates ranging from 33 percent to 44 percent (see Leal et al. 2005). Regardless, the great disparity between the preelection and exit polls is remarkable. On the eve of the election, Survey USA gauged a 37-point lead for Kerry among Latinos, whereas the exit poll showed he had only a 13-point lead. Given the state's overall results, it is unlikely that Bush got as high as 43 percent in New Jersey, but 30 percent is too low given the 53 to 46 statewide margin of victory for Kerry. Table 11.2 shows the results of several surveys that estimate Latino support for all the candidates.

A potentially more instructive way to look at these results is to examine only the New Jersey counties with significant percentages of Latinos (table 11.3). At least 15 percent of the population in Cumberland, Essex, Hudson, Passaic, and Union Counties is Latino. With the exception of Cumberland County, all these counties are located in northeastern New Jersey. A comparison of how these counties voted in 2000 and 2004 might shed some light on the impact of the Latino vote. Bush increased his vote share between three and seven percentage points in all of these counties. In Cumberland County, which has the lowest percentage of Latinos, Bush did seven percentage points better. Kerry did worse than Gore in all five counties, ranging from a deficit of one to six percentage points.

Table 11.2. New Jersey Public Polls Gauging Latino Support

Poll Firm	*Date*	*Bush*	*Kerry*	*Nader/Other*	*Spread*
2004 election result (all NJ voters)	Nov. 2004	46	53	1	Kerry +7
2004 ABC exit poll (Latinos)	Nov. 2004	43	56	1	Kerry +13
Survey USA	Oct. 27–29	30	67	2	Kerry +37
Survey USA	Oct. 16–18	27	66	7	Kerry +39
Survey USA	Oct. 1–3	46	48	3	Kerry +2
Survey USA	Sept. 12–14	32	53	6	Kerry +21
Poll Firm	*Date*	*Bush*	*Gore*	*Nader/Other*	*Spread*
2000 election result (all NJ voters)	Nov. 2000	41	56	3	Gore +15
2000 ABC exit poll (Latinos)	Nov. 2000	35	58	6	Gore +23

Table 11.3. Comparison of the Vote from Top Five Latino New Jersey Counties, 2000 and 2004 (percent)

	2000		*2004*		*Change*		*Turnout Percent*	
	Gore	*Bush*	*Kerry*	*Bush*	*Bush*	*Kerry*	*2000*	*2004*
Cumberland	58	39	52	46	+7	-6	61	65
Essex	72	26	70	29	+3	-2	61	68
Hudson	71	26	67	32	+6	-4	62	63
Passaic	58	39	55	44	+5	-3	66	69
Union	60	37	59	41	+4	-1	70	72

Source: New Jersey Division of Elections.

What about voter turnout in these five counties? Conventional wisdom held that higher voter turnout would help Senator Kerry because of the presumed dissatisfaction with the current administration's policies. In all five counties, turnout slightly increased over the 2000 levels, ranging anywhere from a one percentage point increase in Hudson County to a seven percentage point increase in Essex County. Higher turnout does not seem to have worked to Kerry's advantage, however. Because this is an ecological overview, it is difficult to pinpoint Latino voters as its cause, but in general, higher aggregate turnout in heavily minority and Democratic counties did not help Kerry's campaign.

Table 11.4 shows the 2004 vote for Bush and Kerry in the top ten Latino population cities of New Jersey. In Union City and West New York, Bush performed better than in cities like Newark and Jersey City, presumably because the remaining concentration of the population in the latter two cities was predominantly African American. Of all ten cities, total turnout was the highest in West New York, followed by Union City, home to large Cuban American populations. Unlike Miami, however, Cuban Americans in New Jersey vote predominantly for Democratic candidates, although a substantial percentage of them seem to have voted for Bush, as table 11.4 illustrates. Kerry's margin of victory was highest in Newark, with a 30 percent Latino population, and a majority African American population, followed by Camden, which has a 39 percent Latino population.

Table 11.4. Comparison of the Vote from Top Ten Latino New Jersey Cities, 2004 (percent)

	Kerry	*Bush*	*Spread*	*Turnout*	*Latino*
Newark	86	13	K +73	57	30
Paterson	79	16	K +63	57	50
Jersey City	74	23	K +51	59	28
Elizabeth	67	31	K +36	60	50
Union City	65	32	K +33	61	82
Passaic	66	30	K +36	62	63
West New York	61	36	K +25	66	79
North Bergen	65	33	K +32	64	57
Perth Amboy	71	27	K +44	56	70
Camden	84	13	K +71	50	39

Source: New Jersey Division of Elections.

The real reason that Bush closed the gap with Kerry was because Kerry severely underperformed in other parts of the state. That is to say, Kerry outperformed Gore in only one of the twenty-one other New Jersey counties (Hunterdon), and even that was by just one percentage point. On the other hand, Bush increased his vote share in every New Jersey County by at least two percentage points. In heavily white Ocean County, Bush increased his margin by eleven points between 2000 and 2004. While Bush improved his margins in the heavily Latino counties, it was not the result of specific outreach to Latino communities. Rather, the Rove strategy of reaching out to Republican voters regardless of race, gender, or anything else clearly worked across the state.

In Passaic County, Mike Mecca, the Republican chair, noted that Cuban Americans have always helped Republicans win in local elections, but he also argued that more Puerto Ricans and South Americans have been trending Republican. Juan Malave, a Puerto Rican–born councilman in the county, argued that the Republican emphasis on family values has attracted many Latinos to their party (White 2004). In addition, the number of Mexican immigrants in Passaic County tripled in the past ten years, leading to the establishment of Casa Puebla, a political action group that aims to empower Mexican immigrants to vote and run for political office. Representation is important to this growing population because only one of the nine elected officials in Passaic County is Mexican American; the rest are Puerto Rican or Cuban American (Ortiz 2004).

In the end, however, no serious follower of New Jersey politics expected John Kerry to lose the state's fifteen electoral votes in the general election. New Jersey has not elected a Republican statewide since Governor Whitman's narrow victory in 1997. The only way for a Democrat to lose statewide is if a moderate, pro-choice Republican runs and the Democratic candidate is particularly weak, as was the case with Robert Torricelli and James E. McGreevey. Indeed, the latter two were so politically debilitated that both opted not to run rather than face defeat in the general election. Barring such circumstances, unlike the case in the South, not enough white voters in New Jersey vote for Republican candidates in order for Republicans to win statewide. In particular, white Republican-leaning women are less likely to vote for national Republican candidates because of their positions on abortion and environmental policy.

IMPLICATIONS FOR LATINO PARTY LOYALTY

While the majority of New Jersey Latinos voted for Senator Kerry, President Bush made several efforts to appeal to the Latino community by appointing Latinos such as Alberto Gonzales and Mel Martinez to high-profile cabinet posts, attorney general and secretary of commerce, respectively. At the same time, according to a poll taken by the Hispanic Federation, registered voters in New Jersey had indicated the economy and jobs as the number one issue (26 percent), followed by the war in Iraq (19 percent) and education (15 percent). To the extent that President Bush can help improve the economy and temper the situation in Iraq, he may become more popular among New Jersey Latinos, although Latino voters did not give the president high marks on these two scores just prior to the 2004 election. As the 2008 election season intensified, President Bush's handling of either the economy or the situation in Iraq had not inspired confidence among the general electorate, including Latinos. The president emphasized education policy during his first term by touting the No Child Left Behind (NCLB) Act as a solution to closing the achievement gap for Latinos. To the extent that Latinos see real progress in this area, Bush may receive some credit. Democrats, however, have criticized the president for not adequately funding the NCLB Act.

New Jersey's Latino voters are not wedded to any political party. Sixty-five percent have voted for a candidate from another party at some point in their lives. Fifty-four percent indicate that the candidates and their issue positions matter more than party affiliation when making vote choices. These numbers are much higher than for African Americans, who vote overwhelmingly Democratic. Republicans can take solace in these numbers, while Democrats must work extra hard to win the support of Latino voters. Democrats are taking note. On May 9, 2005, Senate Majority Leader Harry Reid (D-NV) formed the Hispanic Affairs Team to appeal to Hispanic voters. He will need Latino support not only for his own reelection in Nevada but also in national elections (Pratt 2006). Latinos win in such a competitive political environment.

CONCLUSION

New Jersey's rapidly growing Latino population will no doubt influence the state's electoral politics in the years to come. When Senator Jon Corzine (D-NJ) became governor, it cleared the way for U.S. Representative Robert Menéndez to be appointed to the U.S. Senate, making him the first Latino senator to represent New Jersey. This, in turn, created an opportunity for General Assembly Speaker Albio Sires (D-West New York) to replace Menéndez in the U.S. House. Latinos of both political parties represent New Jerseyans in the General Assembly. It is only a matter of time before Latinos start to get elected to the state senate.

In the 2004 elections, Latinos turned out to vote for Senator John Kerry, although President George W. Bush marginally improved his numbers among them. New Jersey's Latinos will no doubt continue to vote primarily for Democratic candidates, especially with Menéndez as one of the most powerful officeholders in the state. While the Latino vote generally does not influence the outcome of statewide elections in

New Jersey, politicians in the state have increasingly found it necessary to consult Menéndez and pay attention to his Hudson County machine, which can make or break candidates. Because neither presidential campaign heavily invested in New Jersey, voter interest in the campaign was not as high as in other parts of the country.

Although voter turnout was up in 2004, this did not help Kerry vis-à-vis Gore's performance four years earlier. Bush gained ground in nearly all parts of the state, but he increased his margin of the vote in heavily white counties rather than in the minority counties of northeastern New Jersey. The Republicans clearly focused on getting their base to the polls in order to increase their vote share, which they were able to do. The Democrats won the state rather convincingly because of a coalition of minorities, labor, and suburban women who were uncomfortable with Bush's social conservatism. In DeSipio and de la Garza's framework from the 2000 edition, New Jersey remains a state in which there appears to be "no Latino influence" in the outcome of the general election. The last time New Jersey Latinos arguably made a difference in the outcome was 1992, when Bill Clinton, George H. W. Bush, and Ross Perot battled for the presidency. Because of New Jersey's unusually high number of independents, Perot performed quite well among working-class white voters.

New Jersey has become a blue state and will remain so barring unforeseen circumstances. Like its neighboring states, Pennsylvania, New York, and Delaware, New Jersey has become a predictable northeastern state in presidential elections. While Pennsylvania's electoral margins have no doubt been closer in recent years, this region of the country is reliable territory for Democratic presidential candidates, although this may change depending on the response of white working-class voters and Latinos to the candidacy of Senator Barack Obama. To the extent that both parties reach out to Latino voters, they have wisely spent more resources in states that make more of a difference in the aggregate, such as Arizona and Florida.

NOTE

1. This analysis is based on a surname listing from the New Jersey Department of Elections. It is possible that some Latinos with non-Latino names were represented, although probably not a significant number.

REFERENCES

Bush, Laura. 2004. "Remarks by First Lady at Bush-Cheney '04 Rally in Hamilton, New Jersey." www.whitehouse.gov. Accessed June 2005.

Connors, Richard J., and William J. Dunham. 1993. *The Government of New Jersey.* Lanham, MD: University Press of America.

de la Garza, Rodolfo, Louis DeSipio, F. Chris García, and Angelo Falcón. 1992. *Latino Voices: Mexican, Puerto Rican, and Cuban Perspectives on American Politics.* Boulder, CO: Westview Press.

Donahue, Joe, and R. Marsico. 2004. "Despite GOP's Overtures, Jerseyans Side with Kerry." *Newark Star Ledger,* November 3.

Duran, Nicole. 2005. "A Formidable Bloc to Chip; GOP Touts Gains among Hispanic Voters." *Roll Call,* January 4.

Faruque, Zinnia. 2004. "Registration Drive Urges Latinos to Get to Polls." *Bergen County Record,* July 8.

Grofman, Bernard, and Chandler Davidson, eds. 1992. *Controversies in Minority Voting: The Voting Rights Act in Perspective.* Washington, DC: Brookings Institute Press.

Hispanic Federation. 2004. "Hispanics in New York City and New Jersey Findings." July. www.hispanicfederation.org/. Accessed February 3, 2009.

Kidd, Lauren. 2004. "Edwards Stumps in N.J." *Home News Tribune,* October 8.

Kocieniewski, David. 2004. "Governor Puts Communion Aside after Upsetting New Jersey Bishops." *New York Times,* May 6.

Latino Coalition. 2004. Media Press Release. www.thelatinocoalition.com/news/2004/PresidentBushendorsement.pdf.

Leal, David, Barreto Matt, Jongho Lee, and Rodolfo de la Garza. 2005. "The Latino Vote in the 2004 Election." *PS: Political Science and Politics* 38: 41–49.

Mulvihill, Geoff. 2004. "Cheney, in South Jersey, Sees State in Bush Column." *Home News Tribune,* October 11.

National Association of Latino Elected and Appointed Officials (NALEO). 2004. *2004 Latino Election Handbook.* Los Angeles: NALEO Educational Fund.

New Jersey Republican State Committee, "Goals of the Hispanic Leadership Council." www.njgop.org/. Accessed February 3, 2009.

Ortiz, Erik. 2004. "A Push to Bolster Mexicans' Political Clout." *Bergen County Record,* September 30.

Pratt, Timothy. 2005. "Reid Reaches Out to Hispanic Electorate." *Las Vegas Sun,* May 9.

Rebovich, David. 2004. "RNC Chair Gillespie Makes it Official: New Jersey Is in Play." www.politicsnj.com. Accessed June 2005.

Salmore, Barbara G., and Stephen A. Salmore. 1998. *New Jersey Politics and Government.* Lincoln: University of Nebraska Press.

Segal, Adam. 2004. "Bikini Politics: The 2004 Presidential Campaigns' Hispanic Media Efforts Cover Only the Essential Parts of the Body Politic: A Select Group of Voters in a Few Battleground States." Hispanic Voter Project, Johns Hopkins University.

Stainton, Lilo H. 2003. "Hispanic Leaders Give McGreevy Ultimatum." Gannet State Bureau.

U.S. Census Bureau. 2000. American FactFinder. http://factfinder.census.gov/home/saff/main.html?_lang=en. Accessed July 6, 2009.

White, Nicolas. 2004. "Republicans Courting Latino Support." *Herald News* (Passaic County, NJ), September 3.

Chapter Twelve

Hearing Footsteps

Latino Population Growth and Anticipated Political Effects in the "New Destination" States

CHRISTINA E. BEJARANO
AND GARY M. SEGURA

In this chapter we examine the current and potential influence of emerging Latino population concentrations in eight states: Arkansas, Georgia, Nebraska, Nevada, North Carolina, Iowa, Washington, and Wisconsin. We use a two-prong standard for judging the importance of the Latino electorate. The first is whether the Latino electorate could conceivably have provided the margin of victory. By that standard, it is apparent that in nearly every state with newly emerging Latino populations, Latinos had—and could have had—little to no effect on the outcome of the 2004 election. This is so because in most of the states where Latino populations are growing rapidly, with the potential exceptions of Iowa, Washington, and Wisconsin, the outcomes of the election at many levels were largely a foregone conclusion.

The second standard is more nuanced. We argue that Latino populations and population growth—and the evolution of their political preferences—have much to say about the political future of a state or locale. There are good reasons, then, for the parties to have made conscious efforts to reach out to Latino voters, even without immediate electoral payoff.

The geography of Latino America is changing rapidly. Latinos, once confined largely to the Southwest, South Florida, Chicago, and New York, are suddenly to be found in large numbers in the South and Midwest. Attracted, in part, by more plentiful job opportunities in industries such as meat- and poultry packing, textiles, and wholesale nursery businesses, Latinos have contributed greatly to population growth in percentage terms in places where they have never before lived in significant numbers. Of the twelve states with the fastest-growing Latino populations, only Nevada (ranked fifth) is from a geographic region usually associated with this phenomenon. All the remaining states are in the South and Midwest. Table 12.1 reports population growth rates and total Latino population in the fastest-growing states.

Table 12.1. U.S. States with the Fastest Rate of Latino Population Growth, 1990–2000

	Growth Rate (%)	*Total 2000 Population*
North Carolina	394	378,963
Arkansas	337	86,666
Georgia	300	435,227
Tennessee	278	123,838
Nevada	217	393,970
South Carolina	211	95,067
Alabama	208	75,830
Kentucky	173	59,939
Minnesota	166	143,382
Nebraska	155	94,425
Iowa	153	82,473
Mississippi	148	39,569

Source: U.S. Census Bureau 2000c.

The aggregate numbers, of course, are usually small. Mississippi's growth rate might be high, but its total Latino population has yet to break 40,000 persons, and Kentucky's Latino community is just over 50,000. Numbers in South Carolina, Iowa, and Nebraska are considerably higher, approaching the 100,000 mark, and the populations in Minnesota and Tennessee exceed that. In comparison, Latino populations in Georgia, Nevada, and North Carolina have very quickly grown quite large.

Two states not listed in table 12.1 also deserve attention. First, Washington now has the nation's tenth-largest Latino population. The rate of growth between the last two census counts might not be as remarkable as in other states, largely because the Latino population has been established and growing for some time. Nevertheless, at 441,000, the population is clearly politically significant. Second, Wisconsin's Latino population is approaching 200,000, the highest concentration of Latinos in the Midwest outside of Chicago. Like Washington, the longer-term presence of Latinos in Wisconsin, especially in and around Milwaukee, prevents the growth rate from being as high as in the new destination states. The population, however, is both sizable and potentially important to election outcomes.

How did the 2004 election transpire in these locales? Were Latinos ignored, catered to, or something in between? We examine the role of Latinos in the 2004 elections specifically in these emerging states, where Latino populations are newer and of significantly lower density. To undertake this examination, we have selected eight of the aforementioned states because of their population sizes, growth rates, or the unique role they might have played in the 2004 election. The states selected are displayed in table 12.2, along with population and growth rate information.

For a variety of reasons, not the least of which are immigration status, noncitizenship, and lower overall participation, Latino population growth does not immediately signal political strength. Though the numbers—especially in some states—are impressive, it will be some time before Latinos exert significant influence on the overall state electoral environment. After Guerra (1992), we recognize that, for Latinos to be an important force, several conditions must be in place, including close contests, generally unified Latino voting, sufficient registration

Table 12.2. Latino Populations, 2000, and Percent Growth, 1990–2000, in Selected States

	Total	*Rank*	*Growth Rate (%)*	*Rank*
North Carolina	378,963	15	394	1
Arkansas	86,666	36	337	2
Georgia	435,227	11	300	3
Nevada	393,970	14	217	5
Nebraska	94,425	33	155	10
Iowa	82,473	37	153	11
Wisconsin	192,921	24	107	19
Washington	441,509	10	106	20

Source: U.S. Census Bureau 2000c.

and turnout numbers to sway the outcome, and an interest by candidates and parties in seeking Latino votes. Although the margin of victory was small enough for registered Latino voters to potentially tip the balance in Iowa, Nevada, and Wisconsin, it is an understatement to say that the above conditions are not yet met in most of these emerging states—where the margin of victory was substantially larger than even the Latino voting age population.

How, then, can we judge the importance of the Latino electorate? We argue here that there are two standards. First, the Latino electorate is important when its votes provide the margin of victory or, by extension, when the absence of their votes permits defeat (de la Garza and DeSipio 2005). To begin with the obvious, in nearly every state with newly emerging Latino populations and voter blocs, Latinos had little to no effect on the outcome of the 2004 election. The reason is simple: in most of the states where Latino populations are growing rapidly, the outcome of the election at many levels was a foregone conclusion.

Though the parties might have publicly protested to the contrary, Georgia, Nebraska, and North Carolina were perceived early on as solidly in the Republican camp. Washington was assumed to be safely Democratic, at least at the presidential level, although history shows that this was not the case at the gubernatorial level. Democrats might have briefly entertained hopes in some of these states—North Carolina is often mentioned—and in other circumstances, they have performed reasonably well in Arkansas (at the presidential as well as the senatorial levels). Nevertheless, we think it is safe to conclude that neither campaign perceived that these states were in play. Data presented in table 12.3 make it clear that the margins of victory for most states in the last election are well beyond the capacity of the Latino population to affect the outcome in any way. By extension, neither camp would then view Latinos as being important to the outcome.

The exceptions are locations where the election could be perceived by both parties to be so close that even the modest Latino electorate could conceivably play an important role. Those four states include Iowa, Nevada, and Wisconsin, where the presidential election was extremely close, and as we mentioned before, Washington, where Latinos may in fact have been among the groups that determined the outcome at the gubernatorial level. We return to these examples momentarily.

Large and growing Latino populations—and the evolution of their political preferences—have much to say about the political future of a state or locale. In Georgia, for example, where the Latino population is approaching the half-million mark, it may not matter that Latino voters were unlikely to determine the outcome of the presidential election in that state in 2004. Rather, their importance might best be understood in terms of their future impact.

Regardless of the forecasts one chooses to make regarding Latino naturalization, registration, and turnout, some degree of political influence will eventually come to this population. Political candidates and parties, we contend, therefore have a clear interest in shaping the political attitudes and identities of these Latinos. While their votes may have had little effect on the 2004 election, their effect on future elections can only grow. For Democrats, a growing and strongly Democratic Mexican American population, combined with existing African American voting strength, could conceivably move Georgia out of the "lock" column for the Republicans and into "battleground" territory. Similarly, a Mexican American population more evenly divided between the parties, or even tilting in the GOP direction, could expand and extend Republican dominance of Georgia and North Carolina's electoral votes. In Arkansas, the southern state where Democrats remain

Table 12.3 Latinos as a Share of State Electorates in 2004

	Latino VAP[a]	*Citizen VAP*	*%*	*Registered Voters*	*Unregistered Potential Voters*	*2004 Margin and Winner*
Arkansas	71,700	40,400	2.0	13,500	26,900	102,945 R
Georgia	389,300	275,300	4.4	133,000	142,000	548,105 R
Iowa	61,800	33,500	1.5	23,200	10,300	10,059 R
Nebraska	71,200	34,900	2.8	16,700	18,200	258,486 R
Nevada	315,400	170.400	11.1	43,800	126,600	21,500 R
North Carolina	341,500	156,100	2.5	43,000	113,100	435,317 R
Washington	318,400	148,700	3.4	112,000	36,700	205,307 D
Wisconsin	142,100	125,100	3.1	79,600	45,500	11,384 D

Source: Data on Latino and Citizen VAP from the U.S. Hispanic Leadership Institute, www.hispaniconline.com/pol&opi/report/Latinoreport.pdf.

[a] VAP = voting age population.

most competitive, Latino population growth and potential politicization could have a long-reaching impact on the state's political future.

In each of the eight states under consideration, then, there are good reasons for the parties to make conscious efforts to reach Latino voters if not to mobilize them. In Washington, Wisconsin, and Iowa, parties and candidates had reason to expect the election—at one level or another—to be close enough that even small voter blocs could alter outcomes. In Nebraska, as well as the aforementioned growth areas of Arkansas, Georgia, and North Carolina, the rate of Latino population growth is sufficient that each party has an incentive to invest in outreach to develop ongoing relationships, even without immediate electoral payoff. In Nevada, both an increasingly competitive present and a huge and growing population share suggest that the importance of the Latino community to electoral outcomes will attract considerable partisan interest. In the next section, we offer a profile of each state, its Latino population, campaign details, and any political success that Latinos might have had leading up to or during the 2004 elections.

GEORGIA

Georgia has experienced one of the most dramatic Latino population increases in the past several years. In 2000 Latinos accounted for 5.3 percent of the population, yet by 2003 they had increased to 6.3 percent (U.S. Census Bureau 2000b, 2003). More specifically, 5.5 percent of Georgia's population consists of foreign-born noncitizens, which has led to a new set of issues being introduced to the state. Most of this newly developing population, much of which is made up of undocumented residents, is concentrated in a few counties, each about 10 to 20 percent Latino. Whitfield, Echols, and Hall Counties have the highest percentage of Latinos in the state, ranging from 19.6 percent to 22.1 percent. The next most heavily populated Latino counties range from Appling, with 17 percent, to Gwinnett, Colquitt, and Chattahoochee, with 10.4 percent to 10.9 percent (U.S. Census Bureau 2000c). Whitfield, Hall, and Gwinnett are located north of metropolitan Atlanta. Whitfield contains the town of Dalton, which has a rapidly growing and especially heavy concentration of Latinos. Chattahoochee is near the western city of Columbus, Appling is outside of Savannah, and Colquitt and Echols are in the southern part of the state outside of the city of Valdosta.

This rapid increase in Georgia's Latino population has not resulted in a sizable political shift, however. In the 2004 presidential election, the margin of defeat for Kerry amounted to 16.6 percentage points. Bush was able to carry the state easily, with 58 percent of the vote over Kerry's 41.4 percent (Georgia Secretary of State 2005). Further, the Edison-Mitofsky (2004) exit poll suggested that the Georgia electorate, about 2 percent Latino, preferred Bush 56 to 43 percent (though these estimates are likely fraught with error).

Although Latinos may not be able to affect the outcome of presidential elections, they have been able to influence their political environment within the state. In 2004 Georgia's three Latino state legislators were able to win reelection. The incumbent state senator, Sam Zamarripa (D), was reelected in District 36, as were the incumbent representatives David Casas (R) and Pedro Marin (D), who represent Gwinett County, home to a large number of Latinos. Georgia has four other Latino elected officials: council members Evelyn Mimi Woodson (Columbus) and Jason R. Anavitarte (Doraville) and state court judges Roland Castellanos (Cobb County) and Antonio Del Campo (DeKalb County). These individuals are among the Latinos emerging as a political presence in Georgia (NALEO 2004).

With their numbers approaching 500,000 in the state, Latinos' political power may grow considerably in the coming years. However, their level of geographic concentration is not yet sufficient to make a case for a majority-Latino electoral district, even with the renewal of the Voting Rights Act. The level of concentration is likely sufficient to increase Latino representation in the state legislature, however. Continued Democratic identity might also create opportunities for black-brown coalitions, as well as bolster the electoral prospects of white Democrats.

NORTH CAROLINA

North Carolina has also experienced a rapid increase in its Latino population—from an estimated 4.7 percent in 2000 to 5.6 percent by

2003 (U.S. Census Bureau 2000b, 2003). This growing segment of society includes an estimated 4.7 percent foreign-born noncitizens. The majority of the state's Latinos reside in six counties, which range from 8 to 15 percent Latino. The most populated Latino counties are Duplin (15.1 percent), Lee (11.7 percent), Sampson (10.8 percent), and Montgomery (10.4 percent). Chatham and Greene Counties also have sizable Latino populations, 9.6 percent and 8 percent, respectively (U.S. Census Bureau 2000c). The northern counties of Chatham and Lee are located southwest of metropolitan Durham and Raleigh, while Montgomery is northeast of metropolitan Charlotte. The eastern counties of Sampson and Duplin are outside of the city of Fayetteville, and Greene is southwest of Greenville.

North Carolina's Latino population does not yet appear to significantly influence the state's political environment. In 2004 Bush was able to carry the state with a sizable margin, 56 percent to Kerry's 43.6 percent of the vote (North Carolina Secretary of State 2005). The margin of defeat in the state for the Democrats was therefore 12.4 percent of the vote. Although the Edison-Mitofsky (2004) exit poll suggested that the electorate was about 1 percent Latino, the Kerry campaign nevertheless targeted the Latino vote by advertising on Spanish-language media (Newspaper Association of America 2005)—perhaps reflecting the Democrats' short-lived hope of winning the state.

While North Carolina did not witness a close contest for the presidential election, Latinos are retaining positions in local offices and the state legislature. Incumbent state senator Tom Apodaca (R) and state representative Daniel McComas (R) both held on to their seats. Moreover, Latinos have attained representation at the local level with Charlotte County commissioner Dan Ramirez (R) and Carrboro alderman John Herrera (NALEO 2004).

That these Latino elected officials are Republicans is a curiosity that necessitates a closer look. If this is a reflection of a more Republican Latino identity emerging in North Carolina, to say nothing of the South more broadly, Democrats may be facing a situation of noncompetitiveness for a generation. Even if there is not an emerging GOP identity, the very presence of elected Latino Republicans—as the sole Latino elected officials in the state—could serve as an important heuristic in shaping the partisan choices of new Latino voters to the benefit of the GOP. On the other hand, if these elected officials are not representative of the majority-Latino sentiment, this is an indication that North Carolina's growing Latino population has yet to secure even a modestly meaningful voice in state politics. The above officials represent areas of the state—Buncomber, Henderson, Polk, and New Hanover Counties—that do not have large populations of Latinos. That they do not emerge from areas of high Latino concentration suggests that their GOP identification may not reflect overall Latino partisan affiliations. However, it does suggest that non-Latinos are willing to vote for Latino Republican candidates under at least some circumstances.

NEVADA

Nevada has been the fastest-growing state for seventeen years running, and the steady increase in the Latino population exceeds that of the rest of the state. In 2000 Latinos accounted for 19.7 percent of Nevada's population (U.S. Census Bureau 2000a). Most of the state's Latino population is concentrated in five counties, ranging in each from 18 to 22 percent. Clark, Elko, and Pershing Counties have the highest percentage of Latinos, from 19.3 percent to 22 percent Latino (U.S. Census Bureau 2000c). The next most heavily populated Latino counties are Humboldt and Lander, at 18.9 percent and 18.5 percent, respectively. Clark County includes Las Vegas in the southern region of Nevada. Elko County is located in the northeast corner of Nevada, north of the cities of Elko and Spring Creek. Pershing and Humboldt Counties are located in the northwestern corner of Nevada. Lander County is located in north central Nevada, south of the city of Battle Mountain.

Latinos have only recently begun to affect Nevada's political environment through a steadily growing group of elected officials, as well as voter impact on the presidential elections. In 2004 Bush was able to carry the state by 21,500 votes, with 50.5 percent of the vote to Kerry's 47.9 percent, but this margin of victory is only about one-fifth the size of the eligible but not participating Latino population (Nevada Secretary of State 2005). Nevada's growing Latino electorate may have been one of the reasons it was considered a swing state in the presidential race, especially since Bush's margin of victory was only 2.6 percentage points. The Edison-Mitofsky (2004) exit poll—its many problems notwithstanding—suggested that about 10 percent of the electorate was Latino. The Bush and Kerry campaigns appeared to have recognized the potential importance of the state's Latino vote, as they both targeted Nevada with Spanish-language advertising.

Further, Latinos have established themselves in other avenues of political power in Nevada. In 2004 incumbent state senator Bob Coffin (D) was reelected to the state legislature representing Clark County, which has a large Latino population. Seven other Latinos have attained various political offices, from attorney general to school board member. Brian Gandoval (R) was elected the state's attorney general in 2002. The other elected officials are county commissioner Dario Herrera (Clark), council members Mike Pacini (Boulder City) and Michael Miera (West Wendover), district court judge Valorie Vega (Clark), and school board members Larry P. Mason (Clark) and Priscilla Rocha (State Board of Education).

Among all the states with new and growing Latino populations, we see Nevada as the state where Latinos are most likely to effect future political change. It has almost three times as many eligible but unregistered Latino citizens as it has voters, its Latino population share is large enough to begin electing Latino officials in significant numbers, and the closeness of the last national election reveals an electoral environment that is increasingly competitive and no longer a GOP stronghold.

WASHINGTON

In contrast to Georgia, Nevada, and North Carolina, Washington has experienced a more continuous increase in its Latino population: from 7.5 percent in 2000 to 8 percent by 2003 (U.S. Census Bureau 2000b, 2003). This steady increase includes an estimated 5.7 percent of the population who are noncitizens. The growing community of Latinos has established a solid presence in several of Washington's counties, especially in the agricultural Yakima Valley. More specifically, Latinos are now firmly established in at least four counties: Adams (47.1 percent), Franklin (46.7 percent), Yakima (35.9 percent), and Grant (30.1 percent). They have also increased their presence in Douglas (19.7 percent), Chelan (19.3 percent), Walla Walla (15.7 percent), Okanogan (14.4 percent), Benton (12.5 percent), and Skagit (11.2 percent) Counties (U.S. Census Bureau 2000c). Skagit, Okanogan, Chelan, and Douglas Counties are located in the north; Yakima, Franklin, Benton, Walla Walla, and Adams Counties are all in southern Washington. The central county of Grant is outside the city of Ephrata.

Moreover, Latinos have also begun to affect Washington's political environment, with a rapidly growing group of elected officials and a newly felt impact on the presidential elections. In 2004 Kerry was able to carry the state with 52.8 percent of the vote over Bush's 45.6 percent (Washington Secretary of State 2005). The growing Latino population in the state may have augmented this 7.2 percent margin of victory for the Democratic Party. The Edison-Mitofsky (2004) exit poll suggested that the overall electorate, about 5 percent Hispanic, preferred Kerry 52 to 48 percent. The Kerry campaign appeared to have recognized the potential of the state's Latino vote, as it targeted Washington with Spanish-language advertisements.

The infamous Washington gubernatorial election—with a margin of victory of just 129 votes—is another matter altogether. Considerable evidence now shows that the campaign of Democrat Christine Gregoire seriously underestimated the strength the Dino Rossi challenge and overestimated the strength of Kerry's assistance down-ticket. Part of this, of course, is due to the particulars of the campaign and the candidates. In addition to winning the state's Electoral College votes, the Democrats comfortably retained control of the lower house of the state legislature, picking up three seats (55 D, 43 R) and taking control of the upper house (26 D, 23 R) by capturing two additional seats. The gubernatorial campaign was clearly the underperforming element.

Further, Latinos have made strides in other avenues of political power in the state. In 2004 three Latino legislators were reelected: incumbent state senator Margarita Prentice (D) and incumbent state representatives Mary Skinner (R) and Phyllis Gutierrez-Kenney (D). Twelve other Latinos have attained political office: deputy mayor Michelle Sandoval (Port Townsend); council members Fred Diaz and Clara Jimenez (Toppenish) and Rick Pruneda (Warden); mayors Gilbert Lubo Jr. (Walla Walla) and Roland Capetillo (Warden); school board members Rolando Cerrillo, Charles Garcia, Bennie Ruiz Jr., Ricardo

Espinoza, and Lorenzo Garza Jr.; and district drainage commissioner Maxmillion W. Jaquez (D) (NALEO 2004). Two of these Latino elected officials represent areas of the state with a high concentration of Latinos: Mary Skinner in Yakima County and Gilbert Lubo Jr. in Walla Walla County.

The majority of Washington's Latino community is Mexican American, and the state's Latino political identity appears to be following the well-developed pattern of a solidly—but not overwhelmingly—Democratic preference. Even a modest margin among Latino votes for the Democratic gubernatorial nominee would allow the Latino community to claim a share of the victory. In short, at least for the Washington gubernatorial race, the conditions appear to meet the ultimate test as operationalized in de la Garza and DeSipio (2005): if no Latinos voted, the outcome would have been different.

NEBRASKA

Nebraska is a low-density state with a rapidly growing Latino population, from 5.5 percent in 2000 to 6.2 percent by 2003 (U.S. Census Bureau 2000b, 2003). Furthermore, 3.2 percent of Nebraska's population are foreign-born noncitizens. Although this Latino population is not as firmly established as that in Washington, it still represents a sizable community in several counties. The majority of the state's Latinos reside in Colfax (26.2 percent), Dawson (25.4 percent), Dakota (22.6 percent), and Scotts Bluff (17.2 percent) Counties and to a lesser extent in Hall (14.0 percent) and Morrill (10.1 percent) Counties (U.S. Census Bureau 2000c). Scotts Bluff and Morrill Counties are located in western Nebraska near the surrounding metropolitan area of Scotts Bluff. Dawson and Hall Counties are in the southern region of the state surrounding Lexington and metropolitan Grand Island. The eastern counties of Colfax and Dakota are near Columbus and Sioux City, respectively.

Nebraska's Latinos have relatively little ability to affect their political environment, and this was especially the case in the last presidential election. In 2004 the state was solidly Republican. Bush won 65.9 percent of the vote; Kerry received 32.7 percent, less than one-third of the votes cast (Nebraska Secretary of State 2005). Therefore, it was very unlikely for the state's Latino population to have countered this 33.2 percentage point Democratic deficit, especially since, according to the Edison-Mitofsky (2004) exit poll, the electorate was only about 2 percent Latino. Latinos also have a minimal presence in Nebraska's elected offices. In 2004 incumbent state senator Ray Aguilar (District 35) was able to retain his seat, as was council member Rita Hernandez (D-North Platte) (NALEO 2004). Aguilar's District 35 (Grand Island and Hall Counties) has a large concentration of Latinos.

Although Latinos are not strong politically in Nebraska, this may be changing. Their numbers are not very large, but with a quarter of the population in some counties and substantial concentration in and around Omaha, we could be witnessing the earliest stages of Latino politicization and electoral success at the local level. The pace at which this develops, however, will be influenced by the extent to which undocumented immigrants contribute to this growth. The size of the Republican majority in the state and the comparatively small Latino electorate to date suggests that Latinos are far from determining outcomes in Nebraska politics.

WISCONSIN

In contrast to Nebraska, Latinos in Wisconsin have established a strong political presence. The Wisconsin population was an estimated 3.6 percent Latino in 2000 and 4.0 percent in 2003 (U.S. Census Bureau 2000b, 2003). Of this community, 2.6 percent are foreign-born noncitizen residents. Further, Latinos are not concentrated in large numbers in any of Wisconsin's counties; they constitute only 4.1 to 8.8 percent of these communities. Latinos have a somewhat sizable population in Milwaukee (8.8 percent), Racine (7.9 percent), Kenosha (7.2 percent), Walworth (6.5 percent), and Jefferson (4.1 percent) Counties, all of which are located in the southwest corner of Wisconsin near the Milwaukee metropolitan area (U.S. Census Bureau 2000c).

In the 2004 presidential election, Kerry won this battleground state by a very narrow margin of victory: 0.4 percent of the vote. Kerry received 49.7 percent of the vote to Bush's 49.3 percent, a virtual dead heat (Wisconsin Secretary of State 2005). Like the Washington gubernatorial race, the presidential election in Wisconsin was decided by a small margin of victory (11,384 votes). That may have been smaller than Kerry's margin among the state's Latino population, but with fewer than 80,000 Latino registered voters in the state, this seems unlikely. The Edison-Mitofsky (2004) exit poll found that the overall Wisconsin electorate, about 2 percent Latino, voted 51 percent for Kerry, 47 percent for Bush, and 1 percent for Nader. Both the Republicans and the Democrats appeared to have anticipated both the razor-thin margin and the potential of Latinos to tip the outcome. The Bush campaign and several conservative 527 groups advertised on Spanish-language media, as did the liberal 527 New Democrat Network. The Kerry campaign did not advertise in Spanish in Wisconsin, however.

Moreover, Latinos have attained diverse political offices in Wisconsin. In 2004 the incumbent state representative, Pedro Colon (D), was reelected to the legislature. The Latino community has also gained representation through county clerk Lorraine Hartung (D-Dunn) and aldermen Shiloh Ramos, Edward Spang (Appleton), Santiago Rosas (Madison), and Angel Sanchez (Milwaukee). Ramona Gonzalez (LaCrosse), Elsa Lamelas (Milwaukee), Kevin Martens (Milwaukee), and Ralph Ramierez (Waukesha) are Latino circuit court judges, and Juan Jose Lopez, Jennifer Morales, and Juan Perez are school board members (NALEO 2004). The majority of these Latinos represent the metropolitan area of Milwaukee, which includes a high concentration of Latinos.

IOWA

In contrast to their success in Wisconsin, Latinos have not been able to gain political office in either Arkansas or Iowa. Iowa's Latino community is small—2.8 percent of the state's population in 2000—but is growing at a rate that far outstrips that of the state. While Iowa experienced only a 2.3 percent population increase in the 1990s, the Latino population grew 153 percent, to 3.1 percent, by 2003. In addition, foreign-born noncitizens make up 2.3 percent of the state's population (U.S. Census Bureau 2000b, 2003). A sizable concentration of Iowa

Latinos reside in Buena Vista (12.5 percent), Louisa (12.6 percent), and Muscatine (11.9 percent) Counties. Latinos are also establishing communities in Woodbury (9.1 percent), Marshall (9.0 percent), and Crawford (8.7 percent) Counties (U.S. Census Bureau 2000c). The northeastern counties of Woodbury, Buena Vista, and Crawford are located east of Sioux City, the southeastern counties of Muscatine and Louisa are south of Iowa City and Cedar Rapids, and the central county of Marshall is east of Ames.

Iowa's growing Latino population has not yet succeeded in attaining political office. However, Latinos are gaining political influence in presidential elections, mostly due to the nature of Iowa's political environment. Iowa is as closely divided as a state can be. After the 2004 elections, the Democrats controlled the governor's mansion, and the Republicans controlled the state's lower house—by one vote. The Iowa senate was exactly evenly divided. Iowa's delegation to the U.S. Congress included two Democratic and three Republican representatives, as well as one senator from each party.

In addition to its distinction as a battleground state, Iowa enjoys a privileged status as the first presidential primary caucus. The peculiar nature of the Iowa caucuses—especially their counting rules—allows for significant shifts of outcome from relatively modest shifts in the preferences of caucus-goers. The 2004 presidential election was highly contested in Iowa and resulted in only a 0.7 percent margin of victory; Bush was able to win the state with 49.9 percent over Kerry's 49.2 percent of the vote (Iowa Secretary of State 2005). Therefore, Latinos could have had a significant impact on this very close vote, especially since the Edison-Mitofsky exit poll suggested that the electorate was about 1 percent Latino. Despite the closeness of the race, the Bush campaign was the only one to buy ads on Spanish-language media.

It is ironic that a state with no Latino elected officials and only a tiny number of Latino residents may allow Latino voters to have more political influence than in almost any other state. For instance, unrealized Latino eligible voters exceed the GOP margin of victory. The closely divided nature of the state would allow even a modest mobilization of Latinos by one party or the other to substantially tip the power balance in the state.

ARKANSAS

The Latino population of Arkansas is small, an estimated 3.2 percent in 2000 and 3.7 percent by 2003 (2.3 percent are foreign-born noncitizens) (U.S. Census Bureau 2000b, 2003). The majority of Latinos reside in Sevier (19.7 percent), Yell (12.7 percent), and Carroll (9.7 percent) Counties and to a lesser extent in Hempstead (8.3 percent), Bradley (8.3 percent), and Washington (8.2 percent) Counties (U.S. Census Bureau 2000c). Bradley, Hempstead, and Sevier Counties are located in the southern Arkansas. Yell County, in the east, is located southeast of the city of Fort Smith. The northeastern counties of Washington and Carroll surround the cities of Fayetteville, Springdale, and Rogers.

Arkansas's small but growing community of Latinos has not yet gained political power. The Latino vote did not likely influence the 2004 presidential race in Arkansas, where Bush won 54.3 percent to Kerry's 44.5 percent—a 9.8 percent margin (Arkansas Secretary of State 2005). This is because, according to the Edison-Mitofsky (2004) exit poll, the electorate was only about 1 percent Latino.

Like Iowa and Nebraska, the small number of Latino residents has not found a meaningful political voice in Arkansas. The prospects of Latinos in Arkansas, however, appear to be brighter than those in Nebraska. Arkansas is not as solidly Republican as Nebraska, and Democrats have been quite successful in winning elections to the U.S. House and Senate. In addition, while Bush's margin was solid, it was not as insurmountable as the GOP advantage in Nebraska.

On the other hand, Latinos in Arkansas do not appear to have the prospects of shaping outcomes that Latinos in Iowa enjoy. Arkansas enjoys neither the political privilege of the caucuses nor the politically interesting characteristic of being so closely divided. Political opportunity would appear to be a bit further off for Latino Arkansans.

DISCUSSION

After our preliminary examination of these eight low-density Latino states, we found that both the Democratic and the Republican Parties did not target Latino voters. Following our aforementioned standards for which Latino communities are most important in a political context, we examined the ability of Latinos to provide the margin of victory in a state as well as their potential future impact in each state. Are the numbers of Latinos living in these states enough to provide a margin of victory? Can rising growth rates in Latino populations, accompanied by Latino political preferences, lead to more political power in the future? Will the Latino effect on election outcomes grow at the state and national levels?

Iowa, Wisconsin, and Washington are three states that have a sufficiently large population of Latinos to have provided the margin of victory for either of the parties. However, neither of the parties strategically mobilized these Latino voters. The Kerry campaign only targeted Spanish-language media in Washington, while Bush's campaign targeted only the battleground states of Iowa and Wisconsin with Spanish-language advertising. While the outcome of the presidential election indicates that Bush was the clear victor in courting the votes of Americans, the Bush campaign also did a better job of courting Latino votes in most states.

Looking back, in the two states where we argue Latinos had an effect on the vote, the margin of victory for Kerry could have been even larger had more of an effort been made to mobilize Latino voters. Looking ahead to the potential political role of Latinos in the 2008 election, we know that Latinos exert nontrivial political influence in Georgia, Washington, and Wisconsin. In these states, Latinos are attaining a wide variety of elected offices and are demonstrating their potential in the state's political environment. Moreover, the growing Latino electorate and the rising number of Latino elected officials in these states, as well as the formation of alliances with African Americans and African American elected officials, show notable promise for stronger Democratic electoral support. That is, Latinos in these states may wield greater political influence in the future because of their large and growing Mexican American and Puerto Rican populations that identify primarily with the Democratic Party, especially if Latinos form coalitions with established African American populations.

REFERENCES

Appleman, Eric M. 2004a. "George Bush-Campaign Organization, General Election Mode." www.gwu.edu/~action/2004/bush/bushorg.html. Accessed February 3, 2009.

———. 2004b. "John Kerry-Campaign Organization, General Election Mode." www.gwu.edu/~action/2004/kerry/kerrorggen.html. Accessed February 3, 2009.

Arkansas Secretary of State. 2005. 2004 Election Results. www.sosweb.state.ar.us/elections.html. Accessed August 26, 2008.

de la Garza, Rodolfo, and Louis DeSipio, eds. 2005. *Muted Voices: Latinos and the 2000 Elections.* Lanham, MD: Rowman and Littlefield.

Edison-Mitofsky. 2004. 2004 Presidential race exit poll. MSNBC Web site. www.msnbc.com/id/5297146l. Accessed April 2005.

Georgia Secretary of State. 2005. 2004 Election Results. http://sos.georgia.gov/. Accessed August 26, 2008.

Guerra, Fernando. 1992. "Conditions Not Met: California Elections and the Latino Community." In *From Rhetoric to Reality: Latino Politics in the 1988 Elections,* ed. Rodolfo O. de la Garza and Louis DeSipio, 99–107. Boulder, CO: Westview Press.

Iowa Secretary of State. 2005. 2004 Election Results. www.sos.state.ia.us/elections/results/index.html. Accessed August 26, 2008.

Nadler, Richard. 2004. "Bush's 'Real' Hispanic Numbers." *National Review Online,* December 8. www.nationalreview.com/comment/nadler200412080811.asp. Accessed February 9, 2009.

National Association of Latino Elected Officials (NALEO). 2004. "Election Profile." www.naleo.org/PRA/Post_Election_Profile_2004.pdf. Accessed June 2005.

Nebraska Secretary of State. 2005. 2004 Election Results. www.sos.state.ne.us/elec/prev_elec/index.html. Accessed August 26, 2008.

New Democrat Network (NDN). 2005. Hispanic Project. www.newdem.org/. Accessed February 3, 2009.

Newspaper Association of America. 2005. "Print Ads Targeting Hispanics." www.naa.org/r2/printads.html. Accessed February 3, 2009.

North Carolina Secretary of State. 2005. 2004 Election Results. www.sboe.state.nc.us/content.aspx?id=69. Accessed August 26, 2008.

U.S. Census Bureau. 2000a. Population Quick Facts. www.census.gov. Accessed August 26, 2008.

———. 2000b. Facts on the Hispanic or Latino Population. www.census.gov/pubinfo/www/NEWhispML1.html. Accessed August 26, 2008.

———. 2000c. Mapping Census 2000: The Geography of U.S. Diversity (Hispanic or Latino Origin: All Races). www.census.gov/population/www/cen2000/atlas.html. Accessed December 7, 2001.

———. 2003. American Community Survey. www.census.gov/acs/www/. Accessed August 26, 2008.

Washington Secretary of State. 2005. 2004 Election Results. http://vote.wa.gov/general. Accessed August 26, 2008.

Wisconsin Secretary of State. 2005. 2004 Election Results. http://elections.state.wi.us/section_detail.asp?linkcatid=491&linkid=155&locid=47. Accessed August 26, 2008.

Chapter Thirteen

Conclusion

The 2004 Election: More of the Same or a New Foundation?

RODOLFO O. DE LA GARZA

Was 2004 different from other presidential election years in terms of Latino influence on the outcome in particular and campaign dynamics in general? That is, did Latinos move away from their traditional irrelevance at both the state and national levels, as has been the case, with notable exceptions, since 1964? In addition, were there developments in 2004 that might foreshadow the future of Latino political influence and activism? This chapter addresses these core questions.

The case studies presented in this volume indicate that Latino influence in the 2004 election followed its established pattern when viewed from a state-by-state perspective. That is, the Latino vote once again had little impact on either national- or state-level results (de la Garza and DeSipio 2004). Indeed, the Hispanic vote was less consequential in 2004 than it had been in 2000 when it (like the vote of numerous other small groups) helped Republicans carry Florida. Ironically, if Latinos influenced any state's outcome, it was in New Mexico, where their inaction—a failure to mobilize and unite behind the Democratic ticket—contributed to the Republican victory in that state. Thus predictions that have become common since the mid-1970s about the increasing clout of the Latino electorate were again unrealized in 2004.

Despite this continuing pattern, I suggest that in time the chronicles of Latino electoral involvement are likely to record 2004 as a signpost year, because it serves as a bridge between elections characterized by Latinos exercising minimal clout, despite increasing levels of symbolic appeals from both major parties, to elections in which they will play increasingly substantive roles. This transformation will result from several key factors. The first is the possible development of a Republican strategy that links Republican core voters and substantial segments of the Latino electorate around a distinct set of issues salient to both groups. The success of this approach in 2004 suggests that future campaigns may emulate it. In other words, the experience of 2004 sets the stage for focusing on substantive appeals rather than on the failed rhetoric of the past.

The second is the success Republicans enjoyed with their Hispanic outreach. Since the 1960s, with the exception of Cuban Americans, there is no evidence of Latinos voting for the GOP on policy grounds. This changed in 2004. That experience taught Democratic strategists that they could no longer treat Hispanics cavalierly and still count on winning at least two-thirds of their vote. Democrats learned that, like Republicans, they needed to court Latinos.

The election's results thus created the conditions for increasing Latino influence within both the nation's electoral institutions and the national electorate per se. At the party level, the Democratic leadership should have learned that high levels of Latino support from a mobilized Latino electorate could not be taken for granted. Republican leaders, by contrast, finally attained the level of Latino support they had falsely claimed they were winning since the 1990s. Nonetheless, the Republicans continue to misunderstand the basis of their inroads by claiming it is policy rather than candidate based, which may fuel exaggerated expectations regarding the likelihood of maintaining the level of Hispanic support they received in 2004. Moreover, these gains set the stage for internecine GOP battles regarding how to balance the interests of their conservative core while institutionalizing a successful Hispanic strategy.

In my judgment, together these developments have created a new foundation for Latino influence in future national elections. The remainder of this chapter focuses on how this came about and discusses its short- and long-term implications.

NEW DEVELOPMENTS

Historically, although Latinos have not been an essential focus of either party's presidential campaign, Democrats have symbolically pursued them while Republicans have either ignored them or negatively targeted all but the Cuban Americans. Democratic outreach patterns have been based on the assumption that Hispanics are, like African Americans, committed partisans. While this was true of Mexican Americans historically (Garcia and de la Garza 1977), the number of Latino Democratic identifiers has declined as the population has become more heterogeneous in terms of class, geographic diffusion, and national origin composition. In 2002, for example, 64 percent of African Americans identified as Democrats and only 5 percent identified as Republicans. By comparison, 49 percent of Latinos identified as Democrats and 19 percent saw themselves as Republicans (Pew Hispanic Center/Kaiser Family Foundation 2002).

Republicans, on the other hand, have courted and invested significantly in the Cuban American vote while treating other Latinos with disdain or hostility. President Richard Nixon, for example, adamantly defended California grape growers at the height of the César Chávez–led grape boycott, and Senator Robert Dole ran on a platform that openly opposed bilingual education, even though his campaign included Spanish-language outreach initiatives (de la Garza and DeSipio 1999). Strategically, such an approach was rational because Latino policy preferences have long been incompatible with core Republican interests (Alvarez and García Bedolla 2003). Consequently, to win Latino support would have required abandoning the principles and policy positions that define the Republican core. Moreover, as has been evident since the Gingrich revolution, Republican leaders targeted conservative white Democrats to the exclusion of Latinos as they worked to become dominant. Clearly, they did not need Hispanic voters to take control of Congress and the White House, so they paid no price for ignoring Hispanic voters.

In addition to neither party treating Latinos as an important constituency, Democrats and Republicans also used the same tactics to feign genuine interest. Both engaged in what analysts label "taco politics," so called because such outreach emphasized highly publicized brief visits highlighted by public fiestas and ample Mexican food and beer while ignoring specific Hispanic policy concerns during and after the election.

Changes to this pattern were evident in the 2004 election. Most significantly, the Republicans abandoned taco politics for the first time in favor of a carefully focused strategy that capitalized on the themes of their overall campaign. Central to their effort was their emphasis on the need to stay the course on patriotism and antiterrorism—issues that played relatively well among Hispanics.

Although they were less focused than Anglos on the war and less supportive of the Bush administration's Iraq policy, almost half of all Hispanics reported that the war against terrorism and the Iraq war would heavily influence their vote—compared to slightly more than half who identified traditionally salient problems such as education and employment as issues likely to affect their vote (Pew Hispanic Center/Kaiser Family Foundation 2004: 4). Moreover, slightly less than half of Latino registered voters (46 percent) supported the decision to go to war, while slightly more than half (55 percent) of the nation's electorate overall supported that decision (Pew Hispanic Center/Kaiser Family Foundation 2004: 5). What is noteworthy here is the relatively high support Latinos voiced for core Republican themes, support that created a unique opportunity to establish a solid foothold among non-Cuban Hispanics.

A second set of related issues Republicans used to expand their Latino vote were abortion and same-sex marriage—even though these issues were much less salient to Hispanics than to Republicans, and recent research suggests that such issues may not hold significant promise for the GOP (see Abrajano 2005; Nicholson, Pantoja, and Segura 2006). Latinos, for example, were slightly more likely than the nation at large to oppose abortion, and they were less likely to support a constitutional amendment banning gay marriage. Nonetheless, these were the only policies that Republicans could use to try to bridge the differences between their concerns and those of most Latinos. Reinforcing the importance of these issues to the Republican outreach strategy was the public condemnation by some Catholic bishops of pro-choice candidates (i.e., Senator John Kerry). While it is impossible to determine the impact of these proclamations with available data, such views were in effect echoed by the almost 40 percent of Hispanic Catholics and fundamentalist Protestants alike who reported that they could not vote for a candidate who was pro-choice; it is noteworthy, however, that 51 percent of Latino Catholics voiced pro-choice views (Pew Hispanic Center/Kaiser Family Foundation 2004: 10–11). Thus 2004 offered Republicans the unique opportunity to increase their Latino support by linking a major part of their message to two issues on which Latinos were almost evenly divided but which were opposed by religious organizations, which are probably the groups Latinos most respect. Consequently, Republicans, rather than win Latino votes by emphasizing these issues, became the beneficiaries of political messages delivered by many religious groups that were not directly affiliated with the Republican Party, thereby obviating the need to resort to partisan appeals to recruit Hispanic support.

A third factor that was key to abandoning taco politics was President George W. Bush's personal appeal. As has been widely noted, he developed a solid relationship with Mexican American voters during his gubernatorial years in Texas, and his advocacy of pro-immigrant policies was the foundation of expanding that support to Hispanics beyond Texas. Indeed, no Republican presidential candidate, including Ronald Reagan—who received comparable levels of electoral support—has ever enjoyed Bush's levels of popularity. The president's relationship with Latinos, his respect for them, and, according to senior staff members, his genuine belief that he could carry the Hispanic vote all contributed to explaining why Republicans replaced taco politics with genuine outreach.

Their claims notwithstanding, although Republicans did not come as close to carrying the Latino vote as President Bush expected, they did much better than their norm; the Bush-Cheney ticket received approximately 40 percent of the Hispanic vote (Leal et al. 2005; Suro, Fry, and Passel 2005). The three factors previously discussed are the principal reasons for what should be recognized as a Republican success. However, the limit of these gains is most clearly evident in that the only

Latino subgroup Republicans carried was Protestant voters, 59 percent of whom voted for Bush-Cheney. Since Protestants total only 18 percent of the Latino electorate, Republican supporters were too few to sway the overall Hispanic vote.

The legacy of 2004, then, is that it should now be clear to Republicans that their political future requires winning a substantial share of the Latino vote. Latino support helped solidify the Bush-Cheney reelection, and the 2004 results make it clear that Republicans can no longer resort to taco politics if they hope to hold on to and enlarge their share of the Latino vote. This means that the 2004 results may be read as a real warning to Republicans to be attentive to Latino voters or suffer the consequences. This should enhance the chances of John McCain, who has an established relationship with Latinos.

It is important to add, however, that it would be a mistake to overstate the probability that Republican outreach will greatly increase the party's Latino support or membership. Latino policy priorities differ from those of whites (or "Anglos"), as table 13.1 illustrates.

Moreover, research shows that Latinos are unlikely to support the Republican party unless it substantially alters its policy positions (Alvarez and García Bedolla 2003) and that the increase in Latino support for the Republican ticket in 2000 and 2004 reflected support for George Bush rather than for Republican policy preferences (de la Garza and Cortina 2007).

Table 13.1. Issues Hispanics Identify as "Most Important" in Determining Their Vote

	Latino Registered Voters (%)	*White Registered Voters (%)*
Education	40	21
Economy	18	21
National defense	6	10

Source: Pew Hispanic Center/Kaiser Family Foundation 2002.

The legacy of 2004 for Democrats is quite similar. Most significantly, Republican gains loudly trumpeted a death knell for any lingering temptation Democrats might have to engage in taco politics. To do so is to invite both short-term losses and the possibility of long-term defections, which would prevent the party from regaining control of the White House and retaining control of Congress. In addition, the Kerry-Edwards campaign's ethnic pandering, as manifested in the efforts to have Maria Theresa Heinz Kerry (John Kerry's millionaire Mozambique-born Portuguese wife) campaign as part of the effort to demonstrate the ethnic sensitivities of the ticket, was insultingly ridiculous. It was so patronizing that it may have contributed to dampening what little enthusiasm Kerry had generated.

The 2004 elections also taught the Democratic leadership that ignoring Latino policy concerns could directly benefit Republicans. That is, unlike African Americans, who seldom find any reason to vote Republican and thus are likely not to vote when they feel ignored or betrayed by the Democrats, Latinos can find reasons to vote Republican when Democrats turn against them. Thus more than has been the case with any previous national election, the lesson of 2004 for Democrats is they must be respectful and solicitous of the Hispanic vote or risk losing substantial portions of it to the GOP.

As this volume documents, the continued growth and dispersion of the Latino electorate to states such as Nevada and Washington, as well as to states across the South and Midwest, drives the point home to both parties that they must respect and court the Latino vote. While this growth is not the result of any event specifically related to 2004, it does illustrate the continuation of a pattern that will be increasingly important in future elections. The growing importance of the Latino electorate makes it clear that future victories must be built around a coalition that includes Latinos. For Republicans, ignoring this faction means losing states like Nevada, North Carolina, and Ohio, where Latinos are becoming increasingly concentrated and are likely to register overwhelmingly as Democrats unless they are explicitly and effectively cultivated. For Democrats, mobilizing Latinos means adding these states to the victory column, which could produce Democratic presidential victories in 2008 and beyond.

A final legacy of 2004 is its impact on leadership. Two Hispanic senators, one from each party, were elected in 2004; thanks to them, Latinos finally attained a truly national voice. This became evident almost immediately as both senators played important roles in the immigration reform debate. Furthermore, their success illustrates the institutionalization of the nonethnic Latino campaign. Historically, even when candidates such as Henry Cisneros tried to run nonethnic campaigns (i.e., campaigns that did not focus on their ethnicity), the contours of the election still defined the contest in ethnic terms. The first major candidate to break this pattern was Los Angeles's Antonio Villaraigosa in his mayoral campaign. Colorado's Ken Salazar and Florida's Mel Martinez successfully emulated his approach, proudly acknowledging their ethnicity while emphasizing that they were running to serve their state and not just their ethnic group. These 2004 triumphs suggest the approach future Hispanic candidates will take even if they run within majority-minority districts.

In my judgment, 2004 also killed whatever chances Governor Bill Richardson had of becoming a nominee for the vice presidency. However stellar his international accomplishments may be—and they are superior to those President Bush had when first elected, as well as to those of current aspirants such as Senator Edwards, Hillary Clinton, and Barack Obama—his political standing was gravely damaged by New Mexico's 2004 results. His inability to create a coalition of Anglo Democrats and a Hispanic electorate that exceeds 40 percent strongly suggests he would be unable to play the mobilizing role that is essential to creating the Latino-white coalitions that are essential to carry states like North Carolina and Nevada.

A NEW ROLE FOR LATINOS

I have argued that the 2004 election has two major facets. Most obviously, it stands as a repetition of the past. Despite a large and growing electorate, Latinos played a very minor role in the election's outcome, reflecting a mix of established patterns and new factors. The former includes the concentration of the Latino population in noncompetitive states where their vote had little impact and turnout rates so low that, as was likely the case in New Mexico, they lost the opportunity to affect the outcome. The latter consists of Republicans receiving enough of their votes to prevent Latinos from moving any state to a Democratic victory.

A second and more long-term perspective is that 2004 can be seen as the beginning of a new phase in Latino national electoral engagement. Their population growth and national dispersal will require both parties to pay more attention to them. In particular, the Republicans will need to reach out to them because, realistically, no other demographically identifiable group is available for them to court. The Democrats will need to take their votes more seriously because, as 2004 shows, sizable portions of Latinos share fundamental interests with Republicans. Democrats cannot return to or hold power without gaining a significant share of these socially conservative segments of the Latino vote.

In addition, 2004 saw the rise of a new type of Latino leadership, more moderate but probably more effective, which bodes well for Latinos and may serve the nation well also. If both parties must become more attentive to basic human needs and more tolerant of civil rights to win the Latino vote, then we will all be better off. Perhaps this is the promise of the changes that will result from the 2004 elections.

REFERENCES

Abrajano, Marisa. 2005. "Who Evaluates a Presidential Candidate by Using Non-Policy Campaign Messages?" *Political Research Quarterly* 58: 55–67.

Alvarez, Michael, and Lisa García Bedolla. 2003. "The Foundation of Latino Voter Partisanship: Evidence from the 2000 Election." *Journal of Politics* 65: 31–49.

de la Garza, Rodolfo, and Jeronimo Cortina. 2007. "Are Latinos Republicans but Just Don't Know It? The Latino Vote in the 2000 and 2004 Elections." *American Politics Research* 35 (2): 202–23.

de la Garza, Rodolfo, and Louis DeSipio, eds. 1999. *Awash in the Mainstream: Latino Politics in the 1996 Elections.* Boulder, CO: Westview Press.

———. 2005. *Muted Voices: Latinos and the 2000 Election.* Lanham, MD: Rowman and Littlefield.

Garcia, F. Chris, and Rudolph O. de la Garza. 1977. *The Chicano Political Experience.* North Scituate, MA: Duxbury Press.

Leal, David L., Matt Barreto, Jongho Lee, and Rodolfo de la Garza. 2005. "The Latino Vote in the 2004 Election." *PS: Political Science and Politics* 38: 41–49.

Nicholson, Stephen P., Adrian Pantoja, and Gary M. Segura. 2006. "Political Knowledge and Issue Voting among the Latino Electorate." *Political Research Quarterly* 59: 259–72.

Pew Hispanic Center/Kaiser Family Foundation. 2002. "National Survey of Latinos: The Latino Electorate." Pew Hispanic Trust, Washington, DC.

———. 2004. "The 2004 National Survey of Latinos: Politics and Civic Participation." Pew Hispanic Trust, Washington, DC.

Suro, Roberto, Richard Fry, and Jeffrey Passel. 2005. *Hispanics and the 2004 Election: Population, Electorate, and Voters.* Washington, DC: Pew Hispanic Center.

Contributors

MANUEL AVALOS is currently Associate Vice Chancellor for Faculty Support and Development and a tenured professor in Latin American Studies at the University of North Carolina at Wilmington. His current academic research focuses on questions of racial inequality in the Americas and the political representation and incorporation of the Latino electorate at the state, local, and national levels. His publications include articles in *Sociological Perspectives, Harvard Journal of Hispanic Policy,* and *Policy Studies Journal,* as well as chapters in Roberto de Anda, ed., *Chicanas and Chicanos in Contemporary Society* (Rowman & Littlefield, 2004); and Rodolfo de la Garza and Louis DeSipio, eds., *Ethnic Ironies: Latino Politics in the 1992 Elections* (Westview, 1996), *Awash in the Mainstream: Latino Politics in the 1996 Elections* (Westview, 1999), and *Muted Voices: Latino Politics in the 2000 Elections* (Rowman & Littlefield, 2004).

MATT A. BARRETO is an associate professor of political science at the University of Washington, Seattle, and a founding member of the Washington Institute for the Study of Ethnicity and Race. His research examines the political participation of racial and ethnic minorities in the United States, and his work has been published in *American Political Science Review, Political Research Quarterly, Public Opinion Quarterly, Urban Affairs Review,* and other peer-reviewed journals. Barreto specializes in Latino and immigrant voting behavior and teaches courses on racial and ethnic politics, Latino politics, and voting and elections. He is also an affiliated faculty member in the Center for Statistics and the

Social Sciences at the University of Washington and an affiliated research scholar with the Tomás Rivera Policy Institute (TRPI) and the Center for the Study of Los Angeles (CSLA). In 2004 Barreto was co-author of the *Washington Post*/Univision/TRPI National Survey of Latino voters, and in 2005 he was co-principal investigator of the CSLA Los Angeles mayoral exit poll.

CHRISTINA E. BEJARANO is an assistant professor of political science at the University of Kansas. Her teaching and research interests are in American politics, with an emphasis on the political behavior of Latinos and women. Her recent work includes "What Goes Around, Comes Around: Race, Blowback, at the Louisiana Elections of 2002 and 2003," *Political Research Quarterly* (with Gary Segura). She is actively involved in the Latino Caucus of the American Political Science Association and the regional Western and Midwest Associations.

JASON P. CASELLAS is an assistant professor of government at the University of Texas at Austin. He specializes in American politics, with specific research and teaching interests in Latino politics, legislative politics, and state and local politics. He is currrently completing a book that examines Latino representation in the U.S. Congress and state legislatures. He is the recipient of numerous fellowships, including the Samuel Du Bois Cook Fellowship at Duke University, where he visited during the 2007–8 academic year.

JERONIMO CORTINA is an assistant professor in the Department of Political Science and a visiting scholar at the Center for Mexican American Studies at the University of Houston. He specializes in political behavior, immigration, and quantitative methods. His work has been published in scholarly and policy journals such as *American Politics Research, Foreign Affairs en Español,* and the *Harvard Journal of Hispanic Policy.*

RODOLFO O. DE LA GARZA is Eaton Professor of Administrative Law and Municipal Science at Columbia University, deputy chair of the Columbia University School of International and Public Affairs, and vice president of the Tomás Rivera Policy Institute. He was twice named by *Hispanic Magazine* one of the 100 most influential Hispanics in the nation. He has served as vice president of the American Political Science Association and is a member of the Council of Foreign Relations. De la Garza combines interests in political behavior, specializing in ethnic politics and with emphasis on Latino public opinion, electoral involvement, and public policy, primarily immigration settlement and incorporation. He has edited, coedited, and coauthored numerous books, including *The Future of the Voting Rights Act* (Russell Sage Foundation, 2006), *Muted Voices: Latinos and the 2000 Election* (Rowman & Littlefield, 2005), *Sending Money Home: Hispanic Remittances and Community Development* (Rowman & Littlefield, 2002), *Latinos and U.S. Foreign Policy: Lobbying for the Homeland?* (Rowman & Littlefield, 2000), and *Bridging the Border: Transforming Mexico-U.S. Relations* (Rowman & Littlefield, 1997). He has also published in leading professional journals, including *American Journal of Political Science, Latin American Research Review, Social Science Quarterly,* and *International Migration Review.* De la Garza received the Lifetime Achievement Award from the Committee on the Status of Latinos in the Profession of the American Political Science Association in 1993 and has served as an expert witness in voting rights cases in Texas, Florida, Massachusetts, Indiana, and New York. He is currently directing studies on immigrant incorporation, Latinos and U.S. foreign policy, and Latino voting patterns.

LOUIS DESIPIO is an associate professor in the Departments of Political Science and Chicano/Latino Studies at the University of California, Irvine (UCI). He is the author of *Counting on the Latino Vote: Latinos as a New Electorate* (University Press of Virginia, 1996) and the coauthor, with Rodolfo O. de la Garza, of *Making Americans / Remaking America: Immigration and Immigrant Policy* (Westview Press, 1998). He is also the author and editor of a seven-volume series on Latino political values, attitudes, and behaviors. The most recent volume in this series is *Muted Voices: Latinos and the 2000 Elections* (Rowman & Littlefield, 2004). DeSipio's research focuses on Latino politics, on the process of political incorporation of new and formerly excluded populations into U.S. politics, and on public policies such as immigration, immigrant settlement, naturalization, and voting rights. He serves as chair of the UCI Department of Chicano/Latino Studies.

JAIME DOMÍNGUEZ holds the position of college adviser in the Weinberg College of Arts and Sciences and lecturer in the Department of Political Science at Northwestern University. His research interests are in the area of race and ethnic politics, urban politics, and Latino politics. He has taught at the University of Chicago, DePaul University, the University of Illinois at Chicago, and Northwestern University.

ROBERT S. ERIKSON is a professor of political science at Columbia University. He has written numerous articles on electoral politics and is coauthor of *American Public Opinion,* 7th ed. updated (Longman, 2007), *The Macro Polity* (Cambridge, 2002), and *Statehouse Democracy* (Cambridge, 1993). He has also served as editor of the *American Journal of Political Science* and *Political Analysis* and as president of the Southwest Political Science Association.

JUAN CARLOS FLORES served as the Miami-Dade field director of the Rudy Giuliani Presidential Committee during the 2008 presidential election cycle. He has served as special assistant to Florida House Speaker Marco Rubio and worked for a variety of private and public institutions, including Quantum Results, Winton Dingwell Partners, and the Metropolitan Center at Florida International University, all in Miami, Florida.

LUIS R. FRAGA is Associate Vice Provost for Faculty Advancement, Director of the Diversity Research Institute, Russell F. Stark University Professor, and Professor of Political Science at the University of Washington, Seattle. He is coauthor of *Multi-Ethnic Moments: The Politics of Urban School Reform* (Temple, 2006) and was a member of the American Political Science Association Committee on Civic Education, which wrote *Democracy at Risk: How Political Choices Undermine Citizen Participation, and What We Can Do about It* (Brookings Institution Press, 2005). He has published extensively in edited volumes and scholarly journals, including *American Political Science Review, Perspectives on Politics, Journal of Politics, Urban Affairs Quarterly, Western Political Quarterly, Du Bois Review,* and *Harvard Journal of Hispanic Policy.* He is one of the co-principal investigators of the Latino National Survey, the first major state-stratified survey of Latinos in the United States.

F. CHRIS GARCIA is Distinguished Professor Emeritus of Political Science at the University of New Mexico (UNM). He is the author or editor of a number of books, articles, and chapters in the areas of Hispanic politics, public opinion and political socialization, campaigns and elections, and New Mexico government. Garcia has taught classes in these areas for over thirty-five years. He has served as an officer of several professional organizations, as well as dean, academic vice president, provost, and president at UNM. During this period, he has provided extensive commentary and analysis of campaigns and elections for local, national, and international media. He is the recipient of many honors and awards, including the APSA Award for Distinguished Service, the New Mexico Governor's Distinguished Public Service Award, and the UNM Regents Meritorious Service Medal.

ERIC GONZALEZ JUENKE is an assistant professor in the Department of Political Science at the University of Colorado at Boulder. His research examines how racial and ethnic minorities turn their preferences into policy in the face of institutional constraints, entrenched majority interests, and policy incrementalism. He looks at these issues from a variety of perspectives, including minority representation in state and local legislatures, Latino and African American bureaucratic representation in U.S. public education, minority political participation and its influence on policy change, interinstitutional interactions over time, and the effects of electoral rules on promoting minority candidates. His most recent publications appeared in the *American Journal of Political Science* and the *Journal of Public Administration Research and Theory.*

FERNANDO GUERRA is Director of the Center for the Study of Los Angeles at Loyola Marymount University. He is also a professor of political science and has served as chair of the Chicano Studies Department and director of the American Cultures program. He has been on the faculty of Loyola Marymount University since 1984. Guerra has written numerous scholarly articles and has also contributed to popular publications. His scholarly work is in the area of state and local governance and urban and ethnic politics, and he is currently working on a book about the political empowerment of Latinos in California. He has also served as a source for the media and has been quoted in approximately five hundred news stories by over twenty publications. Guerra currently serves as a gubernatorial appointee to the California Historical Resources Commission and previously served as a mayoral appointee to the Board of Transportation Commission and the Board of the Rent Adjustment Commission for the City of Los Angeles.

MARIA ILCHEVA is currently a senior research associate at the Metropolitan Center, Florida International University (FIU), specializing in the administration of surveys, polls, and interviews and data analysis and reporting. She has participated in the research and analysis of studies on housing, youth services, health services, business leadership, and hurricane preparedness. Ilcheva has completed her Ph.D. degree in political science at FIU with a dissertation on interethnic relations in Eastern Europe.

JESSICA LAVARIEGA MONFORTI is an assistant professor of political science at the University of Texas, Pan American. As a specialist in U.S. politics, her interests include mass political behavior, public opinion, and urban politics. Lavariega Monforti's current research agenda focuses on the politics of race, gender, and ethnicity, specifically Latino/a politics in the United States. She has published several pieces on the impact of gender on Latino political behavior, exile politics in South Florida, and the political significance of ethnic identity. In addition, she is coeditor (with William E. Nelson Jr.) of *Black and Latino/a Politics: Issues in Political Development in the United States* (Barnhardt & Ashe, 2006). She is a recipient of the Ford Diversity Post Doctoral Fellowship and has been recognized by the American Political Science Association's Latino Caucus and the APSA Committee on the Status of Latinos/as for her research and service.

DAVID L. LEAL is an associate professor of government and the director of the Irma Rangel Public Policy Institute at the University of Texas at Austin. His primary academic interest is Latino politics, and his work explores a variety of questions involving public opinion, public policy, and political behavior. He has published over two dozen articles in scholarly journals, including *Journal of Politics, British Journal of Political Science, Political Research Quarterly, American Politics Research, Political Behavior, Armed Forces & Society, Social Science Quarterly, Policy*

Studies Journal, and *Educational Policy.* He is also coeditor of the volumes *Immigration Policy and Security* (Routledge, 2008) and *Latino Politics: Identity, Mobilization, and Representation* (Virginia, 2007). Leal was an American Political Science Association Congressional Fellow (1998–99), a Spencer/National Academy of Education Post-Doctoral Fellow (2002–4), co-chair of the American Political Science Association (APSA) Committee on the Status of Latinos and Latinas in the Profession (2004–6), and a member of the APSA Task Force on Religion and American Democracy (2006–8).

LISA MAGAÑA is an associate professor in the Department of Transborder Chicana/o and Latinoa/o Studies at Arizona State University. She has published in the area of immigration and Latino public policy issues. She is the author of *Straddling the Border: Immigration Policy and the INS* (Texas, 2005), *Mexican Americans and the Politics of Diversity: ¡Querer es poder!* (Arizona, 2005), and *A Day without Immigrants: Rallying behind America's Newcomers* (Capstone, 2007). Magaña has been a research associate at the Tomás Rivera Policy Institute and visiting lecturer and assistant professor at Pitzer College; the University of California, Los Angeles; and Williams College.

DARIO MORENO is Director of the Metropolitan Center and an associate professor of political science at Florida International University. He writes and conducts research on Miami politics, Florida politics, Cuban American politics, and the voting behavior of new immigrants (Haitians, Cubans, and Latin Americans) in South Florida. He has published over twenty scholarly articles and book chapters and three books. His latest book is an edited volume on Florida politics, and he is currently working on a book on Miami politics. Moreno is a nationally recognized expert on the political, immigration, and demographic issues affecting South Florida and is often quoted in both the national and the local media. He has contributed to the *Harvard Journal of Hispanic Policy* and the *American Political Science Review* and has been a Pew Scholar at the Kennedy School of Government at Harvard University and a Fulbright scholar in Costa Rica. He served as an expert witness for the Florida House of Representatives in the 1992 and 2002 redistricting processes. Recently, he directed the efforts of the Metropolitan Center in drawing the new commission districts for the City of Miami and

Boyton Beach. Moreno has also been a consultant for more than two hundred polls and focus groups in South Florida. His clients have included the South Florida Hospital Association, the Florida Marlins, the Chapman School of Business, Bell South, the Village of Key Biscayne, and the City of Miami.

DOUGLAS MUZZIO is a professor in the School of Public Affairs at Baruch College/City University of New York. He is also codirector of the Center for Transition and Leadership in Government and founder and former director of the Baruch College Survey Research Unit, both at Baruch College's School of Public Affairs. Muzzio is the political analyst and on-air commentator for WABC-TV and has done polling and political analysis for ABC-TV and other news organizations for more than two decades. His governmental experience includes the following: twice-elected trustee of the Pequannock Township (New Jersey) Board of Education; chief of staff to New York City councilmember at large Antonio Olivieri; consultant to the New York City Charter Revision Commission; research director for the Dinkins mayoral campaign; consultant to city agencies and not-for-profit organizations, including the New York City Sanitation Department, Board of Education, and Parks Council, we well as the Hispanic Federation and the Federation of Protestant Welfare Agencies of New York City. He is also in the fourth year of developing and delivering cultural diversity training programs for the New York City Police Department. He is currently writing a book titled *The Reel City: The American City in Cinema, 1896–2001.*

ADRIAN D. PANTOJA is an associate professor of political studies and Chicano Studies at Pitzer College, a member of the Claremont Colleges. His research interests are in immigration studies and Latino politics. His numerous articles have appeared in *Political Research Quarterly, Political Behavior, International Migration,* and *Social Science Quarterly,* as well as in edited volumes. His current research focuses on the intersection of religious identities/beliefs and Latino political behaviors and attitudes.

RICARDO RAMÍREZ is an assistant professor in the Departments of Political Science and American Studies and Ethnicity at the University of Southern California. He is also a National Science Foundation Postdoctoral Research Fellow at the Institute for Social Science Research at the University of California, Los Angeles. His research interests include state and local politics, political behavior, and the politics of race and ethnicity, especially as they relate to participation, mobilization, and political incorporation. He is coeditor (with Taeku Lee and Karthick Ramakrishnan) of *Transforming Politics, Transforming America: The Political and Civic Incorporation of Immigrants in the United States* (Virginia, 2007). His articles include "Segmented Mobilization: Latino Nonpartisan Get-Out-the-Vote Efforts in the 2000 General Election," "Are Naturalized Voters Driving the California Latino Electorate? Measuring the Impact of IRCA Citizens on Latino Voting" (with Matt Barreto and Nathan Woods), "Giving Voice to Latino Voters: A Field Experiment on the Effectiveness of a National Nonpartisan Mobilization Effort," and "Citizens by Choice, Voters by Necessity: Patterns in Political Mobilization by Naturalized Latinos" (with Adrian Pantoja and Gary Segura). Among his current projects are field experiments on the effects of elite mobilization efforts of Latino voters and the political consequences of residential mobility across racial and ethnic groups. He is also principal investigator of a longitudinal study on patterns of gendered career paths among Latina/o elected officials since 1990.

ANNA CHRISTINA SAMPAIO is an associate professor of women's and gender studies at Rutgers University, where she teaches and conducts research in the areas of Latina/o politics, immigration, ethnic/racial politics, gender politics, postcolonialism, and transnationalism. Her major publications include *Transnational Latino/a Communities: Politics, Processes and Cultures* (Rowman & Littlefield, 2002) and *Terrorizing Latinos: Race, Gender, and Immigration Policy Post 9/11* (forthcoming). Her work has appeared in *American Political Science Review, New Political Science, Women's Studies Quarterly, Latino Studies, PS: Political Science and Politics,* and the *International Feminist Journal of Politics.* She currently serves on the governing council of the American Political Science Association and as president of the Women's Caucus of the Western Political Science Association. She has worked with and served on the board of several nonprofit and community-based organizations serving the Latino population, including the Latina Initiative, *Escuela Guadalupe, Escuela Tlatelolco*, and the Mexican American Community Service Agency.

GARY M. SEGURA is a professor of political science at Stanford University. He previously taught at the University of Washington; the University of California, Davis; Claremont Graduate University; and the University of Iowa. His work focuses on issues of political representation. Currently his research involves the accessibility of government and politics to the growing Latino minority in the United States, as well as a book-length project on the links between casualties in international conflict and domestic politics. Among his most recent publications are "Earth Quakes and After Shocks: Race, Direct Democracy, and Partisan Change," *American Journal of Political Science* (2006); "Culture Clash? Contesting Notions of American Identity and the Effects of Latin American Immigration," *Perspectives on Politics* (2006); and "Explaining the Latino Vote: Issue Voting among Latinos in the 2000 Presidential Election," *Political Research Quarterly* (2006). Segura was a co-principal investigator of the Latino National Survey, a national poll of 8,600 Latino residents of the United States conducted in spring and summer 2006, and of the Spanish Translation and Latino Over-Sample in the 2008 American National Election Study. He is a member of the editorial boards of the *American Journal of Political Science, Journal of Politics,* and *Political Research Quarterly* and a former board member of *PS: Political Science and Politics.* He has been appointed to the Board of Overseers of the American National Election Study for 2006–9.

CHRISTINE MARIE SIERRA is a professor of political science at the University of New Mexico. She teaches and researches in the field of American politics, with a focus on race, ethnicity, and gender. Her publications include work on Latino political activism on immigration policy, Hispanic politics in New Mexico, and Latina women in the United States. She is the lead principal investigator of the Gender and Multicultural Leadership Project, a multiyear national study of elected officials of color in the United States. Sierra lectures at college campuses around the country and has been a guest scholar at the Brookings Institution in Washington, D.C., the University of Arizona, and Rutgers University. She frequently appears as an expert in American and Latino politics for local, national, and international media outlets.

Index

www.ingramcontent.com/pod-product-compliance
Lightning Source LLC
Chambersburg PA
CBHW051949270326
41929CB00015B/2586

* 9 7 8 0 2 6 8 0 2 5 9 9 1 *